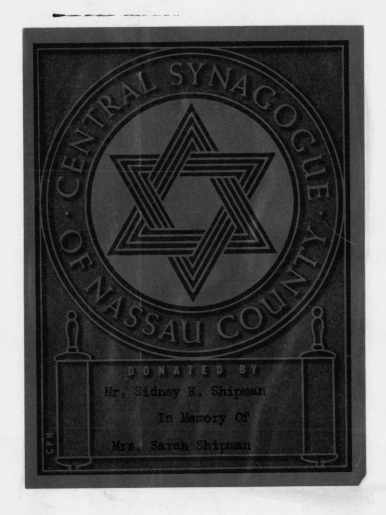

Theodore Herzl, about 1895

Theodore Herzl

A BIOGRAPHY

by

ALEX BEIN

Translated from the German

by

MAURICE SAMUEL

Philadelphia

THE JEWISH PUBLICATION SOCIETY OF AMERICA

5716-1956

60

CONTENTS

Book One — Early Years

Book Two — The Zionist

ILLUSTRATIONS

v

FACSIMILES

BOOK I

EARLY YEARS

CHAPTER I

CHILDHOOD IN BUDAPEST
(1860–1878)

THE ancestral background of Theodore Herzl, like that of many another national hero, is very imperfectly known. According to a family tradition his father was descended from Spaniolo Marranos. Far back in the line two brothers had been compelled by the Inquisition to abjure their Judaism and enter a monastic order, but they clung in secret to the faith of their fathers. Having attained positions of importance in the order, they were sent abroad on a confidential mission and took advantage of this long awaited opportunity to flee. After sundry adventures they reached Turkey, and there renounced the religion which had been forced upon them. From one of these brothers, the legend tells, Herzl's father was descended.

Research so far has failed to transform this legend into anything more substantial. What we do know is that the ancestors of Theodore's grandfather, Simon Loeb Herzl (1805–1879), came from Bohemia, Moravia and Silesia. They settled in Belgrade after that city had passed under Austrian rule with the Treaty of Passarowitz (1718); there they achieved a moderate degree of affluence and married into local Spaniolo families. But Belgrade became Turkish again in 1739, whereupon the Herzls, together with thirty other Jewish families, migrated to the town of Semlin which lay within the so-called Austrian "Military March." As a reward for this exhibition of "faithfulness and devotion" they were accorded the rights of residence for the remainder of their lives. In 1772 and again in 1816 these rights were renewed for their descendants on the ground that (to quote the report of a Military Council): "throughout these many years ... the Jews of Semlin have discharged their duties as faithful subjects," have, further, "served satisfactorily in the local militia and have given sustained evidence of their patriotic activity during the long wars ... they have never engaged in smuggling, have always maintained exemplary order, have given their children public school educations and have always conducted themselves in peaceful, friendly and law-abiding fashion."

From these documents we obtain a glimpse into the life of the Jews of Semlin and of Herzl's forefathers. They had adapted themselves to their surroundings. Though their houses were grouped about the synagogue and school, they do not seem to have constituted a ghetto; certainly they had commercial connections with their neighbors and perhaps served the state as military purveyors. Two of the three sons of Herzl's great-grandfather, Leopold (Yehuda Leib) Herzl, yielded to the temptations held out by the non-Jewish world. Or perhaps it may be that what drew them away from the circle and faith of their fathers was the impulse to pursue to the end the process of assimilation once begun. If this was so, the third son, Simon Loeb, Theodore's grandfather, had in him a similar streak of consistency operating in the opposite direction, for he recoiled all the more sharply into his Jewish loyalty. He observed with scrupulous care the ancient commandments and usages, sounded the *Shofar* on *Rosh Hashanah*, and on *Yom Kippur* led the congregation in the *Kol Nidre*. It is very possible that he already sympathized with the early Zionist efforts of Alkalai. In any case, he was well acquainted with them.

For Yehuda ben Solomon Hai Alkalai (1792–1878) was teacher and *hazan* in the Sephardic community of Semlin. Profoundly moved by the wretched and hopeless destiny of the Jews, influenced no less by the emergent national movement among the Balkan peoples and by the ancient Messianic idea, he came to the conviction that the only salvation for the Jews lay in their return to their original homeland. He propagated his ideal in numerous writings and spread it by word of mouth in the cities of Europe, in Constantinople and in Palestine. Modern in spirit, he was deeply attached to the past of his people in love and knowledge and understanding.

Simon Loeb Herzl died at a very advanced age, when his grandson Theodore had already reached his twentieth year. It would have been extraordinary if the old man had not, on his annual visits to Pest where his son lived, frequently spoken of Alkalai and of his plans and dreams. Who knows whether it was not then that the young and sensitive spirit of Herzl received the decisive imprint which was to determine the course of his life? Who knows if it was not then that the seed was sown which after long and invisible subterranean growth broke out in seed and flower in the sight of all men?

In any case, it is quite certain that in this respect young Herzl owed nothing to his father. Jacob Herzl did not dissolve his bonds with Judaism — but he did not draw them very close, either. Custom and upbringing had made him a Jew, and he remained one. The story of his life is simple, straightforward and direct, just as the man himself was a typically energetic, capable and diligent merchant. At the age of twenty-one he left his native town of Semlin to settle in the city of Pest. Fourteen years later — that is, in 1870 — he was a director of the Hungaria Bank, for it is in this capacity that he is inscribed in the school record of his son Theodore. He could by that time have retired from business, if the idea had occurred to him, but launched instead on new enterprises. He entered the timber business on a large scale, lost his entire fortune in the depression of 1873, began again, and within a few years was again in the saddle. Not a little of his success may be ascribed to his wife, née Jeannette Diamant, whom he married in 1858. She was the perfect mate and comrade for a man of his type.

Of the ancestry of this interesting woman we know even less than of her husband's. Her father, Hermann (Gabriel Hersch) Diamant (1805–1871), Theodore Herzl's maternal grandfather, was a native of Pest, and early in his life had established himself comfortably in the clothing business. He has left behind him the reputation of a clever, witty man, with strong free-thinking tendencies. His wit, as well as his intelligence, he passed on to his daughter Jeannette, who in turn transferred them to her son Theodore. It was from Jeannette's mother that Theodore inherited his deep-set brown eyes, at once dreamy and penetrating — eyes which shone with an inner light of their own and exercised a strange fascination over those upon whom they fell. But the pictures of Theodore's grandmother show those same eyes under a different aspect; they are even deeper, more mysterious and more sombre. They verge almost on the unnatural, laden as they are with suggestions of immemorial sorrows.

An echo of the dying medieval era sounds in the history of Theresa Abeles, the mother of Herzl's maternal grandmother. We know, concerning her, that she became a widow in early years, and that for the rest of her life she sustained herself and her children by house to house peddling. That family name, Abeles, is not unknown in the martyrology of the Jewish people. There was a certain Lazarus Abeles of Prague, a dealer in gloves, who in the year 1694 was accused of having murdered his twelve-year-old son for the sin of apostasy, and was condemned to prison, where he took his own life. Have we here more than an accidental resemblance of name? Something in the appearance of Herzl's grandmother leads us to think so.

In Herzl's mother this touch of mournfulness and fatefulness was mitigated by the admixture of her father's brighter nature. Those who had known her in her girlhood carried to the end of their days the recollection of her striking beauty. The thick, jet-black hair, the lofty forehead balancing the straight lines of her nose, the little mouth which in repose looked serious to the point of bitterness, but which could liven suddenly into wit and mockery and brilliance — all these made up a highly individual appearance. In her little world she was definitely a personality, and she knew it. But she was equally known for other qualities: for goodness of heart and sincerity.

These characteristics of feature and spirit reappeared intensified in her son. The gifts of poetry and satire which were so deeply rooted in Theodore Herzl and, still more, that extraordinary, vibrant sensibility, came from his mother, together with the peculiar expression of his features. But the framework of his body came from his father: the broad, square head, the open forehead, the stature, and the touch of energy in the lips. In father and son, again, the well-formed nose was slightly curved at the tip. The most striking difference was in the eyes. Jacob Herzl's were bright, clear and sharp; they bespoke the man of common sense, whose feet were firmly planted on the earth, the man of action, pedantically systematic and attentive to detail. His harmonious, well-balanced being expressed itself in a high ritual of formality. An amazingly happy blend of paternal and maternal gifts emerge in the son, the vibrant side by side with the orderly, the formlessly impulsive side by side with the disciplined, preparing the way for great achievement.

Theodore (Tivadar) Herzl — or, to give him his Hebrew names, Benyamin Ze-ev Herzl — was born on Wednesday, May 2, 1860, in the city of Budapest. More exactly, the place of his birth was Pest, on the left bank of the Danube, for the union of Buda and Pest as the capital of Hungary did not take place until 1872. His childhood impressions must have been happy ones. The relationship between his parents was one of deep love strengthened by mutual respect for the qualities each needed in the other; if anything, there was in Theodore's childhood an excess of affection and attention rather than the opposite; and to this was added the proximity of his maternal grandparents, the Diamants.

His earliest and nearest playmate was his sister Pauline, a year older than he and the image of her mother. With her he learned to read, to her he first declaimed poetry, and she made other playmates almost superfluous.

The first glimpses of life beyond the family circle must have been unusually stimulating for the little one. When the mother and children went out for their first walks together, making up an extraordinarily beautiful picture, they found themselves at once in the center of the city and of the Jewish district. In those days the Hungarian capital was in process of rapid expansion. In 1850 it had a population of 178,000; by 1873 the number reached 300,000 and by 1880, 371,000. The proportion of the Jewish population rose even more rapidly. In 1873, shortly after the union of Buda and Pest, the capital of Hungary contained 48,306 Jews (16.3% of the total population); by 1880 the number had risen, by natural increase and immigration, to 71,940, or 19.4% of the total.

The Jews of Budapest carried on a long struggle for social and civic rights. The emancipation voted by the Hungarian Reichstag in 1849, after many bitter anti-Jewish demonstrations, did not take effect; for within two weeks of the enactment the Hungarian revolt for freedom — in which Herzl's uncle, Wilhelm Diamant, took part as first lieutenant — was crushed by a union of Austrian and Russian forces. It was only after the famous *Ausgleich*, the compromise arrangement according to which Hungary was to enjoy the broadest measure of autonomy within the framework of an Austro-Hungarian union, that the Constitution of 1867 completed the emancipation of the Jews.

The measure sprang not merely from a feeling for human rights; it had a definite political purpose. Franz Deak, the leader of the liberal party, stated openly that he sought by this act to bind the Jews to the Magyar population and the Magyar program. Until that time the Jews of Hungary generally and of the two cities Buda and Pest more particularly had been German in language, education and upbringing. German had been the language of the powers that were, German had been likewise the language of the Jewish *Aufklärung*, or modern rationalism; for it was from Germany that the impulse to liberal religious reform, carrying with it the philosophy of adaptation to the surrounding world, had proceeded, to precipitate the struggle for Jewish leadership between Orthodox and Reform.

This was the setting of Theodore's childhood. Almost next door to his father's house rose the liberal-reform temple, a red-brick building in Moorish style, its two towers, almost one hundred and fifty feet in height, lifted with a strange, foreign effect above their surroundings. To this house of worship the little boy went regularly with his father on Sabbath and Holy Days. At home, too, the essentials of the ritual were observed, with particular emphasis on the celebration of two festivals, Hanukkah and Passover, the feast of lights and the feast of the Exodus. One touching ceremony which Theodore learned in childhood remained with him in his adult years; before every important event and decision he sought the blessing of his parents.

Even stronger than these impressions, however, was the influence of his mother. Her education had been German through and through; there was not a day on which she did not dip into German literature, especially the classic. The Jewish world, not alien to her, did not find expression through her; her conscious efforts were all directed toward implanting the German cultural heritage in her children. Of even deeper significance was her sympathetic attitude toward the pride which showed early in her son, and her skill in transferring to him her sense of form, of bearing, of tactfulness and of simple grace.

The teacher who was brought into the house when Theodore was five and a half years old, to instruct the youngster for one hour a day so that he might enjoy his freedom from school for an extra year, describes his charge as follows: "He was strong and lively, but at the same time modest and well-behaved. He learned very easily and had an amazing gift of comprehension." When Theodore entered the *Pester Israelitische Normalhauptschule*, one of the folk schools maintained by the Jewish community of Pest, in 1866, the reports were similar in tone. But it does not appear that this school had a positive influence on the boy. In later years Herzl even accused the authorities of discrimination: he felt he had enjoyed a certain superior status because his father had been a well-to-do merchant. Even more significant was a recollection of another kind, which the grown man retained forever out of his childhood.

This early memory has reached us in two versions: one is contained in Herzl's brief autobiographical sketch, written in 1898; the other is recorded by the Hebrew writer Reuben Brainin, as received orally from Herzl himself. When the two versions are fused, we obtain the following:

The story of the Exodus, as he read it in the Bible, had made upon the boy a profound, almost shattering impression. But when the teacher recited the thrilling epic of the liberation from Egypt, his words were cold and dry, his features betrayed not a spark of emotion; it was as if the whole incident were of the most commonplace character. Thereupon Theodore concluded that it was nothing but a fairy tale, made up for the sole purpose of torturing little boys. The first profound impression was replaced by dislike, and by a spirit of opposition. When, some time later, the teacher examined Theodore on the details of the Exodus from Egypt, the boy was unable to answer and received, in keeping with the pedagogic technique of the time and place, the prescribed thrashing. Thirty years later, when Herzl was writing his autobiography, the memory of the thrashing was still strong in him. "Today," he added with bitter irony, "there are scores of teachers who would like to thrash me because I remember the Exodus from Egypt only too well."

The incident itself, and, still more, the attitude it reveals in the teachers, must have done a great deal to discourage the boy's interest in things Jewish. In any case, his mind shifted at about that time to technical matters. The period was one to stimulate this sort of preoccupation in an imaginative youngster, for it was the first great modern era of technological development. The steam-engine was conquering new fields of usefulness. The network of railroads was spreading rapidly over the world, and steamships were taking on their modern imposing proportions. Further, in 1869 the gigantic and difficult project of the Suez Canal, bringing together the Mediterranean Sea and the Indian Ocean, was completed, and the name of Ferdinand de Lesseps, the engineer, filled the whole world. This was the man whom Theodore accepted now as his model.

And this was the time, it appears, that young Herzl was aware of something stirring within, the impulse to some great and extraordinary achievement. He confided his ambition to one person — his father. When he grew up, he said, he was going to duplicate the work of de Lesseps; he was going to cut a canal through the Isthmus of Panama, and bring together the Atlantic and Pacific Oceans.

The parents, anxious to discover and encourage the boy's gifts, took this confession and revelation very seriously. In the autumn of 1870 they enrolled him in the Technical School of the City of Pest.

It appears, however, that both Theodore and his parents had over-estimated the seriousness of his scientific leanings. Such, at any rate, is the conclusion to be drawn from his school record of that time. What young Herzl possessed was indeed constructive imagination but he lacked definitely the capacity to think in technical forms. The fact is that throughout his life he displayed an alert interest in the literature of technical discovery, and in his own literary work the significance of technology played an important role. But, however high his admiration of technology, however skillful his descriptions of its wonders, what interested him most in reality was not so much technology in itself as its function for the solution of human problems. This is of course not the attitude of the engineer but of the leader of men, not of the technical constructor but of the inspirer of construction.

In this same connection much is revealed in the curious report which, half a year before his death, Herzl gave Reuben Brainin. We have already referred to the strange reawakening of memory which has left us the story of the boy's experience with the Exodus and the teacher. This dates from Herzl's seventh year. There is another story from a later time. At about the age of twelve — so Herzl told Brainin — he read somewhere in a German book about the Messiah-King whom many Jews still awaited and who would come riding, like the poorest of the poor, on an ass. The history of the Exodus and the legend of the liberation by the King-Messiah ran together in the boy's mind, inspiring in him the theme of a wonderful story which he sought in vain to put into literary form.

A little while thereafter Herzl was visited by the following dream: "The King-Messiah came, a glorious and majestic old man, took me in his arms, and swept off with me on the wings of the wind. On one of the iridescent clouds we encountered the figure of Moses. The features were those familiar to me out of my childhood in the statue by Michelangelo. The Messiah called to Moses: It is for this child that I have prayed. But to me he said: Go, declare to the Jews that I shall come soon and perform great wonders and great deeds for my people and for the whole world."

This dream Herzl kept to himself. But a few days later there came to his hand one of the popular science books by Aaron Bernstein. There he read that the stream of electricity built a bridge over the entire world, that electricity was the real Messiah, and that its wonders would bring liberation to all nations and all enslaved human beings. Young Herzl was outraged. "What! The electron as Messiah! What blasphemy!" The Messiah of the legend seemed to him to be much nobler and more beautiful.

"Then after a few days a sort of revolution occurred within me. I said to myself: who knows, perhaps the electric stream is really the Redeemer whom we are awaiting and who will liberate us from the bondage of the body and the spirit."

This experience acquires a deeper psychological meaning if we connect it with the time of his *Bar Mitzvah*, one year later. Only a few weeks had passed since the celebration of the Passover, and no doubt the history and the ritual had found him all the more sensitive in view of the solemn religious apotheosis which was approaching for him. Then came the ceremony of the *Bar Mitzvah* itself. With all the solemnity proper to the occasion, Herzl was called up to the Torah and read forth the portion for which he had been prepared — an experience never forgotten even by less sensitive natures than his. For the first time he, as the center of attention, faced a large audience, and stood next to the *hazan* before the unrolled Torah, the mind tense, the soul receptive, the spirit awaiting something extraordinary and memorable.

The family had done everything to heighten the solemnity of the occasion. There had gone forth from their house on the Maria Valerie Street, to friends and relatives, announcements in which Herr and Frau Jacob Herzl requested the honor of their attendance at the "Confirmation" — as it had already become the custom to call it in Reform circles — of their son Theodore, on May 3, 1873, at the Temple. In the afternoon a celebration was to be held at home, to which crowds of friends and relatives were invited.

It may be to this period of reawakened Jewish sensibility, of heightened responsiveness to the expectations of his elders, of resurgent interest in Jewish historical studies (according to the testimony of one uncle) — it may be to this period that the dream of a dedicated life belonged. It is almost certain, too, that for the great event of the *Bar Mitzvah* the old grandfather of Semlin came to Pest. About this time, again, Alkalai, that early, all-but-forgotten Zionist, passed through Vienna and Budapest on his final journey to Palestine. Whether or not each one of these circumstances had a direct effect on the boy, the whole complex surrounds his *Bar Mitzvah* with the suggestion of the mission of his life, and, certainly, occasion was given for the awakening in him of the feeling of dedication to a great enterprise.

As a sort of counterpoint we learn that a wave of anti-Semitism was then passing through young Herzl's school. In the spring of 1873 the period of expansion ensuing on the union of the two cities came to a close, a depression followed, competition grew sharper, and Herzl's father among others lost all he had. It should be borne in mind that this period saw the birth of modern political anti-Semitism in Germany, Austria and Hungary. The Emancipation of 1867 had been followed by a large increase in the Jewish population of Budapest; as against this, Magyar nationalism had grown stronger and taken on a radical character. The stage was therefore set for an intensification of anti-Semitism, reaching its climax in the Tisza Eszlar ritual murder trial of 1882.

Attendance at school must have become more and more of a burden for the self-conscious boy. We know that his reports in most subjects showed a turn for the worse; in the summer of 1874 he received a bare passing mark in "Effort." Herzl had lost all interest in school.

What came to replace it was an ever-increasing preoccupation with literature. The boy had always been a great reader. Now he sought to emulate the creativity of his idols, among whom were Heine and Lenau. He brought forth his literary first fruits. With few exceptions they are in German. He had made his decision in favor of his mother's language, the language of his world of culture; definitely and consciously he dissociated himself from the wave of Magyarization which caught up the Jews of Budapest.

Interesting in itself, and illuminating for the character of the leader and organizer to be, was the manner in which he united and organized the literary talents of his circle of friends. At the beginning of 1874 he founded a school society under the not particularly modest name of "We". It seems to have lasted about two months. The following is an excerpt from the "constitution" which he submitted at the first session, on February 22, 1874:

"We are founding a society for the purpose of increasing our knowledge by the writing of short stories and fables, also adding thereby to our knowledge of the language . . . these works may be taken from history, may be fictional, and may be founded on actual experience; they must, however, always have elegance and grace of form."

Then follow exact rules for the method of handing in and criticizing the literary productions of the members in such manner as to avoid partisanship and discrimination. "Unjust criticism is forbidden, therfore every work shall be criticized by two members." Only when the criticism of both readers was favorable could the author read forth his production before the assembled society, the entire membership of which then voted whether it was or was not of a sufficiently high standard to go into the permanent archives.

The society had officials with definite duties, and care was taken that the privileges of officials should not encroach upon the rights of ordinary members. The highest post was that of the "President"— to wit, Theodore Herzl. His task was to formulate the agenda of each meeting, preside over the sessions, and "perform all duties relevant thereto." A new president could not be elected until after ten meetings.

Childish enough all these rules and regulations must seem, with their imitations of the world of the grown-ups, with their joy in ritual and formality. What schoolboy has not passed through a similar phase? And yet the adult observer can detect here in the formulation of these particular regulations the characteristics of the future leader and negotiator: clarity of phrase, distrust of partisanship, the feeling of tactfulness, the sense of form. Certainly there is a good deal of childishness in the decision that all members of the society shall, during the sessions, address each other gravely as "*Sie*"—"Mr." And still we are inevitably reminded of the Herzl of 1897, who thought it of the utmost importance to wear a frock coat at the opening of the first Congress, and who finally persuaded the rebellious Nordau to go back to his hotel and to change his ordinary street clothes for formal attire . . .

The photographs which have come down from that time give us a clear picture of the president of the "We" association: a tall, slender figure, fresh features which have already lost the soft outlines of childhood, large dark eyes fixed upon the distance. The lightly closed lips seem ready to open in jest and mockery. The bearing, manner, behavior and entire being of this youngster bespeak directed energy and natural mastery of form; there is no doubt that in these characteristics he was already distinguished from his comrades.

His productions, too, lead the list, at least quantitatively. According to the extant minutes, which invariably close with the formula, "Read, approved and passed by Theodore Herzl, President," not a session was held without his reading forth several of his productions: fables, fairy tales, short stories and satires; occasionally, also, some poetry. And he made a great impression once on the members of the society with a longer work, undoubtedly a story, which had to be continued in three sessions. The title of this "distinguished creation," as the report calls it, again has prophetic intimations of the future leader. It is "Obedience and Command."

The attention, energy and time which Herzl devoted to literature, his absorption in himself, his activity in the society meant of course so much less given to his school work. His marks became correspondingly worse. German and history, the two subjects nearest his literary interests, were the two exceptions. He found no time at all for science subjects; Jewish questions likewise disappeared from his interests: he was completely absorbed by German literary culture.

This is all the more astonishing when we reflect that anti-Semitism continued to increase steadily. As a grown man Herzl could recall that one of his teachers, in defining the word "heathen," had said, "such as idolators, Mohammedans and Jews." Whether it was this incident,— as the memory of the grown man always insisted — which enraged him beyond endurance, or the increasingly bad school reports, or both circumstances together, the fact remains that on February 4, 1875 Herzl left the Technical School.

He now prepared himself for admission to a classical institute of learning where the curriculum would correspond more closely to his inclinations. He had always taken private lessons, even while attending the Technical School, in French, English and piano playing. For the next few months his education was entrusted to private teachers. Freed from the distractions of his fellow students and the malice of anti-Semitic teachers, he was able to sink himself wholly into the study of ancient languages and culture. Within a year he had acquired the necessary knowledge of Latin and Greek. The first class attestation given him by the Evangelical High School in February 1876 proved beyond the shadow of a doubt where his abilities lay. In this "Evangelical" School, in which the Jewish students were a majority and therefore secure from anti-Semitic outbreaks, he undoubtedly felt much happier.

To this period of his transfer to the Evangelical Gymnasium, or High School, belongs the story of his love for Madeleine Kurz, of whom we know little more than that she was of Herzl's own age and that she died young. In later years Herzl repeatedly wrote that she had been his one real love; it must have been a shattering experience, and must have led to a great deepening of his spiritual and intellectual qualities.

We do in fact perceive the evidences of a profound inner change in the photographs of that time. The expression in the eyes and lips is dreamy, earnest, almost heavy-hearted; yet it is touched by skepticism and self-consciousness. This fusion tells of inner labor and experience, of bitter conflicts between the spirit and the external world. He had begun to look more sharply at reality and to apply a more critical standard to his own ideas and dreams. The world of nature awoke for him, and when he wandered evenings out of the city along the banks of the Danube, drunk with beauty, he mused on the problems of his life and struggled to find literary forms for the expression both of his romantic longings and his critical perceptions.

The productions which have survived out of those days build up a definite image of the man. He wrote essays, books and theatre reviews, feuilletons and poems; some of the reviews were accepted by the *Pester Lloyd*, then a newspaper of very high standing. He began a novel built up as an exchange of letters, after the style of Goethe's *Werther*. He wrote satires on the demagoguery of the members of the Reichstag. He struggled to define the basic principles of various literary art forms in order that he might see more clearly what he himself wanted to say. He took an active and eager part in the work of the "German Self-Education Society" created by the students of his school. The Jewish world, whose inferior position always wounded his pride, and whose obstinate separatism seemed to him utterly meaningless, drifted further and further out of his mind. The deeper and more earnest his thoughts became, the more wordly and adult were his forms of utterance. To his comrades, who were never permitted to share the intimacy of his inner life, this tall, dark, always elegantly groomed youth seemed to be in perpetual good humor — an ironical, mocking, superior spirit to whom nothing was holy, in short, a complete nihilist.

The exterior was the façade of a genuine shyness; within there went on a ceaseless questing and searching, a ceaseless struggling with the eternal and oppressive human problems of life and death. "I have thought much," he wrote in 1878, "on the purpose of human existence, the highest manifestation of life on earth. Often I thought that I had found the answer; actually it was nothing but the mirror of my years and of the particular phase through which I was passing. At first I thought that the aim of life was enjoyment and freedom from care; then it seemed to me that the only possible aim of life was love for parents, for one's own, and for all human beings. Then suddenly I was submerged in a tide of thought. I saw with blinding clarity the impotence of man. It was as though a flash of lightning had widened and thrust back the horizon of my perception and understanding. Those eternal, insoluble riddles, death and annihilation, I too, an ignorant neophyte, had sought to unravel."

This happened to be the moment which death had chosen to confront him face to face. In February 1878 his only sister fell sick with typhoid fever, and in a few days she was dead.

It was a frightful blow to the parents; and for the mother, who was destined to see husband and son pass away, it was the first of a dreadful series. But it was no less frightful than for the brother. They had grown up together; they had been an ever-present help and encouragement to each other. Now there was a sudden emptiness, never to be filled again. That was death. From that time on he knew what death meant; he had gazed upon its countenance, which was to peer for evermore from the pages of his works. He never forgot his sister. He guarded every keepsake of hers like a sacred relic. His novel *Altneuland* was dedicated to her memory and his father's, and it is his sister's character which is reproduced in that of the clever, self-sacrificing, shyly lovable school-teacher Miriam.

Left alone to his parents, he drew closer to them. He felt it incumbent upon him to mitigate their sense of loss by giving them a double measure of love and tenderness and attention. The relationship between mother and son, which had always been tenderly intimate, acquired a new depth. His attitude toward his father, which had evolved from that of the child into that of the comrade, took on a new warmth. It was as if the three of them closed their ranks in order to hide the gap. These family bonds, which at certain moments might have seemed excessive in their strength, were resolved by death alone, the father passing away first, the mother last.

It was the mother who, crushed in spirit, found intolerable those surroundings — the home, the district, the city — which had once been filled with her daughter's presence. Within a week after Pauline's death the family moved to Vienna.

Theodore had to make one more return to Budapest, in June of that year, to sit for his finals at the Evangelical Gymnasium. These he passed with only moderate success. Then he too abandoned for ever the place of his birth.

CHAPTER II

STUDENT YEARS IN VIENNA
(1878–1884)

DEATH had hastened at least one departure from Budapest; for sooner or later young Herzl would have left for "the larger world." Not that Budapest could, in those days, be called a small place; but for some time now Herzl had longed for the more tumultuous centers of life to the north and west. Now the change came. He passed from the Hungarian capital to that of the Austro-Hungarian Empire, and passed at the same time from the close confinement of schooldays to the broader limits of university life, and from the narrow circle of old friends and familiar scenes into a wide arena of new personalities among whom he would have to conquer a place for himself.

Herzl never revealed in any direct utterance what impression Vienna made on him; but from innumerable hints scattered through his later works, and from the more significant record of his lifelong habits, it is easy to see with what eagerness and love and readiness to understand he became part of the city of Vienna. The streets and buildings must have spoken to him from the day of his arrival; the graceful baroque architecture, with its delicate message of beauty unstifled by rigidity of form, must have been a perpetual and daily inward provocation to his feeling for music and

23

shapeliness. The population of Vienna, music-loving, theatre-loving, and gay, rooted in a folk spirit, lightly moved to jest and mockery, and yet not untouched with a darker, deeper and more painful self-searching, ran to no extremities of expression. It was the population of a center of empire; it moved warily, lightly, gracefully, delaying decision, seeking compromise, harmonizing the clash of interests. In this city young Herzl's natural inclination to sharp, unmerciful criticism was toned down, his manner softened, while his style as feuilletonist took on that inimitable mixture of melodic and suspended cadence and of clarity of meaning which was to set him apart.

Herzl had already reached the decision to become a writer before he left Budapest. Rabbi Kohn, who visited the family during the time of their mourning, gave his opinion on the subject — to the effect that writing was not really a profession and career. The parents too felt that the writer needed an economic basis in some other activity. Thus it was that in the fall of 1878 Herzl enrolled as student in the law faculty of the University of Vienna. He was, however, still haunted by scientific inclinations; he therefore attended classes in the natural sciences, particularly chemistry, and sometimes continued to wonder whether that was not his natural field.

Among his studies it was Roman law which made the deepest impression on him. He himself has said so frequently, and traces of Roman law are visible in the *Judenstaat*; it is implicit in his contention that a small minority can exercise the right of acting on behalf of an entire people. Herzl very obviously had little interest in other branches of the law; but they cannot have been without creative value for him. It was in his nature to pursue the meaning of human relations as between person and person, group and group, person and group, and since this is, after all, the substance of legal study, Herzl must have absorbed certain views without being aware of it.

No doubt there was in him an instinctive rebellion against forcing life into hard molds and standards, but at the same time the art disciplines which he sought also represented a search for form. Like many poets and writers before and after him, he learned from the juristic approach to human relations certain insights into the life of the state and of society. In addition, he heard the views of men like Anton Menger and Lorenz von Stein (on economics and the philosophy of law) each of whom had his special critique of the social structure; he attended lectures on general philosophy and history, with special emphasis on the new Austro-Hungarian empire of nationalities. There cannot be any doubt that his mature views were profoundly, if unconsciously, affected by what he learned in his student days.

What his conscious mind carried away into later years came from anywhere but the classrooms. In this respect he expressed himself sharply enough. "I myself," he writes in his diary, in the year 1895, "was in my youth a playboy, like Lessing and Laube and many others, who managed nevertheless to grow up into decent persons. But if I was a playboy it was only because my will to action had not found its outlet." And in his autobiographic sketch of 1898 he tells us that he "had a part in all the ridiculous pranks of the student body."

His first act was to become a member of the *Akademische Lesehalle* or student cultural association. He found there the men who were to stand closest to him in this period of growth and in his first years of literary activity — men like Heinrich Kana and Oswald Boxer.

The *Lesehalle*, with its close to one thousand members, was a non-partisan organization, with no class or religious distinctions. Adolph Bachrach, later Doctor of Laws and *Justizrat*, a Jew, was its president in its palmiest days, and his slogan was: "In the temple of knowledge all worshippers are equal." This might be so, but it was impossible to keep from within the organization the clash of political and national and general views — an echo of the turmoil which was rending the Austro-Hungarian monarchy and which threatened to split the *Lesehalle*.

Those were the closing days of the Prime Ministry of Auersperg; a new spirit of friendship for the German Reich had arisen, and with it a spirit of expansion which found expression in the occupation of Bosnia and Herzegovina. Simultaneously there was a strong growth of internal nationalisms. The recognition of the national rights of Hungary in the Compromise Arrangement of 1867 had given a powerful impetus to similar demands in other national groups, and German nationalism, threatened in its hegemony, responded with an intensification of its own spirit. The tension grew steadily since the accession to power of Taaffe, a childhood friend of the Kaiser, whose policy was to play off one group against the other so that the dominant Germans would remain in control. The German liberal movement, which had never had the courage of consistency, and had therefore never lent its aid to the struggling, suppressed nationalities, like the Poles and Czechs, was, since the 'eighties, more and more opposed by the German National movement, and soon also by the Christian Socialist movement when the latter found a capable leader in Lueger. Those anti-liberal movements had in common a tendency to exploit the latent anti-Semitism to be found in the lower middle classes.

Herzl, who accounted himself a liberal and an Austrian patriot, plunged eagerly into the activities of the Society, attended its discussions and directed its literary evenings. His fellow member, Arthur Schnitzler, remembered many years later Herzl's sharp manner of utterance at these evenings. He seldom spoke at the larger gatherings; there he listened and took notes which afterwards were incorporated in his plans for literary work and in satirical poems which he read forth on festive occasions. He had occasion, too, to deride certain Jewish fellow members, who in his view displayed an excessive eagerness in their loyalty to various movements.

This was the extent to which, in these days, he occupied himself with the Jewish question — at least externally. He concerned himself little or not at all with the official Jewish world which was seeking to submerge itself in the surrounding world. He seldom visited the synagogue. His impulses carried him beyond the old and out-lived sphere — as he considered it — which had no more significance for him; beyond the "invisible Ghetto" into a more sincere and more aesthetic world, as the hero of his drama, *The New Ghetto* was later to express it. In the outlines and notes for larger works dating from that period we may see clearly what ideals attracted him then and in what direction his spirit was pulled.

As early as 1878, that is shortly after his admission to the University, he had already outlined a great comedy, *Die Ritter vom Gemeinplatz*, the theme of which kept on reappearing under different titles in subsequent enterprises. The satire was always to be directed against the man of big

phrases "who out of the holiest of human emotions manu-
factures contentless hypocritical and treacherous phrases."

As foil to this commonplace word-peddler he would
present his ideal of a man, as he then conceived it. It is no
accident that the hero of this piece was to be a nobleman.
He was to conceal, so read Herzl's notes, "the warmest and
most passionate sensitivity under an immovable exterior of
iciest calm." In reality noble, dedicated to the highest aims,
in love with all that was good and beautiful, he was to
present himself "out of an exaggerated nervous pride" as a
fool, a mentally limited adherent of a decayed caste, the
"living, silent protest against the revolting fashion of the
time, which prostitutes all tender sentiments and perceptions
by exhibitionistic display."

These plans and figures recur in numerous fragmentary
sketches and outlines belonging to the years that follow, as
well as in the few works which he definitely finished: the
superficial mocker, whose one aim is the facile enjoyment of
life, the moralist, the highborn nobleman — and the synthetic feminine dream — forms which were the projections
of the longings of a shy youth.

In 1880 was printed the harmless and unimportant
comedy, *Kompagniearbeit*. More revealing was the novel
Hagenau, which Herzl completed in the summer of 1882.
The center of it is again a nobleman, Count Robert Schenk
von Hagenau, scion of an ancient line fallen from power,
a shy artist whose close friend is a middle-class Doctor of
Laws (!). The latter does everything possible in imitation
of his highborn companion, apes his quiet, undemonstrative
pride, affects the same calm readiness to help all human
beings and the same simple and natural certainty of bearing.
The Doctor of Laws is provoked by the intolerance of a

certain medical man, who considers the aristocratic synonymous with the dishonest, the mean and the pretentious —
till in the end the medical man is won over to the jurist's
point of view. The old distinctions of race and class have
long since disappeared and live on only in the imagination
of obstinate doctrinaires.

And the novelist shows us, foregathered at the ball given
by the new owners of the Hagenau estate, the old and the
new aristocracy, the latter drawn from the middle-class and
including even Jews. "Herr Moritz Loewenstein was there
too. He came in on the arm of his oldest son, Karl. Symbol
of the levelling spirit of the time, Karl's nose in profile was
an absolutely straight line. As for the ladies, it was impossible to distinguish between them, they were so alike in dress
and bearing and speech. Baroness Loewenstein, who sat next
to Countess von Wortegg, was not a bit louder in her dress
than the latter, and she spoke as pure a German." It was
quite true, of course, (these are the thoughts which Herzl
puts into the mind of the old democrat) that this was all on
the surface; the line of demarcation between the classes had
only shifted further. Beyond the walls of this brilliantly
illumined hall lay somewhere the dark quarters of the poor,
"into which a beam of happiness never strayed. An un-
bridgeable gulf separated the decaying peasantry and the
oppressed factory workers from the carefree son of this rich
parvenu."

One does not have to be a profound psychologist in order
to reconstruct from these pictures and figures the character
of their creator: a shy, proud spirit striving to build itself
into an honest and essential being, penetrated with feelings
of responsibility and justice. But that same spirit was also
haunted by a nostalgic attraction toward the world of easy

and superficial success; it was filled above all with admiration for the men who could unite both worlds in themselves — honesty, loyalty and nobility within, and lightness of touch, worldly grace, the "French" inspiration in commerce with the world. Here is what Herzl wrote, with an irony directed at himself, in the introduction to an article: "I have already told you that I am capable of a great enthusiasm for the quality of knightliness; and this one enthusiasm could easily serve to explain, directly or indirectly, all my other enthusiasms, however contradictory."

It was only natural that this young man should be pulled into the life of the organized student bodies. In March 1881, following on an address by the Pan-German anti-Semitic member of the Reichstag, Schoenerer, who was winning a great following among the sons of the small bourgeoisie, the *Akademische Lesehalle* was dissolved. During the winter term Herzl became a member of the student Fraternity *Albia*. This duelling organization had not yet determined its political direction. The question of its program was hotly debated by the Liberals and Conservatives, the Austrian patriots and the German nationalists. Herzl was certainly attracted more by the human side than by the ideological, and perhaps primarily by his friendship for some of the members. Undoubtedly again it was the general style and manner of the Fraternity which fascinated him. Its members were known and respected as vigorous, bold and clean-cut young men. They were skilled and ready duellists, and in the one year 1881 they accepted as many as seventy-five challenges.

As "Young Fox," the name given to the freshman or neophyte, Herzl took a lively part in the proceedings. Proudly he wore the little blue Fraternity pillbox hat and the gold-blue-white band; he attended all the drinking parties, swallowed his quota of beer, joined in the choruses of joyous student songs, played cards and chess, and wrote innumerable articles for the Fraternity paper.

During the first term of his membership he participated daily from 1 to 3 and from 5 to 7 in the official duelling activities and even took a special course under the fencing master. And though it was remarked to his discredit that he had fought only a single duel, he was still regarded, at least during the first period, with considerable respect because of his literary gifts, and liked because of his high spirits and lively temperament.

Herrmann Bahr, who entered the Fraternity after Herzl, recorded later the unforgettable impression produced upon him in a casual encounter by the "exceptional though some-what exotic beauty" of this tall young man and by his "gracious, off-handed and mocking manner of address." A companion of his *Lesehalle* days remembers him for his liveliness and flow of wit. "The dark eyes," he reports, "were fixed penetratingly on the listener." As such he appears, too, in a photograph dating from that period: towering above his comrades, dressed with unobtrusive elegance, he shows his sharp cut profile, on which rests an expression of determination and of haughty disregard for human beings.

The rush of his participation in Fraternity life soon abated. He was undoubtedly writing of himself when he said of the bourgeois hero of the novel *Hagenau*, that "he had con-scientiously gone through the customary buffooneries ex-pected of the sons of rich parents, and had given them up in good time as his understanding ripened." On July 27, 1880, he passed his first legal examination, with distinction in canon and German law. He had to settle down now to prepare for the second examination. Apart from this, he had something better to do with his time than continue to squander it on wild student gatherings.

He was an omniverous reader. His extraordinary knowledge of books was evident in his conversation, for he liked to adorn his speech with quotations, which came readily to his memory. In the *Lesehalle* there were few students who used the library to the same extent, and in the "Suggestion Book" were frequently to be found regular articles by Herzl recommending subscription to this or that periodical. In January 1882 he began to keep a diary in which he analyzed and criticized his own course of reading. From this diary, from the letters to his friend Kana, and from various surviving notes, we are able to reconstruct what he read during several months, what he thought of the material he read, and what he thought worth while as an unfolding writer.

The range of the material is in itself astounding: between January and May 1882 he gives us in his diary detailed observations on more than forty works. He read the great philosophers and the most diverse poets and writers: Rueckert, Byron, Lenau, Macaulay, Mark Twain, Voltaire, Lesage, Balzac, and many others, showing a definite preference for French literature and for the realistic school. Among the Germans there was Jensen. Gottfried Keller received special attention. Herzl's entries show a mind which is sharply critical. He turned away from magniloquence, from over-emphasized pathos, from sickly romanticism, from everything that projected the stereotyped. Then again he expresses himself with cutting severity with regard to the stifling sensuousness which characterized many novels; he was equally severe with the unmeasured realism of many

French writers who turned all life, in his opinion, into a "pornographic goat dance," or portrayed it as "a wanton's couch." For all that, he was ready to perceive the hand of a master even in a "free" novel, as long as the naturalistic scenes were not exalted as ends in themselves.

He was moved and excited by Henry Murger's stories of the life of Bohemia. Here everything moved within the framework of good taste and of beauty. He calls the Frenchman, the "Horace of the Parisian Bohemia," and notes with admiration and envy that "there is hardly a suggestion of friction in the transformation of the idea into the word." How hard Herzl himself still finds the passage from inspiration to execution! "Happy Murger, who is able to say what he wants and to say it so wittily, attractively and profoundly!"

Balance and perfection in form and content is what he dreams of and strives after. It follows then that a book like Dostoyevsky's *Crime and Punishment* must be repellent to him. The only great passage in the work is the interview between Raskolnikov and the investigator. The remainder of the book he finds "disgusting." The feverish criminality of the hero makes the sensitive reader actually sick.

Hard and uncompromising as he was with others, he was equally so with himself. His external utterances were firm and decisive, but internally there was an everlasting struggle with doubt. In February 1882 he competed for three prizes offered by the *Wiener Allgemeine Zeitung* for the best feuilleton; he did not win so much as honorable mention. He took himself severely to task: "For three months I did nothing but dream of this. A whole month of unremitting labor I devoted to the writing itself. I experienced all the pangs of birth, all the ecstasies of creation, all the horrors of discouragement; I knew all the dark lifeless moments of the pitiful wretch whose head is emptied of ideas, whose hand is emptied of strength. And all for nothing! Am I really incapable of producing what seven other mediocre people have produced?"

Was he not, he asked himself, just a commonplace nobody who out of a mixture of futility and laziness, of self-delusion and vanity, had chosen the career of a writer? "And thus," he writes in an excess of sentimental despair, "die all my dreams of success and happiness." But suddenly he is lifted again on a flood of determination. "Back to the yoke. If I am not first on the list, I am not last either. More than one man, more than one hero even, has drunk this cup of bitterness!" And on his twenty-second birthday, May 2, 1882, his impatient ambition broke out in his diary: "I haven't even the tiniest success to show, not the slightest achievement of which to be proud."

He no longer even cherishes the illusion that he will make his mark among the spirits of his time. "Twenty-two years! And damn all done!" Then, after a few sentences in the same style, he turns away angrily from this "literary onanism:" "Here I am, playing the litterateur again! *Satis*! . . . I feel that I am not being sincere in my writing: that is the curse of a diary!" Then, when two days later his feuilleton does after all appear in the *Wiener Allgemeine Zeitung,* he expresses himself with inflated modesty: "Pah! *Post tot discrimina* . . . It really wasn't worth the trouble to pick up the few shabby compliments I got for this 'achievement.'"

We find him quarelling with the Jewish question, too, in this diary. On February 8, 1882, he read Wilhelm Jensen's *The Jews of Cologne,* an episode out of the Jewish persecutions of the middle fourteenth century. The picture of human wretchedness afforded by the medieval ghetto lay like a stone on his heart; that pain was relieved only by the generous emotions and the humane outlook with which the author had informed the work. The medieval Jews, "in their oppression, in the nobility of their spirit gleaming through the walls of their ghetto prison, in their oriental robes and manner of speech," reminded Herzl of the Moors of Spain.

"In the eyes of Jensen," he writes, "the Jews, too, emerge as a sort of aristocratic people which has come down in the world (God! How they have come down!); and then sometimes they make the miserable impression of those descendants of ancient aristocracies who are capable of everything — save earning an honest living by the labor of their hands." Still, Herzl found an excuse in the pressure of the outside world and — quaintly enough — in the prohibition of intermarriage which prevented the Jews from improving their racial stock. It was his conviction, according to the notes dating from that period, that only intermarriage could lead "to the improvement of the figurative and literal racial profile," and thus lead to a satisfactory solution. "The crossing of the western with the oriental races on the basis of a common state religion — that is the great solution to be desired."

Complete assimilation, then, disappearance without a trace in the ocean of the surrounding world! "Without the dull compulsion of the ghetto," Herzl believed, "a compulsion which long outlived the actual ring of walls within which it had been exercised, without that ghetto which still survives in the narrow views of certain men who pass for 'educated,' that ring-finger on the hand of humanity which we call the Jews would not have taken on the form it now has." What was needed now was release from the compulsion of the ring of the ghetto, the reintroduction of free motion and growth into the stunted or twisted limb. "The Jews have too long prided themselves on being just this — the ring-finger of humanity." But the posture, he intimated, had become paralysis, compulsion had deformed the original shape and destroyed the original character.

The day after he made these observations Herzl read Eugen Dühring's book *The Jewish Problem as a Problem of Race, Morals and Culture* — the first and most important effort to find a "scientific," philosophic, biologic and historical basis for the anti-Semitism which was sweeping through Europe in those days (1881). Dühring saw the Jewish question as a purely racial question, and for him the Jewish race was without any worth whatsoever. Those peoples which, out of a false sentiment of humanity, had permitted the Jews to live among them with equal and sometimes even with superior rights, had to be liberated from the harmful intruder, had to be de-Judaized. Inasmuch as the Jews could not be settled in a state of their own, they had to be dealt with on the basis of special enactments. Their influence on public affairs, via the press, for instance, had to be taken from them; their possessions had to pass under the control of the State; their participation in the public service had to be restricted to their proportion of the general population; intermarriage with Jews was to be, if not forbidden, then certainly subject to social ostracism. In brief, there was to be a complete reversal of the "emancipation," or, as the twentieth century followers of Dühring have expressed it, "a return to the ghetto."

It should be quite clear, from those views of Herzl's which have been reproduced here, that the reading of this book must have had upon him the effect — approximately — of a blow between the eyes. The observations set down in his diary burn with indignation: "An infamous book . . . If Düh-ring, who unites so much undeniable intelligence with so much universality of knowledge, can write like this, what are we to expect from the ignorant masses?" Were the Jews really what Dühring said they were, a miserable and revolting race, without a single decent trait of character? "But how could a race so devoid of gifts and character have resisted for a millenium and a half the inhuman pressure of a surrounding world? How could it do this without possessing something good?" And how was it that Dühring, who was forever speaking of "loyalty," failed to be deeply impressed by this Ahasuerian people's loyalty to its God?

"The first chapters of the book," notes Herzl, "are, in spite of their exaggerations and their spirit of hatefulness, so informative that every Jew ought to read them. The peculiar twist in the Jewish morality, and the lack of moral seriousness in many (Dühring says in *all*) spheres of action, are mercilessly exposed and characterized. There is much to be learned therefrom! But as one reads further it becomes apparent that a certain element of truth has been made the implement of much that is false, of much that has been delib-erately *falsified*, and Dühring passes from the dangerous to the downright ridiculous . . ."

"Let us take as an example the medieval regulation, so fateful for the Jewish character, according to which the prac-tice of usury was permitted to the Jews and forbidden to the Christians. The Jews became the leeches of the age; but the blood which they drew into themselves was not destined to nourish them; it was in turn squeezed out of them, partly through taxation and partly through direct dispossession. And now a Christian-German professor comes along and reproaches the leeches with having fed on the blood of others!

But what else was there for the leeches of the medieval era —
and if you like of the modern era too — to do? They were
compelled to be usurers! What else were they Jews for? . . .
But when they had filled themselves with the blood of their
victims, they in turn poured out the same blood to the
Christian upper classes. What were the Jews, in effect, but
a method of indirect taxation? But were they happy to
fulfil this function? Would they not have preferred a thousand times over to be admitted to the handicrafts?"

What had Dühring done? He had merely presented the
legend of the middle ages in modern dress. "The sacrificed
Christian child became sacrificed Christian capital;" the
primitive, bloodthirsty legend which had been discredited
by modern education re-appeared in an economic interpretation. The modern agitators who spoke so glibly of "the
anti-capitalistic social-democratic pest" would finish up,
soon enough, as the instigators of terrific mass passions.
"You may even find," notes Herzl, "an analogy to the ancient accusation of Jewish poisoning of wells in the modern
talk about the 'Judaization of the press,' which poisons the
sources of 'public opinion.' "

Since religion played no role in modern conflicts, the field
shifted to the racial. Modern gasolene poured on medieval
stakes! And after the fire comes the plundering. "The
hunger for loot is the base, stinking motive of all movements
against the Jews; the centuries have brought no change
into this Christian morality . . . But even these nursery tales
of the Jewish people will disappear, and a new age will follow, in which a passionless and clear-headed humanity will
look back upon our errors even as the enlightened men of
our time look back upon the middle ages."

The passionate reaction to Dühring's book, breaking forth in every sentence written down by Herzl, shows us how deeply he had been moved, and how fearfully he had been shaken in his belief that the Jewish question was on the point of disappearing. We shall find echoes of this experience in the pages of the *Judenstaat*. For the time being, however, he shrank from the logical consequences of his reactions. Only his inner pride began to build itself up. The next few pages of his diary are devoted to indifferent matters.

But whether he willed it or not, whether he knew it or not, the reading of Dühring's work was the beginning of a deep process of change. How could it be otherwise? The impression he carried away from the experience remained with him for the rest of his life. He himself said in later years that his serious and troubled preoccupation with the Jewish problem dated from that point. The veil of illusion had been violently torn away from before his eyes. For a certain period he could thrust the realization into the lower reaches of his mind by violent activity: the moment he suspended activity to listen to his innermost self he heard the echo of the experience.

The more immediate reaction was undoubtedly a sharpened perception and evaluation of his fellow-members in the Fraternity. Here too anti-Semitism was breaking through; student after student expressed himself favorably toward the Jew-baiting speeches of Schoenerer, who was making a special effort to win over the universities. In the Fraternity debates Herzl expressed himself sharply against any open or covert manifestation of such sympathy. But he was already known for the sharpness of his tongue and the individuality of his views. Thus he won to himself neither the few co-religionists who belonged to the Fraternity nor the mass of the Germanic students. "He did not feel at ease among his comrades, and was to almost all of them an alien element."

It was the rule in these student bodies that every member should be given a new name. Was it pure accident that Herzl was given that of Tancred, the hero of the first crusade immortalized by Tasso as the conqueror of Jerusalem? Was it pure accident that his additional mock titles were "Prince of Galilee" and "Duke of Antioch?" Had his vigorous and manly defense of Jewry moved his comrades to this choice, or had he already spoken in those days of Palestine? Was there within him a premonitory flash of the ideas which were later to be incorporated in the *Judenstaat?* Perhaps not much was needed to set loose this inspiration after his reading of Dühring: nothing more, in fact, than the discovery of Pinsker's appeal, *Auto-Emancipation*, which appeared in 1882. Herzl himself, speaking long after to Stefan Zweig, could not decide whether it would have been for better or for worse if he had recognized his mission in Vienna, in the full strength of his youth — but without having yet achieved a reputation in the literary field and without the experiences of the Paris years.

In that same crowded year of 1882 there was founded *Der Verein deutscher Studenten in Wien* — a Pan-Germanic anti-Semitic organization. On March 5, 1883, this body arranged a great memorial demonstration in the Sophien Hall in honor of Richard Wagner, recently deceased. The climax of the program was an address by a member of the *Albia*, Herrmann Bahr, in which the speaker spoke approvingly of what he called "Wagnerian anti-Semitism," and declared himself a convert to the Pan-Germanic anti-Semitic movement. The address was received with a wild outburst of enthusiasm. Thereupon the police intervened and dissolved the society. Bahr was rebuked by the University Senate — and idolized by the *Albia*. Thus the Fraternity had taken a definite turn in a direction which made participation impossible for a self-respecting Jew.

Herzl had not been present at the memorial demonstration. Two days later, on March 7, 1883, he wrote a letter to the governing body of the *Albia*. He had learned from newspaper reports, he wrote, that the Wagner memorial meeting, in which his Fraternity had taken a part, had been transformed into an anti-Semitic demonstration. He had not, since then, seen in the public prints any declaration from the Fraternity dissociating itself from the incident. He could not hope, he went on, that such a declaration of dissociation would result from his letter. His Fraternity had, therefore, identified itself with a movement which he, as a believer in liberty, was bound to condemn, even if he had not been a Jew. "It is pretty clear that, handicapped as I am by my Semitism (the word was not yet known at the time of my entry), I would today refrain from seeking a membership which would, indeed, probably be refused me; it must also be clear to every decent person that under these circumstances I cannot wish to retain my membership." In this honorable fashion Herzl withdrew from the organization.

The *Albia* was outraged by the tone of this letter. The plenary session of the Fraternity decided to refuse the "resignation." It insisted instead on "cashiering" or expelling Herzl: it was the severest penalty within the jurisdiction of that body, and was tantamount to a dishonorable discharge. However, there arose within the ranks a protest against this punishment of a dignified act: the resolution was withdrawn, and a letter written to Herzl on April 3 informed him, in a few dry lines, that his name had been removed from the roster, and that he was requested to surrender his insignia.

"And so I said farewell to those gallant young fellows," Herzl wrote long afterwards, in a mocking tone. The matter touched him much more closely at the time. To Dankwart, a former fellow-member in the Fraternity, he wrote: "If I may add a purely personal man-to-man observation here: I did not come to this decision lightly." And in his diary, he writes under date of April 13 — ten days after the incident and after a year without any entries: "Irony of ironies! A few of my closer acquaintances are actually beginning to believe in me — and I myself can't do it ...' Gifted young chap,' or 'man of wit and spirit' seem to be the phrases used about me ... Ah, they don't know how much loneliness and pain and despair this 'forward-thrusting young man' carries concealed under his vest. Doubt! Despair! An elegant doubt, a perfumed despair — which is why the one man who can sometimes look into me, and perceive what the vest conceals, I mean Heinrich Kana, does not believe them to be genuine... And when I reflect that this is the way it will probably go on, year after year, that I shall gradually make my way forward in the world's regard, while within me my unhappiness and despair will rise like a tide! Miserable, charming life!"

This mood of helplessness and resignation had, to be sure, also other grounds than the spiritual struggle round his Jewishness. Herzl himself attributed it mainly to disappointments in love and — even more — his consistent inability to attain literary success; and the latter became all the more urgent for him as he found less and less possibility for a free, generous and honest outlet in his student life.

In the fall of 1882 he completed a one act comedy, *The Hirschkorn Case*, and sent it to the popular actor Ernst Hartmann with the request that it be submitted to the Hofburg Theatre, the leading institution in Vienna. Herzl's ambition could take no lower flight. In a somewhat affected letter he described the play as "the offspring of a union between legalistic boredom and a passing young man who calls himself modestly 'the great inspiration.'" Hartmann sent back a friendly reply and forwarded the piece to the Hofburg Theatre, which rejected it.

He tried his luck with feuilletons, and hit the mark from time to time: we shall deal with this side of his productivity in the next chapter. But the successes were few and far between. One of the feuilletons, *The Commonplace*, has already been mentioned in connection with a competition. The rejection slips continued to accumulate.

The human material with which his student life had brought him in contact was unapt for transformation into dramatic forms: his will to creation, moreover, and his fantasy, outran his manipulative gifts. Then, toward the end of November 1883, he managed to complete one play out of the cycle *Die Ritter vom Gemeinplatz*. It bore the significant title of *The Disillusioned*. But by this time he felt himself to have advanced so far that he treated this completed piece with contempt, and would not submit it to any theatre. *Tartarin*! was the word Kana flung at him.

There was a compensating factor in his life; if the world at large refused him recognition, his parents tried to make up for it. Their lives were dedicated to the welfare of their son; their utmost admiration was reserved for him. They provided him with the means for frequent journeys. He passed the summer months at the Austrian countryside, he visited his relatives in Budapest, he went on a trip to Switzerland in July 1883, after he had passed — and none too easily! — his second legal examination. In May of 1884, having finally graduated as Doctor of Laws, he set out, via south-west Germany, for Paris, the dream world of his literary ambitions.

It was the high point of fulfilment for him thus far in his life. Paris! It meant the loosing of those bonds of the ordinary and the commonplace which were his perpetual fear, and which threatened to reduce him to that most hateful of conditions — the average man. Here he could give full freedom to his wild playfulness, as if he were in a world of children. Here he could change his audiences and table companions from day to day, send out the flashes of his spirit to ever-renewing circles of acquaintances, and feel himself admired afresh each day as he strode, erect, graceful, nonchalant, through the streets, a vision of elegance in his faultless clothes and in the sideburns which he had begun to affect. He took lonely walks through the country, and let himself sink into melancholy harmony with the landscape, calling up elegiac moods tinged with secret self-satisfaction. He wrote down his sad meditations on the nature of life, worked himself into a sweetly painful romantic state of mind, and dreamed of light flirtations and passing affairs deepening into the intoxication of love for which his spirit longed.

Above all, however, he made use of this visit for purposes of self-instruction. He was assiduous in his attendance at the theatre, he haunted the museums, he listened to parliamentary debates and scientific lectures, he frequented public meetings and court sessions. He sought life everywhere. And he was learning in another sense, too: skillful, compact expression was becoming more habitual. He found himself condensing into a few lines the essence of some spiritual or external experience; and these scattered exercises, flowing freely from within, had more grace and simplicity than his programmatic "works" belonging to that time.

On July 30, 1884, Herzl was admitted to the bar in Vienna. His student days were over. A new era opened for him, with its challenge to prove whether or not there was something in him to establish and proclaim to the world. His youth was finished.

That youth of his had started with every advantage and had been attended by every external promise of happiness. But it had not been a happy youth in reality. The internal struggle had been too harsh, the strength that seethed in him had found no outlet, and had been forced inward, to torment him with its imprisoned energy. He was of those men to whom God gives perception before he gives them the liberating word, and who therefore grow younger as they achieve ripeness and the gift of expression and externalization.

In one of the uncompleted sketches of that period, *Die Jungen*, the hero asks bitterly: "Is there really such a thing as youth?" And the answer is provided in one of Herzl's feuilletons: "No, youth is only a fairy tale invented by the old who want to deceive themselves and others into the belief that once upon a time they were strong, honest and full of enthusiasms."

CHAPTER III

THE WRITER IN THE MAKING

ON AUGUST 4, 1884, Herzl entered on his law practice in the service of the state. Until December 13 of that year he was attached to the *Landesgericht* or Court of General Sessions, working on criminal cases; from then till April 15 of the following year he was attached to the *Handelsgericht* or Court for Commercial Disputes; and then, from April 15 to June 14, he was back at the *Landesgericht*, working on civil cases. When, in June, he was transferred to the provincial *Landesgericht* of Salzburg, the Presiding Judge of the metropolitan *Landesgericht* commended him for his abilities, his diligence and his faultless behavior. A similar attestation was given him later by the Court of Salzburg.

But from the beginning his juristic work played a secondary role in his life. The writing of briefs was subordinated to the writing of sketches and outlines of literary creations to come. On New Year's night, 1884, he wrote in his diary: "I spend the mornings filling out forms at the *Handelsgericht*, but my afternoons are beautiful, yes, beautiful. I read, I dream, I smoke, I write. So day flows into day, and one day I shall be old without ever having known youth. But come what may, we shall always burn with activity." This was his summing up of a year which all in all had been a good one, but which had not yet brought him any measure of success.

There had been times when impatience had consumed him. The mornings, with their forms and reports, were interminable; the long devotion to literature, without any sign of adequate return, oppressed him.

Service in Salzburg was pleasanter than in the metropolis. Even the legal work seemed more attractive. His official room was in an old fortress tower, immediately under the bell tower, "And three times daily the chimes rang prettily in my ears." The beauty of the surrounding country heightened both his enjoyment of life and his capacity for work. "In Salzburg," he wrote later, "I passed one of the happiest interludes of my life."

Yet it was in Salzburg that he took the final and fateful decision to devote himself exclusively to literature without the economic covering protection of the legal profession. It seemed to him afterwards that he would gladly have remained in the beautiful city of Salzburg if he could have foreseen steady promotion there in the service of the state. But though he may at that time have been so far from Judaism that only pride and a decent respect for the feelings of his parents stood between him and baptism, he could not help perceiving that as a Jew he would find the higher levels of the civil service hierarchy closed to him. His wounded honor told him that he could have fitted very well into those circles, and even better into higher military service. Had he not, in the early months of 1885, avoided two duels only because in each instance his challenge had extorted an apology from his opponents?

He could, of course, have followed the example of certain school comrades, Jews like himself, with his training and equipment, who became practicing lawyers at large instead of civil servants; he too could have earned a livelihood thus and achieved a certain reputation. But this called for more love of the law than he possessed, and for a pride less ambitious than his. He wanted success, standing, reputation, and he wanted them quickly. So much is clear from all his utterances. He had, as we shall see, achieved a certain reputation as a feuilletonist, enough, at any rate, to justify his faith in his own talents. He had, above all, the ceaseless urge to write. And then there were his parents, who loved him and believed in him, and who attached even less importance than he to the business of achieving economic independence with the least possible loss of time. Here, as a matter of fact, was one of the strongest driving forces in his hunger for success: his pride found it intolerable that he should still be dependent — perhaps for a number of years to come — on his parents, even though, or perhaps because, he considered them the "best" parents in the world, and loved and honored them as parents have seldom been loved and honored. All these considerations led to his final resolve; and on August 5, 1885, he withdrew from the service in order to seek fame and fortune as a writer.

Brimming with hope, he set out on a journey which was to be the introduction to his literary life. He went first to Belgium and Holland in order to acquaint himself with the art masterpieces of those northern countries. The Dutch and Flemish masters left an unforgettable impression on his soul. He listened "to the eternal melody of the sea." But mind and heart were alert for first-hand impressions of life, too. He began at this period to display his inimitable skill at setting down in a few short phrases the essence of a little world. Thus in Bruges: "In the suburb street, Rue du Cote, the lace-makers sit before the doors. The needles fly, earnings are small. The dealers in the Rue Montagne de la Cour in Brussels make the money."

But on the high excitement of that journey followed inevitably the dullness of ordinary days, with the laborious struggle for the right word, for recognition, and — now added to the rest — the need to earn at least a part of his keep by his pen. In what ludicrous contrast with the splendor of his dreams was the actuality of some of his works; for sixty gulden a month he wrote a weekly column of silly jokes for a humorous periodical by the name of *The Flea*. But he did carry on industriously toward the completion of the comedy, *Muttersöhnchen*, which he had begun in Salzburg. In November he submitted it to his parents and to friends. They found it good. So he packed it, together with *The Hirschkorn Case* and *Tabarin* (based on a sketch by Catulle Mendès), into a bag and left for Berlin, to seek a producer.

During his stay in Berlin copies of the *New Yorker Staatszeitung* arrived from overseas with reports — which were soon reproduced in the German newspapers — that Herzl's one act comedy *Tabarin* had been played in New York by the famous actor Mitterwurzer during his tour, and had been enthusiastically received. This announcement, together with the letters of introduction he carried, and his own winning personality, opened all doors for him, and he was received everywhere with the utmost friendliness. He met innumerable people, dined out night after night, went from gathering to gathering. "Yesterday there was a *grande soirée* at Treitel's," he wrote to his parents after one such reception. "Thirty or forty ugly little Jews and Jewesses. Not a very refreshing sight." He was of course an eager visitor at the theatres. It was not until the day before his departure that he took time out for the city sights.

The visit to Berlin had resulted in valuable connections and in no less valuable insights. But the longed-for stage success in the German capital had evaded him. Not one of its many theatres accepted any of his plays. Herzl consoled his parents, and himself, too, with the reflection that the chief purpose of his journey had really been to get to know the metropolitan theatre and to make important personal connections; and in this he had succeeded. But to his friend Kana, who was even less successful than he, but also less easily bribed in his judgments, he wrote of the humiliations which he had had to suffer, the dirt in which he had been compelled to crawl, until his friend, worried by the tone of the letters but merciless in his honesty, wrote back:

"Is that what you call 'humiliation'? Is it crawling in the dirt when you have to spend your time with a couple of hateful people and show them a friendly face?"

He, that is, Herzl, who was forever quoting the categorical imperative, was intolerant and inhumane in his judgment of people — so his friend wrote; he was domineering and hyperegotistic. What were others, "who do not, like me, know that at bottom you are a decent and modest person," to think of his wild superlatives? "Here is a young fellow who has written a good play. To get it produced, in order that he may achieve recognition and success, is the very purpose of his life. Naturally. But what he demands is that everyone else should also conceive it as his life's purpose to have the play produced, should put all other business aside and think of nothing else. And because they refuse to do this, as they have a perfect right to do, the young man becomes embittered, the whole world goes awry before his eyes, its bad features swell up to the skies, its good features suddenly disappear. Whichever way he looks he sees dirt, nothing but dirt, and he is racked by disgust ... there are 1300 million human beings on this planet, 1300 million centers of the universe, and here comes one of these little 1300 million points and demands that all the others stop functioning!"

At that, seen from the outside, Herzl really had no right to complain of a lack of recognition or to despair of success. None of the persons who had declined to produce his plays had put his talents in question, while in the field in which he could now show a definite degree of achievement, namely that of the feuilleton, his reputation was steadily increasing. The notices of the successful production of his *Tabarin* in New York, together with his widening circle of acquaintances, were opening for him the editorial doors of the big newspapers. In some of them he was already regarded as a steady contributor.

Thus the range of his connections and relationships widened from year to year, and when he travelled again it was an ever-widening audience that waited for his impressions and observations. When, toward the end of July 1886, he made a second journey to France, to recuperate after his completion of the play *Seine Hoheit*, his parents begged him to limit his communication to them to a single daily postcard. Whatever he picked up on the way in the shape of impressions, moods and ideas, said his mother, he was to use as literary material, "for it belongs not to us but to the world."

This time he remained in Paris only a few days, on his way to and from Normandy, and these days too were filled to the brim with new sights and sensations. He travelled slowly and comfortably through Rouen, Dieppe and le Havre, to Trouville, where the brilliant life made up a fascinating picture. "Trouville is incomparably the most beautiful and the most elegant of the seaside resorts that I have seen. Only in England, that is if anywhere, can there be anything superior" (August 9, 1886). Refreshed and in excellent health he returned home.

In October 1886, he tried his luck again in Berlin, this time with the new comedy *Seine Hoheit*, a satire on the power of money in bourgeois society which evaluates all human beings according to their possessions and transforms even the human emotions into commodities to be bought and sold. As it turned out, Herzl's second visit to Berlin was more important for his journalistic than his dramatic career. He renewed and deepened the acquaintanceship which he had begun that summer with Arthur Levysohn, editor-in-chief of the *Berliner Tageblatt*. The acquaintanceship became a friendship growing warmer through the years. Levysohn at once recognized the journalistic talent of the young man; he was eager to find advancement for him and did in fact a great deal in that direction. He commissioned Herzl to send him a regular weekly article from Vienna for the *Berliner Tageblatt*, a kind of commentary and review. This was more than Herzl really had expected.

Until the spring of 1887, and again in the autumn of that year, he wrote at weekly or bi-weekly intervals for Levysohn's paper. The articles were exceedingly diverse in content as in value, and they touched upon an extraordinary variety of loosely connected themes — society, politics, drama, literature. The author nowhere attempted to give in these sketches, which he called "The Seven Day Journey," anything like a coherent account of events. The material merely furnished him with an occasion for the display of his lambent wit. But these little trifles constituted a novelty for Berlin. The novelty made a certain impression in literary circles, but, it must be admitted, left the Berlin reading public cold.

The over-exertion in the pursuit of success, the futile knocking at the doors of the theatre, disappointments of one kind and another, resulted in an attack of depression during the winter of 1886–87. The physical symptom was a painful pressure at the back of the head. Herzl did his best to conceal his condition from his mother, but she was not to be deceived and strongly urged upon her son a journey to those southern lands which had so often brought healing to creative spirits.

Herzl, the professional litterateur, set about this journey systematically. He planned in advance a series of articles and feuilletons, and arranged for their publication. In the the course of one week he wrote a pleasant little one-act play for a newspaper. In this fashion he would finance his journey. Before he left he impressed it on his father that the latter was to come forward with financial help only when this was absolutely unavoidable.

It was the Italian journey of a feuilletonist. It unwound comfortably over Venice and Pisa, Leghorn and Rome (where he stayed only a week), over Naples and Capri and Amalfi; then it swung back again through Naples and Rome to Florence, and led finally over Bologna, Padua and Venice toward home. At first Herzl tried to maintain his regular tempo of work; but before long the warm and brilliant cities and skies of Italy, more apt for enjoyment than for labor, overcame him. By the time he reached Naples he had decided to be carefree for once in his life, "just as if I were a young man," and write feuilletons only when he felt like it. From Capri he wrote on March 17 to his parents: "My glorious and enchanting trip has reached its high point here, and this peak is silent, lonely and wonderful, like the topmost reaches of a glacier ... That wild nerve-destroying method of work which I have pursued during the last year and a half must come to a stop. What is the good of success if you have rendered yourself incapable of enjoying it? Certain positions I have had to storm at the point of the bayonet; from now on I shall storm no more. I shall conquer."

We find the same tone in all the feuilletons of that journey — the calmer, more patient spirit, the easier tempo of work, the proud determination to let each achievement ripen to perfection. They read more easily, they are not forced, they are less programmatically witty, they are much more individual and independent in conception and language, even though now and again the shadow of Heine's immortal Italian Journey inevitably falls across the pages. One of the feuilletons, "Emmelfey" (the pronunciation which he heard Englishmen give to Amalfi) caused a minor sensation among the more sophisticated readers of the *Wiener Allgemeine Zeitung* when it appeared on March 25, 1887. Here Herzl attained a fascinating blend of witty observation, chastened sentimentality and a beautiful, mild style in which every word fitted perfectly into its place. It was the unveiling of a new and original talent in the field of the feuilleton so beloved among the Viennese.

The Italian journey proved to be Herzl's conquest of the press. With it he entered on his career as an accepted writer. On April 1, 1887 he returned from Italy and on the 15th he was installed as the feuilleton editor of the *Wiener Allgemeine Zeitung*. He had "arrived."

But he did not retain this position long, for on July 15 he was no longer on the editorial staff of the paper. Just about this time he was apprised that his comedy *Seine Hoheit* had been accepted for production by the Wallner Theatre in Berlin, and by the end of the month he had the contract in his hands.

It was an important year for Herzl. That same summer appeared his first book, a collection of articles, sketches and stories under the rather unfortunate title of *News from Venus*. Some of the material had already appeared in print; some was new. The unifying theme was love as it comes to expression in a variety of circumstances and societies. It was all light, chatty, and distinguished in a minor way.

The introductory *causerie* was devoted to disillusionment, which always resulted, according to the author, when the object of longing was transferred from the dream-distant horizon into the proximity of reality; Venus, the bright star, examined too closely and realistically by the scientist, loses its charm, and so does love when it is similarly treated. It is only the earthy, the massively real, which can sustain such scrutiny, and the dreamer stands before it helpless and disillusioned.

This theme recurs not only in Herzl's first collection of theses; it is one of the basic psychic motifs of all his life.

The closing sketch, "The Thought-Reader," tells of a man who has the peculiar gift of sensing in human beings the transition from the true to the false, from the fullness of feeling to the emptiness of the gesture. "The division into good and bad people is as old fashioned as blood and thunder melodrama," Herzl has this character say. "I believe that in the beginning everyone is good, or as I would put it, genuine . . . Then something intervenes, it may be only the passage of time, and they become ungenuine. Of love nothing remains then but the tender glance, of friendship nothing but the warm handshake. But I observe the change at once, however deceptively alike the two phenomena may be . . . I have a nose for the decay of the genuine . . . I see the transformation into the ungenuine going on all about me . . . Put yourself in the condition of that unhappy man who can with the naked eye see the infusoria swimming about in the water which he drinks. He perishes between revulsion and thirst. In such case am I . . ."

This closing article supplied the basic motif of Herzl's second collection of journalistic pieces, which appeared a year later under the imprimatur of the same publishing house. He chose as his motto the following quotation from Swift's *Tale of a Tub:* "This is the sublime and refined point of felicity, calling the possession of being well deceived, the serene, peaceful state of being a fool among knaves." After long hesitation he chose for this collection the title of *The Book of Folly* and dedicated it to his "honored friend, Dr. Arthur Levysohn."

It differed from the first collection no less in value than in form. It was a definitely superior work. Instead of a loose succession of scenes, dialogues and monologues, we have a genuine orchestration of feuilletons — that art-form which Boerne and Heine had transferred from the French to the German and which reached its highest form in literary Vienna.

The most characteristic section of the book is the very first, and the theme unfolds most clearly in the story "Second-Class Gods." Here Herzl tells us how he travelled with a fourth-rate theatre, working among the actors, putting up and taking down the tent, arranging the benches for the audience — and participating as an equal in the lives of his fellow artists. Each one of them considered himself a genius, and by means of this self-deception and of hearty mutual lying, they made life tolerable for themselves and for each other. "One disillusionment more, my friends! Not every unrecognized poet is a genius; not every one who fights against windmills is a Don Quixote; not every travelling comedian is the pure idealist which I thought him to be in my youthful passion for superlatives . . ." And when one of the friendly actors happens to get a little more applause than usual, his nose is suddenly in the air and he looks down it contemptuously at the others. "Ah, you second-class gods, how well I know you now! A little success, a little luck and sunshine, and the weeds shoot up like a thicket: dishonesty, hypocrisy, arrogance, ingratitude! For all of us are like that."

This feuilleton reflects adequately the tone of his mind and the tenor of his thoughts. It is the disillusionment of a kindly spirit: "For all of us are like that." All of us live by the grace of lies. None of us is morally any better, and the height of happiness is, in Swift's phrase, "to be a fool among knaves."

A total of seven or eight lines is devoted to Jews — Herzl's impressions of the Ghetto in Rome. "What a steaming in the air, what a street! Countless open doors and windows thronged with innumerable pallid and worn-out faces. The ghetto! With what base and persistent hatred these unfortunates have been persecuted for the sole crime of faithfulness to their religion. We've travelled a long way since those times: nowadays the Jew is despised only for having a crooked nose, or for being a plutocrat even when he happens to be a pauper." Pity and bitterness inform these lines, but they are written by a detached spectator. He did not know how much of the Jew there was in him even in this detachment of his, in this feeling of remoteness from a world which offered him not living reality but folly.

These fragmentary productions of Herzl's pen are relatively unimportant when placed side by side with his later creations; they are not those masterpieces of craftsmanship which he was yet to produce in the realm of the feuilleton. But the best of them are already luminous with those characteristics which stamp the inspirations of his maturity: originality of perception, clarity of outline, gentleness of expression, perfect balance between content and phraseology. The slight affectation of the grand manner was already evident in his prose, giving it its individual and inimitable features. He has not yet achieved for every sentence that exactitude and relevance which is the mark of perfection, but neither has he reached that super-refinement of style which later on was to emerge occasionally as the excess of a virtue. In very few instances does he content himself with straightforward, simple narrative; for the most part it is *causerie*, casual conversation. He seems to be addressing a listener, and his remarks flow from him effortlessly, carrying with them no part of his own emotions; or if there is an emotional attitude, it is restricted to a kind of self-irony. No cry of the heart of a poet breaks through; and if now and again there is a hint of the heart's participation, of sorrow or indignation, it is served up delicately, like a finely prepared dish at a gourmet's banquet, in such wise as to make no heavy calls on the digestion of the guest.

It would have been extraordinary indeed if these two little books of Herzl's, distinguished in form, directed in manner and content toward the best social circles, had made any considerable impression on the public at large. The few reviews which they received were laudatory — but the sale was small. "Why don't you do some advertising?" the publisher wrote to him. But whatever the public reception, the books served to keep his name before the eyes of editors — and that was about as much as he looked for.

For between the first and second books Herzl had scored his first dramatic success. In February 1888 his comedy *Seine Hoheit* was produced by an excellent cast in Prague, and was well received by public and critics alike. On March 18 the play was transferred to Berlin. "Its success there was considerably greater than in Prague, even though the production was immeasurably inferior," the triumphant author wrote his parents, who had travelled to Prague to attend the *première*. The Berlin critics were for the most part generous in their treatment of the beginner. There were a few sharply negative pieces, but in the big newspapers the comedy "was either mildly praised or gently criticized." There was, however, complete unanimity in the allusions to "the superb feuilletonist."

Invitations now poured in on him from countless newspapers. There remained only one more citadel to be stormed — the illustrious *Wiener Neue Freie Presse*. And this he achieved effortlessly with his feuilletons on his summer travels.

These carried him across Belgium into England, the country which he was to visit so frequently in later years as a Zionist. It seemed as though he was not destined to make a single journey without at least the fleeting intrusion of the Jewish theme. On this occasion the experience occurred in Mainz. He heard for the first time, with his own ears, the dread medieval cry of "Hep! Hep!"

"I dropped in one evening at a cheap concert hall," he recounted afterwards, "drank my glass of beer and began to make my way out. As I was moving through the noisy room a young lad shouted 'Hep! Hep!' after me, and a tumult rose around him." He did not mention the incident until many years later, for it is first recorded in his diary for 1895, in the days which witnessed his awakening.

At that time his mind was receptive only to happier impressions. London, the tremendous world city, made a profound impression on him. It was, he wrote his parents, the most beautiful city he had ever seen, not excluding Paris. He went to the sea-side, in England and again, soon after, in Trouville; and as always the contact had a revivifying effect on him. Of the dozen feuilletons which he produced on that journey he sent the best to the *Wiener Neue Freie Presse*. They were printed immediately. He could now say that the entire German and Austrian press was open to him.

All that remained now was to achieve a comparable first place in the theatrical world. He therefore turned his attention once more to this field. He addressed a short and businesslike letter to Hugo Wittmann, the leading feuilletonist of the *Neue Freie Presse*, proposing collaboration. Wittmann agreed, on condition that the collaboration remain a secret. The idea which Herzl submitted to him impressed him favorably, and so from their joint labors there soon emerged the comedy *Wilddiebe*. The theme was regulation comedy bordering on farce. It dealt with three men of the world, two of them belonging to the aristocracy, one to the upper middle class, and their three distractingly beautiful women. We find the usual dramatic complications, misunderstandings and cross-purposes, and the usual happy ending which consists of the loving reconciliation between

Philipp von Sorau and his neglected and abandoned wife. Most of the stuff was, in theatre parlance, "hokum," but (or therefore) it was enthusiastically received by producers and public. The piece ran for some years, on and off; it was a success everywhere, even in the financial sense — unlike Herzl's other theatre pieces. But what mattered most to Herzl was that it achieved the supreme distinction of being produced by *the* theatre — to wit, the *Hofburgtheater* of Vienna.

In later years Schnitzler reminded Herzl, in a letter, how the two of them had once taken a walk, on a late autumn evening, past the new *Hofburgtheater* which was then in the process of building. Herzl was at that time still far from his great triumph. "I remember your telling me, with a modest, winning glance directed at the rising walls of the theatre: 'I'll be in there some day'." Now he had attained his ambition; he had scaled the peak, he had been received in the holy of holies of the German theatrical world, and he was to be readmitted several times with other plays of his.

He had every reason to consider himself a definite success as dramatist and prose-writer. He had reached the point which could permit him to think seriously of founding a home for himself.

During all the years of his upward struggle he had longed for the woman who was to be his comrade throughout his life. The dream of this fulfilment stares out from page after page of his published works and his private letters; sometimes it glimmers between the lines, sometimes it finds explicit utterance. Except for that one shattering experience of his adolescence, Herzl had not, during the years of his early manhood, known love and disappointment in their most powerful manifestation, even though there are not wanting numerous hints of emergent love and quick disillusionment. It is only thus that we can explain the blasé tone which runs through his treatment of the subject of love. Of his "successes" there cannot be any doubt. He was strikingly handsome, his voice was as beautiful as his features, his eyes were magnetic. But these successes did not play an important role in his life, and he hardly seems to have taken advantage of them. As a matter of fact this "blasé" man of the world was, in his heart of hearts, too much the sensitive spirit, the enthusiast and the moralist to permit himself to pluck whatever flowers happened to offer themselves to his senses. With concealed shyness and timidity he sought the *one* flower, the asphodel of the poets — the helpmeet who would be to him what his mother had been to his father.

In his student period Herzl had already frequented the home of the Naschauer family. Joseph Naschauer was the son of an immigrant from Bohemia. A man of wide culture, with special emphasis on Jewish philosophy and literature, Naschauer was also an exceptional business success. He had accumulated a considerable fortune in Hungarian petroleum and in the Danube shipping industry. His youngest daughter, Julie (for some reason or other the French form of her name had been adopted by everyone in the family), was born in Budapest on February 1, 1868, and was therefore eight years younger than Herzl.

The time of their first meeting is unrecorded; it appears that at first he paid little attention to her. In any case, there is no mention of her name in his diaries or letters before February 1886. Indeed, he records that in January of that year he fell in love with a thirteen year old child, Magda Fuchs. "Magda! Whom eleven years ago I carried in my arms —

just when I had fallen in love, for the first and only time in my life, with her aunt Madeleine, then fourteen years old, and since dead. In the years between I have known the touch of love, but not the full weight of its hand." Such is the entry under the date of January 10, 1886.

The little one, with whom he danced at a children's ball, hardly noticed him. And, toward the end of February, we have the first mention of gold-blond, blue-eyed Julie. It began with a "touch of love" — a *Liebelei*, to use the untranslatable Viennese term — a few stolen kisses, and a light intoxication which deepened into something of permanent power and significance.

As soon as he observed that the girl was more deeply implicated than he (or perhaps than he admitted himself to be), a sense of honor moved him to break off the relationship between the daughter of a rich man and an as yet unsuccessful author. But after six months the relationship was resumed. "I have found my dear, good Julie again," he wrote on September 7, 1887. "My last and latest love. She has always loved me. I am going to marry her. I have already told her so." And now he would exert himself to the utmost to win a place for himself; "for I don't want her to forfeit her youth for my sake."

His exertions carried him far within the next few years. On July 25, 1889, the marriage was celebrated in the watering place of Reichenau. Thither the young married couple returned, too, after their eight-week honeymoon in Switzerland and France, to await the completion of their home in the Marcus Aurelius Street in Vienna.

The letters which passed between Herzl and his wife after their marriage have not yet been made available to the biographer, and we find little in other sources on which to build the detailed history of their life together. Only the basic outlines can be indicated. It is quite clear that from the beginning there existed the seeds of discord. There was Herzl's mother, to begin with. She was an unusual woman, who idolized her son and who in turn was idolized by him. With the best intentions in the world, could such a woman share the love of her son with another woman? On the other hand, was it possible for this son to satisfy the possessiveness of his mother without throwing a shadow across the happiness of his wife? How was the daughter-in-law to adapt herself toward the mother-in-law, who sought not so much to instruct as to control her son's wife? How was the new wife to fit herself into the style of life of her husband, a style which his parents had understood so wonderfully? Julie came from a rich home; Herzl was comfortably off, but his external style was modest. Would she, who had until then known no duties and responsibilities, have the understanding and imagination needed in marriage to a man who did not belong to the upper bourgeoisie, who was still developing, and whose temperament was not likely to harmonize at all points with the world she had known? And to come down to details: now that she was to be the wife of a well-known writer, one could almost say a famous writer, how was she going to be content with fewer dresses — she who knew so well how to choose and wear the best — than in her girlhood, or serve her guests less lavishly, or think twice before she ordered a carriage?

The outcome of it was that Herzl, faced with a money-need he had not known before, had to press harder than ever toward stage successes. Unfortunately the first rush of luck soon died down. By the early part of September 1889, he had already completed a new comedy, *Was Wird Man*

Sagen?, which dealt with the conventionality of fear of public opinion, and satirized the proneness of men and women to judge their deeds by the reactions of their class. The play was refused by the *Burgtheater* in October, but in March 1890 it was produced in Berlin and Prague, and was an ignominious failure with both critics and public.

Then followed a number of attempts with varying degrees of success and failure. There was the musical comedy *Das Teufels-Weib*, the libretto of which Herzl adapted from Henri Mailhac and A. Mortier's *Madame le Diable*, with music by Müller; it was well enough received, but did not make up for the failure of *Was Wird Man Sagen?* Then Herzl collaborated again with Wittmann in *Die Dame in Schwarz*, which was produced on February 6, 1890 by the *Burgtheater*, and was damned by the critics as hokum. Then followed the comedy *Prinzen aus Genieland*, which was excellently received at the *Carltheater* in Vienna on November 21, 1891, but achieved only a short run.

How was it that this successful and gifted feuilletonist could not achieve enduring success in the theatre, even when he put into his dramatic work something more than the play for popular acclaim? There are many reasons. The foremost — it would suffice of itself — was that he did not populate his plays with genuine, living figures. They were schematic, synthetic puppets, whose existence was justified by the witty things they said in behalf of the author. They were inventions, not the transcriptions of observation. "Let life itself be your source, and not your brain," Hartmann wrote to Herzl in 1887. "Take actual persons as your models, instead of clay figures in the museum of the theatre. You are obviously gifted, you have talent, inventiveness, everything that a playwright needs. But it seems to me that you ought to have a somewhat more respectful attitude toward humanity, you ought to look deeper into it."

But Herzl's attention was unfortunately riveted more on the public, and not on the reality of life. He frequented society and, as we have seen, tried to make of his dramatic productions a sort of criticism of society. But the flood of life beyond society, the thunder of that tide which Hauptmann clearly caught, came through to him as a faint murmur, for there intervened not only his own middle class attitude but the delicate musical attunement of his ear. He was frightened off by that realism in art which was, in those days, about to conquer the theatre. But it was impossible to fob off the great social problems of the time with superior and sceptical psychological ingenuities — which is what Herzl tried to do.

To this inadequacy must be added another: Herzl lacked the quality of genuine humor. He had wit, spirit, the sense of the comical in human situations, which accounts, indeed, for his success with the more concentrated form of the feuilleton. But genuine humor, which provokes hearty and liberating laughter, and which calls, in the author, for the power to lift himself clear of his own life and the life of those around him, was denied him; he took himself too seriously.

This subjectivity was an advantage in the semi-philosophic form of the feuilleton, within which he passed on steadily to higher and higher achievement. He poured into it the results of his daily experience, he was able to convert to its purpose his contact with the theatre, and to liven it with the observations gathered on his frequent travels. Other values were also created in him. He came in contact with the masses, for the first time, via his audiences, and obtained his first glimpses into the art of the manipulation

of the masses. His failures were object lessons in the loss
of such manipulative power, for which another name is —
leadership.

His feuilletons became increasingly earnest and philosophic in the best sense. How much love and insight there
is in that ripe product of his pen, "The Son," written in 1890:
"When he came," the speaker of the piece declares of his
child, "the world suddenly became full for me . . . I had
gone into marriage lightheartedly: it meant a certain relationship secured in permanent form . . . But what shall be
the source of the earnestness of life? . . . It came from my
son . . . Children are our greatest teachers. This little one
has given me a tangible, sensuous love of life, For he is my
son, my never-ending continuation, the guarantee that I
shall forever inherit the earth, forever renewed as my son,
my grandson, forever young, forever beautiful and forever
strong." And he speaks proudly of the boy: "He is loyal,
his heart is true, he responds instinctively to all that is noble,
he knows pity for all that is forlorn."

The words were put in the mouth of a third person, but
it needs no special insight to tell us what had happened:
Herzl had become a father. On March 29, 1890, his daughter Pauline was born, and on June 10, 1891, there came a son.
The effect of fatherhood is given us in the quoted feuilleton.
But there was an outpouring in letters, too. He was no
longer a mere spectator in the world. He was tied to tasks
and to futurity. His life was to be changed by these facts;
his outlook was to take on new clarity and new depth.

There were other lessons imbedded in that period. His
disappointment in the dramatic field was to turn to gain in
later years. But on top of that there was a heavy blow dealt

by the hand of fate: he lost his best friend. There were only two men to whom he could honestly give that title; Heinrich Kana and Oswald Boxer. They were an extraordinarily contrasted pair. Boxer: vital, vigorous, fresh, a man without great illusions about himself, but courageous, gifted, skilful, and an inventive journalist; and Kana: a profound critic of life and men, but of limited creative powers, sensitive in feeling and understanding, too gentle for the rude struggle of the world. He sought the highest alone, and achieved little more than the average. In the end he gave up the struggle in despair. On February 6, 1891, he shot himself. The next day Herzl received his parting words: "My dear, good Theodore, your old friend sends you this farewell before he dies! I thank you for all the friendship and the goodness you have shown me. All earthly happiness to you and yours. I kiss you. Your Heinrich."

It was a shattering experience for Herzl. He never forgot the tragic fate of his best friend. In almost all his plans for larger works the image of Kana recurs again and again. It was only after the passage of ten years, when this memory found poetic expression in the novel *Altneuland*, that the ghost of his dead friend ceased to haunt him with the old oppressiveness.

From this loss and from the disappointments which crowded upon him he found neither consolation nor refuge in his home. For the seeds of discord dormant in his marriage were growing apace. Mother and daughter-in-law could not find their way to each other, and the strain between them bore hard on the man. He had remained the son, and had entered on the career of fatherhood without really achieving the status of husband. Things went from bad to worse through the interference of relatives. Very possibly his theatre failures at a time of mounting expenses had something to do with it. It became evident that his wife was not the right partner and helpmeet for him and there was no genuine community of interests. What she offered him was not encouragement but frustration of the freedom of his development. Finally, with a heavy heart, he decided on separation from her and the children.

At the beginning of August 1891, he left Vienna for the south of France, and for two months wandered among the cities of the Pyrennees. His restlessness gradually died down as he meditated on himself and on life and as he pursued his work. In his free time he learned Spanish. And as peace returned to him together with the enjoyment of his work, he passed through a period of genuine spiritual growth. Life became more earnest, deeper, more authentic for him — we perceive it in the lighter as well as in the more serious feuilletons. His observations became more objective, more penetrating, more understanding, less prone to intellectual snobbery; his natural kindness and gentleness penetrated his words. He realized to a greater degree than hitherto the motto he had chosen for himself the year before: "To know human beings and to love them just the same." And out of this new, affectionate seriousness grew a more authentic humor.

There is a whole world of wisdom, kindliness, human knowledge and description in his sketches of that period. He tells us of St. Jean de Luz, that quiet retreat in which he found himself again. He tells us of his ride along the deep gulley of the Gave River, during which the driver slept soundly until he collided with another carriage. He gives us a picture of Saint Sauveur les Bains. There is a mocking witticism on the feminine question, a tart observation on

Napoleon III's bridge, on which the gilded insciption has faded away — "Just like the Byzantinism of that period." Then he stands before the springs. "And it is all so desolate, so oppressive." But behind him a feminine voice says in English: "Isn't it pretty?" And another voice answers affirmatively in the same language: "Really very nice!" And Herzl thinks with love of his little village of Luz, which isn't even very nice, and where his friends live, "the black-smith, the cobbler, the barber and many others, who appeal to me so much because they wear the dark-blue beret of the painter."

In Lourdes he studied the faithful who had come to be healed, and watched the grand ceremony of the reception by the Bishop of Meaux. He was deeply moved by the humble piety of the sufferers, which expressed itself as it had done for centuries — the world changes but little — in the inward flood of hope and strength which is awakened by the blessing of their spiritual leader. "Ah, Bishop of Meaux, you are after all a great benefactor of mankind!" But he notes that not all the cripples are moved by such religious trustfulness. "I stood there a long time and watched an old man who was using the waters of the spring to heal his sick eyes ... He began by dipping in his sack and sprinkling the water be-tween the lids. And when he opened his eyes again he saw just as badly as before. He tried the same thing a couple of times. Then he gave it up. And as he went away, he heaved a deep and bitter sigh. *He sighed like a Jew!*"

"He sighed like a Jew!" The phrase reveals as much as a whole treatise: the anguish of the Jew had become patent to him, and with it its peculiar utterance. The fate of his poor friend Kana, whom life had broken, appears to him as such a typical expression of the destiny of the modern Jew that he weighs the idea of writing a Jewish novel. He even went so far as to choose the title, *Samuel Kohn*. Under that name he projected the plan of a contrast between the life of the "suffering, decent and despised group of poor Jews" and that of the Jewish rich. "The latter feel nothing of anti-Semitism, for which in reality they are principally responsible." This was how he recorded at a subsequent period his views and intentions of that time. But the plan came to nothing, just like his other plan to extend his travels to Spain and perhaps even to Africa.

For his feuilleton on St. Jean de Luz, which had meanwhile appeared in the *Neue Freie Presse*, had created a sensation in the literary world. Not less favorable was the impression it made on the editors of that paper. To this impression was added the recommendation of Wittmann. Early in October Herzl received a telegram from the *Neue Freie Presse* asking whether he would accept the post of Paris correspondent. He replied at once in the affirmative, and without even returning home, proceeded to the French capital at the end of the same month.

CHAPTER IV

PARIS CORRESPONDENT

THE *Wiener Neue Freie Presse* was by far the most distinguished newspaper in the Austro-Hungarian Empire. It had been founded in 1864 by the Austrian, Michael Etienne, and Max Friedländer, cousin of Ferdinand Lassalle. The two founders had originally been revolutionaries, but their views had with the passage of time become less extreme, and the *Neue Freie Presse* never went further than a moderate liberalism. Very early it established a high reputation by the excellence and rapidity of its reporting and by the extraordinary quality of its literary supplement. Before long it was regarded abroad as the best channel of information on Austrian conditions. The double function of the newspaper, as Austria's mouthpiece to the world and as the world's mirror for Austria, was developed to new levels of effectiveness under the successors of the founders, namely, Eduard Bacher (1846–1908) and Moritz Benedikt (1849–1920), able journalists, German liberals, like the majority of Austrian Jews, and cheerful compromisers like their predecessors.

Herzl's assignment, as his employer described it to him, was "to furnish the paper with everything of interest to be found in Paris." Chiefly, however, the *Neue Freie Presse* would be interested in French domestic and foreign politics as these were mirrored in the French press. But Herzl was also to devote attention to finance and the stock exchange, art and literature, local events and social problems; the last happened to be greatly to the fore, for it was a time of economic depression and labor unrest.

It was no light task which Herzl had undertaken. He fulfilled it so satisfactorily that at the end of the probationary period of four months he was confirmed in the position with an increase in salary. Besides his expenses he was to receive, from the beginning of March 1892, a regular monthly salary of 1200 francs (instead of the 1000 paid him until then) and for each feuilleton 100 francs (instead of 80). For a thirty-one year old journalist this was, in the last decade of the nineteenth century, no ordinary position and no ordinary income.

Years before, when there had been some talk of his appointment as Paris correspondent of the *Frankfurter Zeitung*, Herzl had spoken enthusiastically to his parents about the glory and distinction of that position: "Heine was a Paris correspondent. So were Lindau and Wittmann. Singer of the *Neue Freie Presse* and Blowitz of the *Times* had almost the rank of ambassador." Now he wrote to his parents: "The position of Paris correspondent is the springboard to great things, and I shall achieve them, to your great joy, my dear beloved parents."

Herzl sustained successfully the comparison with his great models and predecessors. In style as well as in substance his reports and articles were masterpieces of their kind. He came to his task with the equipment of a perfect feuilletonist; his style was polished and musical; he possessed in an exceptional degree the capacity to describe natural scenery in a few fine clear strokes and of hinting at rather than of reproducing a mood with a minimum of language. His verbal dexterity and wit, his rapid comprehension of a situation, his practice in the art of condensed dialogue, all contributed to give his work an exceptional character. He managed to impart to each separate field the wider implication of the total scene of life. Even his financial reports were the basis for fascinating reflections of a general character. What distinguished him above all was his form: his political reports had the aesthetic tonality of literary feuilletons. Every telegram of his was a work of art. However rapidly he had to file his reports, he never perpetrated a slipshod or unnecessary sentence. Everything was there, background, mood and development of action in plastic balance. It was only now, when a great opportunity provoked him to the highest effort, that all the lessons of the years of his apprenticeship built up a many-sided perfection.

Herzl's correspondence from Paris won his newspaper many new readers. For himself, however, the work had a different creative significance: he stood for the first time in the broad arena of life. True, he was to this extent detached from the *mêlée* that he was observer and recorder; but with all the freedom of expression he permitted himself he could not choose his material at will. The range of his activity was circumscribed. He had definite duties; he was no longer his own master even in the matter of time, but had to observe certain divisions of the day called for by the exigencies of his tasks. Nor could he permit himself the intellectual pleasure of letting form take precedence over content. In newspaper work the perfection of literary style is a luxury sometimes offered free of charge to the gourmets among the readers; the prime consideration is rapidity and accuracy of reporting. Or as his chief, Bacher, wrote to him in December 1892: "The first thing is fodder, and plenty of it, for the wide open jaws of the public curiosity. If you have no time to cook it, then for God's sake shovel it down in the raw."

Herzl had come to Paris alone, and had taken up his quarters in the Hotel Rastatt, in the Rue Douon. In November 1891 his wife joined him there, seeking a reconciliation. We gather, from indirect reports, that in the course of the months that followed some sort of reconciliation was effected. But the marriage remained what it was, a clash of interests and personalities; there were perpetual conflicts between husband and wife, between daughter-in-law and mother-in-law. For Herzl remained permanently bound to his mother. How much the world at large, and how much the Jewish world in particular, owes to his unhappy marriage! In one of his most mature philosophical pieces Herzl rehearsed the story of a man whom he invented as the symbol of his own condition, a man whose home life had been so embittered by his marriage with an unsuitable woman that he finished up by running away to Africa, where he became a famous discoverer! "The world of science," says Herzl in that sketch, "owes much to that woman. Yes! The foundations of our achievements are sometimes downright comical. Sometimes they are also tragic. The good, respectable middle class has not the slightest notion of the manner of birth of those songs which fill it with such delight, and of those deeds which it admires so extravagantly." Be that as it may, Herzl's transformation from the writer into the national leader and statesman, which occurred within the ensuing years, awakened no understanding in his wife. Her life did not keep pace with his. She remained what she had been until her marriage with him: a beautiful, spoiled, hysterically sensitive woman, easily — and, it seems, without reason — stirred to jealousy. She was an affectionate mother. It was, indeed, this common love of their children which held the marriage together, and gave Herzl the strength to go on. "Children," wrote Herzl in 1893, when one of his children fell sick, "are equally sources of joy and pain, and love for them is rooted in both causes alike." As early as 1892, when his wife and children came to join him, he wrote to his parents: "Life has recovered its charm for me."

We learn a good deal concerning the transformation which was unfolding in him during that period from an exchange of letters between him and Schnitzler which began toward the latter part of July 1892. The two men had known each other since Herzl's student days, but they had not become intimate. In Paris, Herzl happened to read one of Schnitzler's short novels and was so enchanted by it that he wrote the author forthwith. He says, among other things: "My experience with the theatre — I am through with it now — was unpleasant and silly. The pieces in which I believed, and into which I had put true artistic effort, never saw the light of day. When, in a fit of despair, I manufactured something for the stage, I was produced — and despised. When I stop to reflect on my place in German literature — and I do that very rarely — I am moved to laughter ... And yet I must tell you that this does not embitter me. All pain is a process of education. And it is with a cheerful kind of philosophy, such as I did not possess before, that I watch the ways of the world. Old ones, realists and so on — *je m'en fous.*

"But when I see a talent like yours breaking into bloom, then I rejoice; yes, I rejoice just as if I weren't a litterateur myself — that is to say, a narrow-hearted, envious, grudging, meanspirited little fellow; I am filled with the same joy as by the violets blooming in the garden. Don't take offense if I speak somewhat pontifically; don't regard it as evidence of any feeling of superiority, as though I were an elder brother speaking to a younger. The fact is that your manner of writing gives me a genuine feeling of kinship. It is just in this manner, my dear fellow, that I would like to be able to write myself." And then he advised Schnitzler always to remain true to himself. "A horrid example of what compromise can do you may see in myself."

Schnitzler answered in a warm and witty letter; he reminded Herzl of their meeting long ago in the *Akademische Lesehalle*. He admitted that he had looked up to Herzl and had been filled to bursting with envy at the sight of the writer, the elegant, ironic, superior man who, walking down the same path as himself, had always kept twenty paces ahead. There were very few people in the world, he added, whose opinion he valued as highly as Herzl's.

Herzl answered: "If you always saw me twenty paces ahead of you, at least you ought to know that this advantage of distance has been paid for with exhaustion; today, as I have told you, I sit upon a stone by the roadside and watch the others overtake me and pass me by." He declined to send his manuscripts to Schnitzler, in spite of the latter's repeated offers. "My manuscripts! They've gone clean out of my mind. My preoccupation with art has left me with a kind of love of art and, on certain days, in the midst of my lost hours, with a kind of homesickness for poetry and creation" (January 2, 1893). "Forgive me, but I don't want to know anything more about myself — from now on I am the journalist... I think I have already had this out with you ... There's much less bitterness in me over my failures than regret over my early, flippant, artistically dishonest, vulgarly successful productions. I have condemned myself, in punishment, to self-burial. But were I free, were I filled with hope, as in my youthful years, I could find it in me to break out and wander freely, singing my songs, in some open landscape under God's sky. I believe I would not write anything more for the theatre. I believe I would commune with my own soul and reason, and I would smile, and I would not feel the need to woo the applause of the *première* audiences of Berlin or Vienna or any other city" (May 13, 1893). "Honestly and truly, I don't want to know anything more about myself" (May 19, 1893). Early on in that year, in January, he had written: "He who becomes a journalist does not escape punishment. I am doing my very best ... to practice this trade as honestly as possible, and I watch closely the political game. Sometimes I think of myself as young David Copperfield, sitting in the gallery of the House of Commons and taking stenographic notes ... And then sometimes I actually think of myself as a statesman."

He was done with his career as success-hunting playwright. He threw himself seriously and diligently into the journalistic craft. He observed with close attention all that went on about him, and listened with sharpened ears. But the moment had not yet come for the unveiling of a mission within him. Only, he was on the way; the process of preparation had begun.

How, in this mood of his, could he possibly have avoided clashing with the Jewish question? As far back as the time of his Spanish journey, when he had sought healing from his domestic and spiritual torments, the question had presented itself to him and had cried for artistic expression. His call to Paris had been a welcome pretext, perhaps, for putting off the writing of his Jewish novel — the more so as he probably was not ripe enough for such an undertaking. Now that he was in Paris, where his eyes were opened to the full range of the social process, he began to draw nearer in spirit to his fellow-Jews, and to look upon them more warmly and with less inhibition. True, he found them as difficult aesthetically as before, but he tried hard to grasp the essence of their character and substance, and to judge them without prejudice.

In June 1892 he wrote a detailed and thoroughgoing criticism of Lavedan's play, *Prince Aurec*. He made this the occasion for a number of observations on the aristocracy — his favorite theme from of old — and on the modern Jews, who were gradually becoming his new favorite theme. For Herzl, as he writes about the play, Prince Aurec is the typical aristocrat in decline, trading on the glories of his ancestry, as well as in the more substantial heirlooms of the family. Whenever he needed money and could not get it from his parents or relatives, he applied to Baron Horn, a Jewish parvenu, who had spent huge sums in order to work his way into high society. This Jewish success-hunter had, according to Herzl's view — a view which merits our attention — been quite missed, as a character, by the author of the play. "Horn doesn't brag enough about his high connections; he doesn't show himself sufficiently honored, he doesn't stammer with pride and happiness when a Duchess happens to address him. The inner uncertainty of the Jew has not been portrayed in this character. But this uncertainty is the very stamp of the real Horn, in real life; it is his specific characteristic, it asserts itself in every circumstance, finds itself in every gesture of humility. A compassionate understanding realizes, of course, that this insecurity is the fruit of a long, long era of suffering, which has not yet come to an end."

"Which has not yet come to an end . . ." Here we have the source of the humiliations inflicted on Herzl the Jew. They are not personal humiliations! For after all, he is successful as journalist, he is highly regarded, he mixes with writers and political leaders. He passes "unrecognized" through the crowd; no one shouts "Hep! Hep!" after him. But the humiliations which are visited upon Jewry as a group he draws upon himself; and as an honest, objective journalist, who looks round upon the world, and refuses to put on blinkers, he is also compelled to take into account the tide of anti-Semitism.

For it was rising in France too; it was the revival of ancient instincts in new forms and with new rationalizations; it was the parallel phenomenon to the German anti-Semitism which began to surge up in the 'seventies, and which was baptized with that new name in 1879. French anti-Semitism too was based, at least ostensibly, on German books, though these, in turn, had taken as their point of departure the race theories of the Frenchman Gobineau. Gobineau was likewise the inspiration of Edouard Drumont, whose *La France Juive* appeared in 1885 and in the course of one year ran through a hundred editions — one of the greatest book-selling successes of the nineteenth century. Drumont's book goes much further than his predecessor's; it provides the foundation for a definite, rounded-out system of anti-Semitism. Drumont sees all history under the aspect of anti-Semitism. The emancipation of the Jews in 1791 was a blunder; the Jews of France are not Frenchmen but a guest people, which exploits the expanding economic system for its own benefit and for the achievement of world domination. As the representatives of an impersonal capitalism, with a racial flair for commerce, they have created everywhere the implements of "big business," which have destroyed the emergent Christian middle class and concentrated the wealth in the hands of the Jews (Rothschild). With their unclean racial characteristics they corrupted the spirit of France, and were responsible for the decadence of the latter. Their assimilation was impossible, their infiltration into the people via intermarriage undesirable: they were, and would remain, an element alien to the country, fundamentally diverse from the French, possessing no real fatherland, subject to no real bonds, a state within the state or — what is synonymous in the French language — a nation within a nation. It is on this basis, according to Drumont, that the Jews are to be regarded and treated: their emancipation was to be withdrawn, their possessions were to be confiscated and applied to the creation of means of production for the exploited working classes.

The tremendous sales of the book were sufficient index of the responsiveness of the public to such views. There was, for thousands of readers, something extremely attractive in this linking up of social discontent with national sentiment, especially among those who had suffered, or who believed they had suffered, under the social development which was instituted by the Third Republic. In their eyes, as in Drumont's, the Jews had been the allies of the Germans in the defeat of the glory of France. When Herzl arrived in Paris this political tendency had not — in spite of Drumont's exertions, and in spite of his paper, *la Libre Parole*, founded in 1892 — achieved the dimensions of a genuine movement, nor was it destined to become one in the German sense. But it served as the focus for all kinds of discontents and resentments; it attracted certain serious critical spirits, too; its influence grew from day to day, and the position of the Jews became increasingly uncomfortable. It was ultimately to produce a crisis in the life of French Jewry not less than in the life of the French Republic.

Herzl's contact with anti-Semitism dated back to his student days, when it had first taken on the form of a social political movement. He had been aware of it as a writer, though the contact had never ripened into a serious inner struggle or compelled him to give utterance to it. As we have seen, he had already made the acquaintance of one of the basic books of modern anti-Semitism, and had reacted with passionate violence.

Now he read Drumont, as he had read Dühring. The impression was again a profound one. What moved him most in the work was the totality of a world picture based on a considered hostility to the Jews. "I have Drumont to thank for much of the freedom of my present conception of the Jewish question, because Drumont is an artist," Herzl wrote in June 1895, in the midst of the crisis which was to bring forth his *Judenstaat*.

Was it Drumont, again, who led Herzl later on "to understand and to excuse anti-Semitism as a historic phenomenon," as Herzl himself phrased it? Or was this intellectual liberation the result of his daily observation of the world around him, and of the objective reports of conditions which he had to prepare for his newspaper on the subject of the Jews and anti-Semitism? For whether he was interested or not, his duties as a journalist compelled him to a study of the phenomenon, both at first hand and as it manifested itself in the French press. The best we can do towards answering this important question is to set down chronologically the records — in so far as they are obtainable — of his impressions.

On January 26, 1892, occurred the death of the journalist Oswald Boxer, who, after Kana's suicide, had remained as Herzl's sole surviving friend in the more intimate sense of that word. Boxer died of the yellow fever in Rio de Janeiro. He had gone to Brazil, as Herzl knew, on behalf of a Berlin committee to investigate the possibility of settling Russian Jews in that part of South America. Boxer had preceded Herzl in placing himself at the service of a great Jewish enterprise — one which pointed the way, moreover, in the direction which Herzl was subsequently to take. Herzl had received a letter from Boxer, written shortly before the latter fell sick. The letter was filled with details of the task and of the heavy responsibility which rested on the writer. In the obituary which he wrote for the *Neue Freie Presse* Herzl quoted the letter. If the death of his first friend, Kana, had seemed to Herzl the echo of Jewish destiny, that same intimation must have echoed even more loudly from the death of the second friend; and his spirit must have understood the message which was now ineluctably directed toward him, the third and last of the triumvirate of friends.

In January 1892, there took place in Paris the trial of a certain Laurent, a clericalist and anti-Semite, who had conducted shady dealings on the stock exchange while in the employ of the secret service. The failure of his get-rich-quick schemes had led to his arrest. In his self-defense Laurent tried to cast upon the Jews the blame for the leakage of information from the archives of the secret service. Herzl sent a complete report of the proceedings to the *Neue Freie Presse*. "Monsieur Laurent," he wrote, "will have to do a lot of cursing against the Jews to cover up his misdemeanors."

On February 24 and 27 of that year, and again on March 2, the *Neue Freie Presse* printed long letters and reports dealing with a prospective Jewish colony in "Madian" (probably a misprint for Midian) on the northwest coast of Arabia. The project was the result of collaboration between a baptized Berlin Jew, Paul Friedmann, and a retired Prussian officer, Seebach; they had in mind, it appears, the founding of the beginnings of a Jewish state. "It is my hope," wrote Friedmann, who was trying to obtain the cooperation of Baron de Hirsch, a friend of his, "to convert these weak, bad elements into strong, active men, to build up a tribe round which the nation can rally." The clumsiness of the ambitious initiators, the quarrels of the colonists, and the opposition of the Turkish government ruined the plan, which Herzl was to remember later, and from which he was to draw certain conclusions.

On February 22, 1892, the *Neue Freie Presse* printed a long excerpt from the reports of the American Investigation Commission on the persecution of the Jews of Russia, and on February 23 another detailed report (perhaps the work of Herzl himself) on the critical condition of the Jewish colonies in the Argentine, founded by Baron de Hirsch. The paper also carried many reports of debates on the Jewish question in the Berlin and Vienna Reichstags.

On May 24, 1892, the *Neue Freie Presse* printed a report on the proceedings of the general meeting of the Society for the Combatting of anti-Semitism, an organization founded the preceding year in Vienna.

From July 1892 on, the articles, reports and communications on Jewish matters became ever more frequent. To that period belong Herzl's observations on the play *Prince Aurec* and his report on the Burdeau-Drumont trial (July 15), which he attended, thus obtaining his first glimpse of the anti-Semitic leader; it was there that the cry of Drumont's followers, *A bas les Juifs*! was first heard openly in France. Two weeks earlier had taken place the duel between a Jewish officer of the French army and a French anti-Semite, a duel which was only the beginning of a series. The climax of this miniature war was reached on June 24, 1892, when the anti-Semite le Marquis de Morès killed the thirty-four year old Jewish captain and professor at the Ecole Polytechnique, Mayer. The incident created a storm in France and abroad; press and parliament alike were occupied with it; the Minister for War and the Military Governor of Paris declared it a national crime to introduce this sort of disunity among the officers of the French army, but they did not come out with an open declaration against anti-Semitism as such.

The funeral of Captain Mayer was used by the population of Paris as the occasion for a great demonstration. Fifty thousand men and women followed to the cemetery the coffin, which was buried under a tremendous mass of flowers.

During the ensuing weeks the papers were filled with interviews in which leading personalities vented their views on anti-Semitism; and at the same time a ritual-murder trial was in progress in the town of Xanten, in the Rhineland.

On August 31, 1892, Herzl, dealing with this subject as with all other subjects of public interest, summed up the general situation in a long report entitled "French anti-Semitism."

It was a frank and fearless document, but nowhere in it did Herzl indicate that he saw the way out. The best he could do was to try to get past the question with a sort of Heine-esque irony. He added a number of serious observations on the sociological-political foundations of French anti-Semitism, drawing a parallel between anti-Semitism in France and anti-Semitism in Germany and Russia. He came to the conclusion that "for the time being" the French people were cool and uncomprehending in their attitude toward anti-Semitism.

Then he turned his attention to a book, *Les Anti-Semites en France*, by a former Boulangist, Mermeix. He praised highly "the distinguished calmness of spirit" and the "love of objective truth" which characterized the work. The author, Herzl reported, "showed that it was possible to discuss the Jews quietly, without being at all prejudiced in their favor ... What a change and a relief from the treatment accorded by Capucins and rabbis to this question, which has become such a source of income for publishers, national leaders and other businessmen."

According to Mermeix French anti-Semitism had its origin in the activities of the clericalist aristocratic groups; it was reinforced by the financial decline of the country, and was a reflex of the transient socialistic crisis. "Deep down in the French people there lies imbedded a healthy core of reason and love of justice," writes Herzl, agreeing with the author. "Monsieur Mermeix is undoubtedly right. The movement will pass in this country, but perhaps not before it has manifested itself in excesses and individual catastrophes." And Herzl proceeds, in his characteristic ironic style, to make his deductions — which were often to be repeated: "For the Jews this will be a hard but valuable school, such as they have passed through frequently before. A historian, summing up the phenomenon from a distance, must be moved to ask himself, 'Why is it that the benefits of such a hard schooling are visited so frequently on the Jews?' The answer is perhaps that the Jews have from of old shown themselves wonderfully adaptable for exploitation by governments who make them responsible for all the blunders and abuses, for all the misery and wretchedness, for all the corruption and dishonesty that come upon the masses. And so every genuinely conservative statesman will extend a certain moderate measure of protection to the Jews in order that they may survive."

We see that by now Herzl is no longer content with a simple acceptance of the facts: he is looking for the deeper significance of the universal enmity directed against the Jews. For the Jews this enmity is a hard school. For the world it is a lightning conductor. But he does not drive his inquiry further; so far it is only a flash of insight which ends in nothing more than a literary paradox. Thus his whole manner now shows a deeper and more insistent preoccupation with the Jewish question. From now on it gives him no peace.

At first he contents himself with heroic romantic dreams. He thinks of challenging to a duel the great Austrian anti-Semitic leader, Prince Alois Lichtenstein, or else it is to be Schönerer, if not Lueger himself. Should he be killed in the duel (all this Herzl set down on paper years later) a post-humous letter was to declare to the world that he had fallen as a sacrifice "to the most unjust movement in the world." His death was to shake to the innermost the hearts and the thoughts of mankind. "If, however, it had been my lot to

kill my opponent and be brought to trial, then I would have
delivered a brilliant speech which would have begun with my
regrets for the death of a man of honor — after the fashion
of Morès, who killed Captain Mayer. Then I would have
turned to the Jewish question and delivered an oration
worthy of Lassalle. I would have sent a shudder of admiration through the jury. I would have compelled the respect
of the judges, and the case against me would have been
dismissed. Thereupon the Jews would have made me one of
their representatives and I would have declined because I
would refuse to achieve such a position by the killing of a
man."

This idle dream of the time of his mental confusion died
in him, to be resurrected ultimately only on paper. But the
Jewish question haunted him persistently, compelling him
to unremitting effort toward the discovery of a solution.

At the turn of the year 1892–93 there came a sharp clarification in his ideas, recorded in documents made public after
his death. He had followed closely the evasive debates in the
Austrian Reichstag — debates which forever dodged the
reality by turning the question into one of religion. "It is no
longer — and it has not been for a long time — a theological
matter. It has nothing whatsoever to do with religion and
conscience," declared Herzl brutally. "What is more, everyone knows it. The times are past for men to slaughter each
other on a question of the [Lord's] Supper. Today it is
not a question of the supper, but of the dinner, of our
daily bread. The Jewish question" — he has reached a
clear formulation — "is neither nationalist nor religious.
It is a social question."

He has taken a step forward. The Jewish question is a
social question; it is therefore no longer a question of assimi-

lation and adaptation. It lies deeper and is linked up with profound considerations affecting the existing order. This outlook, it appears, was expressed in attempts which Herzl made in correspondence with the editors of the *Neue Freie Presse* to influence the plans on foot for the combatting of anti-Semitism. In January 1893, Herzl was approached by Regina Friedländer, the widow of the founder of the *Neue Freie Presse*, for cooperation with the *Verein zur Abwehr des Antisemitismus*, an organization founded by well-meaning and noble hearted friends of humanity like Baron von Suttner (the husband of the famous pacifistic writer Bertha von Suttner) and the captain of industry Friedrich Leitenberger. The motto they had adopted was: "For us the Jewish question does not exist." Herzl answered with a criticism of their program and an outline of his views on the Jewish question and on anti-Semitism.

In this letter he said that the question of social discrimination against Jews was by far the less important one. Effective action fell into two divisions. First there was the combatting of the symptoms, or external manifestations, of anti-Semitism. For this the best method was the brutal one of the duel. "Half a dozen duels will do a great deal to improve the position of the Jews in society." If the evil was to be cured, then the Jews were to get rid of those characteristics which were justly charged to them and thus do away with the prejudice against them. "A long, difficult and hopeless path. The best we can expect is to succeed with the exceptional Jew." The real and definitive solution could only lie in the complete disappearance of the Jews through baptism and intermarriage.

Frau Friedländer passed the letter on to Baron Leitenberger who, on January 23, 1893, wrote Herzl and took issue

with him. He was completely unable to accept Herzl's substitute program ."That all Jews who are looked at askance
should issue challenges to duels, and that all Jews without
exception should get themselves baptized, is really nothing
more than charming salon chatter. It is not the kind of
thing to be taken into serious consideration by earnest men
who have made up their minds to proceed in all seriousness
against the racial war."

Herzl was stunned. "So — nothing but idle chatter! It
is a sharp retort. But is he right?" In a strongly worded
letter of twenty-two pages he rebuts the Baron's views and
unfolds a plan of action in all the colorful detail which was
later to characterize his more mature plans.

"Do not believe" he says," that I am so fond of intellectual paradox that I find it a pleasure to issue hard judgments
against the Jews. On the contrary, I find that they cut an
astoundingly good figure when we take into consideration
the long oppression to which they have been subjected and
under which they have been morally fragmentated. When
I observe here in Paris how cautiously, shyly and timidly
many a German bears himself, hesitating to reveal his identity, then it occurs to me that there is much to excuse in the
Jew who has been living perpetually in enemy territory."

This, from Herzl, is startling enough: "who has been living perpetually in enemy territory!" Was not this violent
perception going to provide the basis for a revolutionary
revaluation of the problem? But for the moment he continues to defend his proposal that the Jews shall let themselves be absorbed completely in that enemy territory. In
all these reflections on sociological problems we perceive,
glimmering through, the spiritual pattern created in him by
his own family life. "The idea of a general baptism is half

jest and half earnest. I am permitted to say it, I who would not baptize. But what about my son Hans? When I think of his future I am ready to admit that the pressure of his Jewishness will teach him much concerning humanity. But I ask myself whether I have the right to make life so super-fluously difficult for him as it has become for me and will become in increasing measure. When he grows up I hope he will be too proud to renounce his faith, even though he has as little from it as I. That is why we must baptize Jewish children while they are still incapable of giving themselves an accounting, and while they can still feel nothing either for it or against it. We must submerge in the people."

These observations take up only one-tenth of the letter. By far the greater part is devoted to the program which he recommends to the Society for the Combatting of Anti-Semitism. Herzl guards himself against unjust criticism of the means adopted. He finds them very humane and honorable — but they have come too late. When the first stirrings of anti-Semitism were felt, it might have been useful and effective to provoke this public protest on the part of leading men and women. Now that anti-Semitism had become a great folk movement, such well-meaning humani-tarian action could achieve nothing. "The answer to a move-ment is another movement," or to speak openly, the answer to anti-Semitism was — Socialism. "It is my conviction that the Jews driven thus into a corner will ultimately find no other escape than into the arms of Socialism." Those who wanted to prevent the extruded Jews from linking up with an extreme radical party working for the revolutionary transformation of the existing order had only one course before them, the creation of a Socialist movement which would retain the foundations of a liberal social system. For the propagation of such a movement the Society for the Combatting of anti-Semitism needed not "circulars which circulated nothing" but a real newspaper, a daily in a new style. And Herzl goes on to give all the instructions for the founding of such a paper. One of the very definite planks in the platform is that no Jew, not even a baptized Jew, shall work on the paper.

"What a letter! As long as I can remember I haven't written at such length. But it seems to me to be worth the effort."

It goes without saying that the letter achieved precisely nothing, but it is instructive to note that it was written when the famous Panama trial — in its first phase — was drawing to a close, and great debates were being held in the Chamber of Deputies on the outcome. In 1889 the Panama Society, founded by Ferdinand de Lesseps, the engineer of the Suez Canal, collapsed before a third of the work on the Canal had been completed. Thousands of workers had died in vain; 1400 million francs, most of which had been obtained under false pretenses from the savings of small people, had been lost. The mismanagement of this huge sum had led to state intervention. In November 1892, after long delayed investigation, the directorate of the Panama Society was brought to trial. At first a financial scandal, it soon became a political affair of the first magnitude. Boulangists and anti-Semites openly accused French politicians — large numbers of leaders among them — of having been bribed to vote in favor of the last public loan made by the Panama Society. There ensued wild debates in the Chamber of Deputies; revelation followed revelation; personality after personality was implicated in the dubious business. Public passion rose to an ever higher pitch. France became a volcano.

There Herzl was, in the midst of this fury, reporting for his Austrian newspaper. He did a staggering amount of work during those months. There were days when his reports and observations took up four full pages in the *Neue Freie Presse*. In fact, he was doing much more than he was strictly obligated to do. It was impossible to avoid the impression that he was personally gripped by the unfolding of events. There is only one way to describe what was happening in France at that time: it was as if the last day had come for this planet of ours and in the tumult of dissolution all the secret machinery of human action had been brought into the open. The economic, social and political processes of France were uncovered to the eye of the spectator. Herzl took full advantage of the opportunity, penetrating to the innermost structure of the social and political world. His eyes were wide open, he looked, he grasped, he described — and he meditated.

But however organically the life of France was involved in this tremendous scandal, the Jewish question did not fail to put in its appearance. The fact is that from beginning to end the Panama Society had been built up of clericalist elements; there were no Jews in it; in fact, its complexion had been anti-Jewish; no Jews had been involved in its collapse. That certain Jewish names should be pulled in by the anti-Semitic press was inevitable, with the result that the affair was given a specifically Jewish tinge and the French Jews were cowardly enough to accept the implications of what Nordau calls "this blood libel of a Jewish Panama." France was being prepared for the grand climax of the Dreyfus case.

Herzl followed up to their logical conclusion the intellectual consequences flowing from this drama: "There is a

Jewish question, there can be no doubt about that. Those
who deny it are wrong." Such is the observation he set down
in April 1893. He then went on to conclude that the solution
of the Jewish question in Germany would be found in the
Jewish espousal of Socialism, while in Austria it would be
found in the Jewish conversion to Catholicism.

In July 1893, Herzl lived through those violent scenes in
the French Chamber which were evoked by the implication
of Georges Clemenceau in the Panama scandal. At the end
of the month he left Paris for a much needed rest, accompanied by his wife and his three children, the last of whom,
Margaret (always known as Trude), was born May 20, 1893.
The family went first to Lucerne, then to Austria. To this
interlude no doubt belong his conversations with the publishers of the *Neue Freie Presse* mentioned two years later
in his diary. The idea of a radical dissolution of world Jewry
had gone on working in him, ripening gradually into an extraordinary plan.

The Jewish question — at least in Austria — was to find
its solution with the help of the Catholic Church. Herzl's
idea was to reach the Pope through the Catholic hierarchy of
Austria, and to say to him: "Help us against anti-Semitism,
and I in return will lead a great movement amongst the Jews
for voluntary and honorable conversion to Christianity."

"Voluntary and honorable" meant that the adult converts — with Herzl at their head — were to remain Jews,
while agitating for Christian conversion among the Jewish
people. "In the broad light of day, at noon on a Sunday, a
solemn and festive procession accompanied by the pealing
of bells, shall proceed to the St. Stefan Cathedral in Vienna.
There shall be no furtiveness and no shamefacedness, as
hitherto; it shall be done proudly and with a gesture of dig-

nity. And inasmuch as the adult leaders are to remain Jews, they shall lead the procession to the threshold of the church but shall not enter themselves. The entire enterprise should take on a mighty character of integrity. We, the intermediary generation, are to remain where we are; we shall stand by the faith of our fathers, but our children shall pass over to Christianity before their conversion can bear the character either of cowardice or of interested scheming."

Moritz Benedikt, Herzl's chief, naturally refused to have anything to do with the plan. Benedikt's argument that it was utterly unfeasible, and that the Pope would not even receive Herzl, had no weight with the dreamer who was trying to become a man of action. There was, however, one consideration which had some effect on Herzl: "Throughout one hundred generations your people has sustained itself as Jews. And *you* want to become the limit of that process. That is something which you cannot and may not do." This appeal to his feeling for the relationship between father and son, for the dignity and meaning of the past generations, went home with the man who was himself so loving and so faithful a son.

In any case, after this exchange of views he gave up his baptism plan. He was unquestionably influenced by the consideration that without the cooperation of his newspaper it would lack weight and authority. But that this was his sole reason for relinquishing the idea is false — and when Herzl himself makes this out to be the case, as he does in subsequent records, he is deceived by his memory. But he soon got over his disappointment, and came to the conclusion that his "solution" was no solution at all.

Almost immediately after his return to Paris, and at most two or three weeks after his conversation with Benedikt, he expressed himself publicly on this question, and the circumstances under which he did so are proof sufficient of the degree to which he was preoccupied with it. Writing on the Panama affair, he draws a direct comparison between the Jewish Marannos and the French Monarchist Catholics, who, on the advice of the Pope, had suddenly declared themselves in favor of the Republic: "These Catholics," he writes, "will pass through the same experience as the Jews of the Middle Ages, who submitted in vain to baptism. They were persecuted just as vigorously in their new status and under their new name: for they were called *Nuovos Christianos* — the new Christians!" Could the futility of Jewish baptism have found clearer illustration?

The period of his Vienna visit seems to have given birth also to the idea of a letter to Baron Chlumecky, leader of the German Liberals and Speaker of the Austrian Chamber of Deputies. The subject matter of the letter was the plan of *Assistance par le Travail*, or work relief, which Herzl had become acquainted with in Paris. Baron Chlumecky showed himself sympathetic to the idea, and Herzl returned to it in an article which was printed in the *Neue Freie Presse* on August 2, 1893. The principle, which had first been tried in Belgium and Holland, and had subsequently reappeared in England, Germany, America, Switzerland and France, was that of employment for the destitute instead of outright charity — a principle which has since then taken on new significance in the world.

Herzl's quick understanding of the essence of the plan shows his social and moral alertness. He did not believe that this was the solution of the social problem, but he did perceive that "in contrast to the usual charitable enterprises, which are a kind of premium paid for laziness, 'relief through work' introduces a new element of intelligence and justice into the solution. The great problem, which continues to haunt us, is not solved thereby, but certain attendant questions are answered. How shall we take away from society the reproach of a situation in which human beings who are prepared to work are condemned to starvation or suicide? How are we to combat the sort of crime which springs from sheer need?"

Herzl's sympathetic and sensitive reaction to the idea of work instead of philanthropy as a solution of the social question is a forerunner of his comprehension of the right approach to the Jewish question: for he was to submit a solution which differed in just this spirit from all the old suggestions, with their demoralizing philanthropic basis. He went on to talk of the re-adaptation and restratification of the defeated classes, the rediscovery of creative ability in men who had been frustrated by maladjustment. Men who had failed in the city would succeed on the land. It was an astoundingly prophetic document, which reads as if it had been produced by a thinker of the fifth decade of the twentieth century.

It was a more earnest and more sombre man who returned to Paris in July 1893. Herzl's education was proceeding apace. He had looked deep into human problems. For three years he had watched closely the workings of the faulty machinery of government, in the case of the Panama scandals. Elections were now approaching in France, and he made up his mind to give to the study of their conduct a degree of attention going far beyond the call of his journalistic duties. For reasons he could not yet justify he had a special and passionate interest in the workings of the parliamentary system in general, in that of France in particular.

He went about listening to all sorts of speakers; to the little urban bourgeois occupied with his local problem, to the peasant occupied with the land, to fanatically excited socialists. He heard the demagogue and the place-seeker. The lesson rose to a climax in September and October, when a wild wave of enthusiasm swept over France, occasioned by the visit of a squadron of the Russian fleet. Herzl went to the naval base in Toulon, and paid a heavy price for this devotion to duty, for while he was in the south of France he contracted malaria, and was bedridden for seven weeks. The cure included subcutaneous quinine injections which produced an abscess in his ankle, so that for a long time he was compelled to limp along with the aid of a stick, like a cripple. It is quite possible that this sickness had a permanent, adverse effect on his constitution, and that the tremendous strain which he put on his heart in later years found it already undermined.

The weeks of his recovery were a period of enforced external idleness; but within him the process of his transformation was swiftly approaching its climax. When he returned to his work in Paris new excitements came to keep alive the ferment in his soul. A bomb was exploded in the Chamber of Deputies; it was the opening of a second series of attempted assassinations of political leaders. These violences, as Herzl wrote, were serving to focus attention on the basic problems of society, on the social structure and on fundamental law. He wrote for his newspaper a number of profound and penetrating articles, in which he analyzed, under the rubric of "The Bourbon Palace," the essentials of the difficult period through which the French nation was passing.

On the surface his attention was devoted to the problems of France; below the surface his spirit was unceasingly at work — to some extent unconsciously — on the Jewish problem, so that he transferred as it were from French to Jewish territory the intellectual and spiritual consequences of his observations. The first fruit of this period was a one act play in verse — dashed off in eight feverish and happy days — *Die Glosse*. But this was only a beginning. His energies were still concentrated, at least as far as his conscious will was concerned, on his newspaper work, and it is remarkable that in spite of this strange cleavage his journalistic achievements rose to their peak in that period. His story of the assassination of President Carnot, his account of the presidential struggle from which Casimir Périer emerged as victor, his record of the fierce public debates round the anti-anarchist press laws — the flight to Brussels of the arch-anti-Semite Drumont was one of the consequences — his word-pictures of the trial of Caserio, as well as of the execution of the assassin of Carnot, were masterpieces of description.

Then came the summer, and at its close Herzl took a much needed vacation. He spent the month of September in Baden, near Vienna, in the company of his fellow-feuilletonist on the *Neue Freie Presse*, Ludwig Speidel. They went for long walks in the green meadows and philosophized at each other — landing, inevitably, in the midst of the Jewish question. Herzl has left a record of the conversations. What he gave Speidel was more or less what he had felt, many years before, after his reading of Dühring. He admitted the substance of the anti-Semitic accusation which linked the Jew with money; he defended the Jew as the victim of a long historic process for which the Jew was not responsible. "It is not our fault, not the fault of the Jews, that we find ourselves forced into the role of alien bodies in the midst of various nations. The ghetto, which was not of our making, bred into us certain anti-social qualities ... Our original character cannot have been other than magnificent and proud; we were men who knew how to face war and how to defend the state; had we not started out with such gifts, how could we have survived two thousand years of unrelenting persecution?"

Modern anti-Semitism, he said, was the consequence of the emancipation, which had been "an error of doctrinaire libertarian thought, the illusion that men are made free when their rights are guaranteed on paper. We were liberated from the ghetto, but we remained, we still remain, ghetto Jews. We need time in order to accustom ourselves to freedom, and the surrounding peoples have neither the patience nor the magnanimity to grant us the time needed. They see us as we are, but they do not realize that we incorporate the characteristics of men who have served long prison sentences unjustly."

It is fascinating and touching to watch Herzl blundering around the logical issue of his views without actually coming through. He projected his personal experience into a philosophy of the mass. Personal suffering had helped develop his own character; he therefore considered that "anti-Semitism has been useful in the development of the Jewish character. It is the education of a group by the action of the masses, and it will perhaps lead to the absorption of the group ... The Jews will adapt themselves through a process of Darwinian mimicry."

For the time being Herzl was stuck half way along the road of discovery. He came across the Zionist solution, and definitely rejected it. Discussing the drama *Femme de Claude*, by Dumas the younger, he says of one of its characters:

"The good Jew Daniel wants to rediscover the homeland of his race and gather his scattered brothers into it. But a man like Daniel would surely know that the historic homeland of the Jews no longer has any value for them. It is childish to go in search of the geographic location of this homeland. And if the Jews really 'returned home' one day, they would discover on the next that they do not belong together. For centuries they have been rooted in diverse nationalisms; they differ from each other, group by group; the only thing they have in common is the pressure which holds them together. All humiliated peoples have Jewish characteristics, and as soon as the pressure is removed they react like liberated men."

But in throwing up to Dumas the reproach that he, the offspring of a mixed marriage, the "half-breed," as many would have called him, should have been the first to approach the Jewish question "with greatness of spirit," Herzl contradicted his own thesis of the educational value of suffering. "What tremendous power he — Dumas *fils* — showed in combatting those prejudices which were directed against him. But when we examine the total situation with detachment, we are compelled to ask ourselves, what was the creative value of these prejudices if they failed to bring a Dumas to full human growth?"

The inner apotheosis was drawing nearer and nearer for Herzl. Its footsteps rang ever louder in his spirit. In October 1894, they sounded on the threshold. On the nineteenth day of that month Herzl was in the studio of the sculptor, Samuel Friedrich Beer, who was making a bust of him. The conversation turned to the Jewish question and to the growth of the anti-Semitic movement in Vienna, the hometown of both Herzl and Beer. It was useless for the Jew to turn artist and to dissociate himself from money, said Herzl. "The blot sticks. We can't break away from the ghetto." A great excitement seized Herzl, and he left the atelier, and on the way home the inspiration came on him like a hammerblow. What was it? The complete outline of a play, "like a block of basalt." The next day he said to Beer: "Man, if I weren't a hired laborer, and could run off to the heights of Amalfi for fourteen days, I could produce that play." As it was, he produced it in seventeen days! Between October 21 and November 8, 1894, a period of spiritual intoxication, he completed *The Ghetto*, or, as he later renamed it, *The New Ghetto*.

The story of the play is easily told. Its hero is the young lawyer Dr. Jacob Samuel, the son of simple, decent people (modelled faithfully after Herzl's own parents). Samuel marries the good-hearted but spoiled and showy Hermine Hellman, daughter of a wealthy merchant. Until the time of his marriage a pure idealist, whose friends have been almost exclusively non-Jews, Samuel, who was introduced to the Hellman family by Dr. Bichler, a baptized Jew, becomes linked with the wealthy class of Jewry, till then an unknown world to him. His closest friend, the Christian Franz Wurzlechner, breaks with him because he dislikes the contact with stock exchange Jews, and also because the association would be harmful to his political career. Samuel's new brother-in-law, Rheinberger, a typical parvenu who toadies to the aristocracy, and his partner Wasserstein, a good natured, ignorant broker, are stock exchange speculators. They see life only under the money-making aspect, and in their eyes Samuel, who continues to stand by his ideals, is an impossibly high-strung individual.

The action of the play develops round the business relationship between Rheinberger and Wasserstein on the one
hand, and a certain Rittmeister von Schramm, the owner
of a mine, on the other, with Samuel between them. Samuel
is called in to draw up the articles of incorporation of a
company which is to take over the mine, and of which the
chief shareholders are to be Rheinberger, Wasserstein and
von Schramm. It so happens that von Schramm, the distinguished descendant of a long line of aristocrats, was no
stranger to Samuel. They had met years before, and had quar-
reled; Schramm had challenged Samuel to a duel, and Samuel
had avoided the duel by tendering an apology — the un-
revealed reason being that he dreaded the effect of a duel not
on himself, but on his old, sick father.

Samuel has no illusions about von Schramm's opinion of
him; the gallant aristocrat undoubtedly thinks of him contemptuously as a coward. Nevertheless he accepts the
assignment offered him by Rheinberger and Wasserstein —
and that chiefly because he wants to protect the Christian
aristocrat against the possible machinations of his brother-
in-law, who is infinitely more skilful in business than his
new partner.

In the midst of the negotiations Samuel, who has already
defended without charge a number of socialists, receives a
visit from the delegate of Schramm's miners. The delegate
complains that the mine is in bad condition, and a catastrophe may take place any day. Samuel, who has borrowed
some money from his brother-in-law, returns the loan and
withdraws from his assignment, to take up the cause of the
workers. He proceeds at once to the town of Dubnitz, where
the mine is situated, and calls the miners out on strike. The
strike collapses. On the day when the miners return to work,

the waters, which have been accumulating during the period
of the strike, break through, and a frightful accident ensues.
The result is — on the business side — that the shares of
the mine take a sharp fall; the value of the shares held by
Rittmeister von Schramm no longer covers the loan which
he has made. He is ruined. Rheinberger, whom Schramm
holds responsible for the situation, refuses to receive the
ruined aristocrat. Samuel interviews him instead and de-
nounces him in the sharpest terms for his treatment of his
workers. Von Schramm retorts that Samuel is hand in glove
with his thievish brother-in-law. Samuel: "That is a lie!"
Schramm: "Jewish pack of thieves!" Samuel: "Take that
back!" Schramm: "And if I don't? You'll apologize, just
as you did last time. I know you! You'll apologize for yourself, and you'll apologize for your brother-in-law! Jewish
pack of thieves!" Samuel flies into a rage and slaps von
Schramm. There is a duel. Rittmeister von Schramm kills
Dr. Jacob Samuel.

With this play — by far the best of his dramatic creations
— Herzl completed his inner return to his people. Until
then, with all his emotional involvement in the question, he
had stood outside it as the observer, the student, the clari-
fier, or even the defender. He had provided the world-his-
toric background for the problem, he had diagnosed it and
given the prognosis for the future. Now he was immersed
in it and identified with it.

He has become its spokesman and attorney, as he is
spokesman and attorney for other victims of injustice. It
is no accident that the hero of the play is a lawyer by voca-
tion and avocation. For the hero is Herzl himself, and the
transformation which unfolds in Dr. Jacob Samuel is the
transformation which is unfolding in Theodore Herzl.

There are powerful scenes in the play which throw a blinding light on the working out of the transformation. When Franz Wurzlechner tells Jacob Samuel that, without feeling differently toward his old friend, he is compelled to give up the friendship because he would ruin himself politically if he associated with these stock exchange Jews, Samuel is deeply stirred, but quite clear as to what he is to do. He had learned much from Wurzlechner, he admitted: bearing, manner, gestures. "I have learned from you how to honor a man without crawling at his feet, how to be proud without being arrogant." With the help of Wurzlechner he had "taken a number of steps out of the Jewish street," so that now he was able to continue the exit by himself. At the same time he knows that no credit for this is due his friend. "To be frank with you, what I have admired in you is your family, just as you despise my family now. For some hundreds of years you have been citizens — while we . . ." he smiles painfully. "You became a lawyer because the Wurzlechners of Vienna have always been lawyers or doctors. And Wasserstein, too, is what his forefathers were, he is that which destiny made his ancestors. It's not his fault. Neither is it your achievement. The moral element comes in later, when conscious effort begins. It comes in when the deliberate effort is made to overcome that which has always been instinctive. As for us Jews, we have been made what we are not even by nature, but by history."

"It's all over between us, Wurzlechner! But if you were to offer me your friendship again, if you were to give me the choice, to go with you or with Wasserstein, I would know where I belong. I belong with Wasserstein, whether he is rich or poor. I can't reproach him with anything, any more than I can praise you. Each of you stands there where your history has placed you. But we must not be satisfied with that. We must go onward, upward. Do you hear me? That is what it means to be a man!"

He belongs utterly to the Jews; it is for them that he fights, and, dying, he still sees himself as the fighter for their future. "Jews, my brothers," are his last words, "there will come a time when they will let you live again — when you know how to die. Why do you hold me so fast? . . ." Murmurs: "I want to get out! . . ." With all his strength: "Out! Out — of — the — ghetto!"

What future Jacob Samuel foresaw for the Jews in his dying moments remains unclear. It would appear that Herzl himself still believed that a deepening of mutual understanding between Jews and non-Jews might bring the solution. It is only thus that we can interpret another passage in the dying speech of the hero of the play: "Do you know what else I want? I want reconciliation and forgiveness . . ."

But Herzl had travelled so much further by this time that he could not have in mind the "reconciliation" which would come by the capitulation of baptism. Indeed, the play emphasizes as a first prerequisite in human relations the element of self-respect. "If you become untrue to yourself," says the clever mother to the son, in the play, "you mustn't complain if others become untrue to you." A man could only be true to himself if he continued to stand by the particular world in which he had grown up and in which nature and history had placed him. And it was the duty of every man to rise consciously, in vision and comprehension, above the limits of his particular little world. The ghetto, Herzl teaches in the play, brings frustration in bearing and being; it is the narrow, the oppressed, the unmanly, it is the distortion of character. The emancipation took away the physical ghetto; the internal ghetto, however, the invisible ghetto, has to be destroyed by ourselves. It is in this sense that Jacob Samuel stands forth as the symbol of a better future.

What Herzl sought, in the writing of this play, was to unburden himself of his crushing obsession. We shall see that he did not succeed in this. But *The New Ghetto* was a tremendous step forward in his development; it was the beginning of a new Jewish political method. Henceforth the Jewish question was to be lifted out of the trivial atmosphere of minor groups and obscure tea-party meetings, and put by the Jews on the stage of public action. It was like a fresh wind blowing suddenly through the choking atmosphere of a lightless room. It was a new attitude: decent pride!

"This piece *has* to be produced! It has to speak from the stage!" Thus Herzl wrote to Arthur Schnitzler, the one man to whom he revealed his authorship of the play. For it was his intention to have Schnitzler make a copy of the manuscript and submit it to producers as the work of one "Albert Schnabel." Herzl wanted the authorship to remain veiled in anonymity. No established name was to handicap the production. "It must reach the people. I have written it in this form for this purpose. They will not hear me to the end otherwise. I have written it for a nation of anti-Semites." And then, toward the middle of December, he wrote again to Schnitzler: "Under no circumstances is this play to be taken as defense of the Jews, or as an attempt to come to their rescue. I only seek to force the issue to open and wide discussion! Let the critics and the people do the defending or attacking. Once I have reached the stage my purpose is fulfilled. What happens afterwards is not of the slightest importance. I despise money, though I have almost none, and I despise fame, though I have none at all. I don't want to be a sentimental-pathetic poet. I want to utter myself, I want to unburden my heart. And if this piece reaches the world, that will be my unburdening."

Schnitzler had been correct in guessing that the play carried with it the implication of other works, which Herzl was compelled to put to one side for the time being. "There are greater songs asleep in these strings," Herzl admitted. "Some day I may be liberated from my daily labor, then I will reach for those higher themes. There is a whole spring-tide still within me, and some day it may break into bloom."

It called for a frightful effort to descend from the intoxicating heights of creativity to the ordinary round of work. For weeks now his regular employment had filled Herzl with revulsion. The first reports of the Dreyfus trial, which appeared while he was working on his *New Ghetto*, therefore made no particular impression on him. It looked like a sordid espionage affair in which a foreign power — before long it was revealed that the foreign power was Germany, acting through Major von Schwartzkoppen — had been buying up through its agent secret documents of the French general staff. An officer by the name of Alfred Dreyfus was named as the culprit, and no one had reason to doubt that he was guilty, even though Drumont's *Libre Parole* was exploiting the fact of the man's Jewishness.

In November the death of Alexander III, Emperor of Russia, took up more space in the newspapers than the Dreyfus case. Then the latter gradually forged to the front. Herzl himself sent in several reports, and like the rumors which then filled the air, they were contradictory. On December 6 he wired his paper the final results of the preliminary investigation. Dreyfus denied having written the note on which the prosecution was basing its case. The handwriting experts were not unanimous as to the authorship of the note. Public excitement mounted from day to day. An atmosphere of mystery had begun to envelop the case, which was taking on international significance. The actual trial, following on the preliminary investigation, began on December 19, 1894.

Herzl was present in his capacity as representative of the *Neue Freie Presse*. He wrote: "Today this affects more than the army, this question whether Dreyfus betrayed his fatherland, or whether it was possible to arrest him on the most frightful charges without sufficient evidence, and then to disgrace him publicly. At the beginning the vast majority demanded the head of the accused without delay, but soon after a great deal of doubt was expressed as to his guilt." Herzl then goes on to describe in detail the actual scenes of the trial. "A few moments pass. Deathly silence in the hall. All eyes are turned toward the little door, and suddenly the accused man appears before the public. There is an extraordinary tenseness in the looks which are directed at him. A trim, erect figure, somewhat above the average height, clad in the elegant dark uniform of an officer of artillery, the three gold stripes of the captain's rank on his sleeves. With lowered head Dreyfus passes through the crowd of onlookers, mounts the three steps to the prisoner's bench, draws himself up before the court, and makes a brief, stiff bow. Then he sits down, and I have a chance to get a good look at his face. He looks ten years older than he really is. It is said that this change came over him in prison. The short hair is tinged with grey, the forehead runs up into a bald patch, the nose is sharply curved, the ears stand away from his head, cheeks and chin are clean-shaven, the thick moustache is close-cropped, the mouth painfully drawn. He wears a pince-nez. Dreyfus's bearing is calm and firm."

The court debates the question whether the proceedings shall be secret or public. Demange, the attorney for the defense, clashes again and again with the presiding judge. The court withdraws to consider. "Dreyfus stands up and looks round the room without a trace of embarrassment. Then he sits down at his ease, fingers his moustache, and exchanges a few words with the lieutenant at his side."

The court returns. It has decided that the proceedings shall be secret. The room is cleared of spectators and journalists. Even the witnesses may be present only when they are on the stand. The trial goes on behind closed doors.

Thus, during the next few days, Herzl can write only about the general impression produced by the trial, and about the particular impression the prisoner has made on him. He observes Dreyfus as the latter marches, in uniform and white gloves, from the guardhouse to the courtroom. "His bearing is calm, his features more relaxed than yesterday." The interest and excitement among all elements of the population reach new levels; nearly everyone is convinced that he will be condemned; there are rumors that additional evidence of his guilt has been uncovered.

The public proclamation of the verdict came as the relaxation of a tension which had become almost unbearable. Here is Herzl's description :

"The public was admitted to the courtroom at six o'clock in the evening, after the attorney for the defense had made his last plea. The room was jammed, and the spectators were gripped by a nameless and breathless excitement. At seven the judges entered, to the cry of 'Attention!' The silence became deeper. In a firm, clear voice Colonel Maurel announced that the court-martial had unanimously declared Dreyfus guilty (a deep 'Ah!' from the audience). Maurel went on to pronounce the sentence of the court: military degradation and deportation for life. Someone in the courtroom cried out *'Vive la Patrie!,'* but already there was a rush for the doors on the part of those who wanted to be first to spread the news."

The nation received the verdict with satisfaction; the general belief was that the man was guilty. No one knew as yet what was to be revealed by years of courageous investigation, namely, that the verdict had been based on a forged document which neither the accused man nor his attorney was permitted even to look at. Nor did it as yet occur to anyone that "the foreign power" to which Dreyfus was supposed to have sold his country's secrets would permit an innocent man to be condemned without declaring openly that it had had absolutely no relations with him. When however, such a declaration was actually made — later — it found no credence. Only his family expected him to be set free, and on the day of the verdict his place was set at home for the family dinner. Dreyfus himself at once appealed the case. Shortly before the trial, wrote Herzl on December 27, the accused man had told the non-commissioned officer on guard that he was the victim of a personal plot and of private vengeance, and that the case against him would collapse at the trial like a house of cards. "I am being persecuted because I am a Jew," were his words.

Such was the report. But it is improbable that Dreyfus whose bearing throughout had been proud and confident, and who was moreover an assimilated Jew, should have expressed himself thus to his guard. What is interesting is the fact that Herzl should have written this report. It indicates the direction his mind had taken, and is the first mention of the Jewishness of the prisoner appearing in Herzl's articles on the Dreyfus affair.

At about this time Herzl wrote for his newspaper a review of the internal situation in France in the year 1894. "Anyone who has lived in France during this period," he observed, "has been the witness of important events." He was referring to the struggle of the French Republic against Anarchism and Socialism, those two movements which stand in diametric opposition to each other. The red flag of the Socialists was countered by the old cocarde of the tricolor. The national idea took on new life and penetrated into the most diverse sections of society. At the same time Socialim was making practical progress, as was evidenced by the introduction of the income tax. This did not mean, however, that the French bourgeoisie had given up. "The forces of the French Republic are not yet exhausted, and the world may still rivet its attention on this land, where all-human matters are being dealt with. It is the land of experimentation. It is a great honor to fulfil this function—an honor which must be earned. France is the great pot in which new political preparations for the entire civilized world are simmering."

In this same France, "where all-human matters were being dealt with," there took place on Saturday, January 5, 1895, the public degradation of Captain Dreyfus. Herzl's description of the event appeared in the evening edition of the *Neue Freie Presse* of the same date:

"On this dismal winter's day the degradation of Captain Dreyfus, which was carried out in the grounds of the Military

Academy, drew large numbers of the curious to the vicinity. Many officers were present, not a few of them accompanied by ladies. Entry into the grounds of the *Ecole Militaire* was permitted only to army officers and some journalists. Outside the grounds swarmed the morbid crowds which are always attracted by executions. A considerable number of police were on duty. At nine o'clock the great open court was filled with a detachment of troops in square formation: five thousand men in all. In the centre a general sat on horseback. A few minutes after nine Dreyfus was led forth. He was dressed in his captain's uniform. Four men conducted him before the general. The latter said: 'Alfred Dreyfus, you are unworthy to bear arms. In the name of the French Republic I degrade you from your rank. Let the sentence be carried out.' Here Dreyfus lifted his right arm and called out: 'I declare and solemnly swear that you are degrading an innocent man. *Vive la France!*' At that instant the drums were beaten. The officer in charge began to tear from the condemned man's uniform the buttons and cords, which had already been loosened. Dreyfus retained his calm bearing. Within a few minutes this part of the ceremony was over.

"Then began the parade of the condemned before the troops. Dreyfus marched along the sides of the square like a man who knows himself to be innocent. He passed by a group of officers, who cried: 'Judas! Traitor!' Dreyfus cried back: 'I forbid you to insult me!' At twenty minutes past nine the parade was over. Dreyfus was then handcuffed and given into the custody of the gendarmes. From that point on he was to be considered a civilian prisoner and treated as such. When he had been led away the troops defiled off the grounds. But the crowd surged toward the gates to watch the condemned man being led way. There were passionate shouts. 'Bring him out here, and we'll tear him to pieces!' But the crowd waited in vain. There was a curious excitement amongst those who had been able to witness the ceremony of the degradation. The strange, firm bearing of the prisoner had made a profound impression on some of them."

Later in the day Herzl sent off a supplementary report which appeared in the Sunday edition of his paper:

"To complete the picture of the ceremony it should be added that as Dreyfus was being paraded before the troops, among whom there were numbers of recruits, he kept calling out: 'I am innocent!' When he passed near a group of journalists he stopped for a moment and said: 'Tell all France that I am innocent!' Some of the journalists retorted with insults. Part of the crowd outside, which was able to catch a glimpse of the ceremony, shouted again and again: 'Death to the traitor!' "

It was indeed in a state "of curious excitement" that Herzl left the scene. What was it that moved him so? He was — as the tone of his report showed — becoming more and more convinced of the innocence of the condemned man. He had not the slightest external evidence on which to base this feeling; it was an insight born of his new understanding of the problem of the emancipated Jew. He did not believe that a Jewish officer was capable of committing an act of national treachery. "A Jew who, as an officer on the general staff, has before him an honorable career, cannot commit such a crime... The Jews, who have so long been condemned to a state of civic dishonor, have, as a result, developed an almost pathological hunger for honor, and a Jewish

officer is in this respect specifically Jewish." That Captain
Dreyfus, a well-to-do Jew who had been prompted to a
military career by pure ambition, should have committed
such a crime therefore seemed to Herzl a psychological im-
possibility. This was the view expressed in a conversation
with the Italian military attaché Panizzardi, who was later
to play an important role in the breaking of the case. At
that time, however, the Italian was convinced of Dreyfus's
guilt, for to this honest soldier it seemed impossible that
seven officers should have condemned a comrade without
overwhelming proof of his guilt. But just this happened
to be the problem which lifted the case out of the ordinary
class of judicial error.

For even if we grant, on insufficient grounds, that it was
really a traitor who was being condemned and degraded,
the attitude of the crowd was — according to the printed
report — a strange one. We read, in the *Neue Freie Presse*,
that the crowd shouted: "Death to the traitor." This is
quite comprehensible — but there is something incomplete
about it. We cannot avoid the impression that Herzl's
telegrams were edited before they were printed, and it was
fear that motivated the excisions. It is unlikely that Herzl,
in the condition in which he then was, had himself colored
the report. Four years afterwards there still rang in his ears
the shouts of the crowd, which left him shattered: "*A mort!
A mort les juifs!*" What! he asked himself. Death to *all* the
Jews because *one* of them is a traitor? "The Dreyfus case,"
he wrote in 1899, "embodies more than a judicial error; it
embodies the desire of the vast majority of the French to
condemn a Jew, and to condemn all Jews in this one Jew.
Death to the Jews! howled the mob, as the decorations were

being ripped from the captain's coat ... Where? In France. In republican, modern, civilized France, a hundred years after the Declaration of the Rights of Man. The French people, or at any rate the greater part of the French people, does not want to extend the rights of man to Jews. The edict of the great Revolution has been revoked."

Illumined thus in retrospect, the "curious excitement" which gripped Herzl on that occasion takes on a special significance. "Until that time most of us believed that the solution of the Jewish question was to be patiently waited for as part of the general development of mankind. But when a people which in every other respect is so progressive and so highly civilized can take such a turn, what are we to expect from other peoples, which have not even attained the level which France attained a hundred years ago?"

We need Herzl's formulation of the situation as set down in 1899 in order to put his impressions of January 1895 in the proper light. In that fateful moment, when he heard the howling of the mob outside the gates of the *Ecole Militaire*, the realization flashed upon Herzl that Jew-hatred was deep-rooted in the heart of the people — so deep, indeed, that it was impossible to hope for its disappearance within a measurable period of time. Precisely because he was so sensitive to his honor as a Jew, precisely because he had proclaimed, in *The New Ghetto*, the ideal of human reconciliation, and had taken the ultimate decision to stand by his Jewishness, the ghastly spectacle of that winter morning must have shaken him to the depths of his being. It was as if the ground had been cut away from under his feet. In this sense Herzl could say later that the Dreyfus affair had made him a Zionist.

But only in this limited sense. For a new question mark
had risen before him, and the answer was not clear: how was
he to feel and what was to be his reaction? His play, which
was to set things in motion by putting the Jewish question
before the public, was rejected by the leading German
theatres. What was he to do?

He was overcome by a feeling of the forlorn and abandoned; an impenetrable loneliness descended on him. He
tried to flee from it. "Why have I heard nothing about your
play? Why don't you send it to me? Haven't I come close
enough to you during these recent months of conspiratorial
secrecy?" Thus he wrote bitterly about mid-February to
Schnitzler, he who as a rule was so proudly reticent. "Really,
I almost feel like putting an ad in the papers: 'Man in prime
of life seeks friend to whom he can confide without fear all
his weaknesses and absurdities . . .' I really don't know, am
I too shy, or too distrustful, or am I seeing too well: I don't
find any such friend among my acquaintances here."

But while he sought a friend frantically, while he felt
himself drowned in loneliness, he saw all about him the ever
fiercer light of a blazing anti-Semitism. In the French
Chamber of Deputies the deputy Denis made an interpella-
tion on the influence of the Jews in the political administration of the country. In Vienna a Jewish member of the City
Council rose to speak and was howled down. On April 2,
1895, were held the municipal elections of Vienna, and there
was such an enormous increase in the number of anti-Semitic
aldermen, all of them followers of Lueger, that the majority
held until that time by the Liberal Party was reduced to ten.
"One little step more," wrote the *Neue Freie Presse*, "and
Herr Lueger will be the head of the municipality of Vienna

and of the only great metropolis to be branded with the shameful mark of an anti-Semitic administration."

Herzl had lived through these elections, for he had made a short visit to Vienna, and was in the city on March 22. It was as if the lonely man, whose faith in mankind had suffered an almost fatal diminution through the Dreyfus affair, had fled to his nearest and dearest, and to the place in which he had passed his early manhood, in order to find strength again. But we cannot be clear as to the mysterious processes then at work in him. Herzl himself could not have given a picture of them even a few weeks later. We do know that there was awakening in him a rebellion against the importance of the Word. "Aren't they inclined to overrate the value of the Word in the Palais Bourbon?" he asked on March 2, 1895, and the question might very well have been directed toward himself. He wanted to burst out beyond the Word. There was in him a fierce urge to the Act. For the first time he went to the religious services in the temple on the Rue de la Victoire. "Once again I found them moving and solemn." There was much to remind him of his youth and of the temple on the Tabakgasse in Pest. Changing plans passed tumultuously through his mind. He wanted to write a book on "The Condition of the Jews," consisting of reports on all the important areas of Jewish settlement in Russia, Galicia, Hungary, Bohemia, the Orient — and the recently founded Colonies in Palestine, about which he had heard from his relative Löbl on his brief visit to Vienna.

There was a conversation between Herzl and Alphonse Daudet, for whom Herzl had translated an article, and the Jewish question inevitably crept into it. Herzl said: "Out of all these faithful and accurate descriptions of Jewish life, there will emerge the proof that the Jews have not merited the misfortunes which are visited on them, that they are men and women who are attacked without being known." Daudet was known as an anti-Semite, but Herzl unfolded to him his views on the Jewish question, and was confirmed in his outlook when he marked what a deep impression they produced on Daudet. Daudet felt that Herzl ought to write a novel; it would carry farther. "Look at *Uncle Tom's Cabin.*"

That was enough to throw into confusion Herzl's idea of a sociological report. He returned to his former plan of a Jewish novel which he had abandoned when he was called to his assignment on the *Neue Freie Presse* in Paris. Friend Kana, the suicide, was no longer to be the central figure. He was instead to be "the weaker one, the beloved friend of the hero," and would take his own life after a series of misfortunes, while the Promised Land was being discovered or rather founded. When the hero on board the ship which was taking him to the Promised Land would receive the moving farewell letter of his friend, his first reaction after his horror would be one of rage: "Idiot! Fool! Miserable hopeless weakling! A life lost which belonged to us!"

We can see the Zionist idea arising. Its outlines are still indefinite, but the decisive idea is clearly visible: only by migration can this upright human type be given its chance to emerge. In *The New Ghetto* Jacob Samuel is a hero because he knows how to choose an honorable death. Now the death of a useful man is criminally wasteful. For there are great tasks to be undertaken. Life! Life is needed!

In essence it is the Act and not the Word that confronts us. What last impulse it was that actually carried Herzl from the Word to the Act it will be difficult to tell — he himself could not have given the answer. Little things may play a dramatic role not less effectively than great ones when a man is so charged with purpose as Herzl then was.

It is possible that something apparently irrelevant was the immediate efficient cause. On April 29 Herzl reported in great detail a catastrophe which had occurred near Epinal: a dam had collapsed, a great flood had burst over the countryside and more than a hundred human beings had been swept to their deaths.

This incident, coming at this moment, appears like a liberating symbol for his own life. In him too a dam collapsed. In him too great floods were released to carry him away.

In the early days of May, Herzl addressed to Baron de Hirsch the letter which opens his Jewish political career.

BOOK II

THE ZIONIST

CHAPTER V

THE *JUDENSTAAT* IN THE WRITING.
(MAY - FEBRUARY 1895)

"Honored Sir:

When may I have the privilege of visiting you? I wish to discuss the Jewish problem with you. It is not a question of an interview, still less a direct or indirect money matter. I want to discuss with you a Jewish political plan the effects of which will perhaps extend to days when you and I are no longer here."

This is the opening paragraph of the letter to Baron de Hirsch which Herzl drafted in the early days of May 1895. He let the draft lie on his desk for fourteen days; his family, which was living with him, returned to Vienna and he, following his usual custom for that period of the year, moved to the Hotel Castille in the Rue de Cambon. Toward the middle of the month he sent the letter off. He asked the Baron to set a day on which he could spare him an hour or two without interruption. The tone of the letter is proud and cool, almost condescending; he wanted to make it absolutely clear from the outset that this was not a journalistic device which was to lead up to a request for money. "It is evident," wrote Herzl, "that there are so many demands being constantly made on you that one cannot be too hasty in anticipating and disarming any suspicion of ulterior intentions."

123

Baron Moritz de Hirsch, Freiherr von Gereuth, was one of the richest men of his time, and the foremost symbol of Jewish philanthropy. In 1891 he had founded the Jewish Colonization Association (*ICA*) with a capital of two million pounds. Its purpose was to solve the problem of depressed Russian Jewry by the systematic, planned transference of some millions of Jews to the Argentine. In that country Hirsch had purchased large areas for colonization. Hirsch had considered the question of Palestine, a country which he had learned to know well at first-hand when he carried through the extension of the first railroad from the Balkans to Constantinople; he had come to the conclusion that for political and economic reasons Palestine was not suited for a permanent and well secured Jewish colonization. He had been in contact with the *Hoveve Zion*, the pre-Herzlian Zionists, who had tried to win him over to the idea of Palestinian colonization. He had acknowledged the deep traditions, worthy of all reverence, which bound the Jew to Palestine. Nevertheless, as he stated in a letter of August 1891, he did not consider these traditions a solid enough basis for the security of the new fatherland and as a protection against a repetition of Jewish misfortunes. However, he soon discovered (in 1891) that the Argentine, too, presented no easy task. When the actual colonization began he was confronted with vast difficulties rising in part from the unsuitability of the human material, in part from the nature of the soil, and in part from the clumsiness and inexperience of the directing personnel. Of what significance, in the light of his original, grandiose intentions, were the four colonies which he had managed to create by 1894, with their total population of 3,000 — especially when one bears in mind that 800 of the original colonists had to be resettled in the United States? And what a disproportion between the sums expended and the results obtained! Perhaps, thought Herzl, the will-power and energies of this man, who had been so obviously and so deeply moved by the plight of his people, were now ready to be diverted toward the great plan which had fired the imagination of Herzl and which seemed to him to promise swifter results: the founding of a new, publicly secured Jewish community.

He received from Hirsch a request to submit his plan in writing. On May 24 he wrote to him: "What you have undertaken till now was as magnificent in conception as it has proved futile in actuality; it is as costly as it is hopeless. Until now you have been only a philanthropist, a Peabody. I want to show you the way to become something more."

A week later, at half past eleven on the morning of June 2, 1895, the interview took place in the palace of Baron de Hirsch. Herzl had prepared notes which took up twenty-two quarto pages. He knew that he, the intellectually superior mocking spirit, the ready *causeur*, was always handicapped by a preliminary shyness when he confronted a personality of high rank or standing, and the copious notes were intended as a safeguard and as a help to his memory.

In these outlines — they were the first written expression of his new idea — Herzl offered the great philanthropist two alternatives: solution of the Jewish question without migration, and solution by migration. Either solution presupposed a preliminary process of education of the Jewish masses. What Herzl sought first was to win Hirsch over to this idea of the education of the Jewish masses in self-sacrifice, moral bearing and capacity for great enterprises. The solution of the Jewish question without migration (i.e., by complete absorption in the surrounding population) would, if at all possible, call for a long period of time.

"But," the notes continue, "if the Jews are to be transformed into men of character in a reasonable period of time, say ten or twenty years, or even forty — the interval needed by Moses — it cannot be done without migration. Who is going to decide whether conditions are bad enough today to warrant our migration? And whether the situation is hopeless? The Congress which you (i.e. Hirsch) have convened for the first of August in a hotel in Switzerland. You will preside over this Congress of notables. Your call will be heard and answered in every part of the world.

"And what will be the message given to the men assembled? 'You are pariahs! You must forever tremble at the thought that you are about to be deprived of your rights and stripped of your possessions. You will be insulted when you walk in the street. If you are poor, you suffer doubly. If you are rich, you must conceal the fact. You are not admitted to any honorable calling, and if you deal in money you are made the special focus of contempt ... The situation will not change for the better, but rather for the worse ... There is only one way out: into the promised land.'"

In the actual discussion Herzl did not manage to reach these, the central points of his thesis. For at the very outset of the conversation, in his basic presentation, he came into sharp conflict with Hirsch's views and practical measures. Herzl began the talk thus:

"Some of the things I have to say you will find too simple, others too fantastic. But it is the simple and the fantastic which leads men." He then leaps into the centre of the problem, and outlines the basis in a few words. It is the logical extension of the thoughts with which he was occupied in *The New Ghetto*. History was responsible for the condition of the Jews, and for the torments which were inflicted on them. "Throughout the two thousand years of our dispersion," he said now, "we have lacked unified political leadership. I consider this our greatest misfortune. It has done us more harm than all the persecutions. It is this that is responsible for our inner decay. For there was no one, not even a king inspired by selfish motives, to educate us as men . . . If we only had a unified political leadership . . . we could initiate the solution of the Jewish question." It is clear now: for Herzl the problem has been transformed from something social into something purely human, taking on for that reason a political character; and its solution could be effected only by political means.

The first thing to be created, therefore, was a political center, from which could issue the leadership of the people in its totality. This was the fundamental prerequisite now insisted on by Herzl. This center would also direct the national re-education, whether or not migration was proposed. For the process of re-education new methods would be called for from the outset. First would have to come total repudiation of the principle of philanthropy: this was the second basic principle involved in the new concept. "You breed beggars," he told the great humanitarian. "It is characteristic of the situation that among no other people is there so much philanthropy and so much mendicancy as among the Jews. It is impossible to escape the conclusion that there must be an organic connection between these two phenomena. This philanthropy debases the character of our people." With this observation Hirsch was in agreement. Then Herzl went on to criticise the Argentinian colonization, which had also been conducted on false

principles — false because they were of a philanthropic character — and which was therefore bound to end in failure.

"You transport these Jews as plough-hands. They naturally feel that henceforth they have a claim on you, and this
certainly does not promote the will to work. Whatever
such an exported Jew costs you, he is not worth it. And
how many individual samples can you transplant in any
case? Fifteen thousand, twenty thousand. There are more
Jews in one street in the Leopold district of Vienna."

The direct method, he went on, was altogether unsuited
for a mass movement. Only indirect methods could be
effective. Great aims, daring and attractive enterprises, were
alone capable of driving masses of men toward higher
objectives.

Along these lines, the first task was to improve the mass
character among Jews wherever they happened to be already. "They must be made strong as for war, filled with
the joy of work, penetrated by high virtues." How was
Hirsch to set the change in motion? By offering prizes for
achievements in science and art, for distinguished moral
actions, etc. "The annual prizes will themselves be of little
importance. What is of importance is the wide-spread effort
which will be made to be among the prize-winners; through
this the general moral level will be raised."

Here Hirsch interrupted him impatiently: "No, no, no.
I don't want to raise the general level. All our misfortunes
come from the fact that the Jews aim too high. We have too
many intellectuals. My aim is to discourage this pushful-
ness among the Jews. They mustn't make such great progress. All the hatred of us comes from this." In the Argentine, to which bad elements had come at first, things were
already going better. After a few years he would prove to

the world that the Jews made good agricultural workers. One of the consequences might be that the Russian government would then give its Jews access to the land.

After these remarks of Hirsch's, Herzl said he considered it useless to unfold his ideas any further. "You do not know," he said, "what fantasy means, and you do not realize that it is only from a certain height that one can perceive the great outlines of men."

Herzl reports further: "Hirsch said that migration was the only way. 'There is land enough to be purchased ...'

"I almost shouted at him: 'Certainly! Who told you that I'm against emigration. Here it is, in these notes. I will go to the German Kaiser; he will understand me, for he has been educated to the reception of great ideas ... I will say to the German Kaiser: Let us go forth. We are aliens here, they do not let us dissolve into the population, and if they let us we would not do it. Let us go forth! I will show you the means and methods whereby this migration can be carried out without causing an economic upset, without leaving a gap behind us.'

"Hirsch said: 'Where will you get the money? Rothschild will donate five hundred francs.'

" 'The money?', I said, smiling scornfully. 'I will create a national loan of ten million marks.'

" 'Fantastic,' smiled the Baron. 'The rich Jews will give you nothing. The rich Jews are bad, they display no interest in the sufferings of the poor.'

" 'You speak like a Socialist, Baron Hirsch,' I said.

" 'This won't be our last conversation,' the Baron suggested. 'The moment I return from London you shall hear from me.' "

This was the end of that dramatic conversation, as Herzl recorded it. These two men, representing two different worlds, parted, feeling a certain sympathy for each other, respecting each other, but without reaching common ground. Herzl's first attempt to win this great power over by storm had failed. Had he set about it in the right way? Had it been wise of him to try and compel this man to new ways of thought? We can, without presumption, assert that he had not set about it in the right way; he had not approached him from the practical angle, he had not given due weight to Hirsch's positive achievements. He should have come to this cool, practical man with a more specific plan of action, on which they could have united. The larger theoretical aspect could have been introduced later, and by degrees. As it was, he began by bringing to focus their theoretical divergence, with the result that Hirsch felt he was dealing with an interesting dreamer, but a dreamer nevertheless, and Herzl did not get further than the sixth page in his voluminous notes. Thus it was, too, that he left Hirsch, who for years had seen the necessity of emigration as part of the solution of the Jewish problem, with the impression that he, Herzl, was opposed to it, and wanted to solve the Jewish problem by training and re-education on the spot.

An objective observer who reviews the incident after this lapse of years must further conclude that Herzl had approached Hirsch too soon, before his own vision of the plan had clarified. His dream of the new Jew, of the new Jewish political movement, overshadowed the question of program.

On the day of his conversation with Hirsch, Herzl wrote him a long letter in which he sought to supplement the information and impressions which had been the result of the meeting. How much better he could do it in writing!

He outlined the steps connected with the carrying out of the emigration plans. First as to money: "I will launch a Jewish national loan. There's always plenty of Jewish money for Chinese loans, for Negro railroad enterprises in Africa, for the most extravagantly adventurous ideas — and will we be unable to find money for the deepest, most immediate, and most tormenting need of the Jews themselves?" With this loan, which was to be "the main fund of the migration plan" the migration itself was to be organized, "cities are to be built and the new land is to be made so fruitful that it shall become the Promised Land."

Where the Promised Land was to be located, how it was to be acquired, is not yet mentioned. Herzl does not seem to have thought this question of decisive significance; it was a scientific matter, as he later intimated. It was the organization of the migration which held his attention, the political preparations among the Powers, the preliminary changes to be brought about among the masses by training, by "tremendous propaganda, the popularization of the idea through newspapers, books, pamphlets, lectures, pictures, songs." All these works "are to be directed purposively and farsightedly, from a single center. But then I should have had to speak to you finally about the flag which had to be unrolled and under which the movement was to march. And then you would have asked me mockingly: 'A flag — what is that? A stick with a rag at the end of it.' No, *Monsieur le Baron*, a flag is a great deal more. It is with a flag that people are led whithersoever one desires, even to the Promised Land. For a flag men live and die; indeed, it is the only thing for which they are prepared to die in masses if they have been brought up to it.

"Please believe me, the political life of an entire people — particularly when that people is scattered throughout the entire world — can be set in motion only with imponderables floating high in the air. Do you know what the German Reich sprang from? From dreams, songs, fantasies, and gold-black bands worn by students. And that in a brief period of time.

"What? You do not understand imponderables? And what is religion? Bethink yourself what the Jews have endured for two thousand years for the sake of this fantasy . . .

"Certainly this national fantasy must rest on practical foundations. But whence have you the impression that I have no practical ideas for the details?

"The exodus to the Promised Land presents itself as a tremendous enterprise in transportation, unparalleled in the modern world. What, transportation? It is a complex of all human enterprises which we shall fit into each other like cog-wheels. And in the very first stages of the enterprise we shall find employment for the ambitious younger masses of our people; all the engineers, architects, technologists, chemists, doctors, and lawyers, those who have emerged in the last thirty years from the ghetto and who have been moved by the faith that they can win their bread and a little honor outside the framework of our Jewish business futilities. Today they must be filled with despair, they constitute the foundation of a frightful over-educated proletariat. But it is to these that all my love belongs, and I am just as set on increasing their number as you are set on diminishing it. It is in them that I perceive the latent power of the Jewish people. In brief, my kind.

"Their withdrawal will in itself suffice to lighten the pressure among the middle classes in anti-Semitic countries."

These were the concepts and methods which distinguished him from the Baron. "You are the great money Jew, I am the Jew of the spirit, hence the differences in our outlooks and methods." Hirsch had indeed tried to do much for the Jews. But his methods, which aimed at keeping the Jews on the lowest possible level, contradicted all the laws of human development and were therefore impractical.

"Do you know that you have adopted a frightfully reactionary policy — worse than that of the most absolute autocrats? Fortunately your powers are not great enough to carry it out. You mean well, *parbleu, je le sais bien*. That is why I want to direct your will to the right channel. Do not permit yourself to be prejudiced by the fact that I am still fairly young. At thirty-five men become cabinet ministers in France, and Napoleon was Emperor at that age."

He closes the letter by declaring that he is ready to continue the conversation as soon as Hirsch desires. But he makes it clear that the movement does not depend on the consent of the Baron. "Very definitely I should like to find, through you, an existing and recognized force, the short-cut to my plans. But you would only be the beginning. There are others. And finally, and above all, there is the mass of the Jews, to which I shall know how to find my way."

In this letter of June 3, 1895, Herzl for the first time imparted his new Jewish policy to a stranger. The writing down of his views, as well as his conversation on the subject, had had a stronger effect on himself than on Hirsch. He had obtained a clear vision of the new and revolutionary

character of his proposals. On the same day or shortly thereafter he began a diary under the title of *The Jewish Question*.

"For some time now I have been engaged upon a work
of indescribable greatness. I do not know yet whether I shall
carry it through. It has assumed the aspect of some mighty
dream. But days and weeks have passed since it has filled
me utterly, it has overflown into my unconscious self, it
accompanies me wherever I go, it broods above all my
commonplace conversation, it peeps over my shoulder at
the comical little journalistic work which I must carry out,
it disturbs and intoxicates me.

"What it will lead to is as yet something at which I
cannot even guess. Only my experience tells me that it is
something remarkable, something which, as a dream of
extraordinary beauty, must be written down — if not as a
memorial for all men then at least for my own memory and
future delight. And perhaps it is something between both
possibilities: for literature. If the fantasy does not become
the deed, the deed can become a fantasy."

So begins the astonishing diary which he was to keep from
that day on until shortly before his death. A unique book,
one of the very strangest books in world literature, emerged.
In it a man uncovered himself completely to the world,
uncovered his thoughts and acts to the extent that these
seemed to him to be essential. He labored — not always
with complete success, as he himself admitted — to set down
without pose, without ulterior motive, that which happened
in and through him, to leave an honest record for his own
later years and for future generations. It was the work of a
writer who in a long apprenticeship of search and experiment
had acquired a complete mastery of language which enabled

him to transmit, "almost without friction" (we recall the longing of his youth) to the written word whatever had been absorbed by heart, eye, and brain. If nothing more had survived of his literary production this astounding diary, *The Jewish Qestion*, would remain forever fresh, forever readable: at once an exciting confession and a literary masterpiece.

He begins with a backward glance at his own development, and attempts to trace his growth to his present state. He enters into the record the first two letters to Hirsch, and Hirsch's replies; he reproduces, like an act from one of his own plays, the conversation. "I've mounted again the beautiful steps, traversed the distinguished court. I was not disappointed, but rather stirred. All in all a pleasant, intelligent man — vain, *par excellence*! — but I could have worked with him. He makes the impression that with all his self-opinionatedness he is reliable. When I got home I was drawn irresistably to my writing table."

Up to this point the story in the diary makes consecutive reading; then it breaks off. The third letter to Hirsch, in which he tried to give more consistent form to his ideas, is not entered.

Then suddenly the storm breaks upon him. The clouds open, the thunder rolls and the lightning flashes about him. A thousand impressions beat upon him simultaneously, a gigantic vision. He cannot think, he cannot act, he can only write; breathless, unreflecting, unable to control himself, unable to exercise the critical faculty lest he dam the eruption, he dashes down his thoughts on scraps of paper — "Walking, standing, lying down, in the street, at table, in the night," as if under unceasing command. He notes on June 16: "During these days I was more than once afraid that I was

going out of my mind. So furiously did the cataract of
thoughts race through my soul. A lifetime will not suffice to
put everything down. But I am leaving behind me a spiritual
legacy. For whom? For all men. I believe that I shall be
named among the great benefactors of mankind. Or is this
feeling of mine the beginning of delusions of grandeur?"
He notes elsewhere: "Am I working it out? No, it is working
me out. It would be an hallucination were it not so informed
by reason from beginning to end. The old expression for this
kind of thing was inspiration."

He has already begun to see himself in a setting of history.
"My migration from Vienna to Paris and back were historically necessary in order that I might learn at first-hand the
migratory process." "Thirteen years were needed at the
least in order that I might reach this simple thought. Only
now do I see how narrowly I missed it on frequent occasions."

And then doubts rise up from the depths. He dines with
well-to-do, educated, oppressed people who confront the
question of anti-Semitism in a state of complete helplessness:
"They do not suspect it, but they are ghetto-natures, quiet,
decent, timid. That is what most of us are. Will they understand the call to freedom and to manhood? When I left them
my spirits were very low. Again, my plan appeared to me
to be crazy." Then at once he comes to. "Today I am again
as firm as steel," he notes the next morning. "The flabbiness
of the people I met yesterday gives me all the more ground
for action."

Clearer and clearer becomes the picture which he has of
himself and of his task in the history of his people. "I pick up
once again the torn thread of the tradition of our people.
I lead it into the Promised Land."

He notes on June 12: "Today the idea came to me that perhaps I am solving a great deal more than the Jewish question. To wit, *tout bonnement*, the social question, I do not know. I can hardly believe it. But if it should really be so," he adds almost piously, "what a gift of God to the Jews."

However, he is careful to explain: "When I say God I don't mean to offend the free-thinkers. For my part they can say World Spirit or something else in place of this beloved, old, wonderful abbreviation . . ."

"The flag has occurred to me," he says two days later. "Perhaps a white flag with seven golden stars. The white flag represents our new clean life. The stars are the hours of work. It is under the sign of work that we draw toward the Promised Land."

"The Promised Land, where we can have hooked noses, black or red beards, and bow legs, without being despised for it. Where we can live at last as free men on our own soil, and where we can die peacefully in our own fatherland. Where we can expect the award of honor for great deeds. So that the offensive cry of 'Jew!' may become an honorable appellation, like German, Englishman, Frenchman — in brief, like all civilized peoples. So that we may be able to form our state to educate our people for the tasks which at present still lie beyond our vision. For surely God would not have kept us alive so long if there were not assigned to us a specific role in the history of mankind."

"While writing," he notes the next day, "and in particular when I envisioned the earnest, festive mood on the ships, and over there, on their arrival, the festive reception, I have often wept over the misfortunes of my people."

"But when I will be leading the people," he at once commands himself, "I must not show any tears. The glance of the leader must be hard." "Above all I must exercise perfect self-control."

"It has occurred to no one," he notes on June 16, "to look for the Promised Land in the place where it is — and yet it lies so near. Here it is: within ourselves! I am not fooling anyone. It is open to every man to convince himself that I am telling the truth. For every man takes a piece of the Promised Land in him and carries it over. This one in his head, the other in his hands, the third in his savings. The Promised Land is where we will carry it!"

He adds: "The Jewish state is a world need." He draws the logical consequence for himself: "I believe that for me life has ended and world history begun."

He let the first storm pass over him, yielding to its imperious will, making no effort to stem its fury, lest he interrupt the inspiration. When it had had its way with him, he took hold of himself again, and gathered up his energies for the effort to reconstruct everything logically and in ordered fashion. He was afraid that death might come upon him before he had succeeded in reducing to transferable form his historic vision. He prepared himself, at the same time, to submit the plan to the Rothschild family, recognizing his failure with Baron de Hirsch. Thus, in the course of five days, he added to his diary a sixty-five page pamphlet — in effect the outline of *Der Judenstaat* — which he called: *Address to the Rothschilds*.

In this *Address* we already find the actual wording of most of his ideas, as they were to be given to the world. It is in essence a speech directed to the family council of the Rothschilds, and in no wise occupies itself with the tasks of the public itself. The Rothschild family, or more correctly the Rothschild fortune, therefore takes a prominent place in the scheme.

Herzl is convinced, and in turn attempts to convince the Rothschilds, that their enormous fortune can be rescued only by the instrument of the Jewish State. This fortune he compares to a tower which keeps on growing interminably without a corresponding broadening of the base. He therefore offers them the means of harmonizing the two dimensions. "This simple old idea," he says, "is the exodus from Egypt."

The fortune of the Rothschilds, which the world regarded as a danger, must acquire aim and purpose. It would do this by serving as the financial basis of the great migration and resettlement; and the manner of the action is given by Herzl in some detail. The liaison between Herzl and the Rothschilds was to be Moritz Güdemann, the famous scholar and rabbi, who had succeeded Jellinek in the chief rabbinate of Vienna. Herzl would first submit his plan for criticism and discussion to Güdemann and to an intelligent layman; he would also consult with them as to the first steps to be taken. On June 11 — while he was still in the midst of the inspirational fever — he wrote to Güdemann and suggested that the two of them meet within a few days at Caux, on Lake Geneva.

Güdemann answers evasively. Herzl presses him, and asks him whether he will undertake to read the *Rothschild Address* to the Viennese branch of the family. Should Güdemann, whom Herzl considers the right man for this task, refuse, then he, Herzl, would have to look elsewhere. "For," he writes, "I have the solution to the Jewish question. I know it sounds mad; and at the beginning I shall be called mad more than once — until the truth of what I am saying is recognized in all its shattering force."

At that time Herzl received a visit from his friend Friedrich Schiff, the doctor and journalist. Schiff was astounded at Herzl's appearance. He looked like a man who had not slept for nights; and his clothes, which were always faultlessly neat, were in shocking disorder. Schiff remarked that Herzl looked as if he had discovered the secret of the dirigible balloon. To this raillery Herzl did not reply. But he entered a note into his diary that evening: "One of my fiercest battles will have to be with Jewish mockery. This mockery is the impotent reflex of the prisoner in his effort to appear a free man. That is why it touches me so closely." But he made up his mind to submit his plan to his ironic friend. He wanted to see the effect on a totally unprepared mind. And so he made his friend sit down, and he read forth to him the *Rothschild Address*.

At first Schiff, who seemed to be shaken to the point of tears, remained silent. When Herzl pressed him for his opinion, Schiff answered frankly: he considered the plan the product of an overstrained mind, and he urgently advised Herzl to take a rest and seek medical treatment.

Herzl had been prepared for opposition; this reaction he had not anticipated. He responded energetically by telling Schiff of the first active steps, and showed him the copy of his letter to Güdemann.

"Güdemann will think you mad!" cried Schiff. "He'll go to your father, and your parents will be plunged into unhappiness. You are making a ridiculous — or tragic — figure of yourself." This mention of his parents had such an effect on Herzl that he sent off a telegram to Güdemann to return the last letter unopened.

After a sleepless night Schiff came to Herzl again. The two men went for a stroll in the Tuileries gardens, and again, with the utmost urgency and distress, Schiff urged his friend to give the whole thing up, lest he be universally regarded as a lunatic. The deep concern for his condition thus displayed by a simple honest man had a profoundly depressing effect on Herzl. To Schiff's suggestion that he submit the matter to Max Nordau, with whom he had been acquainted for some years, he returned a negative. If his ideas, which he considered both true and realizable, called forth such a response in an honest man and faithful friend, there was obviously no sense in following them up.

Crushed to the ground, yet breaking out in fury against the littleness of the Jews, of whom he considered his friend the typical representative, he wrote on that same day a fourth letter to Baron de Hirsch, who had not replied to his last communication: "My last letter calls for a conclusion. Here it is: I have given the whole thing up. There is no helping the Jews for the time being. If someone were to show them the Promised Land they would treat him with contempt. They are disintegrated. And yet I know where salvation lies: in us! In our capital, in our labor, and in that special combination of the two which I have outlined to you. But we shall have to descend deeper, we shall have to fall lower, we shall have to endure more insult, we shall have to be spat upon, despised, beaten, plundered and thrashed even more than till now, before we become ripe for the idea . . . We have not yet reached the right degree of despair. That is why the savior will be greeted with laughter. What, laughter? No, smiles: there is not strength enough left for laughter. There stands the wall — and that wall is the disintegration of the Jews. On the other side of the wall there await us freedom and greatness. But I can't break through that wall, I can't break through it with my head alone. And so I am giving it up ... As far as the practical aspect is concerned, the thing is ended for me. Theoretically I still stand by it with the utmost firmness. And perhaps this only shows that I too am disintegrated. A Christ would go through thick and thin for an idea of such power. But what can you expect? I don't want to look like a Don Quixote. But those little solutions — your twenty thousand Argentinians, or the passing over of the Jews to Socialism, I refuse to accept. For I am not a Sancho Panza, either."

Later on Herzl compared the crisis through which he passed in those days to the plunging of a red-hot body into ice-cold water. "To be sure," he said, "if the body happens to be iron it emerges steel." But for the moment he asked himself whether he was really in his right senses. A trifling incident reveals to us the depths of doubt and despair to which he had sunk. The following day (June 19) Schiff came to him with the bill for the telegrams he had sent off for Herzl. "I was tremendously reassured by the fact," writes Herzl in his diary, "that I added up the figures more rapidly and more accurately than he; he was slow, and he kept on making mistakes. So deeply did he shake me yesterday."

And then, immediately after, this entry: "I have found a way out of this torment of the soul which Schiff's desperate opposition has brought on. I shall turn to Bismarck. He is big enough to understand me — or else to cure me."

In the letter to Bismarck, which he at once outlined, he asked for the privilege of an interview in order to submit his plan for the solution of the Jewish question. He described the condition to which he had been reduced by his friend's reaction. There was a certain personal problem: whatever sacrifices he had to make had to be his own and no one else's. But there were his parents, his wife and his children to think of. If he continued with his plan and was declared a lunatic with messianic obsessions the effect on his nearest and dearest would be almost fatal. If the great statesman, whom Herzl had honored and revered all his life, considered the plan practical and realizable, then it was for him to carry it through, or to move the German government to do so. But if Bismarck refused, or made no reply to the letter, then "my plan is nothing but a literary fantasy . . . Then I shall become calm again. Then I have merely dreamed, like other Utopians, from the days of Thomas More to those of Edward Bellamy."

On June 22 he sent off the letter to Bismarck. "But will Bismarck understand me?" he asks of his diary. "Napoleon did not understand the steamship, though he was then younger than Bismarck is now, and therefore more open to new ideas." But on that day, despite his doubts concerning Bismarck, Herzl found his spiritual balance again. It was as if the mere action of writing to the disgruntled statesman in Friedrichsruh had sufficed to open a new chapter of political action. On the next day Herzl started a fresh volume of his diary. It was in a mood approaching the festive, the result of rediscovered inward faith, that he wrote to Arthur Schnitzler, whom he had long been owing an answer to the latter's inquiry on *The New Ghetto*.

"My dear friend: Thank you for your letter. The piece is in Prague, no decision has been reached. The whole matter, however, has moved into the background of my mind. How right you were when, out of the cleverness of your perception, you told me that the writing of this play would not suffice to take the burden off my heart. That one eruption was not enough. Throughout the weeks which have elapsed, and during which I have not written you, something else, something new, something infinitely greater, has burst open in me. I feel as if a mountain has arisen in me, and the mountain still glows with the heat of its emergence. These have been weeks of tremendous creative excitement, and I have sometimes feared that I was going out of my mind. For what moves me to believe that I have brought forth something of value is the fact that not for one instant have I been occupied with myself as the litterateur; I have been occupied solely with the great sufferings of others. A few days' work more, and the thing is completed in such wise that it cannot be lost, even though I should be prevented from carrying out the minutiae . . . You remember that dear poem of von Heyse's, 'To the Poet:'

'Trembling, he might die in the night,
Ere the full work was brought to light.'

"That is my mood. I have deposited the material created till now in the Comptoir d'Escompte, strong box No. 6, shelf No. 2. The combination is: turn each of the three knobs seven times to the right. Someone must know this, lest 'I die in the night.' You are that one. Do I seem to you to be excited? I am not. I was never in higher or happier mood. I am not thinking of death, but of a life full of manly action, in which everything base, wild and corrupt that has ever been within me shall be extinguished, transformed and uplifted, and in which there shall be utter reconciliation between me and all men, through my work."

There was no reply from Bismarck. The fact did not discourage Herzl. He continued to work on the memorandum which he now planned to submit to the German Kaiser via the diplomat Schön. Before submitting the memorandum, he would communicate with Albert Rothschild, of Vienna. The letter in which he asks for an interview with Albert Rothschild is energetic and cool; it is more objective than any of the letters he has written hitherto on the Jewish question. But Albert Rothschild, too, vouchsafed no answer.

And now again there rises in him the idea of a Jewish novel. "It is to be a novel in which I shall set down everything that I have regretted doing — including my letters to Hirsch, which he perhaps has shown round laughingly" (July 4, 1895). The next day a letter came from Hirsch. The Baron wrote that, without having changed his views, he would be glad to meet with Herzl again, a few months hence, when he would return to Paris.

Herzl answered on the same day. He had been so angered by Hirsch's failure to answer the letter following the interview, that he had written him of his intention to give the whole thing up. "But after your communication of yesterday, I would like to make clear what this means. *For* the Jews I will still try to do something — but not *with* them. If I could have hoped that there was one man who would understand the ideas on which I was determined, you should have been that man. I have even less to expect from other Jews. It is in this political strengthlessness that the decline of our once powerful race displays itself. People will jest about me, or suspect me of God knows what commercial schemes. I must wade through a swamp of disgust — and I am not prepared to make this sacrifice for the Jews."

He lifted himself out of the alternations of despair and hope, out of his hesitations between literature and action which attended those days of waiting, by sheer work.

Between the end of June and the middle of July he wrote the last three articles of his series *Pictures of the Parliamentary Life of France*, which were later to be published under the book title of *Le Palais Bourbon*. The collection represents the most polished, balanced work that Herzl did for the *Neue Freie Presse*. It is not, however, his best book. Many of the individual pieces are too forced, too polished and too deliberately reflective. "There are pages," wrote Max Nordau, the unbending critic, "which are masterpieces of temperamental, artistic prose. But for my taste others are not simple enough; they do not seem to have been written for inner satisfaction but with an eye on the reader, and in a confusion of native impulse and desire for effect. Such confusion does not produce the best work."

Whatever these objections may be worth, the *Palais Bourbon* is for the most part a composite of brilliant pictures and of penetrating thought. One may apply to Herzl the remark which he applied to Deschanel: he thinks, even though he chatters. He observes, and his first question is directed at the essence, meaning and value of what he sees. He uncovers, behind the facade of magniloquence and great gestures, the trivial humanity of the speakers. To use the phrase of a critic, he sees these parliamentarians not as they create laws but as they create themselves. But his study of personalities is only the psychological springboard for his observations on great questions of political and social import, questions of the structure and instrumentalities of the state, their use and their abuse.

In his studies of the elections of 1893, Herzl had already revealed his critical attitude toward parliamentary democracy as it functioned in France. He was critical of the indecisiveness, the rapidity of change, the general lowering of the level of thought and action, to which it led. It exaggerated the significance of the empty word, it dealt carelessly with great personalities, it gave the advantage to mediocrity. Everything is directed toward the applause of the people. The "free" representative of the people exists in theory only; actually this representative is under the thumb of the election committee; he cannot vote according to his conscience if he expects to be re-elected. There are important questions of domestic, and, even more, of foreign policy, which cannot be treated with theatrical boldness, and which do not even permit of a simple yes or no decision. "The public character of the decisions, demanded by democracy, is false and fictitious. Behind that frontage of public discussion things continue to happen which ultimately break out in scandals, like the Panama affair and others of its kind."

On the other hand Herzl perceives clearly that only the normal man, and not the excessively big man such as democracies seek, is fit to direct a government. "These giants, these monster figures, are necessary for the creative eruption, but they are dangerous for the values that exist ... The existing values must be guarded and directed by average persons." A clear distinction must be made between government principle and the form of the state, is the opinion of this admirer of Machiavelli, Montesquieu and Rousseau. "There are only two principles of government: the aristocratic and the democratic. And I believe that the principle of government must stand in complementary contrast to the form of the state. The principle of government and the form of the state must mitigate each other ... For the aristocratic Republic and the democratic Monarchy are certainly the finest forms of the completed state."

From this expression of opinion on the question of state and people, we may gather how difficult it was for Herzl to decide on submitting his plan to the reaction of the public. An admirer of true aristocracy, his general inclination was toward a management of political affairs from above; how much more then would he insist on the propriety of this view in the case of the Jews, who possessed no recognized political center of action, were without political will or education, and lacked the power of decision with regard to their political destiny. His first experiences strengthened his conviction that oppression and assimilation had corrupted this people beyond the capacity to understand a call to liberating action.

Now, in furtherance of his plan, he wrote on July 15 to Güdemann, the occasion being the anti-Jewish excesses which had occurred in Vienna. "This plan ... is a reserve against more evil days." Thus the interchange of letters with the chief rabbi of Vienna was resumed. "These wretched or cowardly men — or perhaps it is their wealth which has undone them — are enough to make one give up the work in disgust; but we must think, all the same, of the poor and decent Jews. They are the majority. We are not a chosen, but neither are we an ignominious people. That is why I am standing firm."

Two weeks later, on July 27, 1895, he left Paris. The day before his departure he made, against his instinctive inclination, and without success, the effort to see Baron de Hirsch, who happened to be in the city unexpectedly. "And today," he wrote in his diary, "I leave Paris. One book of my life closes, another begins. Which?"

He left Paris never to return as resident. He was unable, he tells us, to stand the place any more. He longed to escape from the sense of the alien which haunted him there and which he could not escape even in his own house; he longed for Vienna, for his parents, for warmer surroundings, and for a better center on which to base his political activity. He persuaded the publishers of the *Neue Freie Presse*, who reluctantly relieved him of his post as Paris correspondent, to repatriate him to Vienna as feuilleton editor, at a reduced salary. He had learned everything he could learn in Paris: he had learned the meaning of state and society, he had seen at close range the forces which directed politics, he had lost his respect for men in high positions. And above all, he had achieved self-realization, he knew with the utmost clarity the nature of his own will and his own ideas, and he knew with the same clarity what tasks and duties his destiny imposed upon him. How was he to fulfill them?

He went first to Aussee to relax for several weeks. From that town he conducted by mail and wire a correspondence in varying mood with Güdemann and with the Berlin philanthropist and friend of Palestine, Heinrich Meyer-Cohn. After long negotiations the three men came together in Munich on August 17.

To these two men Herzl read forth his *Address to the Rothschilds*. It took place in other surroundings than those he had originally desired. He had wanted the meeting to take place in Glion, by Lake Geneva, in the unusual setting of the Swiss Alps, so that he might enlist in his cause the overpowering effects of nature. Now, to his distress, the reading took place in utterly different surroundings. The

first session was in an emtpy room of the Jochsberger Res-
taurant and was interrupted at four o'clock in the afternoon
because at that time Meyer-Cohn had to meet a business
acquaintance. Then they met again at six o'clock, and the
reading continued until supper time, at half past eight.
This second meeting was held in Herzl's small hotel room
and he had to sit on the bed because there were only two
chairs. A strange picture indeed, with this elegant man of
the world as its central figure! After the three of them had
eaten supper together, he finished the reading amid frequent
critical interruptions of a most trivial character on the part
of the practical Zionist, Meyer-Cohn.

The impressions produced on the two listeners were highly
divergent. Meyer-Cohn, the democrat, found himself in
sharp opposition to Herzl's opinions and proposals regarding
aristocracy and nobility; he declared the entire plan a Utopia
of the fantasy. Güdemann found himself, in spite of some
similar objections, swept along. In the afternoon, he said:
"If you are right, then my entire philosophy collapses. And
yet I wish you to be in the right. Until now I believed that
we Jews are not a people: that is to say, I believed we are
more than a people. I believed we had been entrusted with
an historic mission as the carriers of the idea of humanity
among the peoples." In the evening, as they went down to
supper, Güdemann, quite dazed, said to Herzl: "It is as if
I saw Moses in the flesh," and when he left him that night
he said: "Continue to be that which you are. Perhaps you
are the one who has been called by God." And he kissed
him.

On one important point the two men chosen by Herzl as
counsellors were agreed: the speech ought not to be read or

addressed to the Rothschilds, who were too self-seeking to understand it. The plan ought to be published as a novel. Perhaps the impulse would take effect and initiate a great movement.

Depressed as he was by the result of this conference, Herzl sat down the next day and actually began the introduction to a novel. But this literary plan occupied him for no more than a day. Güdemann had compared Herzl with Theodore Hertzka, the Viennese economist and journalist who had set forth his ideas of a liberal social commonwealth in two novels, *Freiland*, and *Eine Reise nach Freiland*. Thereafter Hertzka had made unsuccessful attempts to realize his ideal commonwealth in Africa. Herzl at once read the second of these Utopia novels which Güdemann had especially compared with his own plan, because, like the latter, it was filled with artistic details. On August 22 Herzl wrote to Güdemann: "*Freiland* is a complicated machine with many wheels and cogs, but there is nothing in it to convince me that it can be set in motion. As against this, there is for my plan a natural driving force. What is that force? The Jewish plight, the crying need of the Jewish people. Who dares to deny that this force exists?"

Only now had Herzl discovered the practical foundation for his plan. In his *Address to the Rothschilds* the driving force is still the national enthusiasm, an abstraction he had picked up in his observation of the French masses. We perceive at this point to what extent, in the intervening period, Herzl had looked into and meditated upon his own people, how much more deeply he had penetrated into the realities of life. He compares this newly discovered force of the Jewish plight with the power of steam; just as the latter is created by pressure, grows stronger with the increase of pressure, and can be utilized to great ends, so the pressure on the Jewish people created a force waiting to be utilized. "We also know of the steam power which is generated by heat in a teakettle, and lifts the lid of the kettle. It is this teakettle phenomenon which we find in the Zionist attempt and in a hundred other plans for the combatting of anti-Semitism. But I say now that this force is great enough to drive a great machine."

After this new basic discovery there came weeks of hesitation, groping and indecision. He tried out the people with whom he came in contact, and tested their receptivity for his new ideas; he looked in vain for helpers. He perceived that he had the capacity to fill people with enthusiasm, to bring the light of belief into their eyes; but always and ever this enthusiasm died away as soon as the individuals withdrew from the magic circle of his personality. Güdemann, on whom he had at first based great hopes, became more hesitant from day to day. Narcisse Leven, co-founder and general secretary of the *Alliance Israélite Universelle*, with whom he had established contact in Salzburg at the beginning of September via Güdemann, refused to be convinced; instead he told Herzl of the Zionist societies in Russia, France and England, and Herzl heard for the first time the name of Pinsker. Meanwhile he observed the growth of the anti-Semitic movement, and on the occasion of the municipal elections in Vienna, "on *erev Rosh Hashana*," he beheld "the hate and scorn against the Jews at arm's length." It was more in the soft, mild expressions than in the violent denunciations that he perceived how deep in the people anti-Semitism was rooted. And he kept on questioning himself day after day, hesitant and uncertain as to how he should

1. Herzl's Father

2. Herzl's Mother

3. The House where Herzl was born (to the left of the Synagogue) (see p. 10)

4. The Jewish Temple in Budapest

5. Herzl at the age of 6

6. Herzl at the age of 15 (see p. 19)

7. Herzl's sister Pauline (see p. 21)

8. Herzl at the Law-Courts, about 1884 (see p. 46)

9. Herzl as a free-lance writer, about 1886 (see p. 51)

10. Herzl's wife Julie (née Naschauer), 1889 (see p. 63)

11. Pages from Herzl's Diary of a journey to Holland, 1885, with a sketch and description of *The Lute-Player* by Frans Hals (see p. 48)

Ich arbeite seit einiger Zeit an einem Werk, das von unendlicher Grösse ist. Ich weiss heute nicht, ob ich es ausführen werde. Es sieht aus wie ein mächtiger Traum. Aber seit Tagen und Wochen füllt es mich aus bis in die Bewusstlosigkeit hinein, begleitet mich überallhin, schwebt über meinen gewöhnlichen Gesprächen, blickt mir über die Schulter in die komische kleine Journalistenarbeit, stört mich und berauscht mich.

Was daraus wird, ist jetzt noch nicht zu ahnen. Nur sagt mir meine Erfahrung, dass es merkwürdig ist, schon als Traum, und dass ich es aufschreiben soll — wenn nicht als ein Denkmal für die Menschen, so doch für mein eigenes späteres Ergötzen oder Sinnen. Und vielleicht zwischen diesen beiden Möglichkeiten: für die Literatur. Wird aus dem Roman keine That, so kann doch aus der That ein Roman werden. Titel: das gelobte Land!

Ich weiss wahrhaftig heute nicht mehr, ob nicht überhaupt der Roman das erste war, woran ich dachte. Allerdings nicht etwas „Belletristisches" als Selbstzweck, sondern nur als ein Dienendes

12. The first page of Herzl's Zionist Diary, 1895 (see p. 134)

13. Captain Dreyfus, 1894 (see p. 109)

14. Baron Moritz von Hirsch, philanthropist, the first person to hear of Herzl's Zionist plans, 1895 (see p. 123)

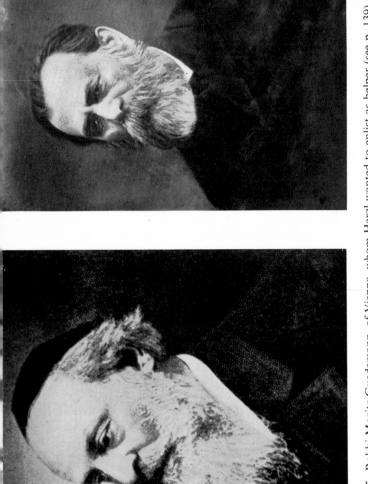

15. Rabbi Moritz Guedemann, of Vienna, whom Herzl wanted to enlist as helper (see p. 139)

16. Dr. Leo Pinsker, of Odessa, author of *Auto-Emancipation* (1882) and leader of the *Hovevei Zion* movement (see p. 174)

15

16

17. Herzl, about 1897

18. Dr. Max Nordau, physician, writer and orator, one of Herzl's first and most influential helpers (see p. 156)

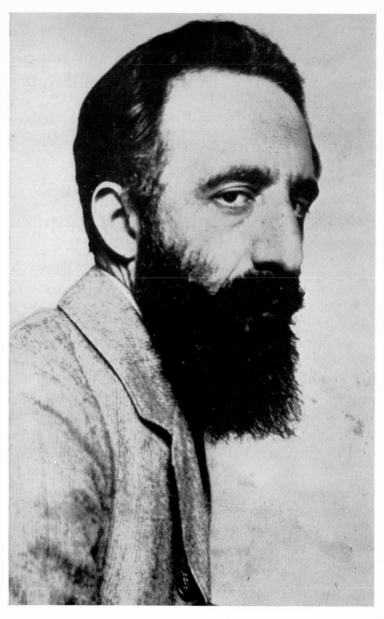

19. Dr. Nathan Birnbaum, of Vienna, who coined the term Zionism
(see p. 185)

begin the realization of his plan, whether by publication or by political action from above, meaning by the latter the presentation of completed acts which should compel the people to move along the lines he had laid down for them.

Then suddenly, out of the multitude of back and forth negotiations, there seemed to him to emerge the road to action. In September 1895, Count Badeni, a capable and energetic statesman, was entrusted with the Prime Ministership. It was widely hoped that he would be able to cope with the difficult language question in Bohemia. Badeni's first thought was for the creation of an instrument for the influencing of public opinion, and to that end revived the *Presse*, the forerunner and now the out-lived rival of the *Neue Freie Presse*. After preliminary negotiations which lasted from September 20 to October 27, Dr. Kozmian, the right-hand man of Count Badeni, officially offered Herzl the editorship of the *Presse* in its new role as organ of the government: such had been the impression created by Herzl's free and independent reports from Paris. A great opportunity seemed to have presented itself. Should he take it, he would acquire at one step that great organ of public opinion which seemed to him to be of the highest value as an instrument of power and as a means of popularizing his ideas. Herzl thus came in intimate contact with the Prime Minister, to whom he was attracted by his personal qualities as well as by his political outlook; he could also hope to win the great man over gradually to the support of his plan. It might then be possible to start the movement simultaneously from above and from below. These considerations, and these alone, prompted Herzl to enter on the negotiations. He declared that he wished to inform the publishers of the *Neue Freie Presse* of the offer on the day it was made, and that he would give his own answer within twenty-four hours. There was thus the possibility that he might compel the *Neue Freie Presse* to a decision as to whether it would or would not go along with him in his Jewish political action. He would neither seek nor accept any personal advantage from the situation. It was his desire, he declared again and again, to conduct this Jewish affair on an impersonal basis.

As far back as September, when he had moved from Aussee to Vienna, he had discussed the Jewish question with Bacher and the latter showed himself to be in disagreement with his plans. On October 21, Herzl had a three-hour consultation with Moritz Benedikt. Now Herzl read the *Address to the Rothschilds* to Bacher and demanded that the publishers decide whether they would place the paper at his disposal for the furtherance of his ideas on the Jewish question or would prefer to dispense with his services. It must be admitted that it was a difficult problem for these men. The newspaper was their life work; they were bound up with it ideally not less than financially. Were they to risk the position of the *Neue Freie Presse* as a liberal world newspaper when they were of the opinion that anti-Semitism was an unpleasant but temporary phenomenon? They rejected Herzl's offer decisively.

Thereupon Herzl resumed his negotiations with Badeni's representative. He submitted as the most important condition that he should at all times be free to approach Badeni personally "like an ambassador." The Prime Minister graciously declared that this was his own wish, and treated Herzl as if the matter were already settled.

While Herzl busied himself during the following days with the details of the form and appearance of the paper, it gradually became more and more obvious to him how little he had to do with these officials who were to be his co-workers, and how intimate were his bonds with the *Neue Freie Presse*. In particular his relationships to Bacher, from whom he had learned much as a journalist, were almost those of a son to a father. Thus on November 1 he told Bacher that he could not bear the thought of losing his friendship. Bacher was naturally delighted to hear this, and declared to Herzl that there was a great future before him on the *Neue Freie Presse*, but Herzl again repeated that he sought no personal advantage. It also seemed to him that there was more prospect of realizing his idea through this paper than through Badeni. The outcome of the various negotiations was the following: Herzl would first attempt to create a Study Commission in Paris or London; the publishers would give him a furlough for this purpose and place their influence at his disposal; should he fail to set matters in motion by this method, he was to publish a pamphlet which would then be discussed in the *Neue Freie Presse*. This was, to be sure, not very much, but it was enough to prompt Herzl at his next interview with Badeni to refuse the offer.

Had he done the right thing? Probably. To have accepted Badeni's offer would indeed have made an impression on the Jews, who always accord their highest respect to one of their own when he has been recognized by non-Jews; at the same time he would have become involved in the politics and the destiny of this particular government, which already fell in November 1897. He would have become an official of the government without any guarantee that he would be able to make use of Badeni or the newspaper for his aims. And then could not his opponents have accused him with apparrent justice of being an agent of the government in the Jewish matter, too?

On the other hand, he had achieved little enough with the *Neue Freie Presse*, and even that little, as he soon discovered, was not to be realized. His admission of friendship had weakened his position, his refusal of the government offer had deprived him of the expected instrument of power. The publishers of the *Neue Freie Presse* drew the logical practical conclusions from the situation, in effect, if not deliberately. Herzl was a valuable employee, and it was as such that he was treated henceforth; i.e. in friendly fashion when there was any danger of losing this journalistic force, irreplaceable in its own way, negatively when he sought the fulfillment of the promise to extend to him even the most modest degree of assistance for his plans.

Toward the middle of November Herzl visited Paris. In the negotiations which he conducted there with Narcisse Leven, Chief Rabbi Zadoc Kahn, and a number of rabbis invited by Zadoc Kahn, no one took him seriously. Zadoc Kahn confessed himself a Zionist but would not admit the slightest reflection on his French patriotism, and showed himself dependent on the opinions of the others. However, he did serve Herzl frequently later on as middleman between the latter, the Rothschilds and the *ICA*.

But the great result of this visit to Paris was that Herzl won Max Nordau over to his plan. Even before he had left Paris for Vienna, Herzl had had a long conversation with Nordau, and the two men had admitted to each other to what an extent anti-Semitism had driven them back to the

Jewish people. At that time Herzl had not dared to say more. Now he encountered from Nordau a "lightning-like understanding." Nordau declared himself ready to co-operate with all his power in the realization of the idea. Eleven years older than Herzl, Nordau, also born in Pest, was the son of Rabbi Südfeld. He had been given an or-thodox upbringing, but in his early manhood he had, as atheist and German writer, become alienated from Judaism. His profession was that of doctor, but he was at the same time the Paris correspondent of the *Vossische Zeitung*. Through his books, among them *Paradoxes*, *The Conventional Lies of Civilization* and *Degeneration*, which appeared in an enormous number of editions and in a great many languages, he had achieved a worldwide reputation as an independent and fearless thinker. It was as a fanatic for the truth and as a destroyer of superstition and of ignorance that he loomed before the educated world — one of the most widely known figures of those days. How much it would mean if this man were to align himself with a move-ment which yesterday had been utterly unknown!

Now Nordau commended Herzl to Israel Zangwill, in London, whither Herzl proceeded in order to set up his Study Commission. He arrived in the English capital on November 21, 1895. The conversation with Zangwill, who understood little French, while Herzl himself was not very familiar with English, was a laborious one. Never-theless Zangwill was soon captured by Herzl's personality and will, even though he was at first not completely convinced by his arguments. He gave him the names of some important people, and used his offices to obtain for Herzl an invitation to a banquet of The Maccabaeans club, at which he could ex-pound his plan. It was the first group to hear Herzl's ideas.

The speech has not come down to us, for he spoke from a few notes, first in German then in French. His remarks were received with applause, and he was made an honorary member of The Maccabaeans. But no Study Commission was forthcoming, either out of this circle or as a result of his visits to other organizations and individuals. The activity of which England was later to be the center did not begin as yet, but he had established contacts of prime importance: with Sir Samuel Montagu, the banker and the good Jew, who responded enthusiastically to Herzl's words, even though he did not let himself be swept off his feet; with Rabbi Singer, an immediate convert; with Asher Myers of the *Jewish Chronicle*, who asked Herzl for an article, with the result that the *Jewish Chronicle* preceded the *Judenstaat* by four weeks in its publication of Herzl's views; and above all with Colonel (then Lieutenant) Goldsmid, who, like Daniel Deronda in George Eliot's novel, was the son of baptized Jews, had grown up as a Christian and had turned back to his people when he discovered his own origins. Goldsmid said to Herzl: "This is my life's idea. We shall work for the liberation of Israel."

None of them wanted to know anything about the Argentine, and on this point the practical men were united with the dreamers: Palestine alone came into the picture for a national concentration of the Jews. Greatly strengthened in spirit by these conversations, Herzl hurried back to Vienna via Paris at the end of November.

These first attempts drove Herzl to the conclusion that the influencing of individuals would not suffice to set the plan in motion. He therefore resolved to approach the public at large. In his conversations with Zadoc Kahn he had made use of his *Address to the Rothschilds*, but had crossed out every reference to the family. He now reworked the address from beginning to end, with thoroughgoing changes of style and content; he took cognizance of his experiences between his first attempts to launch the idea and the stage he had now reached; he laid a wider foundation for the structure of ideas, made the structure itself more logical, and provided a stronger peroration.

It was thus a new work which finally emerged. Its title was: *The Jewish State: An attempt at a Modern Solution of the Jewish Question.** After some vain efforts to secure a well-known publisher, he offered it to M. Breitenstein, the bookseller and publisher of Vienna, and an edition of three thousand copies was printed.

Der Judenstaat may properly be called Herzl's life work. His philosophy of the world, his views on the state, on the Jewish people, on science and technology, as we have seen them developing to this, his thirty-fifth year, are concentrated in the book. It is possible to perceive between the lines the traces of that development, the evidences of old convictions displaced by new ones. When we compare the *Judenstaat* with the original *Address to the Rothschilds* there leaps to the eye the change which had come over the man within this brief interlude. He had grown, he had become clearer, more consistent, more disciplined in the presentation of his views. It is possible that he would have fared better in his earlier negotiations if they had been based on the form now given to his ideas. On the other hand, the perfection of form he had now achieved was itself the result of all those

---

*It is under this title that the English edition of 500 copies appeared in London in 1896, translated by Sylvia d'Avigdor.

unsuccessful conversations and negotiations. Closer analysis reveals without difficulty the effect of almost every individual experience preceding the writing of the book. What masterly clarity, what power and freshness, what proud self-certainty rings from the introduction! The sentences are like trumpet peals.*

"The Jewish question exists. It would be stupid to deny it. It is a hangover of the Middle Ages, of which the modern civilized nations, with the best will in the world, cannot rid themselves. They showed their magnanimity when they emancipated us. The Jewish question exists wheresoever Jews are to be found in larger numbers. Where it does not exist it is brought in by immigrating Jews. We move naturally toward those areas where we are not persecuted; our appearance in those areas is followed by persecution. This is true, and it must remain true, even in highly developed countries — France proves it — as long as the Jewish question is not solved politically. The poorer Jews are bringing anti-Semitism into England; they have already brought it into America.

"I believe I understand anti-Semitism, which is an extremely complicated movement. I examine this movement as a Jew, without hate and without fear. I believe I recognize in it those elements which are merely brutal humor, mean stomach-envy, inherited prejudice, religious intolerance: but I also recognize the element of unconscious self-protection. I consider the Jewish question to be neither social nor religious, even though it takes on these and other colorations. It is a national question, and in order to solve we must, before everything else, transform it into a political

---

*The passages from *Der Judenstaat* are here retranslated. (M. S.)

world question, to be answered in the council of the civilized peoples.

"We are a *people, one* people. Everywhere we have tried honestly to disappear in the surrounding community, and to retain only the faith of our fathers. We are not permitted to do it. In vain do we show our loyalty, and in some places an exaggerated patriotism; in vain do we bring the same sacrifices of blood and gold as our fellow-citizens; in vain do we exert ourselves to increase the glory of our fatherlands by achievements in art and science, the wealth of our fatherlands by our contributions to commerce. In our fatherlands, some of which we have lived in for many centuries, we are denounced as strangers: often by those whose forefathers were not yet in the land when ours were already sighing there. It is the majority which decides who is the stranger in the land: it is a question of power, as in all national relations . . ."

True assimilation, an honest equalization in kind and manner, is possible everywhere only through intermarriage. But this can be realized on a large scale only when the Jews shall have achieved beforehand so much economic power that the old social prejudice against them shall have disappeared. "But this preliminary condition of absorption cannot be achieved; for it would represent the subjugation of the majority by a minority which was despised until recently, and which is not in possession of the administrative and military power."

Nor could the external conditions necessary for such a process be expected, to wit, an interlude between persecutions, and a state of political well-being, lasting for one or two generations. "For the ancient prejudices against us are rooted deep in the people. In order to get at the truth of the matter it is only necessary to listen there where the people expresses itself authentically and simply: the legends and proverbs of the folk are anti-Semitic." Thus, as soon as a stage of well-being is achieved anywhere by the Jews, the contempt of the centuries begins to stir, and after a short period of tolerance, the ancient enmity reawakens. But oppression and persecution could never destroy the Jews; they only served to press back into the ranks the best sons of the people; for if they sought to give up their peculiar character, the hatred of the surrounding world turned them into strangers. Even when the Jews made the attempt to give up their existence as a people, the same enmity always flung them back upon themselves as an "historic group of recognizable interrelationship," i.e., as a people.* "He who is able to go under, he who must and wants to go under, let him do so. But the folk personality of the Jewish people cannot, must not and does not want to go under. It can not because external enmity keeps it together. It does not want to—this it has demonstrated in two thousand years of frightful suffering. It must not: that is what I attempt to establish with this book, following in the footsteps of many Jews who have not given up hope. Whole branches of the Jewish people can perish: the tree lives."

The modern form of anti-Semitism, which must be fundamentally distinguished from the old historical Jew-hatred, is, in Herzl's view, the consequence of the emancipation of the Jews. The liberation from the ghetto, the emancipation,

---

*Herzl rejected the race theory. "He accepts the racial point of view," he remarked regarding Zangwill, after their first meeting. "I have only to look at myself and at him in order to reject it. What I mean is: we are a historic unity with anthropological variations. ... No nation has uniformity of race."

came too late. The Jews were not ready to be emancipated, just so, in the areas which they occupied; for pressure of circumstances had resulted in the development of a middle class people, and no sooner were they emancipated than they constituted a tremendous competition with the Christian middle class. Thus the Jews are subjected to a double pressure, as Jews and as members of the bourgeoisie. To all this is added an unceasing over-production of middle-class intellectuals for whom there is no healthy descent into the masses and no healthy ascent into the classes.

Thus, if no radical rescue is organized, the Jews must remain in a definite condition of distress wherever they live in larger numbers. The equality of rights guaranteed them by the law is abrogated in actual effect. A continuous boycott propaganda is exerted to drive them out of business. Public attacks, discriminations and exclusions increase from day to day. The persecutions practiced on them differ in character and name from country to country, from class to class; but in their essentials they remain the same. Everywhere the Jews are surrounded by the same enemy, everywhere the same pressure is exerted against them. "In the economically upper classes it produces discomfort. In the middle classes it produces a dull unhappiness. In the lower classes it produces naked desperation. The simple fact is that everywhere the pressure issues to the same effect, and it is summed up in the classic Berlin cry: *Juden raus!* I shall therefore compress the Jewish problem into its capsule form: Must the Jews 'get out'? If so, whither? Or can we remain? And if so, for how long?"

In this situation, in which to depend on the goodness of people is lunacy and suicide, "there comes to the rescue, from another side, the world spirit of our time." Technology, in which the faithful son of the nineteenth century had beheld the solution of all the great problems of humanity, would solve the Jewish problem too. The technical development of the nineteenth century had brought about conditions which mankind had not dreamed of hitherto. The distances between points on the surface of the earth had shrunk enormously, nothing was impossible any more.

"I am not of the opinion that the electric light was invented merely that a few snobs might illuminate their salons with it, but rather that the problems of mankind might be illumined and solved thereby. One such problem, and not the least important, is the Jewish. In solving it we shall be acting not only in our own behalf, but in behalf of many other depressed and heavy-laden spirits."

It is to be solved by an exodus, by the gathering together of the people out of its dispersion, by its concentration in a land of its own, under its own government, responsible to itself; in brief, by the founding of the Jewish state. Political principle will provide the basis, technology will provide the means, the driving force of the great machine will be the Jewish tragedy, the guiding idea will be the Jewish state. "No individual is strong enough or rich enough to transfer a people from one place of residence to another. Only an idea can do it. The state idea does possess that power. In the long night of their history the Jews have never ceased to dream that kingly dream: 'Next year in Jerusalem.' It is an ancient saying among us. The task before us now is to prove that this dream can be transformed into a thought of the bright daylight."

This is the essence and significance of the plan as outlined in the introduction. The greater part of the book is devoted

to the details of the carrying out of the plan. Let us review
in brief the substance of the method.

Two organs shall be created as the carriers of the movement: "The Society of Jews" and "The Jewish Company,"*
the first to serve as the legal representative of the idea, the
second as the economic instrument of the upbuilding.

"The Society of Jews" is the legal representative of the
Jewish people, its *Gestor*, as Herzl described it, using the
Roman legal expression. It assembles about itself the Jews
who accept the new idea of the Jewish state, and acquires
thereby the right and authority to speak in the name of the
Jewish people. Basing itself on this right and this authority,
it must seek to obtain recognition as "a state-building
power." "With this, the state would already be created in
essence." It then approaches the Powers with the demand
that they transfer to its sovereignty some part of the world's
surface large enough to answer the need of the Jewish people.
This sovereignty is an essential preliminary condition. There
is to be a complete break with the principle of "gradual
infiltration of the Jews," such as has been accepted in the
case of the Argentine and Palestine. For if immigration
were attempted without this condition precedent of legal
recognition, there would result the regular recurrence of an
old phenomenon: "the government, under pressure of the
local population, which would feel itself threatened by the
immigration, would forbid the further influx of Jews. Emigration can therefore have sense only when it has as its
foundation our assured sovereignty of the territory."

---

*It is significant that these terms occur in English in the original text.

Should the Powers show themselves ready to place a country at the disposal of the Jews under these conditions, it shall be the function of "The Society of Jews" to conduct the negotiations.

At the beginning Herzl was by no means definite in his own mind as to the particular country which should be chosen for the ingathering of the Jews. The decision depended on the possibilities which might offer, and on the public opinion of the Jewish people. Both of these were to be determined by "The Society of Jews." Herzl himself mentions in the *Judenstaat*, as he had already mentioned in earlier outlines, two countries, the Argentine and Palestine, without, however, deciding for either or against any other. But when we compare the manner in which the two countries are mentioned in the *Judenstaat* and in preceding outlines, it at once becomes evident that Palestine, as "our unforgettable historic homeland," has moved definitely to first place.

"The name alone would be a tremendously gripping call to our people. If His Majesty the Sultan were to give us Palestine, we could undertake to bring into order the finances of the Turkish government. For Europe we would constitute in that country part of the rampart against Asia, we would occupy the outposts of civilization, stemming the tide of barbarism. For the Holy Places of Christendom a status of internationally secured extra-territoriality could be instituted. We shall be the guard of honor about the Holy Places, responsible with our life for the fulfilment of this duty. This guard of honor would be a great symbol of the solution of the Jewish question after the eighteen centuries of our suffering."

Should the decision be made, "The Society of Jews" will have acquired sovereignty over a country under the protectorate of the European Powers; upon this will follow the work of investigation which must precede every effort at systematic colonization. Then begins the task of "The Jewish Company."

"The Jewish Company" is the executive instrument for the migration and resettlement of the Jews. It is to be a stock company according to English law, with its center in London, "because on the legal side it must be placed under the protection of a Power which at the present time is not anti-Semitic."

Its first task is to liquidate the fixed assets of the Jews in a form useful to the emigrating Jews and not harmful to the economy of their respective countries, and then to direct the migration and resettlement according to plan. "The Jewish Company" is a purely commercial enterprise; in all its tasks, always carried out under the control of "The Jewish Society," it must observe strict business principles.

For the creation of the share capital (Herzl had in mind a sum in the neighborhood of fifty million pounds, or two hundred and fifty million dollars) which, with the right management, should certainly yield high profits, three possibilities presented themselves: the high bank, the middle bank, and popular subscription. The simplest, swiftest and surest method would be the founding of the high bank. For this purpose use could be made of the credit of this mighty finance group; the method also commended itself because it would react most favorably on the political work. "There still lies dormant in the Jewish financial power a great deal of unused political strength. The enemies of the Jewish people represent this power as possessing an influence which it could have, but in reality has not. The poor Jews only feel the hatred which this financial power awakens; its benefits, the mitigation of their sufferings which it could effect, the poor Jews do not enjoy. The credit policy of the big financial Jews must be placed in the service of the national idea."

Should the rich Jews, who are still content with their condition, not show themselves ready to help, then the creation of the funds would have to be entrusted to the middle class of Jews. The third and last possibility would be an appeal to the Jewish people at large, which would, by its participation in the subscriptions, also be carrying out a new form of plebiscite for the registration of its consent to the plan. The migration itself, which would occupy some decades, would proceed naturally according to the pressure in individual countries and the stage of development of the colonization.

The migration would start with the poorest Jews, "the most energetic human material for the taking over of a land; the successful carrying out of great enterprises calls for a touch of desperation." They will be led "by our intelligentsia, which is everywhere persecuted and which we everywhere produce in too large numbers." The work done by these first elements, and the consumers' market which they create, will progressively attract the higher groups. "There will always migrate those individuals who believe that they can thereby improve their condition. First the desperate, then the poor, then the well-to-do, then the rich."

The migration is to take place in groups, preferably by localities. They are to be organized at once when the movement begins. The groups are to form voluntarily round the rabbis. "So many rabbis, so many local groups. The rabbis will also be the first to understand us, the first to become enthusiastic; from their pulpits they will spread their enthusiasm to others."

The upbuilding of the country is to be based on the most modern principles, making use of all the instruments of science and technology. The Jewish state is not to be a state like all others. It is to become, on the technical and social side, a model state. The great work of the opening up of the land is to be carried out by a labor legion, which shall guarantee both the opportunity for work and the hope of individual advancement to every willing worker. Private initiative shall be encouraged, but it shall at the same time be made to serve the public interest. The normal working day shall consist of seven hours. Work as a right and a duty shall be guaranteed to everyone.

What language are the Jews to speak in their new homeland? Herzl is of the opinion that a common language can not be prescribed. As yet he knows nothing of the efforts being put into the revival of Hebrew; it therefore does not enter his mind that this might be the language of the country. "Who of us knows enough Hebrew to ask for a railroad ticket?" Still less does he consider the use of Yiddish, which is for him a ghetto language, "the furtive language of prisoners." He believes that there will simply emerge a language federation, as in Switzerland. The principle language will impose itself without compulsion on the basis of majority usage.

The book closes with an appeal which expresses the profoundest faith. The very initiation of the plan will witness a weakening and retreat of anti-Semitism. The steady flow of greater and greater numbers of Jews out of the lands which harbor the largest masses will of itself diminish the pressure, and with it the degree of hatred.

"There will be prayers in our temples for the success of our enterprise. But in the churches, too! Here is the end of an ancient oppression from which all have suffered. But the light must first break into the minds of men. The idea must radiate out until it reaches the last wretched nests of our poeple. They will awaken out of their dull brooding. For a new content will come into the lives of all of us. Each one of us need only think of himself, and the procession becomes tremendous. And what glory awaits the selfless fighters for the idea! That is why I believe that a race of wonderful Jews will grow out of the earth. The Maccabees will rise again!

"Let the word be repeated here which was given at the beginning: the Jews who will it shall have their state. We shall at last live as free men on our own soil and die peacefully in our own homeland. The world will be liberated by our liberation, enriched with our wealth, made greater by our greatness. And that which we seek there for our own use will stream out mightily and beneficently upon all mankind."

CHAPTER VI

WORLD JEWRY AND THE *JUDENSTAAT*

THE longing of the Jewish people for the return to the land of its past is as old as the diaspora itself. Prophecy had made an eternal bond between the land and the future of the people, and this bond the Jews had never repudiated. Always it had remained *Erez Israel* — the land of Israel. Scattered to the four corners of the earth, the people guarded the memory and hope in its heart, and enshrined them in its religious utterances. There was no praying to the Creator without proffering the supplication for the return. Cast among diverse climates, it celebrated its festivals according to the seasons of the Holy Land. Yearly, in the Passover ceremonies, it sat girded for the call of the Messiah, which would assemble them out of the dispersion and lead them to the Land of Promise. In every period of crisis there arose leaders who gave themselves out as the Elected One, and always there were desperate masses to believe and follow. Men like David Reubeni in the sixteenth century, and Sabbatai Zevi in the seventeenth, half adventurers and half believers in their own mission, called forth a tremendous agitation in Jewry and even found political forces ready to lend them an ear.

The gradual emergence of the Jews from the ghetto and the formal recognition of their civic equality had been followed by a weakening of this sentiment among the Jews of the western countries, and among the more privileged Jews of eastern countries. Here and there the memory of that sentiment was even deleted from the prayer books in acknowledgement of the fact that the land of adoption had now become the homeland.

But parallel with this decline of the sentiment itself, the sporadic plans for the ingathering of the dispersion and the rehabilitation of Palestine took on a more realistic form than in former times, and this was true among non-Jews not less than among Jews. In 1799 no less dominant a figure than Napoleon had for a short time entertained the idea of the erection of a Jewish state in Palestine. Then, from 1818 on, Mordecai Manuel Noah, the Jewish journalist who had been American consul in Tunis, made the attempt to found a Jewish territory, "Ararat," within the confines of New York State. In 1839 the great philanthropist Moses Montefiore submitted to the Governor of Syria his plan for large scale Jewish immigration into the Holy Land. In 1848 the Frenchman Ernest Laharanne proposed the creation of a Jewish state in his book, *On the New Oriental Question.* In the middle of the nineteenth century there arose in England a strong Christian movement, based on ancient tradition, for "the restoration of the Jews." Leading English statesmen were interested in the proposal. In 1847 Benjamin Disraeli produced, in his *Tancred,* the first novel of a Zionist state, and a generation later George Elliot's Zionist novel *Daniel Deronda* attracted wide attention. As a boy Ferdinand Lassalle dreamed, at the time of the ritual-murder accusation in Damascus, in 1840, of leading the Jews, sword in hand, to the conquest of Palestine.

Men like Hirsch Kalischer of Thorn and Yehudah ben Solomon Hai Alkalai of Semlin*, who in many ways anticipated the demands of the later Zionists, encouraged the beginnings of colonization work in Palestine. Moses Hess, the Rhenish-Parisian "communistic rabbi," published his epochmaking book *Rome and Jerusalem* in 1862, and was the first thinker to classify the Jewish question logically among the nationalist struggles set off by the French Revolution, and to give it its right cultural evaluation. A few years later Perez Smoleskin and David Gordon pleaded in Hebrew for the revival of the national language, and the resettlement of Palestine, as the foundations for the rebirth of the Jewish people. And in 1870 Charles Netter was already entrusted by the *Alliance Israélite Universelle* with the founding of the agricultural school *Mikveh Israel*, in the vicinity of Jaffa, its object being the preparation of Jews for the colonization of Palestine.

The decisive forward step occurred at the beginning of the 'eighties among the Jews of Russia. In the famous Pale of Settlement, a small area within which something like half of all Jewry was compulsorily confined, there occurred in the May Days of 1881 a series of pogroms such as the more recent history of Jewry had not yet witnessed. In the western countries only the reflex of these incidents was felt: a migratory flight of desperate human beings, who poured over the frontiers, traversed the ocean, and reached the shores of America, threatening to create a new anti-Semitism among Jewish settlements everywhere.

Much deeper, however, was the influence of this catastrophe on many Jewish intellectuals within Russia itself.

---

* See Chapter One.

Like their more "advanced" brethren in the west, they had also believed until then in the ultimate triumph of the ideas of the Emancipation. In the degree that the Jews would begin to resemble the peoples in the midst of which they lived, the ancient Jew-hatred would dwindle, and the Jews would integrate themselves with their neighbors. Now these intellectuals recognized that though radical assimilation might be feasible for a few individuals here and there, it was utterly impossible for Jewry as such; and they turned back to Jewry, which they now began to understand as a people, and whose national existence they now desired to secure and strengthen in Palestine. In a large number of cities there sprang up, during the winter of 1881–82, groups of the *Hoveve Zion*, Lovers or Friends of Zion, whose program it was to prepare men and means for the colonization of Palestine. Practical work was begun at once. In the summer of 1882 the first fourteen members of the *Bilu* group set out for Palestine, students who exchanged the book for the plough. The colonies of Rishon le-Zion, Rosh Pinah, Zichron Ja'acob and Yesod Hama'alah arose. Petach Tikvah, already founded by Jews of Jerusalem in 1878, received a new access of strength.

In the midst of this agitation there appeared, in September 1882, a small German pamphlet entitled *Auto-Emancipation*. The author, who was at first anonymous, was Dr. Leo Pinsker, a Jewish doctor of Odessa who until that time had been remote from Jewish national efforts. The pogroms of 1881 had brought about a revolution in his views. With him, as with Herzl, the moving principle was the wounded feeling of honor. "To be plundered as a Jew, or to be protected as a Jew," he wrote, "is equally shameful and equally painful for the human feelings of the Jew." Pinsker diagnosed the condition of the Jewish people like a doctor, and very often his formulations and perceptions have a genuine touch of genius.

Whence, he asks, this alien position of the Jews, this general hatred of them? It is born, he believes, from the circumstance that the Jews, having been driven from their homeland, continued to display all the spiritual characteristics of a national entity without being rooted in the earthy realities proper to a national existence. The world therefore beholds in the Jewish people "the eerie figure of a corpse wandering among the living." This "ghost-phenomenon of a wandering corpse" inspired fear, a sort of ghost-terror, Judaeophobia. "Judaeophobia," he writes, "is a psychosis. As a psychotic condition it is hereditary, and as a disease which has been transmitted for two thousand years, it is incurable." All denunciations of the Jews are only efforts to rationalize this instinctive revulsion.

The treatment of the disease can begin only with the recognition and removal of its real cause, the abnormal condition of the Jewish people. But this removal can be effected only by the Jewish people itself through self-help, self-liberation, or "Auto-Emancipation." These plain Jews, without a sense of selfhood, must be transformed into a self-conscious, independent nation, planted on its own soil and living the natural life of a normal people. Wherever the proportion of the Jews to the surrounding population had passed the saturation point, the Jews should emigrate, but not into a new dispersion; the migration should be directed to a territory (which does not have to be Palestine) where, with the consent of the Powers, they would create their own commonwealth.

In this brochure Pinsker far surpassed his predecessors in the clarity and weightiness of his diagnoses, and in the penetrating force of his national appeal. By implication he also anticipated Herzl's own demands in his recognition of political necessities, in his insistence on a politically secured territorial centre for the Jews, and in a great many minor details. Pinsker has with justice been called the first political Zionist. What he lacked, however, was clarity in practical approach; and, more than that, he lacked the compelling power of the born leader. His appeal, therefore, did not produce all the effect for which he had hoped.

But some measure of success he did achieve. It was largely as the result of the impulse he had given to the movement that the Kattowitz Conference was called in 1884, resulting in a certain unification of the numerous *Hoveve Zion* groups which had sprung up over Russia. Pinsker linked himself with these groups for lack of other support, but he could not perceive in them the realization of the great national political ideas with which his utterance had been interpenetrated. The energies of the *Hoveve Zion* expended themselves in the collection of relatively trivial sums of money for the support of the colonies in Palestine, and these minor labors gradually pushed into the background the great concepts on which the colonization had originally been founded.

Because of the inexperience of the settlers, the colonies soon found themselves in the most serious difficulties. They would have collapsed completely had it not been for the intervention of the great philanthropist Edmond de Rothschild (1845–1934). He took most of the colonies, one by one, under his protection and entrusted their direction to his officials. The principle of philanthropic method thus scored a complete victory, so that even Pinsker, who was profoundly opposed to it, saw no way of bringing about a change.

The colonization progressed with great difficulty, passing through one crisis after another. There were wide-spread complaints against the bureaucratic system of the management. The long sought acquiescence of the Turkish government did not materialize; indeed, in 1891, when a series of new repressive measures in Russia coincided with favorable reports from the colonies, and there was a sudden rush in the direction of Palestine, the Turkish government renewed the existing restrictions on immigration and became more stringent in their application. In the midst of these difficulties Pinsker died, disheartened by the whittling down of his plans and ideas. Then came sharp criticism from within the ranks of the *Hoveve Zion* itself, directed against the aims and methods of the movement.

In the year 1889 the Hebrew periodical *Ha-Melitz* published an article, *Lo Zeh ha-Derech*, — "This is Not the Way" — over the signature of "Ahad Ha-am," or "One of the People." It was the first work of Asher Ginsberg, who under this pseudonym continued through the following years to give varying expression to his opinions on the state of the movement. His articles were remarkable for something more than the style, which incorporated the qualities of lucidity and thoughtfulnes to a degree as yet unknown to modern Hebrew, and which became a model for his contemporaries and successors. The opinions which the writer expressed with inflexible courage attracted wide attention and divided public opinion into opposing camps. Particularly effective was his unsparing criticism of the colonization methods and aims of the *Hoveve Zion*, published under the title "The Truth from Palestine," after his visits to that country in 1891 and 1893. The entire national and Palestine movement, declared Ahad Ha-am, had begun with false assumptions. It had undertaken to solve the problem of Jewish need, a task which it could not perform and was not supposed to attempt. More important than the physical need of the Jews was the spiritual crisis in Jewry. The development of Judaism in the *galut* or exile had led to an inner rigidity; Judaism had become alienated from its original source, the national community of sentiment; its center had shifted from the group to the individual. The revival of the national sentiment was therefore the most important task before Jewry, and should be the tacit assumption behind every enterprise. This was also true of the colonization work in Palestine. Not the number and the size of the settlements should be the decisive consideration, but their quality. For the significance of Palestine lay neither in itself as such, nor in its role as the gathering-place of the Jews; much rather was it to become a spiritual-cultural center in the construction of which all Jewry might participate so that there might radiate back upon it the values it had created. This was the ideal which Ahad Ha-am set before his generation.

Soon after the appearance of his first article he issued the call for the founding of the society of the *B'nai Moshe* — the Sons of Moses — the membership of which was drawn chiefly from the leadership of the *Hoveve Zion*. He exercised a profound influence thereby on the leaders of the movement, and these in turn were almost unanimous in acknowledging themselves in later years the pupils of Ahad Ha-am. As far back as 1890 Ahad Ha-am and two of his followers were elected to the executive of the *Hoveve Zion* federation, the so-called Odessa Committee; a three-fold balance was thus established between the cultural factor, the practical (under the leadership of Lilienblum), and the religious (under Samuel Mohilever), in the rebuilding of the Holy Land.

The Palestine colonization societies of western Europe and America, which had sprung up under the influence of the Russian movement, formed a central committee in Paris in 1894.

All this was not calculated to have a vitalizing effect on the movement. It is true that by 1896 there were already eighteen settlements in Palestine, but they were in constant need of help, and where Baron Rothschild did not provide it the *Hoveve Zion* went out to collect it in tiny sums. The work of most of the societies practically began and ended with these collections. The great national political idea faded into the background, retaining some of its original force only among the youth, to whom it served as a romantic vision. A few years more and the entire movement seemed doomed to extinction.

It was into this dull atmosphere of decline that Herzl's *Judenstaat* broke with the effect of a thunderbolt.

The impression produced by the pamphlet, which was translated into several languages, was everywhere strong; the reactions differed. The general German press, to the extent that it did not completely ignore the work, or interpret it in an anti-Semitic spirit, took a negative attitude; and this was especially true of that part of the press which was under Jewish influence. The journalists made their little jokes about the "escaping Maccabees", and about the Jewish Jules Verne, the crackpot and adventurer who wanted to become the Prime Minister or King of the Jews. The publishers of the *Neue Freie Presse* sought until the last moment, by a mixture of threats and promises, to prevent the publication of the pamphlet. When it actually appeared, they broke the promise they had made Herzl at the time of his refusal

of Badeni's offer, and no mention of *Der Judenstaat* ever
appeared in their paper. Levysohn of the *Berliner Tageblatt*
was determinedly opposed to the ideas expressed in *Der
Judenstaat*. The *Wiener Allgemeine Zeitung*, for which Herzl
had worked at brief intervals in 1887 and again in 1889,
declared Zionism to be the madness born of despair. "Away
with such chimeras!" The *Münchener Allgemeine Zeitung*
turned the book over to the literary historian Anton Bettel-
heim, who described it as "the prospectus, poor in ideas, rich
in imbecilities, of a company for the creation of a Jewish
Switzerland," and "the fantastic dream of a feuilletonist
whose mind had been unhinged by Jewish enthusiasm."
The worthy patriot then burst out as follows: "But we, who
have been brought up in equal and heartfelt devotion to our
family memories and our homeland, we who remain faithful
to the teachers and leaders of our childhood and adult years,
do not for an instant hesitate to declare that we reject Herzl's
Judenstaat with greater distaste than the meanest anti-
Semitic pamphlet."

Not much more intelligent was the response of the non-
Zionist Jewish publicists. Not long after the appearance of
the *Judenstaat* the same publishers issued a reply by a
Dr. Ernst, who denounced it as an act of cowardice for Jews
to fly before their enemies. His pamphlet was entitled
No Jewish State, but Freedom of Conscience. The Berlin
publication *Allgemeine Israelitische Wochenschrift* criticized
the pamphlet violently. The orthodox *Israelit* of Mainz
described Zionism as "a modern miniature of medieval
Messianism" and called the author of *Der Judenstaat* to task
for his indifferent attitude toward religion. His book, furthermore, contained nothing new and was both an internal and
an external danger. The *Allgemeine Zeitung des Judenthums*,

the veteran of the struggle for Jewish equality, dealt kindly with the writer and his intentions, but challenged the assumptions on which the work was based, and the conclusions he had drawn from them. The orthodox Jews, declared the critic, should do nothing to further the idea, but should wait for "the visible signs of God's direct intervention;" the Reform Jews could do nothing "because their ultimate ideal was not the re-establishment of nationality but the prophetic promise of a time of all-human ennoblement." The Jews scattered throughout the world had nothing in common but their belief in God and their conviction that Israel had not yet fulfilled its mission. "We cling to this view because it is the life-nerve of our being." Where, the critic asked, was Herzl to find support, then, since the Zionists too would become his opponents if he should finally decide on some other land than Palestine?

The fact was that among many of the leaders of the *Hoveve Zion* he awakened at first nothing but suspicion. Who was this stranger, of whom they had never heard before, and what did he want? Was he serious about the business? Why this tremendous trumpet blast of a proclamation, why this gigantic political program which had no prospect of realization within measurable time? Might he not, with his tactless openness, antagonize the philanthropists on whose money the work depended, irritate and alarm the Turkish government, whom they were constantly reassuring of their non-political intentions, and thus bring danger on the colonization itself, the one thing that mattered? What did he mean by his rejection of the Hebrew language? And why did he ignore so pointedly his predecessors who had written in the German language on the subject of a Jewish state — such as Bodenheimer (*Whither Russian Jewry?* 1891), and Nathan

Birnbaum (*The National Rebirth of the Jewish People in its Own Land as the Solution of the Jewish Question*, 1893)? Why was he silent about the work of Rabbi Rülf of Memel, of Gustav G. Cohen, the Hamburg banker, of Heinrich Loewe, and others? And if not these, why did he not at least mention Hess and Pinsker?

Actually Herzl did not know a single one of these names at the time he first put down his ideas. Of Pinsker he heard for the first time from Narcisse Leven, in September 1895. He promised himself to read *Auto-Emancipation* at the first opportunity but did not get round to it until February 1896, when he had already received printed copies of *Der Juden-staat*. He noted down at the time: "Staggering agreement on the critical side, great similarity on the constructive." He further noted down, and also told Wolffsohn later, that he might perhaps never have written his own book if he had known of the existence of Pinsker's. Hess's *Rome and Jeru-salem* he began to read in Jerusalem, in 1898; but a thorough reading did not come until May 1901, and then Herzl was profoundly impressed by it. Of the other mentioned works he learned shortly after the publication of *Der Judenstaat* through their authors, or through Wolffsohn. At the time when his inspiration broke forth from him so violently he did not feel the need of reading; nor was he looking for solutions. He was merely setting down that which was pent up in him. And precisely this was the remarkable element in the situ-ation, the element which imparted historic power and identity to his ideas, namely that, as if driven by destiny itself, he had broken through to the path which others, more intimately bound up with the history and being of Jewry, had trodden before him. These facts were, however, un-known to the men who had been part of the Palestine movement for years and decades. They took Herzl's silence on his predecessors as a sign of arrogance and criticized him accordingly.

Powerful as the impulse to action was within him, Herzl was by no means certain, when he published his book, that he would actually take the matter in hand himself. "I myself," he wrote in the introduction, "consider my task completed with the publication of this work. I shall speak again only if forced to by the attacks of opponents worthy of my attention, or if it is a question of answering unforeseen objections and correcting errors." He was still hesitating. He wanted to wait for the reaction of the Jews, and of the world at large, to discover whether the time was ripe, or whether he was in advance of it. Had he heard no other voices than those which we have already mentioned, voices raised in repudiation and criticism, the act might have remained unperformed. But there were other voices that came to his ears.

For there were wide circles upon which the book had a totally different effect. "When I had read it to the end," Wolffsohn wrote him, "I felt that I had become another man." "The broad perspectives, and the faith, strong as a vision, which speaks from every line of the *Judenstaat*, has opened before me a new world, whose existence I had indeed long suspected, but which I had never beheld." This was also the effect upon simpler members of the *Hoveve Zion*, who had not lost their original outlook, and who longed to escape from the pettiness of their Palestinian tasks. Similar, too, was the response of the Zionist youth. A door had been flung open for them, light streamed in. Clarity, dignity, strong faith and a prophetic, appealing pathos lifted them out of the dreariness of the daily reality. That flutter of eagles'

wings which, as Herzl told later, he had felt above his head
when he wrote the *Judenstaat*, became audible now to these
of his readers. Now they suddenly saw before them a goal,
a great and attainable goal, and the steps which led to it.
And all this from a Viennese litterateur, an editor on one of
the greatest German newspapers, who until now had worried
little about Jewish matters — a man who had lived in the
world of writers, who had moved in the circles of the great,
and who had suddenly turned back to his despised people.

The radical conversion of a man before the eyes of the
world is always an overwhelming phenomenon. It is to be
found at the beginning of every great religious foundation,
as witness Moses, Paul, Buddha, Mohammed. It was as an
improbable and legendary figure that Herzl dawned upon
the eastern masses of Jewry. His book, kept out of the
country by the Russian censorship, was hardly known; only
the name passed over the heads of the masses, and the stories
that accompanied it gripped the hearts and stirred the
imagination of thousands. Was there not about him, in fact,
a suggestion of a prince out of the ancient times when Jews
still lived in their own land? "What we lack," wrote Pinsker,
"is a genius like Moses to lead us; such gifts are not made
frequently to a people." Herzl had called his "Society of
Jews" the new Moses. The masses, however, saw the new
Moses in him, the leader, who had returned "like Moses from
Midian" to liberate the Jews from their wretchedness.*

Responses like these came from every country; sometimes
they were couched in touchingly helpless phrases, sometimes
they revealed a no less touching faith. They came from
Bulgaria, from Galicia, from Germany, from Russia, from

---

* Letter from the Society *Ahavat Zion*, Borislav, Galicia.

Palestine. They called upon him to take over the leadership. "Among our sages of old," wrote to him Reuben Bierer, one of the veterans of the movement, "there was a remarkable saying: 'Some men win the world-to-come in a single moment.' If that saying is true, then there is no one among our people to whom it applies more aptly than to you."

From Semlin, the home of his forefathers, he received the news that all the Jews there were ready to leave as soon as "The Jewish Company" was formed. "Your pamphlet," wrote the society *B'nai Zion*, of Rohatyn, Poland, "is the very embodiment of the Zionist ideal, it has clothed it with flesh and blood, it has converted the idea into tangible reality. We know now what we want and what we will do." The society *Zion*, of Lemberg, sent a telegram calling upon him to take in hand the realization of his plans, all East European Jewry was waiting for him. The *Hasid* Aaron Marcus wrote to him from Podgorze, and in a warm letter mentioned the prospect of winning the cooperation of the three million *Hasidim* of Poland.

Particularly warm was the response of the Zionists of Vienna, and among these the most enthusiastic were the Zionist students. This city, which had been the battleground of the Austrian national forces, had long since witnessed the rise of the Zionist movement. In 1882, when Herzl was still a member of the *Albia*, a number of students, stung to action by Dühring's book, had founded the first student Zionist body, *Kadimah* — "Eastward." Among the founders were Reuben Bierer, Nathan Birnbaum, M. T. Schnirer and Oser Kokesch. In 1893 the Zionist student circles of Vienna and similar bodies in Berlin corresponded on the question of calling a general Zionist Congress. Nathan Birnbaum, who had coined the word "Zionism," had been the initiator.

Since 1894 the idea of a Congress had spread with the increase in the number of Zionist societies. The founding of the Viennese colonization group *Admat Yeshurun* — later the Zion Society — was followed by the founding of similar groups in Czernowitz, Graz and elsewhere. Before long the scattered societies had formed a federation. On these circles of the student Zionist youth Herzl's appeal had an intoxicating effect. Here was strength, purpose, direction. A great struggle beckoned.

The students did everything that lay in their power to encourage Herzl along the path of leadership. Student deputations waited on him with invitations to their festive evenings, where great ovations were prepared for him. Schnirer and Kokesch, co-founders of the *Kadimah* and now members of the Zion Society, delivered to him, early in April 1896, a resolution of these bodies expressing their confidence in his work. They further persuaded the Federation of Austrian Societies for the Colonization of Palestine to circulate a memorandum of a similar character among all their sympathizers in German and Austrian academic circles, and within the next few months thousands of signatures were added and presented to Herzl. The signatories expressed their gratitude to him for the publication of his plan, which had given clear expression to the feelings of the Jewish people, and placed themselves at his disposal for the realization of the idea.

And while the laughter grew louder in journalistic circles, men came forward to press his hand gratefully. Max Nordau, that critic of critics, was swept off his feet by the pamphlet; he described it as a great act, a revelation. In mid-February Richard Beer-Hofmann, the poet, wrote to him: "Even more than to the contents of the book I was attracted to its implications. At last there comes again a man who does not carry his Judaism with resignation like a burden or a misfortune, but is proud to be the legal inheritor of an immemorial culture." And in May 1896, David Wolffsohn sought him out to offer him his homage and cooperation.

The first meeting between Wolffsohn and Herzl merits some attention, for it was to lead to decisive results for the movement. Older than Herzl by two or three years, Wolffsohn was born in a townlet in the Russian Pale of Settlement. His father, the Talmudic teacher Rabbi Eisik, had been a man of modernizing tendencies. From him Wolffsohn had his thorough knowledge of Jewish life, his love of Zion and his hope of a Jewish national liberation. From his mother he had inherited his goodness and cleverness. In the Talmud Torah of Memel he came under the influence of Rabbi Rülf. David Gordon, in whose house he lived during his short stay in Lyck, had strengthened his Jewish national outlook. He had worked himself up from the most modest economic beginnings. After various unsuccessful business ventures he became a traveler and ultimately a partner in a large timber firm. He settled first in Papenburg and then in Cologne. His circumstances were now easy. In Cologne he struggled side by side with Max J. Bodenheimer for the furtherance of the Zionist ideal: the dream of a Jewish state had come to them before they heard of Herzl. Even now all that Wolffsohn knew about the author of the *Judenstaat* was that he was a Viennese editor and litterateur, and he expected "a true Viennese type, well padded and clean-shaven." He was confounded and amazed by the majestic figure of Herzl. It was a fateful encounter. In Wolffsohn, Herzl found not only immediate entree to the German *Hoveve Zion*, but a

devoted and unfaltering follower. He soon became more —
a friend. Deep-rooted in Jewish folk origins, closebound to
Judaism by instinct, reflection and knowledge, and withal
a clever and experienced man who incorporated the best
characteristics of the simple Jew, Wolffsohn was the perfect
complement for Herzl: an admonisher, encourager and
teacher, ever ready to extend his help, independent in action,
glad to accept responsibility and yet prepared, in all lesser
matters, to sink his own opinion and accept that of the leader.
Certainly there were bound to be differences between two
men of such diverse origins and natures, and on one occasion
there was something like a genuine conflict; but these were
only episodes.

The difference in outlook became evident at their first
encounter. Wolffsohn was astounded to learn that Herzl
had not the slightest knowledge of his predecessors in
Zionism, but that he had, on the other hand, a totally false
conception of the Russian Jew. Herzl, on his side, was
equally astounded to learn that he was himself an "Eastern
Jew," and that "there was no difference between the Russian
Jew and the European." Then, when Wolffsohn expressed
the opinion that the success of the plan depended largely on
the reception accorded it by the Jews of Russia, Herzl found
the statement completely incomprehensible at first. He knew
only of the masses of East European Jewry, which would be
needed for the work of up-building when the preliminary
conditions had been created. Of the leaders of Russian
Jewry, of the Zionist movement in that area, and of its
significance, he had no notion whatsoever. But Herzl's
personality and his profound faith had all the more effect on
Wolffsohn for that very reason. "He takes this matter of the
Judenstaat with the utmost seriousness," he wrote to Boden-

heimer, "and he lives in the firm conviction that he will attain his goal, and that quite soon. He has opened a regular office for this business and conducts an enormous correspondence, but he does not wish to speak about it as yet."

It is clear, then, that by this time Herzl had resolved to become the man of action, and the purpose behind the enthusiatic responses he had received was fulfilled. They had proved to him that he did not stand alone; they also gave him a certain confirmation with respect to the outside world. The mockery which he had refused to endure the year before he now took upon himself in all consciousness. "He who prepares the future must be able to look beyond the present." And in his diary he notes: "This people must be educated, and that by our example."

At first he declined to speak at large public gatherings, partly out of the shyness of the "man of the writing desk" and partly because he felt that it would do the work more harm than good if he were pushed into the foreground. Why should he weaken and diffuse the effect of his plan with interminable discussions and debates? Why should he encourage splits when the unification of all forces was the most important consideration?

In a general way, too, he did not think much of discussions; the determined act was what counted. One must go ahead — that was what counted; success would pull along the hesitant, the completed act would force the assent of opponents. On May 12 he noted in his diary: "Great things need no firm foundation. You have to put an apple on the table, if you don't want it to fall down. The earth swims in space. Thus I can perhaps found and buttress the Jewish state without a firm hold. The secret of it lies in motion."*

There were three tasks to be undertaken at once. The first was the creation of "The Society of Jews," for which purpose he had in mind English Jewry, which had shown a certain degree of understanding for his ideas during his visit of July 1895. The second was the initiation of diplomatic work in Constantinople and among the Powers, for the acquisition of Palestine; for, as he wrote at about that time to Max Nordau, his contacts with the *Hoveve Zion* had convinced him that Palestine alone came in question for his purpose. The third was the creation of organs of publicity for the influencing of world opinion as well as for the preparation of the Jewish masses. Later these same organs would be used for the direction of the activities of the masses when the preliminary conditions had been prepared. He set about this threefold task systematically.

He began with the political work, his newspaper plans offering no immediate prospects. He wanted to act alone, backed only by the expressions of sympathy and agreement he had received. Visible and demonstrable results, he told himself, would facilitate the negotiations for the formation of "The Society of Jews." Then, when this instrument had been created, it would in turn react favorably upon the political work.

He found two men, both non-Jews, to help him in the political work. The first came to him out of conviction, and

---

* He adds in parenthesis (vol. I of the diaries): "I believe that it is on this principle that the steerable flying ship will be invented. Weight overcome by movement: it will be the motion, and not the ship, which will have to be steered.

remained faithful to the movement long after Herzl's death; the second was picked by Herzl, and paid by him — and Herzl never found out who and what he was, an effective worker or a treacherous adventurer. But each of the two men was unusual and interesting in his own way.

On March 10, 1896, there burst into his room a clergyman "with the long grey beard of a prophet," and as Herzl started up in amazement at his writing desk, the intruder stammered: "Here I am!" "I see that," said Herzl, "but who are you?" "I understand your astonishment," answered the man, "but it was I who first brought the great tidings to the Grand Duke of Baden, and now I want to help you." Thereupon the stranger showed Herzl a book which he declared he had written himself. It was entitled *The Restauration of the Jews to Palestine According to the Prophets*, and in it he proved, on the basis of prophecies made in the time of Omar, and of the interpretation of certain biblical passages, that Palestine would be given back to the Jews about 1897-1898. While he, the author, was waiting for the fulfilment of the miracle, he had heard from the Zionist journalist S. R. Landau of Herzl's *Judenstaat*, and had rushed over at once to offer his help. To work for the homecoming of the Jews to Palestine was, for him, "to fulfil prophecy."

Finally he explained who he was. He was the Reverend Hechler, chaplain to the English Embassy in Vienna. He was also a great collector of Bibles and of models of the ancient Temple in Jerusalem. He had so many of the latter that they lined the walls of his room as high as the ceiling. When Herzl, a few days later, returned the strange man's visit, the latter showed him a tremendous military staff map of Palestine and the haversack he would wear when he would accompany Herzl into and through the Holy Land.

"Next to Colonel Goldsmid," noted Herzl in his diary, "this is the most extraordinary man I have encountered in the movement." He recognized, however, that Hechler might very well prove to be a valuable coadjutor. It might even be possible to reach, through him, the German princes and ultimately even the Kaiser. For besides being chaplain at the British Embassy, Hechler had for many years been tutor to the children of the Grand Duke of Baden, and was on good terms with this Prince as well as with his nephew, the Kaiser himself.

Until now, Herzl told Hechler, he had encountered nothing but opposition, which threatened to use up his strength completely unless new help came. The most important thing for him, he said, was "to meet with some responsible and authorized — or for that matter unauthorized — government official" — a minister, or a prince, and through him to build up a visible and impressive system of external connections. Then the Jews would follow him. The most suitable figure would be the German Kaiser. Hechler declared himself ready to proceed to Berlin and to talk with the court preacher Dryander and the Imperial Princes Günther and Heinrich. Herzl supplied Hechler with the expenses for the journey. Uncertain of the impression which the naive dreamer and enthusiast would make in court circles, Herzl charged him specifically not to reveal that he had been sent, but to act as if he were coming entirely on his own initiative to the imperial personages.

At about that same time Herzl made connection with his second political helper, Nevlinski, and again it was S. R. Landau who was the middleman.

Philip Michael, Ritter von Nevlinski, the descendant of a long line of Polish nobles, was born in 1847 in Antoniny,

Volhynia. The family fortune, which had enabled him as a boy to lead the wild life of a young aristocrat, had been confiscated by the Russian government because of the share of the Nevlinskis in the uprising of 1863. Thus young Nevlinski was compelled, against the family tradition, to find some calling at which he could earn his own living. He had studied law in St. Petersburg, and in 1865 he had found employment as a journalist on some of the leading papers of St. Petersburg and Moscow. In 1872 Andrassy had offered him a post in the Austrian Foreign Ministry.

He advanced steadily, was transferred to the Austro-Hungarian Embassy in Constantinople, and a brilliant career seemed to be opening for him. But in 1879 he suffered an irreparable check. The accumulation of debts forced him out of the service of the state. Since then he had put his experience and his connections to use as diplomatic agent at large and as journalist. Shortly before meeting Herzl he had begun to publish a periodical called *Correspondance de l'Est*. This daily was intended to serve as a source of original information for the Austrian and foreign press, as well as for diplomatic and political circles, on general international questions, but particularly on the affairs of Russia, Turkey and the Balkans. The paper seems to have begun with a fairly wide circulation, but this had shrunk considerably by the time under discussion. Nevlinski himself was an imposing figure. His style of life was that of the *grand seigneur*, spending money to right and left. He was thoroughly experienced in all the forms of diplomatic intercourse, and even if it might be said of him that he belonged more to the *demi-monde* of diplomacy, he had the great manner to his finger-tips. In any case, he created a considerable impression on the Jewish journalist in process of becoming a statesman. But Herzl was by no means swept off his feet. In fact he swung to and fro considerably in his estimate of Nevlinski; he admired him and saw through him, he despised and respected him in alternation. What is certain is that he learned a great deal from this diplomatic adventurer. It was under Nevlinski's guidance that he took his first steps out of the bourgeois journalistic world into the general European, learned the niceties of diplomatic form, and was introduced to the complications of Turkish politics. In part as the result of his former position, and in part as the publisher of the *Correspondance de l'Est*, Nevlinski enjoyed excellent political connections in Constantinople, even though it may be strongly doubted whether he had such frequent access to the Sultan as he claimed to have.

Meanwhile the "prophetic" Hechler set about his task. On April 14 the German Kaiser came on a visit to Vienna. Hechler hastened to the Hofburg, imparted to the Major Domo the contents of the *Judenstaat*, and informed that astonished official that the time had come "to fulfil prophecy." Hearing that the Kaiser would be leaving the next evening for an extended visit to the Grand Duke of Baden, Hechler proposed that Herzl and he proceed there in advance. Herzl declined. "If the high personages should not feel disposed to receive me, I would find myself in a most embarrassing and unworthy position," he said, and instructed Hechler to go on alone and to ask for an audience. Should he obtain one, he had only to telegraph to Herzl, who would set out at once.

Hechler left the next morning. Tense days followed for Herzl. He threw himself into his work with greater energy than ever to overcome his restlessness. First came very hopeful telegrams, then silence, then again satisfactory telegrams, then again days of silence. The newspapers reported at last that the Kaiser had left the court of Baden. The manoeuvre was, it seemed, a failure.

On April 20 Herzl drafted a long letter to Nordau, suggesting that the latter attempt to make connection with Baron de Hirsch. Perhaps the Baron could be persuaded to contribute a couple of million francs to the cause, This would "make a ringing impression on public opinion,"and at the same time they would have the *baksheesh* needed for negotiations with Turkey. How far he had outgrown his own pride in thus proposing to approach once more the man who had so coolly let him leave Paris! The next day he completed the letter and sent it off. An hour later he learned that Baron Moritz de Hirsch had died the night before on one of his estates in Hungary. He recalled the letter telegraphically. "What a strange coincidence," he noted in his diary. "For months the pamphlet has been ready. I gave it to everyone except Hirsch. The moment I decide to do it, he dies. His cooperation could have hastened our success tremendously. In any case, his death is a loss to the Jewish cause. Among the rich Jews he was the only one prepared to do something big for the poor ones. Perhaps I did not know how to handle him. Perhaps I should have written that letter to Nordau fourteen days ago. For it was always in my mind to win Hirsch over to the plan."

The day passed in that mood of introspection, of self-searching and clarification. He is preparing for a journey to Budapest. Then, late that evening, he receives a telegram from Hechler bidding him set out at once for Karlsruhe, where he will be received in audience by the Grand Duke. To Herzl, with his Spinozistic-Goethean inclination to view all transient things as images of the eternal, that day was

almost like a symbol of the end of Jewish philanthropy and
the beginning of Jewish political action.

The next morning, as the Orient Express carried him
through the spring landscape toward Karlsruhe, he continued these reflections in his diary: "A Viennese newspaper
says, in its obituary today: 'Hirsch could not help the poor
because he was rich.' And it is true. I approach the same
matter in a different and, I believe, in a better and more
powerful way, because I shall carry it out not through money
but through the idea."

Herzl prepared with the utmost care for this audience,
the first of its kind in his life. Very much would depend, he
told himself, on the impression he left with the Grand Duke;
for it was through the latter that he hoped to reach the
Kaiser.

"All the same," he noted, "I must not become dizzy on
these heights. I shall think of death, and that will make me
earnest." He wanted to be cool, calm, firm, modest and yet
determined. He succeeded. During the hours of waiting
he walked about the city and studied the pictures of the
Grand Duke in the shop windows. And when, at the appointed hour, four in the afternoon, he stood in the presence,
he was amazed and overwhelmed by the simple naturalness,
the quiet goodness, the noble modesty, the deep faith of
the Grand Duke. "I thought it best to speak in a low voice,
so that the usual self-intoxication of speech disappeared."
But before long he was completely master of himself and
unfolded his plan in bold, large strokes.

He laid particular emphasis on the beneficent effect of the
movement on Germany; and in writing to the Grand Duke
a few days later, he was even more precise on this point,
as if he were making sure that it would be transmitted to the

Kaiser. If some of the royal heads of states were prepared to express their benevolent attitude toward the movement, "The Society of Jews" could start out with greater authority, and the migration could be organized more rapidly and with greater discipline.

Responding, the Grand Duke thought it would be better to create "The Society of Jews" first, and then he would be able to judge whether he ought to cooperate with it. He said repeatedly that he was afraid of having his motives misunderstood; his attitude toward the Jews was one of benevolence, but as the plan was one for the migration of the Jews, his support of it might bring him under suspicion of anti-Semitism. On Hechler's suggestion, he granted Herzl the permission to let it be known abroad that he, the Grand Duke of Baden, was interested in the enterprise. He was won over — by Herzl's personality. The interview lasted for two and a half hours, and at the parting the Grand Duke held Herzl's hand for a long time.

It was a great success for Herzl and for the movement. For the first time he had been heard and understood by a ruling Prince. This was in itself a considerable gain. But should the Grand Duke go further, and transmit his interest to the Kaiser, then, in the constellation of the Powers as they then stood, with German influence strong in Turkey, the most far-reaching consequences might reasonably be expected. It was this combination which inspired Herzl's activities throughout the months and years to come: Baden was to be his bridge to Berlin.

The immediate effect, however, was a mighty access of courage and energy, and a thrust forward along the whole line. On May 19 he was received by Agliardi, the Papal Nuncio in Vienna. The latter was negative in his attitude.

He did not believe that this was the solution of the Jewish problem. His allusions to the Jews were tinged with anti-Semitism. On the other hand Herzl had Samuel Montagu send a copy of *Der Judenstaat* to Gladstone, and had the satisfaction of learning that the venerable English statesman was not unfavorably impressed by the book. And the *Neue Freie Presse* went so far as to make mention of this fact in a little paragraph on an inside page — the only mention ever made by that paper of the subject of Zionism until the death of Herzl.

But Herzl now concentrated his main energies on the effort to establish contact with the Sultan. He urged Nevlinski, whom he paid generously out of his own pocket, to proceed to Constantinople and set the business in motion. Nevlinski, for his part, was less anxious to further Herzl's ends than to promote his own. Herzl might help him to bring about a reconciliation between the Turkish government and the Armenians, and to put an end to the ghastly reign of terror under which that people was suffering. Nevlinski promised Herzl that if he could achieve something in that direction he would thereby come favorably to the notice of the Sultan, and the contact could easily be established.

As to Herzl's urgent pleadings that he take immediate steps to arrange an audience for him with the Sultan, Nevlinski showed himself little inclined to action. The hostile attitude of the journalistic world, not excluding that part of it which was constituted by Herzl's own newspaper, seemed to Nevlinski to render the plan hopeless. It was only when Herzl showed himself ready to go to Constantinople alone, and to employ the services of another agent, that Nevlinski came around. At Herzl's expense the two men

left Vienna on June 15, 1896. On the same train were travelling the three Turkish statesmen Ziad, Karatheodory and
Tewfik Pasha, to whom Nevlinski presented Herzl.

Herzl was in Constantinople from June 18 to 29. He
arrived in the Turkish capital filled with high hopes. Nevlinski had, for months past, talked so much about his excellent relations with the Sultan that an audience seemed to
be assured. More than an audience with the Sultan, as
external evidence of the fact that his plan was being taken
seriously, Herzl did not need for the moment. Actually he
did manage to meet, through Nevlinski, a number of highly
placed individuals, including the vizier. He visited the latter
twice, the first time in his capacity as Jewish statesman, the
second in his capacity as one of the editors of the *Neue Freie
Presse* seeking an interview on the Armenian situation. Ar-
menia was occupying the front pages of the European press
at that time, in consequence of the frightful massacres
perpetrated in that country by the Turks. Herzl also
visited the Austrian ambassador, Calice.

The plan which he submitted to the Sultan's advisers was
a very simple one, and had already been mentioned in the
Judenstaat. Ever since the middle of the nineteenth century
Turkish finances had been in a shocking condition. By the
end of 1881 the total external indebtedness of the country,
including accumulation of unpaid interest, had reached the
enormous figure of 253 million pounds sterling. At the end
of 1881 the Turkish Debt (that phrase became one of the
familiar terms of European politics toward the end of the
nineteenth century) was consolidated by a union of the
creditors, and was reduced to 106 million pounds, but the
administration of it was transferred to a council of the debt-
ors, known thereafter as the Administrative Council of the

Public Debt. This body was entrusted with the management of certain domestic Turkish monopolies (tobacco and salt) and with the collection of certain taxes. A large number of officials served the Council. This situation, in itself a disgrace to the status of an independent country, gave the European Powers the opportunity to interfere in the internal affairs of Turkey. It was only by the removal of this foreign tutelage that Turkey could hope to recover genuine independence, and it was toward the achievment of this end, argued Herzl, that the Jews, and the Jews alone, could be used. If they were given Palestine as an independent state, they would undertake the regulation and normalization of Turkish finances and liberate the country from foreign control. In his conversation with Turkish leaders Herzl intimated that influential English Jews like Montagu stood behind him.

But with all the pressure that Herzl exerted, he could not obtain his audience with the Sultan. Nevlinski ran all over the city, and assured Herzl repeatedly that he himself had seen the Sultan but that the latter had shown himself unfavorable to the plan, and therefore refused to receive Herzl and discuss the transference of the sovereignty of Palestine. Improbable as some of Nevlinski's stories were, Herzl, as yet a neophyte in international politics, had boundless confidence in the Pole, and not only believed him implicitly, but also admired him.

With all that, there was no denying that Herzl had now carried on serious discussions with important Turkish statesmen; this was in itself a gain and a step forward, and it had provided him with an insight into the reaction of Turkish governmental circles. It became clear from the outset that a complete renunciation of sovereignty over Palestine was out of the question: the more so as the Viennese journalist who was negotiating for this important change could not yet prove that he had the slightest backing. Should he however succeed in obtaining the backing of Jewish finance, then — from all the evidence — he could reasonably hope to get Palestine for the Jews, if not as an independent state, then as a vassal state of Turkey: at the very least there was the prospect of securing permission for large scale Jewish immigration under Jewish management. But everything now depended on the help which Jewish financiers were prepared to extend to Turkey.

With this knowledge, and in possession of the Commander's Cross of the Order of the Medjidje, which Nevlinski had obtained for him as visible evidence of the seriousness with which the negotiations were regarded, Herzl left Constantinople, thoroughly satisfied with developments. His next point was London, where he would now attempt to found "The Society of Jews."

On the way to and from Constantinople he passed through Sofia and was able to observe at first hand what an impression his appeal had made on the Jewish masses. When he went through toward Constantinople hundreds of people waited on the railroad platform to get a glimpse of him. "There was an old man in a fur hat who resembled my grandfather Simon Herzl." The crowd called him "Lord and Leader in Israel," and shouted "Next year in Jerusalem." On the way back to Vienna he spent a few hours in the Bulgarian capital. The crowd conducted him, amid continuous cheering, to the Zionist Society, and then to the synagogue. Hundreds of people were assembled there, as though he were the bringer of messianic tidings. They pressed forward to kiss his hand. As he, the assimilated West European, stood on the pulpit, and showed his embarrassment because there was a cry for a speech and he did not know how to address them without committing what might be the impropriety of turning his back to the Torah, one man called: "You can stand with your back to the Ark, you are holier than the Torah!" He had already been reminded more than once of Sabbatai Zevi; and he saw now that his personality was being assimilated in the fantasy of the people to that of the seventeenth century cabalistic leader and misleader, who had aroused such a storm of belief in the Jewish masses of his day. Herzl's sense of responsibility revolted from this development. He warned the people against conducting street demonstrations, which could only rouse the non-Jewish masses against the Jews. In the evening he dined with the Bulgarian minister Natchevitch, and discussed with him the fear of the local Jews that they were about to be deprived of their synagogue. Natchevitch promised his benevolent intervention.

In London his journey to Constantinople had been reported by the press. His reception by the influential London Jews, who were the focal element for him, was cool, distant and hostile. Yet Herzl had come to them with a very moderate program. The representatives of the various Jewish organizations were to unite in a federation which was to be "The Society of Jews." As the aim of the Society he formulated "the acquisition of a territory secured by international law . . . for those Jews who cannot assimilate."* And in order to show that he was approaching the work quite

---

* Soon after he added the words "or who do not want to do so." He used this formula frequently, even after the First Congress, although a different wording had been adopted there.

objectively, and that no personal ambitions were involved, he pleaded for the acceptance of his program on condition that he be allowed to withdraw from the leadership of the movement. He was even ready to content himself at first with the formation of the Study Commission. On the day of his arrival he sat down in conference with Claude Montefiore and Frederick Mocatta, two prominent liberal Jews, representatives of the Anglo-Jewish Association. They asked for time to think the plan over, then rejected it.

At the banquet of The Maccabaeans, arranged for him the next evening, he fared no better. He was very warmly received, and replied to the toast in French and German. The speech of the evening he delivered in English. Linguistically this was very difficult for him; he had always neglected the English language in favor of the French. After his removal from Paris he had, indeed, again taken up the study of English; but now, speaking before The Maccabaeans, he found it necessary to make notations of the English pronunciation of the more difficult words. The substance of the speech, too, was not easy to transmit. He could only throw out hints with regard to the nature and results of his diplomatic negotiations, in part because he had promised the Grand Duke of Baden and others not to give any publicity to the conversations, and in part because he was not prepared to put his cards on the table. He was well qualified for this kind of half concealment; he had shown his skill at it in his feuilletons, which derived much of their charm from the allusive style. But he was speaking in English now, and this was an enormous handicap. Nevertheless even his English speech conveyed the impression of a statesman who knew, and was doing, much more than he could reveal to the public.

As guarantors of the fact that there were genuine achievements behind his guarded utterances, he cited Colonel Goldsmid, Sir Samuel Montagu and the Reverend Singer, to whom he had imparted in private much more than he could put into his address. He then pointed out that considerable progress had been registered in the serious reception which his plan had obtained among leading political figures. He was not, he said, concerned with the details set forth in his book. "Mine is a political plan, and in politics it is frequently necessary to allow oneself to be guided by utility, of course only in so far as is consistent with the object in view." The mass response to his book, which he had originally intended only as the starting point for the awakening of public interest, had shown that "the Jewish state is no longer the isolated dream of an individual, but rather shared by innumerable human beings. Today I know, and tomorrow the world will know, that the Jews wish to have a state wherein they may at last live and thrive as free citizens." To spread and strengthen this will to a state was the historic significance of the emancipation of the Jews. It was not the emancipation itself. Thus he revised, in great strokes, the generally accepted interpretation of that historic event. Every country, he said in Pinsker's formulation, could accept only a certain number of Jews, in accordance with its absorptive capacity for their assimilation. Assimilation as such was therefore inapplicable on a grand scale. "Smaller nations than ourselves have ventured to claim proprietorship of a portion of the earth's surface."

Again he attacked, as solutions of the problem, both philanthropy and infiltration, which offered no guarantee for the security of Jewish settlements. "If we offer a home — be it even a historic one — to the people who migrate on account of persecution, we ought at any rate be able to assure them that they will never more be persecuted on religious or national grounds . . ."

He spoke in high terms of what had already been achieved in Palestine, and of the demonstration which the Jews had given of their ability to transform themselves again into land workers. "There the old land renews its youth under men's active labor. It bears flowers once again, and fruits, and perhaps one day, one beautiful day, the land will bear again the prosperity and honor of the Jews."

The personal impression which Herzl produced was profound, but practical issue, in the form of a Study Commission, there was none. Nor did Herzl make any progress in this direction during the next few days of effort — not to mention his idea of raising a loan of two million pounds sterling for Turkey as the first step in giving a practical turn to the interest of that country in his plans. All he achieved was the agreement of Sir Samuel Montagu and Colonel Goldsmid to work with him for a vassal Jewish state under the sovereignty of Turkey if a) the Powers agreed, b) the Baron de Hirsh Fund (*ICA*) would place its ten million pounds at the disposal of the plan, and c) Baron Edmund de Rothschild entered the executive committee of "The Society of Jews."

What was remarkable at this point was the fact that the very hesitations of the people who had declared themselves as being with him now strengthened in Herzl the determination to carry on. "All these people," he noted in his diary on July 12, "decent and sympathetic though they be, compel me, by their hesitancy, to become the leader."

This consciousness of inevitable leadership was confirmed in him the following day. In contrast to the spirit shown by the leaders of the *Hoveve Zion*, the young people, members of the *B'nai Zion*, had arranged a mass meeting in Whitechapel, the heart of that east side Jewry which had not achieved the economic status or the assimilatory philosophy of the members of the Anglo-Jewish Association. The ghetto masses streamed that evening toward the Working Men's Club in such numbers that before long the hall was filled to overflowing. Thousands jammed the surrounding streets. Tremendous cheers went up when Herzl appeared. Was it Herzl they were cheering? The leadership of the meeting, turned down by the important personalities of London Jewry, had been accepted by Moses Gaster, the Chief Rabbi of the Sephardic community, a scholar and a fiery orator, and by the Hebrew teacher Ish-Kishor. The latter, in his speech, compared Herzl to Moses and to Columbus. While Herzl thus confronted his first mass audience, he was aware, in the midst of strange emotions, that already legend was busy with him. "The masses," he noted afterwards in his diary, "are sentimental. The masses do not see clearly. I believe that they already have no clear concept of me. A faint mist is already rising about me; perhaps it will become a cloud in the midst of which I will walk."

He admonishes himself to become worthier of the love and the confidence demonstrated by these poor people. One phrase uttered by a speaker that evening sank deep into him: "The east is with us." What the speaker meant was that the east side of London stood behind Herzl; but in the messianic mood of that evening the phrase was interpreted and perpetuated as the slogan of the return of the Jews to their homeland. That evening he recognised what his impassioned followers like Ish-Kishor and young de Haas confirmed to him the next day: that it depended solely upon him whether or not he became the leader of the masses. But he did not want to accept — at least, not before he had tried to secure the help of the Rothschilds by his offer to withdraw from the movement.

The next evening Herzl was invited to attend a session of the *Hoveve Zion* society. The leaders of this organization were not disinclined to cooperate with Herzl if the latter would only undertake not to attack their method of slow-tempo immigration and colonization without legal guarantees, which was also the method of Baron Rothschild.

What was Herzl to do? Should he seek the support of the *Hoveve Zion* by surrendering his leading principle? Would not the entire movement then decline and disintegrate, just as it had done after Pinsker's appeal? Herzl had no intention of yielding; but stung by the refusal of the leaders to have anything to do with his mass meeting of the evening before, he expressed his refusal in much sharper terms than was either wise or necessary. He wanted only the kind of colonization which would be protected by its own army. He was particularly outspoken in his attack on Rothschild, whose philanthropic activity he stigmatized as a kind of rich man's sport. Rothschild had to put himself at the disposal of the national effort, then Herzl would be prepared to accord him the highest place in it, while he himself withdrew from it. The attack let loose a storm, and the meeting was closed by its chairman, Joseph Prag. After it, Colonel Goldsmid wrote a letter to Baron Rothschild, in which he warned him against Herzl.

From London Herzl went to Paris, and sent a message to Baron Rothschild asking for an interview — a bitter sacrifice for a man as proud as Herzl. On July 18, 1896, the meeting took place in the reception room of the bank on the rue Laffitte. It was a strained, almost hostile affair. Rothschild was some years older than Herzl, but, shy and nervous by nature, he was even less at ease than usual in the presence of the calm, self-certain critic of his life's work. He felt himself to be the more practical man; he knew, or at any rate believed, that he had done a great deal more for Palestine than Herzl, who made on him the impression of a dangerous and undisciplined enthusiast. He began to criticize the whole idea of a Jewish state, and Herzl interrupted him brusquely: "You don't know what it's about, let me explain it to you," and once again expounded his basic ideas. He reiterated the proposal he had made in London, that Rothschild take over the leadership; he himself would withdraw if he had Rothschild's word of honor, and the word of honor of his associates, that they would carry on the work in the spirit in which he had begun it.

Rothschild declined, obviously influenced by, among other things, Goldsmid's letter. He did not believe in the possibility of the creation of political conditions favorable to a mass immigration; and even if there were such a possibility an uncontrolled mass immigration to Palestine would put the whole enterprise in danger. He remembered the effect produced in the colonies by the sudden rush of immigration in 1891. A hundred and fifty thousand Jewish paupers would suddenly land in Palestine, and they would have to be fed and looked after. He therefore could see before him no other method than that of slow colonization, carried on in a fashion which did not attract hostile attention. All of Herzl's objections were futile. The Baron's refusal was decisive.

It was a historic decision. By his refusal Rothschild assumed at least as definite a responsibility as he would have done by an acceptance. Herzl, with his innate sense of the symbolic in external events, recognized this fact at the end of the two-hour conversation. "Wherein," he asked Baron Rothschild, "do I recognize the power of an idea? In the self-involvement which is implied by an affirmative answer, and in the self-involvement which is also implied by a negative answer." Rothschild's refusal, which carried with it the refusal of the Hirsch Fund and of the leading London Jews, put an end to the hope that the enterprise might be directed from above. Now Herzl saw himself forced to make use of propaganda and agitation which would excite an even greater unrest among the masses. "And it was just what I wanted to avoid. I have shown my good intentions ... You refuse — I have done my share."

Four days later he was in Karlsbad, where Nevlinski obtained an audience for him with King Ferdinand of Bulgaria. From that city Herzl sent a telegram followed by an explanatory letter to Chief Rabbi Zadoc Kahn, asking him to use his offices in arranging a *modus operandi* with Baron Rothschild. He himself, he wrote to Zadoc Kahn, had perhaps been too clumsy or too impatient. "But the enterprise should not suffer because of my shortcomings."

But Herzl's decision had already been made, swiftly, as was his wont. He had drawn the logical conclusion from Rothschild's doubts and hesitations. On July 21 he wrote to de Haas, his honorary secretary in London: "There is only one reply to this situation: let us organize our masses immediately." The next day he turned to the Russian Jewish students in Paris: "The word is not yet, 'Forward march;' I only say, 'Youth, attention!' (*Jeunesse, debout*)!"

And a week later he wrote to Wolffsohn: "The day after tomorrow I shall be in Vienna and will call our chief men together for a conference in which the first point will be the early convening of a Zionist Congress ... My answer to Rothschild is, begin organizing at once." He sent similar letters to his correspondents in Sofia, Vienna, Paris, London. Day after day the call went out: Organize the masses, organize our followers!

The "organization of the masses" as Herzl had it in mind at the moment did not actually mean the creation of a movement. All he sought was the organization of the cadres, which would accustom the masses to the idea of discipline and prepare for the great migration. At the same time he wanted to prove that such organization was possible, and thereby exercise pressure on the rich. In reality it did not matter what his ultimate intentions were: his action initiated the movement which in turn exerted a decisive influence on the leaders. Thus the breaking up of negotiations with Rothschild may be designated as the beginning of the new Zionist movement.

The first step was the organization of his followers in Vienna. The Zionist Society of that city was, in its existing state, futile. It had neither life, nor money, nor even as much as a decent hall for its meetings. Its few faithful and reliable members — graduates of the *Kadimah*, like the physician Dr. Schnirer, the lawyer Dr. Kokesch, the two engineers Kremenezky and Seidener, the Galician Shakesperian scholar Leon Kellner, Herzl's relative Löbl, the stockbroker from Semlin, and a few others — gathered every Tuesday evening, without any action resulting. Now Herzl attended these meetings regularly. The little circle became the initial cell of the organization, its "Actions Committee." At the beginning of September, Herzl was officially installed as the leader of this circle, the head of the organization in the making. The first battalion had been formed.

In other countries, too, in England, Germany, Galicia, Bulgaria, the first cells were crystallizing. Toward the middle of September, Herzl received, among others of its kind, an enthusiastic memorial from Jerusalem signed by the director of the Lämel School, Ephraim Cohn, the Hebraist David Yellin, Eliezer ben Yehuda and Wilhelm Gross. Representatives of Russian Zionism wrote Herzl that they "accepted with enthusiasm the basic idea" of his pamphlet. In October 1896, the *Hoveve Zion* of Johannesburg (South Africa) added their approval.

Now Herzl came out of his reserve, and on November 8 for the first time addressed an open meeting in Vienna, accepting at last the frequently repeated invitation of the Austrian Union of Israelites, a middle-class anti-Zionist organization. What is noteworthy about this address is that in it Herzl referred to his predecessors, among whom he named Montefiore, Rothschild and Hirsch; nor did the word *Judenstaat* occur in this or in most of his public utterances of that time. He had by no means given up his plan in all its essential points. But his negotiations had made him more cautious, and he avoided those expressions which would irritate his opponents or prejudice his political work in Constantinople.

The speech was received with applause by the large audience, but it would have accorded the same applause and interest to the speech of any other well-known personality. And there is no doubt that Herzl was by now well known, even popular. Jokes and anecdotes were already current about him, he aroused amazement, and in some circles admiration and reverence. But he was making no progress to speak of either in his external politics or among the Jews.

Early in September he was sent by the *Neue Freie Presse* to Görlitz and Breslau to attend the manoeuvres, at which the Kaiser was also present. He was therefore able to observe the ruler of Germany fairly closely, but in spite of Hechler's efforts could not get to him personally. Equally futile were the efforts being made in England to obtain an interview for him with Prime Minister Salisbury. At the end of September, Prime Minister Badeni renewed his offer to Herzl, and sought his cooperation in the founding of a great daily. It was a brilliant opportunity, since Herzl's condition precedent, namely, the backing of Zionism by the Austrian government, was not turned down. But in spite of tremendous exertions Herzl could not create the funds for the newspaper; one reason may have been that he was over-sensitive in money matters and did not understand how to engage the practical interests of the big givers.

A painful incident added to his distress. An official of the Austrian foreign office spread the statement that Herzl had demanded and received a subvention of £3,000 for the *Neue Freie Presse* during his visit to Constantinople. To combat the unpleasant rumors thus set afloat, the *Neue Freie Presse* published sharp editorials advocating the partition of Turkey. This was of course a setback for Herzl. Even so he could make no progress in Constantinople. The Armenian massacres had aroused world opinion against Turkey, making Herzl's position more difficult than ever. Toward the end of January 1897, a new financial arrangement among the creditors relieved the immediate pressure on Turkey, so that this basis of negotiations, too, was destroyed. Nevlinski was disappointed in Herzl because of

his failure to start the newspaper and because of the mounting opposition among the Jews. Herzl had several conversations with the Turkish Ambassador to Vienna, but they were
pointless, helpless, irrelevant and politically valueless.

It was no better in the Jewish field. His negative attitude
toward the policy of infiltration, expressed so sharply in
London, strengthened the opposition to him among the
Hoveve Zion. From Paris, Zadoc Kahn wrote that the
directors of the Hirsch Fund were less than cool toward
Herzl's plans; he would do well therefore to let the matter
rest for the time being.

He encountered resistance on every hand, and very little
practical assistance even from among his most faithful
followers. His spirits sank from day to day. "If it should
come to a point where the Zionists fight me," he wrote to
Wolffsohn, "then I give the whole thing up. For the Jews
do not deserve that I should go to pieces trying to help
them." That was in August 1896. Toward the end of
October he expressed himself even more drastically to his
Hebrew secretary Berkowitz, after the latter had read out
to him a violent article which had appeared in *Hazefirah*.
He was fed up, he said, with the struggle against lies and
meannesses; he wanted to have nothing more to do with the
whole business. These were momentary outbursts. But in
his diary, too, similar expressions of despair became more
numerous. Then weeks passed without a single entry.
On January 18, 1897, he wrote bitterly to Wolffsohn: "People
look down from their window balcony and watch my work
with the liveliest interest." And again in his diary: "I feel
myself growing exhausted. The belief recurs to me much
more frequently now that my movement has come to an end.

I am still completely convinced of its practicability but I cannot overcome the initial difficulties."

As far back as March 1896, his doctor told him that his heart had been affected by the excitement which had attended the creation of the *Judenstaat*, and even more by his frequent clashes with the publishers of the *Neue Freie Presse*. This may have contributed to his growing depression, which at the beginning of 1897 actually filled him with thoughts of death. On February 12 he wrote a "literary testament:" "It is proper to be prepared for the end. I do not want to use empty phrases. What I was for the Jews the future generation will judge better than the contemporaneous masses ... My name will grow after my death ... I am conscious today, as I have always been, that I have used my pen like a man of honor. I have never sold my pen, never used it to mean ends, never even made it an instrument for the promotion of friendships. This last testament may be published."

He looked death in the face, and like the host in his philosophic story, *Das Wirtshaus zum Anilin*, who needed only to be confronted by death in order to feel a tremendous call to life issuing from his uncompleted task, Herzl recoiled in a sudden access of utmost resolution. If he had felt till now that the empty applause and the inactivity of others had called him to the leadership, now his will asserted itself to give his leadership an affirmative foundation. From this time on he is the real leader. A new characteristic, or one that had been dormant in him till now, emerged mightily — will. The time of stagnation and depression was over.

Ever since the failure of his attempt to win over Baron Rothschild, the idea of a "General Zionist Conference" had been ripening in Herzl. Such a Conference would be a sort of review of the forces at his disposal and an indication of the readiness of the people to accept the migration. There, also, the Zionists of all countries would assemble for united action. The idea of the conference was also in part a consequence of his failure to create a great organ of publicity for the popularization of his plan. The journalistic method was closer to Herzl; since it could not be applied, he would use a Congress in order to place his solution of the Jewish problem before world opinion.

It so happened that his recurrent efforts to found a great daily initiated the first active step toward the realization of the Congress idea. The report of Herzl's plan for a newspaper had reached Berlin. Since the beginning of the 'nineties there had existed in that city a small group of men interested in the Palestine work. Among them were Hirsch Hildesheimer and the clever and gifted Willy Bambus, whose approach to the problem was that of pure philanthropy. There was another and smaller circle made up of Leo Motzkin's Society of Russian Jewish Students and Heinrich Loewe's Young Israel, which was occupied with the broader aspects of the Zionist idea and which had even made some unsuccessful attempts before Herzl's time to call together a Zionist Congress. This latter group was now drawing closer and closer to Herzl, especially encouraged in this by Wolffsohn and Bodenheimer.

On January 24, 1897, Willy Bambus and Theodore Zlocisti addressed a letter to Herzl. They had heard from the Berlin Zionist, Dr. Holzmann, on his return from a visit to Vienna, that Dr. Herzl was prepared to meet with the Berlin Zionists in order to discuss all differences of outlook which might exist between him and them, and to cooperate in the carrying out of any plan of action which they might agree upon. Dr. Holzmann had mentioned, as projects of immediate interest, the founding of an agrarian bank in Palestine and the transformation of the monthly publication *Zion* into a multi-lingual organ.

In his reply of January 27, 1897, Herzl stressed his desire for an understanding: "There can be really nothing more than shades of difference in our opinions." He was quite sure that at the General Zionist Conference which he planned to hold in Zurich, they would come to a closer understanding. The bank project he considered sound but premature. It had to be preceded by propaganda, but he considered a monthly journal as inadequate. Attempts should be made to win over the right forces for the founding of a great daily. "Until now Zionism has been dumb. We must loosen its tongue. That is the first task. When it has been fulfilled everything will be easier, will even move of itself." Bambus did not or would not understand this cautious allusion to their differences. He replied that the public agitation, the necessity of which he fully recognized, had already been carried so far by the years of practical work that a certain advance could now be based on it. A great daily newspaper could hardly be expected. But the successful colonization work, small though its scope, had already provided the basis for a reasonable amount of propaganda, and he hoped to obtain Herzl's cooperation in this positive activity.

At this point Bambus received a communication from the Galician Zionist leader, Dr. Salz, to the effect that a certain person had pledged himself to contribute 300,000 gulden for a newspaper if the remaining 700,000 could be raised elsewhere. This was a great practical project which stirred the imagination of the Berlin group. The young theologian Josias Thon at once advised Herzl, and proposed a conference in Breslau. Herzl was soon satisfied of the seriousness of the offer, but could not get away to Breslau. There-upon Thon, Bambus and Birnbaum called the conference in Vienna, for March 6 and 7.

There were present, in addition, some of the members of the Vienna circle (Kremenezky, Kellner, Kokesch, York-Steiner), Dr. Salz of Tarnow, Rabbi Ehrenpreis of Diakovar, M. Moses of Kattowitz and N. Turov of Breslau. Herzl's personality captivated the newcomers at once, even though, in Jewish knowledge, they were all superior to him. In the sessions, the main subject was — the newspaper. Bambus and Herzl, the two most dynamic men present, tried to find their way to each other, and they managed, superficially at least, to overcome the differences which divided them. Herzl's proposal that a general Zionist Congress be called was adopted, with the reservation that the consent and cooperation of the Russians be obtained. The city of Munich was chosen for the Congress.

It soon became evident that the "understanding" between Herzl and Bambus had been more apparent than real; each of them had believed that he had convinced the other, and neither had yielded anything of his own views. What Herzl was aiming at was a "World Congress of Zionists;" and in a "Preliminary Announcement" he communicated the plan to a number of journalists and prominent individuals. Bambus wanted to avoid the compromising word "Zionist" and merely to call a "Conference of pro-Palestine Societies." For the latter the primary consideration was the practical work, which seemed to him much more important than "the Zionist dreams of the future." The last were good in their way, but ought not to be discussed publicly, lest they frighten off the non-Zionist philanthropists who were helping Palestine. But it was just this public discussion of the Jewish question which meant everything to Herzl. The combating of the philanthropic concept of Jewish self-help was of the essence of his ideas. "The Jewish question," he said in his preliminary announcement, "must be taken away from the control of the benevolent individual. There must be created a forum, before which everyone acting for the Jewish people must appear and to which he must be responsible." He wanted a "national assembly," a parliament, which should meet at stated intervals, and which should, between its meetings, entrust to an elected council the direction of Jewish affairs. The Jewish people was to become articulate, was to address itself to the world and formulate its needs and demands.

There were to be reports on the condition of world Jewry, with an opening review by Max Nordau; he himself was to give an account of his actions, and deliver an address on "The Jewish Question and the Next Diplomatic Council of the Powers." The Congress itself was to be preceded by mass petitions of the Jews describing the state of need among them, and their readiness to migrate.

A contrast like this between Herzl's and Bambus's concept of the Congress was bound to lead to a conflict. Bambus published, in the *Allgemeine Zeitung des Judenthums*, a declaration deprecating the aims of Herzl's "Preliminary Announcement." The name and form and aims of the Congress, he declared, had not yet been decided on; everything was in the preparatory stage. When Herzl, in response, reiterated his intentions, Hildesheimer published a sharp rebuttal and dissociated himself from the enterprise — at least in Herzl's form. Hildesheimer too had envisaged "nothing more than a general discussion of the immediate tasks confronting the Palestine funds." He had not consented "to discussions of the future plans and hopes of Zionism which could only serve to hinder and compromise the practical and realizable aims of the movement." Bambus also withdrew officially from the arrangements committee; his reasons, like Hildesheimer's, may have revealed a paucity of faith and imagination, but they were sincere and sprang from a genuine feeling of responsibility. Herzl, on his side, was bound to counter-attack, the more so as he considered the methods "unfair" — though he did not for a moment doubt the honorable intentions of his opponents. In a letter to Hildesheimer, which the latter was asked to publish in his *Jüdische Presse*, Herzl declared: "The Congress will take place. That is all that matters."

"The Congress will take place!" This was the slogan which Herzl launched and reiterated with increasing emphasis in the weeks and months that followed. His resolution grew stronger as the attacks upon him increased in number and vigor. For now his opponents threw off all restraint. The opposition which he had encountered till now was like a quiet prelude to the ferocity of the general assault. What? they asked. Was this man mad, to be calling together a Jewish Congress to discuss the Jewish problem in the presence and hearing of the whole world, to publish openly the view that the Jews were not just a religious community, but a people? Was not this what the anti-Semites had been waiting for? As long as Herzl had confined himself to writing and to private effort, there had been the hope that he could be ignored into oblivion. Now that he was pushing the fight into the public arena, there was nothing for it but to declare open war on him.

Dr. Adler, Chief Rabbi of the Ashkenazi community of Great Britain, led the attack. Herzl alluded to him sarcastically as "a man who came from Germany to England and who would undoubtedly like to think of himself as a descendant of the Anglo-Saxons." Dr. Adler was followed in mid-April by Dr. Güdemann, Chief Rabbi of Vienna, who in a pamphlet entitled *National Judaism* exposed the irreconcilability of the national idea with the Jewish religion, and attacked Herzl without mentioning him by name. What? Our old friend Dr. Güdemann? He who had been the first to give his blessing to Herzl's plan, had seen the new Moses in him, and had kissed him in sign of his love and reverence? None other. But his doubts had begun to set in the very day after the reading of the *Address to the Rothschilds*. And yet, when Herzl had sent him the galleys of *Der Judenstaat*, he had written back: "I have read it all and find absolutely nothing to object to." He had encouraged Herzl, he had sent in his suggestions for little improvements in the text, and he had spoken with the highest enthusiasm of the work and its author. Apparently Güdemann had forgotten that Herzl was a gifted writer, and that he wielded his pen with the deadly skill of a great duellist. Herzl replied; in restrained, brief sentences he alluded to Güdemann's original attitude. He spoke ironically of the changes that had taken place; these, of course, could be due only to spiritual reasons. "For it goes without saying that the Chief Rabbi of Vienna is so independent that there can be no conceivable external reason why he should take up the cause of the rich against the poor." He indicated the contradictions in Güdemann's arguments and refuted him with his own phrases. And then, the "Mission!" "We must not," wrote Herzl, "confuse this application of the word with that given to it in speaking of those poor monks who set forth for the wild places of the world to carry the Christian gospel to cannibalistic tribes. The Jewish 'Mission' is something sated, comfortable and well-to-do. For years now I have been observing the people who retort with 'Israel's Mission' whenever I come to talk to them about the wretchedness of the Jewish poor. These missionaries are all excellently situated." And how was this revaluation of the symbolism of the Return, so frequently mentioned in Jewish prayer, to be understood? "Why, whenever the Return to Zion is spoken, the very opposite is to be read into it."

It was from the liberal rabbis, "the soul-shepherds," that Herzl, in his naive ignorance of Jewish reality, had expected the first call to action after his. It was the liberal rabbinate which was fiercest in its attack.

The Jewish Community of Munich protested openly and officially against the holding of the Congress in that city. The Congress was moved to Basle. The battle raged on. In July 1897, the executive of the Federation of Rabbis published a statement in the *Berliner Tageblatt* and other leading newspapers. It protested against the "nonsensical distortion of the meaning of Judaism and of the ideals of the confessors of the Jewish faith" as implied in "the calling of the Zionist Congress and in its published agenda." The aims of "the so-called Zionists" contradicted the "prophetic message of Jewry and the duty of every Jew to belong without reservation to the fatherland in which he lives." "Religion and love of the fatherland, no less than our regard for the welfare of Judaism, lay upon us the duty to repudiate the aims of Zionism and to ignore the call to the Congress."

The Congress document was an unworthy, cowardly con-.
coction "one of those contemptible utterances which play
into the hands of our enemies."

The author of the denunciation, Rabbi Maybaum, and
his co-signers, were soon to regret its publication. Herzl's
reply was devastating. He began by pointing out that those
who did not feel that they belonged to a Jewish people had
no business to interfere in its affairs. "To belong to Jewry,
to exploit this relationship as it were professionally, and to
fight it at the same time" was something monstrous. For
"Zionism is not a party. Jews of every party can enroll in
the movement, just as the people contains within itself all
parties. Zionism is the Jewish people on the march."

Thus, in every counter-attack which he launched, Herzl
found new and deeper formulations of his purpose. He
became increasingly sharper, even though his language continued to be moderate and restrained. "When they speak of
Zion," he wrote, "they mean, in God's name, anything but
Zion." Fortunately the Rabbinate was not unanimous in
this view. There were rabbis like the venerable Mohilever
of Bialystock, Zadoc Kahn of Paris, Rülf of Memel and
Gaster of London, who placed themselves at the service of
the national idea. In order that the latter might not be
confused with the former, Herzl coined for these the name of
"Protest Rabbis."

For the publication of the article on the "Protest Rabbis"
Herzl was no longer dependent on the uncertain hospitality
of Bloch's *Oesterreichische Wochenschrift*. After taking counsel
with his father, whom he always consulted on such matters,
Herzl decided to put his own money into a weekly publication for the defense and propagation of his ideal. The name
on the masthead was *Die Welt*, and between the two words

appeared a Shield of David across which ran the outline of
the coast of Palestine. The design was York-Steiner's. Herzl
threw himself into the launching of the publication with
the feverish intensity of creative inspiration. He attended
to the minutest details. On June 4, 1897, the first issue
appeared.

Yellow had been the color of shame for the Jews of the
Middle Ages: yellow was the color chosen for the covers of
Die Welt, so that what had been the badge of shame should
become the badge of honor. *Die Welt* was to be a free organ
of expression, its columns open even to criticism of the movement, and to the exposure of that which was shameful in Jewish life. It would report on past events, it would anticipate
the future of the people. "And between memory and hope
stands the deed ... *Die Welt* is to be the instrument of
those men who are leading Judaism out of our times into
happier times to come."

It was a high promise, and Herzl kept it. The journal
was something utterly new in Jewish life. It was, in fact,
the preliminary trumpet-peal of the Congress. Particular
attention was given to the contributions made to the movement by the predecessors of the new Zionist movement and
to expressions of opinion on Zionism by the leading personalities of the time. Herzl wrote innumerable letters to prospective contributors. At first he himself contributed numerous articles; he wrote on the Congress; he critically analyzed
Leroy-Beaulieu's book on anti-Semitism; he was responsible
for many shorter unsigned articles and notices. He contributed a regular weekly review of all activities connected
with the movement, whether directly or indirectly. His
comments were cool, moderate in form, but always clear and
direct in their ideological content. He directed the paper in

all its details, though he refused to figure as its official editor and publisher. His open association with *Die Welt* would have meant a break with the *Neue Freie Presse*.

As it was, his activities led to constant clashes with the daily which provided him not less with his public position than with his livelihood. It was a difficult situation for the *Neue Freie Presse*, as well as for Herzl. Its publishers were responsible for what was publicly referred to as a "Jew-paper." Opponents of the Zionist movement, they were identified by the anti-Semites with *Die Welt* and its program. But Herzl stood firm — whatever was happening in his heart. He saw the threat to his position; he did not let it interfere with his furious activities for *Die Welt* and the Congress.

The amount of work he did during the months preceding the Congress was utterly fantastic. A participant in the preliminary conference reported later: "We took counsel, we laid our plans, formulated our resolutions, and returned to our regular occupations. But the Congress was made by Herzl alone, it was his money and his labor which brought it into being." The man of the pen was suddenly revealed as a first-class man of action. He worked without surcease, he encouraged, admonished, pleaded, persuaded, threatened and fought. He wrote to every country calling for the election of representatives to the Congress. He refused to be disheartened by the fact that the *Hoveve Zion* in England and France would have nothing to do with the Congress, and that sections of the Russian *Hoveve Zion* worked against it. New attacks were launched against him, he became the target of an unceasing campaign of ridicule, accusations, rumors of all sorts. He listened, and he caught the sound of a gathering force; the movement was progressing in

Bulgaria, in Roumania and even in Russia, where the government censorship made open participation in his plans impossible. He had become nothing but work and will. He had written, once, that he was doing the work only because it was streaming out of him from within. Now he scribbled down: "The greatest happiness is to be that which one is."

It was granted him to see the effect of his labor; he did not die on the day of fulfilment, like Faust. On August 29, 1897, the first Zionist Congress assembled in Basle.

CHAPTER VII

THE FIRST ZIONIST CONGRESS

ON AUGUST 25 Herzl arrived in Basle to superintend the completion of the office which had been opened at the beginning of the month. He knew that in the preparation of this first public appearance of the Jewish people in the world's political arena, every detail counted. A participant in that preliminary work reported in later years: "The whole world outside of the Congress had actually ceased to exist for him. He gave his attention to all the minutiae of the work. He let nothing slip past him. He issued the instructions, and supervised the carrying out of the instructions. And all this in a gentle voice, with a friendly smile, and yet so categorically that it simply occurred to no one to disobey or contradict."

The development of the last few months had placed upon his shoulders the entire responsibility, so that the weight of it threatened to crush him. He relied only on himself, his glance was turned inward, he followed his instinct, his insights and his sense of duty. But he also demanded implicit execution of his orders. This corresponded to his nature; it corresponded also to his concept of the state whose foundations he was trying to lay during those days.

He was, in fact, the only one who knew what he was aiming at through the Congress. The majority of the participants in the Congress were guided by mood rather than insight.

There was a vague feeling of great things about to happen, a union of all the friends of Palestine, a unification of the Jewish people. Perhaps this strange man from Vienna, who could speak and write so mysteriously, was prepared with a revelation of great diplomatic successes, only dimly suspected by others. But hope was also mixed with grave concern. Professor Shapira of Heidelberg, a man advanced in years, was forever admonishing Bodenheimer to moderate his utterances, lest the masses be further divided and the Palestine work run into new obstacles. The responsible leaders of the *Hoveve Zion* shared his concern. The Russians had a difficult problem of their own; they were afraid that incautious utterances emanating from the Congress would be taken up by the Russian government, with disastrous consequences for the Jews of that country. There was also the fear of a setback for the colonies in Palestine through the alienation of Baron Rothschild. At a preliminary conference held by the Russian leaders in Karlsbad on July 28, all these considerations came into the open.

Stiassny of Vienna and J. Kremenezky were delegated to confer with Herzl and to see to it that "the names of Rothschild and Russia should not be mentioned in the public statements of the Congress." Herzl gave them satisfactory assurances. There were individuals, like Bambus, who, having failed in their efforts to prevent the Congress from convening, came in order to save what could still be saved. And until the last day no one really knew how many delegates there would be, what kind of people they were, and whether they could be welded together into an instrument of common declaration of purpose and action. Only a few days before his departure for the Congress, Herzl noted mercilessly in his diary: "The fact is that I have only an army of *schnorrers.* I stand at the head of a mass of youths, beggars and jackasses."

He saw all the difficulties clearly. He had to go forward, and at the same time take into consideration the most extraordinary diversity of interests and viewpoints. He had to avoid offending the orthodox Jews; but he also had to keep the peace with the free-thinking Jews. He had to take into account the patriotic sentiments of assimilationists and half-assimilationists, whose support he would like to win; he also had to bear in mind the views of the Christian Churches with regard to the Holy Places. And in all this he had to stand by his principles if he was not to compromise his aims. His natural moderation and self-control were put to the utmost test. It may be said that the difficult task could not have been carried out more skilfully than it was.

Two days before the opening of the Congress he presided over a preliminary conference attended by a large number of delegates, most of them from Germany and Austria. Its task was to determine on the proceedings and agenda of the Congress. There was agreement on the general outlines to be followed, but for the formulation of the program of aims to be accepted by the Congress a separate commission was appointed. Its members were Nordau, Siegmund Mintz, Shapira, Siegmund Bromberg, Birnbaum and S. R. Landau.

The delegates began to arrive several days before the date set for the opening. Every train brought new ones, from Russia, from Germany, from Austria-Hungary, from Bulgaria and Roumania, from England and Holland and Belgium, from Palestine, from the Scandinavian countries, from America and Algeria. There were veteran leaders of the *Hoveve Zion* and recent converts to the movement; there were orthodox Jews and atheists, well-to-do members of the middle classes and representatives of the socialist movement, white-haired septuagenarians and young students. Many came out of sheer curiosity, others as opponents. The total number of the delegates on the opening day was one hundred and ninety-seven.

The majority of them saw Herzl for the first time. Until then they had only heard of him, or had read his articles and his appeals for the election of delegates. In these latter he had drilled into their minds the necessity of imparting to the Congress, by the representative character of its delegates, by the weightiness of its deliberations, a dignity which would make a lasting impression on the world at large. "This Congress," he had instructed them, "is to be the great council which must and will be followed by greater acts."

His call to pride and dignity, his double invocation of a glorious past and a more glorious future, was repeated in all the details of his preparations. The delegates' cards carried the two-fold symbol of the ancient Wailing Wall and of the new Jewry of modern Palestine. Over the portals of the Casino which Herzl had designated for the sessions, a large sign displayed the Star of Zion and the word: ZIONISTEN-KONGRESS. At one side hung a flag: a white field with two blue stripes and the Star of David. Wolffsohn, clever, practical and steeped in tradition, had chosen the colors of the *tallit*, or prayer-shawl, and the majority of the delegates actually took it for granted that this was the old Jewish flag.

The deliberations took place in a dignified concert hall with grey, unadorned walls. "The long green table on the platform, with the raised seat of the President, the green decorations, the table for the journalists and stenographers" made a striking picture, and Herzl notes that he himself was deeply impressed when he went to the back of the hall at a moment when Nordau was presiding and glanced over the scene. How much deeper must have been the impression on the delegates, whose sensitivity had not been dulled by participation in the preparations. To emphasize the solemnity of the occasion, Herzl had prescribed — and it was printed on the delegates' cards — that every delegate must wear a frock coat and a white tie. "The people must accustom themselves to associating the Congress with everything that is festive and dignified," he told Nordau, when the latter came in an ordinary suit of clothes and was persuaded to go back to his hotel and put on the official uniform. There were of course some who laughed at all these externalities, and cracked jokes about Herzl's theatrical experiences and impulses. Yet behind the instructions lay something deeper than the mockers understood. Something was needed to symbolize for the delegates the break with the ordinary, the proclamation of the something great and beautiful in the dream which had brought them together.

On Sunday, August 29, 1897, the delegates assembled in this hall for the first time. The galleries were crowded with visitors, most of them Jews and Christians of Basle, who did not want to miss the spectacle of a "Jewish Congress." Herzl had also invited, as his and the Congress's guests, the Reverend Hechler, Lieutenant-Colonel Bentinck of London, and Baron Manteuffel of St. Michele, Christian Zionists to whom he wanted to show the nation in the making. The leading Jewish and non-Jewish newspapers had sent their reporters. There were represented the *London Times*, the *London Daily News*, the *London Daily Mail*, the *New York Herald*, the *Frankfurter Zeitung*, the *Kölnische Zeitung*, *l'Echo de Paris*, the *Pester Lloyd*, the *Jewish World*, the *Jewish Chronicle*, the Hebrew newspapers and the Swiss dailies: proof sufficient of the thoroughness with which the event had been prepared in spite of the lack of time. The delegates were filled with a festive mood, a mixture of suppressed joy and painful hope. The world about them had melted away. There was a tense silence.

Three taps of the gavel opened the Congress.

The dean of the Praesidium, Dr. Lippe of Jassy, a *Hovev Zion* since the time of the founding of the first colony in Palestine, covered his head, and amid the tears of many of the listeners, uttered the prayer *Sheheheyanu*: "Blessed art Thou, O Lord our God, King of the Universe, who hast kept us alive and brought us to witness this day."

Then he passed on to the business of the opening session, and moved that a resolution of thanks and devotion be sent to the Sultan of Turkey. It was Herzl who had called for this gesture of friendliness. But many of the delegates read into it a great deal more than it actually implied.

Then Herzl rose and, calm, completely self-possessed, erect, walked over to the tribune, the focus of attention. "It was extraordinary! What had happened? This was not the Dr. Herzl I had seen hitherto, and with whom I was in discussion as recently as last night. Before us rose a marvelous and exalted figure, kingly in bearing and stature, with deep eyes in which could be read quiet majesty and unuttered sorrow. It is no longer the elegant Dr. Herzl of Vienna; it is a royal scion of the House of David, risen from among the dead, clothed in legend and fantasy and beauty. Everyone sat breathless, as if in the presence of a miracle. And in truth, was it not a miracle which we beheld? And then wild applause broke out; for fifteen minutes the delegates clapped, shouted and waved their handkerchiefs. The dream of two thousand years was on the point of realization; it was as if the Messiah, son of David, confronted us; and I was seized by an overpowering desire, in the midst of this storm of joy, to cry out, loudly, for all to hear: '*Yehi hamelech*!' Hail to the King!" These are the impressions set down by Ben Ami, the *Hovev Zion* and Hebrew writer.

Others were overcome by similar feelings. Zangwill compared him with some king of ancient Assyria. There was felt, streaming out from him, something majestic and mysterious, which cast a charm over all. It was not just the physical beauty and stature of the man, now in their prime. Those who beheld him were aware of wells of strength opening within them; it was from within themselves that the princeliness of the leader derived its overpowering strength. Gratitude, admiration and hope were in the applause which greeted him like a storm.

In the midst of this reception Herzl remained externally calm. He knew that at this moment every response, every gesture, had symbolic significance. Pale with excitement, neither bowing nor making any other acknowledgement of the demonstration, self-controlled, erect, he stood on the tribune until the applause had subsided. Then he read out his opening address.

Without loss of words he set forth, in a single sentence, the task of the Congress: "We are here to lay the foundation stone of the house which is to shelter the Jewish nation." The community of destiny of the Jewish people had long been shattered, even though a community of suffering had been its lot everywhere. It was only now that "the wonders of modern methods of communication" had made possible a bringing together of the divided and dispersed. "In this epoch, in other respects one of such high achievement," the

Jews were everywhere surrounded by the ancient Jew-hatred in modern form — anti-Semitism. It had hit hardest just those Jewish elements which it had probably not wanted to reach primarily: "The modern, educated, de-ghetto-ized Jew, who felt himself stabbed to the heart. Today we can say this calmly, without being suspected of making a play for the tearful compassion of our enemies. Our conscience is clear. The world has always been badly misinformed about us. The feeling of unity among us, which the world so often and so bitterly throws up to us, was in process of dissolution when the tide of anti-Semitism rose about us. Anti-Semitism has given us our strength again. We have returned home." Then came the sentence which has been so long and so widely discussed, and to which we shall have to return in another connection: "Zionism is the return of the Jews to Judaism even before their return to the Jewish land."

Zionism, he went on, had already brought about that which till then had been considered impossible: the uniting of the most modern with the most conservative elements, without unworthy spiritual and intellectual compromises on either side. The basis of unification was the recognition of the fact that the Jews were a people. At this point counsel was to be taken on the formation of a strong organization. "The organization is the evidence of the common sense of a movement." But immediately Herzl, taking cognizance of the fears which such a declaration might rouse, explained that this was not to be looked upon as an international organization like that of Social Democracy, the terror of the middle classes and of all governments. "We Zionists," he stressed, "seek, for the solution of the Jewish question, not an international society, but international discussion . . . We have nothing to do with conspiracy, secret intervention or indirect methods. We wish to put the question in the arena and under the control of free public opinion."

There were numerous facets and approaches to the work of promoting the movement. The Congress would therefore occupy itself with "the spiritual means of reviving and nursing the Jewish national consciousness." But, even more than its spiritual, the physical condition of the Jews called for attention. The recognition of this fact "had also moved the predecessors of present-day Zionism to attempt the creation of an agricultural class among the Jews." "Concerning the colonization efforts in the Argentine and in Palestine we shall never speak except in terms of the most genuine gratitude. But these were the opening, and not the closing words of the Zionist movement. This movement must become greater, if it is to be at all. A people can be helped only by itself; and if it cannot do that, then it cannot be helped. We Zionists seek to awaken the Jewish people everywhere to self-help."

It was not through the continuation of the old, slow colonization methods, with no basis of legal recognition, that the Jewish problem was to be solved. The form which an agreement guaranteeing this recognition to the Jews would take, was a matter for future negotiation. This much had to be set down as an indispensible condition precedent: "The basis can be only that of recognized right, and not of sufferance. We have had our fill of experience with toleration and with the protected Jew. Our movement can be logical and consistent only in so far as it aims at the acquisition of a publicly recognized legal guarantee."

"All this my friends and I have repeated over and over again, and we shall not tire of repeating it until we are everywhere understood ... On this occasion too, which witnesses the bringing together of Jews from so many scattered lands in reponse to the ancient call of the nation, we shall repeat it. Must we not feel, hanging over us, the intimation of great things to come, when we reflect on the hundreds of thousands of Jews whose eyes are now fixed on us in hope and expectation? Within a few hours the results of our common counsel will be carried to the ends of the earth. It is therefore our duty to send forth a message of clarification and reassurance ... That which the individual says or writes may pass unnoticed, but not that which issues from this Congress ...

"And finally, it is the duty of this Congress to see to it that when its sessions have come to an end, we do not relapse into our previous condition of disorganization. We must create here and now an organ, a permanent organ, which the Jewish people has lacked till now. The enterprise is greater than the ambition or wilfulness of any individual. If it is to succeed at all, it must rise to a level of high impersonality. And our Congress shall endure far into the future, not only until the day when our need has been met, but far beyond — perhaps then more than ever. Today we meet on the soil of this friendly nation. Where shall we be a year from now?"

This address, the first which Herzl delivered as it were before the world at large, contains no ideas which he had not already expressed in previous speeches and articles. The same ideas were offered in concentrated form. Some of them were given greater weight, some were passed over rather lightly, for there was ever present in his mind the impression they would make on the non-Jewish as well as the Jewish world. What a difference between the *Judenstaat* and this speech! Not in the aim, but in the cautiousness of utterance. In the first you still feel, radiating from every sentence, the heat of the great eruption. It is full of devastating criticism, it glows with the colors of the dream of original inspiration, it is wild with the unrestrained vision of the seer. The second is the carefully considered public statement of one who knew he represented tens of thousands, perhaps hundreds of thousands, of followers. Not only experience had filled the intervening years, but the acquisition of a following which laid upon him new responsibilities. His words had to be those not of a seer but of a statesman. And to be a Jewish statesman was in its own way a prophetic fulfilment; for since the dispersion there had been no Jewish statesmen; there had been only English or French or German statesmen of Jewish birth.

Almost as profound was the effect produced by Nordau's speech. He too came from an alien world; he had moved so far from Judaism that he had actually changed his name, from Südfeld to Nordau. His European and world reputation was far greater than Herzl's. In addition he was incomparably the superior orator. He spoke freely, only referring to notes now and again. A clear-sighted spirit was his, an explosive temperament, an incorruptible love of truth. Herzl was the prince and statesman of the Congress; Nordau was the expression of its passion.

But whatever the surface appearances, there was no comparison at all between the two men when it came to originality of spiritual insight. Nordau's speech was built, ideologically, on foundations supplied by Herzl; but with his superiority in systematization and organization he made the superstructure more imposing and all-embracing. His address, "The General Picture of the Condition of Jewry at the Close of the Nineteenth Century," did more than grip the audience to which it was addressed, and their contemporaries who read it in the public prints. It remained, as Herzl foresaw it would, a permanent memorial of that time.

Herzl's and Nordau's addresses were the two highlights of the Congress. They were placed on the same level by the delegates; or perhaps the advantage was with Nordau. The subsequent proceedings were to show that in leadership Herzl was first — without a second.

The Praesidium of the Congress had been elected, in accordance with the plan adopted at the preliminary conference, before Nordau delivered his address. Herzl was President, Nordau First Vice-President. Herzl's election was intended as an act of homage; he very soon showed that he was President of the Congress by virtue of something more. Not for nothing had he sat for four years in the Palais Bourbon, following with close and critical attention the conduct of a parliament. He presided gracefully — but he was always master of the situation; he had both a natural and a trained skill in the manipulation of debates. He always had the right word and gesture with which to smooth out the frictions which threatened to develop into dangerous clashes, or to eliminate the irrelevances which might lead to pointless delays. He knew what he wanted the Congress to do — and he saw that it was done.

After Nordau's address came the reports from the various countries. Only Russia was silent — and that silence was more instructive than any report. Then Nathan Birnbaum and David Farbstein, in supplementary addresses, dealt with the sociological and economic aspects of the movement.

The opening day was in the nature of a demonstration, the first of its kind in Jewish history for nearly two thousand years. For the first time in that millenial interval the scattered Jewish people had sent its representatives to a deliberative assembly of its own, symbolizing thereby its will to unification. The beginning of the second day strengthened the symbolism of the incident. Herzl reported that telegrams and letters had arrived from every part of the world, expressing the support and goodwill of the senders. The petitions or memorials from Galicia and Roumania alone carried six thousand signatures.

With this the demonstration was at an end. The practical tasks now called for attention.

Nordau had been entrusted by the Commission of the Preliminary Conference to formulate the program of the movement. The opening sentence of his report, and the most important in it, reads: "Zionism seeks to establish for the Jewish people a legally secured homeland (*Heimstätte*) in Palestine." The word *Heimstätte*, which falls short of the stronger word "state," was a compromise between Herzl's original intentions and the suggestions of Bodenheimer and others. It is a word which carries certain overtones of the philosophy of cultural Zionism. Nordau was responsible for the choice. Then a stormy debate developed. Motzkin and Fabius Schach of Cologne, speaking for the younger generation, demanded that for "legally secured" the phrase "secured by international law" be substituted. They and their supporters had long been disillusioned by the small-scale work and the narrow-spirited outlook of the *Hoveve Zion*, and they could not forget the tragic decline from the high ideals which Pinsker had represented. Would not the same decline ensue now, they asked, if from the very outset the new movement accepted so drastic a compromise? Nordau himself, like the other members of the Commission, also felt that only on the basis of international guarantees could a great colonization plan be developed; they had compromised on the weaker formulation for fear of offending the *Hoveve Zion* and of alarming the Turkish government. Herzl, participating in the debate, repeated the phrase he had chosen in his address — *öffentlich-rechtlich* — (the nearest English translation is: "publicly recognized, legally secured") and secured its adoption. This became, and has since remained, the official program of the Zionist movement, the so-called Basle Program. "Zionism seeks to secure for the Jewish people a publicly recognized, legally secured home (or homeland) in Palestine for the Jewish people." For the achievement of its purpose "the Congress envisages the following methods:

"1) The programmatic encouragement of the settlement of Palestine with Jewish agricultural workers, laborers and artisans (see page 271);

"2) The unification and organization of all Jewry into local and general groups in accordance with the laws of their respective countries;

"3) The strengthening of Jewish self-awareness and national consciousnessness (*Volksbewusstsein*);

"4) The preparation of activity for the obtaining of the consent of the various governments, necessary for the fulfilment of the aim of Zionism."

The program bears on its surface the evidences of the attempt to compromise between the various tendencies in the Zionist movement. Several points were formulated with admitted vagueness, and Herzl did his best to evade a clear interpretation. What seemed most important to him there and then was unity, and this he seemed to have achieved by the wording of the program.

The second important task was the creation of an organization. Here the difficulty consisted of the possible clash with the laws of the various countries: in many places membership in international organizations was forbidden by law. The Congress therefore had to content itself with the creation of a general framework; the integration of the various local bodies and the form of membership had to be left to each country. Herzl and Bodenheimer stressed the provisional character of the formulation. In actual fact the permanent organization was launched there and then, in its essential features, of which the foremost was, the principle of representation. The Congress was declared to be "the chief organ of the Zionist movement." The basis of electoral right was to be the payment of at least a *shekel* — which was taken at that time to be the equivalent of one German mark. The Congress was to elect an "Actions Committee," with its permanent seat in Vienna. Of its membership five were to be residents of Vienna, and these were to constitute the actual Executive (or, as it was then known, the Inner Actions Committee); the remainder were to be elected from the various national organizations.

Next followed the creation of specific instruments of action. Bodenheimer reported on the numerous plans which had been suggested, and proposed, amid general approval, the formation of a bank and of a National Fund. Professor Shapira had already proposed the latter in *Die Welt*, and he now urged the adoption of the plan. Schnirer proposed that no further immigration into Palestine be undertaken before the status of "legal security and public recognition" had been accorded to the aims of the movement; the existing colonies were to be looked upon and supported as "experimental stations." New ones were to be created only from the human material already available in Palestine, and should be of a cooperative character. To this compromise between his own views and those of the *Hoveve Zion* Herzl gave his assent and support both at the Congress and subsequently. Kaminka reported on the colonization work done till that time; Adam Rosenberg of New York spoke on general conditions in Palestine; all the speakers criticised the system of tutelage under which the colonies existed. Bambus defended the Paris Committee and the practical work. Heinrich Loewe, part of whose address was delivered in Hebrew, announced in enthusiastic terms the agreement of the Palestinians to the plans of the Congress, even when the plans ran counter to the immediate interests of the colonists. At the close of the debates, Marcus Ehrenpreis delivered an address on the Hebrew language and literature, and Professor Shapira demanded, at the very launching of the movement, the creation of a Hebrew University in Palestine. Everything that was to unfold later in Zionism, both in the way of affirmative forces and inner contradictions, was already visible or latent in the first assembly of Zionists.

The first and second day of demonstration and deliberation were marked by a spirit of exaltation. On the third day the mood had declined, but was lifted again when Rabbi Cohn of Basle, who until then had been an opponent of the movement, declared that some of the utterances he had listened to had made an unforgettable impression on him. Like all other orthodox rabbis he had been deeply concerned lest the upbuilding of the Jewish homeland result in a weakening of the religious spirit of Jewry, and in particular of the sanctity of the Sabbath. Herzl thanked him, and declared that Zionism envisaged no action "which might wound the religious susceptibilities of any group in Jewry."

The Congress was now drawing to a close. Professor Max Mandelstamm, one of the oldest delegates, asked for the floor. In a tremulous voice he thanked all those who had contributed toward the creation and success of the Congress. But above all he expressed his and everyone else's gratitude "to that courageous man who is primarily responsible for this gathering of Jews from all countries taking counsel on the future of our people." The delegates rose to their feet and shouts of loyalty and gratitude sounded in all languages. When the venerable speaker pleaded with them to prosecute the enterprise in the face of all discouragement and discomfort to a successful conclusion, a wave of enthusiasm and determination passed visibly over the assembly. The shouts of applause broke out again and Zangwill, the sceptic and critic, sprang on to one of the tables, applauding with all his strength.

It was in the midst of this outburst of joy and devotion that Herzl closed the Congress.

CHAPTER VIII

THE BUILDING OF THE ORGANIZATION

ON HIS return to Vienna Herzl made the following entry in his diary: "If I were to sum up the Basle Congress in a single phrase — which I would not dare to make public — I would say: In Basle I created the Jewish State. Were I to say this aloud I would be greeted by universal laughter. But perhaps five years hence, in any case, certainly fifty years hence, everyone will perceive it. The state exists as essence in the will-to-the-state of a people, yes, even in that will in a single powerful person ... The territory is only the concrete basis, and the state itself, with a territory beneath it, is still in the nature of an abstract thing ... In Basle I created the abstraction which, as such, is invisible to the great majority."

A few weeks later he stated publicly: "In order to achieve the homeland secured by international law we had first to present to the world the evidence of our existence as a people. If the people is there, then the piece of land which it needs comes of itself ..."

What was the great, the essential experience of those who had participated in the Congress? The realization that this people existed. It was an unhappy people which as a people had been declared dead. Here it had demonstrated not only its factual existence, but its ability to bring together its constituent fragments from the ends of the world, and to dedicate itself to a creative future. With this experience in their minds and hearts the participants had returned to their homes, to tell what they had seen and heard, to spread the vision and to win converts. The masses of east European Jewry received all this as the tidings of a happier time to come, and some were disappointed that the great exodus did not begin at once. From every part of the world Herzl received letters which expressed this hope, and he was touched deeply by the countless, pitiful expressions of a childlike faith in the early triumph of his cause.

Herzl's most important experience was, as he himself declared, the intimate contact which he had established with eastern Jewry. East Europe was till then a terra incognita to him; none of his early travels had taken him in that direction. He had known only of the existence of masses of the poor, an element which by its readiness for physical labor could be counted on to provide the pioneer foundation of the Jewish state. He had listened, with mingled doubt and amazement, to Wolffsohn's first accounts of a great spiritual leadership among the *Ost-Juden*. Later he had been shaken in his doubts by his first-hand observations. He had met Mandelstamm; Ussishkin had visited him in 1896. Even so, he had retained his general idea that the Russian Jews would have to depend on leaders coming from the west. "And then, at the Basle Congress, there rose before our eyes a Russian Jewry the strength of which we had not even suspected. Seventy of our delegates came from Russia, and it was patent to all of us that they represented the views and sentiments of the five million Jews of that country. And what a humiliation for us, who had taken our own superiority for granted! All these professors, doctors, lawyers, industrialists, engineers and merchants stand on an educational level which is certainly not lower than ours. Nearly all of them are masters of two or three languages, and that they are men of ability in their particular lines is proved by the simple fact that they have succeeded in a land where success is peculiarly difficult for Jews."

Yet not this was the essence of the discovery. What impressed him, the Westerner, most was the spiritual stature, the natural will and determination of these men. The former had won through to inner unity after a long struggle; for the latter it was, by comparison, something tacit and self-understood. "They possess," he summed it up, "that inner unity which has disappeared from among the westerners. They are steeped in Jewish national sentiment without betraying any national narrowness and intolerance — though, of course, these last would hardly be comprehensible in a Jew. They are not tortured by the idea of assimilation, their essential being is simple and unshattered. They do not assimilate into other nations, but they exert themselves to learn the best that there is in other peoples. In this wise they manage to remain erect and genuine. And yet they are ghetto-Jews! The only ghetto-Jews of our time! Looking on them, we understood where our forefathers got the strength to endure through the bitterest times."

If the impression which the Congress made on eastern Jewry was, with few exceptions, a profound one, the reception accorded it in the west was by no means so uniform. The Swiss press, which for the most part had been detailed and friendly in its reports, commented unfavorably on the telegram to the Sultan, who was everywhere condemned by public opinion. The French press was cool. In Germany, the

Kölnische Zeitung printed long and sympathetic reports.
Other leading German newspapers devoted a fair amount of
attention to the Congress. The Viennese press was for the
most part silent. In the *Neue Freie Presse* Herzl encountered
derision. The most earnest reception came from the English
press. While Oswald H. Simon of the *Times* took up an
uncompromisingly negative attitude, the *Daily Mail*, the
Pall-Mall Gazette and Arnold White in the *Contemporary
Review*, called for a World Congress to take up and elucidate
the Jewish question.

Among the Jews the Congress had the support of those
who were already its partisans, or who were ready to be
convinced. The masses of the assimilated Jews were hardly
affected by it; their leaders renewed, in press and pulpit,
their former attacks and accusations. Herzl was unmoved
by all this. He had mastered himself to the point where he
could not be provoked. As to the accusations, with their
personal implications, these did not matter; he reacted to
them only to the extent that they reflected on the movement.

It was of course difficult to draw a line of demarcation
between the movement and its leader, particularly since the
Congress. Herzl had insisted, and continued to insist, that
his leadership in the movement was impersonal, and that
now the direction of the movement was vested in the instruments, the Congress and the Actions Committee, which the
movement had created. But for the mass of his followers
he was the leader, and his will was identified with the will
of the movement. Nor, since his experiences in Basle, could
he himself wholly suppress the feeling that he had been
elected, not merely to the presidency of the organization, but

to the position of its representative. He was, in fact, its personification. This status was confirmed more emphatically from day to day by a positive and by a negative circumstance; the first was the growing volume of affirmation which reached him through the mails; the second was the inactivity of the people who surrounded him. The Viennese group which constituted the Actions Committee was composed of men who devoted to the movement whatever time they could spare from their daily occupations. But by comparison with Herzl's feverish self-dedication their participation seemed to be almost trivial. Herzl recognized their human qualities, but he found their prudence and hesitation a brake on his own stormy will to work. He coined for the inner circle the bitter name of "Inactions Committee;" it seemed to him that everyone was prepared to let him work himself to death in order that he might make of himself a target for criticism, or provide others with the opportunity of claiming the credit for themselves.

The result was that he developed a dictatorial attitude; he instructed, commanded, demanded, though always with the same restrained courtesy. He was the only one whose will-power was proportionate to the greatness of the cause. The lower the creative potential of the others, the higher he had to make his own, if the movement was not to decline into complete futility.

Step by step he became more hostile in his expressions toward the opponents of the Congress and the Zionist movement, always finding in the general constellation of forces — insofar as they impinged to any degree at all on Jewish life — additional demonstrations of the justice of the Zionist demand. The world picture as a whole became for him a

Zionist argument; from day to day his involvement in the destiny of the Jews became more organic and more passionate. He felt himself to be both leader and father, the manager of every aspect of the Jewish problem. And the masses of East European Jewry in Galicia, Roumania and Russia saw him in the same light.

Immediately after the Congress he wrote a leading article in *Die Welt* on the significance of that event, emphasizing the miracle of the revival of the Jewish people and of the unification of the "linguistic, social, political and religious" fragments of Jewry. "Brothers have found each other again," he proclaimed. This was followed by a more detailed article which appeared first in the *Contemporary Review* and was afterwards republished as a pamphlet under the title of *The Basle Congress*. We have already referred to his new conception of the significance of East European Jewry. But he now turned his attention to the political possibilities and consequences of the Congress. Zionism, he pointed out, needed the confirmation of the Powers and of Turkey, whose best interests would be served by the movement. But suppose, in spite of all Zionist efforts to clarify the situation, both the Powers and Turkey remained unconvinced? "In that case we must wait until the crisis in the East comes to a head. A people can wait. Its life-span is longer than that of individuals and governments, and the constellation of events in the East is such that the fateful hour cannot long be delayed."

The growth and evolution of Herzl's conception of the Jewish problem since the day when he looked on at the degradation of Dreyfus can be measured almost with laboratory accuracy by a study of the articles which he wrote

20. David Wolffsohn, Herzl's closest friend and most active helper
and his successor as President of the Zionist Organization (see p. 187)

21. The Rev. William Hechler (see p. 191)

22. Grand Duke Frederic of Baden, the first head of State to receive Herzl (see p. 196)

23. The first meeting of Vienna Zionists with Herzl at the Café Louvre in Vienna, 1896 (see p. 186)

24. The Casino in Basle, meeting place of the first Zionist Congress, 1897 (see p. 229)

25. Delegates to the second Zionist Congress, 1898 (see p. 273)

26. The Closing Session of the second Zionist Congress, 1898: Rabbi
Jizchak Ruelf proposing a vote of thanks to Herzl, who had presided.
Drawing by Okin (see p. 274)

27. Herzl with the Zionist delegation to the Kaiser, on board ship to
Palestine, 1898 (see p. 297)

28. A spoilt photograph taken by David Wolffsohn of the meeting between the Kaiser and Herzl at Mikve-Yisrael, 1898 (see p. 300)

29. The meeting between the Kaiser and Herzl ("rectified" photograph),
1898 (see p. 300)

30. The Kaiser entering Jerusalem, October 1898 (see p. 301)

31. The Zionist delegation to the Kaiser outside the gates of Jerusalem
(see p. 304)

32. Herzl in his study, with his mother

33. Founder's share of the Jewish Colonial Trust, 1899 (see p. 318)

34. Herzl among opposition members at the fifth Zionist Congress, 1901 (see p. 372)

35. The first office of the Anglo-Palestine Company, opened in Jerusalem in 1903, now the Bank Leumi Le Yisrael (see p. 351)

36. Prof. Richard Gottheil, first President of the Federation of American Zionists, founded in 1898

37. Herzl, 1903

38. Herzl and his children

39. Herzl and Prof. Mandelstamm in Alt-Aussee, about 1902

40. Herzl and his family with Prof. Gottheil, his wife and his sister in Alt-Aussee

immediately after the first Congress. He himself was quite
aware of the transformation. Two years before, in December
1895, he had been outraged by Güdemann's declaration
that the use of a Christmas tree in Jewish homes — an
accepted custom in Herzl's household — was essentially un-
Jewish. Herzl had believed then that it was permissible to
interpret the Christmas tree as a "Hanukkah-tree;" or it
might be looked upon as the celebration of the upward turn
of the sun at the winter solstice. Now he wrote an article,
entitled *The Menorah*, in which he told how he had returned
to Judaism, how he regarded the celebration of Hanukkah,
and how this festival affected him. The story begins like
a fairy tale: "Once upon a time there was a man who had
felt deep in his soul the distress of being a Jew." The man
was an artist; he had made his peace with the surrounding
world; he had long since ceased to concern himself with his
Jewish origins and the faith of his fathers. But the ever-
rising tide of anti-Jewish sentiment, the incessant attacks
on the Jews, tore open something within him "so that his
soul became nothing more than an open and bleeding
wound." He came by degrees to "a deep inner love" of
Judaism, and to the conclusion "that there was only one way
out of the Jewish plight, and that was a return of the Jews
to their homeland." Everyone believed that the man had
gone mad. Everyone believed that "the way out" which he
had chosen would result in a deepening and intensification
of the evil. "But he was sure now that the moral catastrophe
in Jewish life was all the sharper because the Jews had lost
that inner compensation which had existed so strongly in
their ancestors."

Undistracted by the mockery and contempt which were
directed at him, the man followed to its logical conclusion

the consequences of his conviction. He realized that the first problem was that of the education of the young generation of Jews. He therefore decided to revive the festival of the Maccabees for his children, and to plant in their young souls a feeling of relationship to the past of their people. As he held aloft the nine-branched candlestick he suddenly recalled, in a strange rush of feeling, his own childhood, and the celebration of the festival in his father's house. He looked at the antique symbol, the prototype of which had so obviously been a tree, and asked himself "whether it was possible to bring new life into this petrified Menorah form, and to water its roots again as if it were really a tree." And thus the first evening of the Hanukkah festival passed.

"The first candle was lit, and the story of the origin of the festival recited: the miraculous origin of the undying lamp, the saga of the return from Babylon, of the second temple and of the Maccabees. Our friend related to his children all that he knew. It was not much, but it was enough for them. When he lit the second candle, it was the children who recited the story to him, and as he heard it from their lips it seemed not only beautiful, but quite new. And from then on he looked forward joyfully to the coming of each evening, always brighter than the evening before. Candle stood by candle in the Menorah, and by their light, father and children dreamed their dreams. In the end it all grew into something more than he had sought to tell them, for it had risen beyond their understanding . . .

"Amid these meditations the week passed. The eighth day came, and now the *shammash*, the servant among the candles, which until then had been used only for the kindling of the others, burned together with them. A great light streamed out from the Menorah. The eyes of the children flashed, but what our good friend saw was the kindling of the light of the nation. First one candle, and dimness all around it, so that the candle was sad and lonely. Then a companion was added to it. Then a third, and a fourth. The darkness is compelled to retreat. The first candles are lit among the young and the poor, and gradually they are joined by all those who love truth and beauty and justice and freedom. When all the candles burn there is admiration and rejoicing for the work that has been done. And there is no office more beneficent and creative than that of a Servant of Light."

From the moment when he began his negotiations with the Turkish authorities Herzl had felt himself hampered by uncertainty; he did not, after all, know whether he could procure the money which he promised the Turkish government. As a matter of fact it proved impossible to raise even the amount for a small loan. Moreover, the Armenian massacres had intervened, with a consequent embitterment of European public opinion against the Turks. Herzl had made no progress in his relationship with Constantinople. This interval in diplomatic activity he sought to employ for the creation of the financial instrument which would provide a basis for his negotiations with Turkey. He would ask no favors of the Sultan. He would come as the representative of one people to the representative of another, with a quid pro quo. "I am now attacking the problem of 'The Jewish Company,' " he wrote in his diary on October 6, 1897. "The Basle Congress represented the creation of 'The Society of Jews' as a facet of the Jewish state, even though with opportunistic modifications and imperfect execution. The work of the next year must be the foundation of 'The

Jewish Company,' temporarily named 'The Jewish Colonial Bank.' "

It need hardly be said that it called for a violent effort on Herzl's part to undertake the creation of a financial institution. He had never had anything to do with the money world; neither in his personal nor in his literary capacity had he tolerated the possibility of any base suspicion being directed against him. In his youth his reaction to anti-Semitic propaganda had been a sharpening of his aversion to money values. In Paris he had learned to understand better the nature and significance of money, and this first insight into the organization of the money market and the meaning of finance had been deepened by his Zionist work. His negotiations with Constantinople had compelled him to give some attention to the structure of the financial world. One of the pillars of his Zionist plan was to find a creative channel for Jewish money; as far back as the time of the *Address to the Rothschilds* he had already accepted this principle. For all that, it did not follow that he himself would have to take in hand the business direction of the Bank, just as it was clear to him that he could under no circumstances have any material interest in it. But now there was no blinking the fact that unless he himself set about it, nobody else would. He would have to overcome his profound reluctance. "Now," he wrote in one of his letters, "the beautiful days are over, the lovely time when I was looked upon merely as a lunatic. From now on I shall be treated like a businessman. But I've got to go through this too."

Mid-November he first presented his ideas on the subject publicly. In the programmatic editorial of *Die Welt* he stated: "The movement must have a financial instrument of high character and adequate usefulness. The national movement must be liberated from the graciousness of benefactors and the kindness of foundations."

The task of the Colonial Bank was the elimination of philanthropy. "All that our benefactions have done till now has been to make the giver a little poorer — and the taker too." For what the latter lost, he said, was some of his feeling of responsibility. The settler on the land, who increased its value by his labor, "merited something more than a gift: he merited credit," and credit is not only more moral both for the giver and taker, it is also worth more, materially, than a gift. The prospective Bank could therefore begin by extending the needed credits to the colonists; later it would expand into the instrument for the bringing in of Jews, and would therefore supply credits for "transportation, agriculture, commerce and construction."

The seat of the Bank, as already intimated in *Der Judenstaat*, was to be London; its share capital was to be £2,000,-000. There were to be 2,000,000 shares at one pound each. The Bank was to be created by a group of "reputable and well-known businessmen," but the political leaders of the movement were to be able at all times to control the policy of the Bank; no one thus connected with the Bank was to derive any material benefit from it.

Herzl at once set about the enlistment of such "reputable and well-known businessmen." Through Rabbi Gaster he managed to interest Seligman, one of the biggest London bankers. Seligman was ready to take up a block of shares, but he felt that his position prevented him from being publicly associated with the new venture. He did not think much of the prospects of a bank which confined its activities to Palestine. A few days after he learned all this, Herzl,

then in Vienna, received a visit from the wealthy Lodz
banker, Poznansky. After long and detailed discussion,
Poznansky expressed himself as completely won over. He
declared himself ready to enter the syndicate which was to
secure the subscriptions, but was of the opinion that the
capital ought to be between five and ten million pounds.

On December 11 Herzl wrote hopefully to Nordau: "With
his entry, the other Russian millionaires are as good as
signed up. The Bank has taken a tremendous step forward."
Now Nordau was to try, through Zadoc Kahn, to win the
Paris Rothschilds, upon whose friendliness — and if not that,
their benevolent neutrality — Poznansky placed great
weight. They did not have to give official approval to the
project. Indeed, their official approval might even, in Herzl's
opinion, be somewhat of a handicap. Only the success of
the guarantee syndicate was now necessary in order to
assure an enormous subscription list, so that the Zionist
movement might become a genuine power ... The Jewish
Colonial Bank (or, as it came to be called, The Jewish Colonial Trust) had to become the Jewish National Bank.
It was to be launched in grand style. Herzl thought, in
April 1898, of chartering a ship and inviting a large number
of subscribers or prospective subscribers to accompany him
on a trip to Palestine. He even obtained figures on the cost
of such an enterprise. Immediately after the return, the
subscription lists were to be opened to the public.

Again his will to action blinded him to the difficulties
before him. Zadoc Kahn promised his help, but Edmond
Rothschild's attitude was one of complete scepticism. Ludwig Stein, the philosopher of Berne, called together a conference of rich Berlin Jews, at which Herzl was present, on
January 6, 1898; there were no practical results. Herzl's

personality made a profound impression on these people; but he could obtain neither their cooperation for the Bank nor their agreement with his political views.

"I know very well," said Herzl, in an impromptu speech to the Berlin Zionists, "that the soil hereabouts is an arid one ... German nationality itself is young and uncertain; it has added its confusing influence to the uncertainty which the Jews feel on other historic grounds." He spoke calmly, almost dejectedly: "If the progress of the Zionist movement is such that we cannot hope to reach forth tomorrow and to take in our hand the heritage which we know to be ours," still he knew that a time would come when the Jewish National Assembly would no longer meet on other soil than its own.

The restrained tone was due to something more than his failure with the rich Jews of Berlin. Herzl had also had two long conversations with Ahmed Tewfik, the Turkish ambassador in Berlin. Tewfik had expressed himself sharply against the idea of a close settlement of Jews in Palestine; if there was to be colonization at all, it would have to be scattered, and there was to be no talk of a Jewish territory or Jewish autonomy. Such a solution Herzl definitely rejected. "It would be the settlement of another Armenian people in Turkey."

Four weeks later the two men came together again in Berlin, and the contact was more cordial. But the practical results remained, as before, nil. The occasion of Herzl's visit was, actually, the production of his drama, *The New Ghetto*. Some weeks before, he had been present at the opening night at the Carl Theatre, in Vienna; the performance had been excellent, and the reception enthusiastic on the part of an audience which was not in agreement with the author

on the Jewish question. The critics weakened the effect:
very few of them gave any serious attention to the Jewish
question, which Herzl had hoped to place in the arena of
public discussion by means of this play. However, the piece
was a great personal success for Herzl both as playwright
and Zionist. It even made money. There were twenty-five
performances in Vienna, and then the drama which had been
refused by one manager after another in 1895, was produced
in Berlin, Stettin, Hamburg, Altona, Augsburg, Baden-
Baden, Libau, Dorpat, Prague, Teplitz, Budweis, Pilsen,
Olmütz, and many other cities. Only in Brünn the leaders
of the Jewish community got the authorities to forbid the
production.

Almost everywhere *The New Ghetto* met with a friendly
reception on the part of the public; but the influence which
Herzl had hoped to exercise thereby on the outlook of the
Jews was nowhere in evidence. Not only were the critics
reserved in their tone — in Berlin they were almost hostile—
but many Zionists too were disappointed by the play, which
was printed in instalments in *Die Welt*, and later appeared
in book form. No one knew, of course, what the writing of
The New Ghetto had been in Herzl's life. It was looked upon
— and the fault was in part Herzl's — as something he had
just produced, as a recent formulation of the views of the
Zionist leader. Actually Herzl had only touched it up here
and there. Reuben Brainin, a warm admirer of Herzl's, had
undertaken to translate the play for the Hebrew publishing
house *Ahiasaf* before seeing the text. Now he wanted to cry
off, and complained to Ahad Ha-am at being forced to introduce into the Hebrew language "such literary trivialities."
Brainin wrote a devastating critique of the play, which Ahad

Ha-am printed only after Brainin had appended his signature, so that it might be known that not an opponent but a follower of Herzl had written it. Ahad Ha-am refused to awaken or strengthen the suspicion that the struggle between himself and Herzl was a personal one.

For Ahad Ha-am's criticism of Herzl the political leader was of the utmost sharpness. Herzl had invited him to attend the first Congress. He had accepted, and he had followed the proceedings in his own, peculiar critical fashion. Like everyone else, he had been deeply moved by Nordau's speech, in part for its prophetic passion and in part for certain ideas which, as he afterwards wrote to Nordau, were closely related to his own. The first day of the Congress, this gathering of the people, this proud and authentic declaration of its need and of its national will to life, had been a great experience for him. But what followed seemed to him to be superfluous and even dangerous. Shortly before the Congress, and again on the last day, he had two short conversations with Herzl; his impression was that Herzl did not think responsibly, that his ideas and plans breathed "the feuilleton spirit," and that the intimations he had given to the Congress of his negotiations in Constantinople had no reality behind them. Herzl appeared to him, in fact, in the light of a misleader, a bluffer, who was diverting the loyalty and attention of the old Zionists from their laborious but fruitful enterprise by his fantastic representations. The day after its closing, September 1, he wrote to Ravnitzky that he could not yet evaluate the significance of the Congress, but that "one thing is clear to me; we have destroyed much more than we have built up ... Who knows whether this was not the last sigh of a dying people! I simply cannot get this thought out of my head ..."

The same tone characterizes the short article which he wrote in *Hashiloah*, the most important Hebrew journal of the time, of which he was the editor. In *Hashiloah* Ahad Ha-am kept close watch on everything that took place in Jewish life, and through it he educated a generation of Hebrew writers. The beginning and the opening of the article warmly acknowledged the value of the demonstration as such. "But that is all. More than demonstrate this asembly could not do and should not have tried to do. For — and why should we deceive ourselves in this? — of all the great objectives which the love of Zion, or as they now call it, Zionism, sets for itself, there is only one which we can actually approach: that is the moral objective, our self-liberation from inner slavery, and the repudiation of the attempt to achieve dissolution through assimilation; we must so strengthen our common labor in all branches of our national life that we shall become prepared for a life of dignity and freedom." Everything else, Ahad Ha-am went on to say, was, at the moment, pure fantasy. He thought it extremely doubtful whether the agreement of the Powers, and particularly of Turkey, could be obtained to Herzl's plan. But the more serious, the more difficult question was "whether we ourselves, in our present moral condition, can accept their consent," and whether the Jewish question would be solved if the Jewish people, after its millennial suffering for its historic task, were restored as a little state which would again become the football of its stronger neighbors.

The conveners of the Congress, therefore, would have done better to be content with the demonstration, instead of making great diplomatic gestures and arousing unhealthy hopes. A similar situation had been created in 1890, when the enthusiastic phrases used by the executive of the *Hoveve Zion* in Jaffa had led to a belief in a vast impending immigration. At that time Ahad Ha-am had told the bitter truth, and had been denounced by many as a traitor. And now, suddenly, all the "practical men" were passing over to the new Zionism, as if the principle of slow colonization had been rejected. "In Basle yesterday, as in Jaffa then, I sat lonely among my brothers, a mourner among bridegrooms. But on this occasion too I shall not use my tongue to conceal the truth. Let others say what they will, I have one call to make: Be careful! Danger is near, the reaction is close. This new enthusiasm, too, is an artificial one, and the result of treacherous hopes will again be despair." And the article closes: "The salvation of Israel will come through prophets, not through diplomats."

It need hardly be said that this article attracted widespread attention. It had been dictated by a stern sense of responsibility, but in the excessive sharpness of expression one felt the bitterness of the writer who saw nearly everyone drawn along in the train of the new movement. He mentioned no names, not even Herzl's or Nordau's, but there was no mistaking whom he meant; so that there were some who believed that he was moved by jealousy. A storm broke out in the Hebrew press. M. L. Lilienblum, a veteran of the *Hoveve Zion*, and long an opponent of Ahad Ha-am, attacked him fiercely. And in *Die Welt* Marcus Ehrenpreis published an article under the title of "Moral Zionism" in which, acknowledging the gifts and standing of Ahad Ha-am, he said: "This great thinker has no understanding for the imponderable values of life, and while he makes his sociological calculations with the precision of a merchant, he fails to perceive that social forces are directed by those invisible

factors which cannot be weighed or measured." Ahad
Ha-am's error lay in thinking too schematically: first there
would be moral education, then would come political action.
Actually the two had to go hand in hand. Diplomacy and
money-gathering were certainly not enough, but neither was
the spiritual wholly independent of the political. Ahad
Ha-am was confusing cause with effect. "The moral condition of Jewry, such as it is, with its good and its bad, is only
the result of its political position; the former can be changed
only as the latter changes."

The numerous attacks and the occasional misrepresenta-
tions of which he had thus become the target moved Ahad
Ha-am to a more complete and detailed exposition of his
views on political Zionism. He did this in two articles,
"Jewish State and Jewish Need" and "Political Work and
Colonization," which appeared at the turn of the year
1898–1899, in *Hashiloah*.

In these articles he avoided the sharp phraseology which had
marked the first attack; but their substance was even more
hostile. He spoke ironically of the messianic enthusiasm
which was welling up in countless mass meetings and written
expressions of opinion. He submitted the phenomenon to a
cutting analysis, in which he came to the curious conclusion
that Zionism really had nothing to do with the *material* needs
of the Jews in their various countries; the object of its concern was the *moral* need of the Jews. This need, he said, was
due, in western Europe, to the spiritual distress of the assimilated Jews; while in eastern Europe the need was that of Judaism. It was impossible to create a homeland for all the Jews
in the world, nor was this the task of Zionism. Its task could
only be the creation of a home or centre for "Judaism,"
which was the guarantee of the existence of the Jewish people.

After this general repudiation Ahad Ha-am proceeded to disagree with Herzl on the details of his utterances and methods, which seemed to him to be shallow and "diplomatic;" and here he showed that he had completely misunderstood both Herzl's philosophy and Herzl's significance.

An abstract Judaism, such as Ahad Ha-am had in mind, contradicted completely Herzl's vision and manner of thought. When, in his first address to the Congress, he had said that Zionism was a return to Judaism before it was a return to a Jewish homeland, he had meant a recognition of relationship toward the Jewish people and its destiny. But Ahad Ha-am's conclusion, that Herzl had not been serious in his demand for "a return to Judaism" was thoroughly erroneous. Herzl always proceeded on the basis of the visible and tangible as a symbol of the intangible; but precisely this showed that he considered the apparent and the essential indivisible. The Jewish people, with its spiritual and physical need, was for him, the artist-seer, a tragic and tangible reality; a Judaism independent of that people was utterly incomprehensible to him. His opponents could justly reproach him with an inadequate knowledge of Jewish history and Jewish tradition, and with the lack of energy or time to make this deficiency good. But he possessed something which they lacked: a deep insight into the essential being of men. He knew their secret longings, he knew what the people was waiting for, how it could be led, how it could be wakened from its lethargy and set in flaming motion, and how its contradictory elements could be fused and united. Ahad Ha-am was certainly not wide of the mark when he criticized the absence of clarity and definition in many of Herzl's utterances and decisions; there was something, too, in his derision of the whole of that procedure which he subsumed under the title of "diplomacy," and which the smaller people among Herzl's followers made ridiculous by their imitation. As a critic Ahad Ha-am was right; but life has a way of moving past the critic. It was quite true that the diplomatic diffuseness of the resolutions and expressions of opinion created the danger of conflict and misunderstanding for the future. But the first result was the creation of unity, the setting in motion of the mass, and Herzl could hope that out of the community of effort and of practical tasks there would come a deeper unification in outlook. With Ahad Ha-am's methods a Zionist movement of any volume could never have been created.

Herzl did not answer Ahad Ha-am's criticism. It is not quite certain that he read the articles in complete translation. If he did, he must have felt that they had something personal in them — and he very rarely replied to personal attacks. The objective criticisms, those that dealt with specific points, were dealt with by Ehrenpreis in his rebuttal. As a thinker Ahad Ha-am, with his rationalist outlook, so remote from Herzl's nature, could not interest the latter. As an opposition leader, the representative of a certain force, he was of little moment, since his followers were moving over en masse to Herzl. Nevertheless Herzl did not fail to appreciate the moral substance of Ahad Ha-am's Zionism. On his visit to Palestine in 1898, Herzl said to Grazovsky: "If we had ten Ahad Ha-ams, we would be much nearer our goal." He also sought to win Ahad Ha-am through personal contact. He invited him in April 1898, to attend the preliminary conference in Vienna which was to prepare the second Congress. Ahad Ha-am did not come; there were external obstacles, he wrote to Herzl.

One point in Herzl's program Ahad Ha-am did understand: what mattered above all else to Herzl was the unification of the movement, and the drawing into it of all those who were standing on the sidelines. Over and over again he emphasized the "community of purpose." "We all want the same thing," he wrote in *Die Welt*, addressing himself to the English *Hoveve Zion*, who on March 6 had called a conference of delegates in the Clerkenwell Town Hall, in London. "One goal calls to all of us, one longing for a happier life fills all of us, and the ideal which we pursue with patience and courage is something to unite and not to divide us."

The winning over of the English *Hoveve Zion* was for Herzl a matter of prime importance. From the beginning he had, as he himself expressed it, looked upon England as the Archimedian point on which to rest his lever. As far back as July 1897, he had discussed in *Die Welt* an article which had appeared in the *Quarterly Review*, and which had advocated the partition of Turkey, with the assignment of Egypt and Syria (Palestine included) to England. England needed desperately this short cut to India. But the Powers begrudged each other this little land. The French claimed it; and now the newspapers were reporting that the Kaiser was contemplating a visit to Palestine in the near future. If the Powers could not agree on the assignment of this country, could they not perhaps agree to turn it into a little state which by its nature could serve as the guardian of the route without entertaining any political aspirations? "The search for the short route to India, wrote Herzl, "has led to many discoveries from which mankind has benefited. The coasts of Africa were investigated, America was discovered, the Suez peninsula was pierced. Perhaps the solution of the Jewish problem, too, lies along the shortest route to India."

The winning over of the English *Hoveve Zion* was important from both points of view, the external and the internal. Their influence on the Paris Committee of the *Hoveve Zion* was considerable; and again, London, the financial centre of the world, was to be the seat of the Bank. At the conference in Clerkenwell Town Hall the English Zionists declared themselves ready to join with the Vienna Actions Committee, and expressed the hope that the latter would be able to unite with the Paris Committee. The location of the new directorate thus formed should then be decided on at the next Congress. Herzl made a bitter notation in his diary: "Why do they repeat the obvious? Because they want to make it clear that the Vienna Committee is to last only till the second Congress. Then the London Committee takes over. I am in complete agreement."

The weary resignation which speaks in this last sentence had been his mood for several weeks. Ahad Ha-am felt lonely because his followers were deserting him. Herzl did not feel less lonely as the head of a movement which was growing from day to day. The rivalries precipitated round him and his leadership embittered him; his impatiently active nature endured with difficulty the obstacles created by opponents and by too easily discouraged followers, and, not less, by the perpetual lack of funds. The total number of subscribers to *Die Welt* was 2400, of whom 280 were in Vienna; it was a constant drain on Herzl's resources. On top of all this came his heart ailment, which his strenuous labors aggravated. In mid-February 1898, immediately after his return from Berlin, he asked Nordau to take over the presidency of the second Congress and the work of preparation for the third, the centre of the movement to be meanwhile transferred to Paris. Nordau had not fitted well into the second role at Basle; now Herzl wanted him to rise to the position of leader, on condition of course that he made himself responsible for the labor and the struggles which lay between the Congresses. For himself Herzl retained only the acknowledgment of later times: that which he had created would be recognized when another leader had taken over. "I stood firm during the darkest days, I was calm during the brightest. That called for something! One had to know how to be silent when a single word could have aroused enthusiasm. One had to sustain the courage of others, even when everything within had collapsed. One had to meet disaster with a smile, one had to consort with blackguards, endure the visits of beggars, put up with the arrogant and the insolent... And then, the envy, the treachery, the base attacks — and no reward, for naturally I shall be accused of having done everything out of vanity."

Together with a longing for rest there came visitations of literary inspiration. He thought of an autobiographic novel in which he would describe the newspaper world. And after a conversation with Leon Kellner, the Shakesperean scholar, "my nearest, dearest friend, whose visits are like rays of light in the midst of all these torments," he put down the outline of a biblical drama, *Moses*. He envisions Moses as "a great, powerful figure, filled with the strength of life and the spirit of humor. The drama is to show how he becomes inwardly weary, while retaining his will to the full. He is the leader because he does not want to be it. Everything is swayed to his will because he has no personal desires. His aim is not the fulfillment, but the wandering. Education and training by wandering... Aging, he recognizes ever again Korah, the golden calf, the eternal characteristics of slaves. All these things weary him, and yet he must urge the others forever forward with fresh energy. It is the tragedy of a leader of men who is not a misleader . . ."

It is thus that Herzl sees himself, and at bottom he rejoices when Nordau, who has stood with him ever since the days of the Dreyfus affair, sends back a refusal couched in warmest terms. He who begins a task must carry on till the end. "At least I know myself; I shall go on until I am stretched out in death."

Internal crises of this kind always unlocked new sources of strength. He envisaged plans for the transformation of the organization; he began to entertain now the idea of the conquest of the Jewish communities. But in first line stood the Bank, which he wanted to be presented as an accomplished fact to the second Congress.

The preliminary conferences were held in Vienna from April 23 to April 25. There were present representatives from Russia, Austria and Germany. The consensus was, on the whole, against the holding of a second Congress so soon after the first. It was feared that there would be a falling off in the attendance, a sharpening of conflicts. But Herzl's fundamental idea in calling the Congress together again after the lapse of a year was precisely the creation of a permanent body. He was perpetually concerned with the fear that the movement would die of inanition. Besides, the reconstruction of the organization, and the confirmation of the Bank by the Congress, seemed to him to be urgent matters. Herzl proposed immediate action. As soon as the details of the forms of the bank had been worked out, shares were to be put on the market. The par value was to be one pound sterling; first payment was to be ten per cent. Since neither his efforts, nor those of Nordau, Wolffsohn and others, had enlisted the interest of the big financiers, Herzl wanted to begin a popular action. He believed that great results would be forthcoming. Perhaps the success would be such as to persuade the financiers to take a hand.

There were difficulties with the Russian and Galician delegates, who were set on furthering the immediate practical work in Palestine. But Herzl carried his point. It was decided to send Motzkin to Palestine to prepare a report for the Congress on the state of the colonies and on the possibilities for new colonization. At the close of the conference, as throughout most of the sessions, the mood was high. It was decided, further, that the second Congress should be held in the city of the first, Basle. (Herzl and the Vienna Committee had originally thought of London.) Herzl was again acclaimed as the leader of the movement.

But as against this, the proclamation of the second Congress and the initiation of action for the founding of the Bank gave the signal for a renewed attack on the part of the opponents of the organization. It was obvious to them that the success of a second Congress and the founding of the Bank would mean a great accretion of power to the movement. Rabbis, communities, societies for the defense of Jewish rights, launched a flood of protests. Herzl worked on unmoved, answering the attacks on rare occasions, and then in a tone of biting irony. Letters passed almost daily between him and Wolffsohn, whom he had appointed as the director of Bank activities, and who later became the first President of "The Jewish Colonial Trust." Herzl demanded daily reports on the progress of the provisional subscriptions. He carried on a ceaseless propaganda. *Die Welt* opened a special section for Bank affairs; but the statements it carried were a little too enthusiastic for the more practical and cautious Wolffsohn.

The subscriptions flowed in, though much more slowly than had been expected. It proved almost impossible to install subscription offices in the West European countries. The Jewish financial world was everywhere hostile. The Frankfort bankers Seligmann and Marx had agreed to the use of their offices, but now that they were called upon to give effect to their promises, they withdrew them, and a new start had to be made at the beginning of August. While in his house his son was slowly recovering from an almost mortal sickness, Herzl wired to Wolffsohn: "Undiscouraged." He called a Bank conference for August 25, three days before the opening of the Congress.

The second Congress which, in spite of all obstacles and attacks, opened on schedule, showed how much the movement had grown since the first Congress. In his report of the Actions Committee, Schnirer showed that 913 groups had joined the organization, which had increased three fold since the previous year. The total number of delegates was now 400, including the majority of those who had attended in 1897. Among the new ones were Rabbi Rülf, of Memel, Professor Gottheil, of New York, Bernard Lazare, of Paris, who was given a great ovation for his work in the Dreyfus affair, and young Chaim Weizmann. Ahad Ha-am was absent. Nahum Sokolow, who had attended the first Congress as a journalist, now came as a delegate. Herzl's father was among the delegates. Nevlinsky and his family were present as the guests of Herzl.

The press representation was much larger than in 1897. Among the hundreds of telegrams and letters of greeting, there was one which made an especially deep impression. Its writer was Cesare Lombroso, the famous psychiatrist, a recent convert to Zionism. But the most moving incident which preceded the opening of the Congress, one which brought tears to Herzl's eyes, and to the eyes of all who witnessed it, was quite impromptu. A throng of delegates was assembled on the outside balcony of the Congress hall, when a procession with banners came down the street. It was the day of the Swiss national festival which celebrates the victory against the Armagnacs, and the patriotic demonstration was returning from its exercises. A woman on the balcony waved her handkerchief, and as if at a word of command all the flags were dipped and "a tremendous, unexpected cry floated up: *Hoch die Juden!*"

More important, however, was the internal victory which was signalized by the presence of a large Russian delegation. Shortly before the Congress, the Russian Zionists had held a conference in Warsaw, and had laid down the lines of their participation. Their presence showed that they had been won over. Kohan-Bernstein paid enthusiastic tribute to Herzl and to his influence over the Jews of eastern Europe. "The moment the report came of the founding of the Bank, a new stream of life flowed through the masses. They did not ask what the aims of the Bank would be; they knew only that its guiding spirit would be our leader, Dr. Herzl." Herzl's influence among the people was greater than that of all the Russian delegates together. "The heart of our people and the heart of our leader have come together and have entered into an eternal bond."

These words were uttered in the course of the debate on the Bank. Herzl had opened it with a brief address and had declared optimistically that the Bank would begin its activities in the course of that year. Wolffsohn, the head of the Bank Commission, reported that in the few weeks of intensive work which had been carried on, four million francs had been subscribed, almost all of it in small sums — a respectable achievement when it was borne in mind that this was a preliminary subscription the chief purpose of which was to investigate the possibilities.

The Bank as such met with no opposition. The necessity of a Bank had been recognized from the beginning of the colonization work, and several unsuccessful attempts had already been made to found one. Differences of opinion arose only as to the formulation of the field of activity of the new financial instrument. In the first draft the Orient alone was named. The Russian Zionist leader, Menachem Ussishkin, demanded the substitution of the words "Syria and Palestine." After a four hour debate the final formulation was accepted as "the Orient and especially Palestine and Syria." The resolution founding the Bank was passed by acclamation.

Next to the question of the Bank, the most important was that of colonization. Before and during and after the first Congress it was this question which had called forth the strongest divergences of opinion. The sending of Leo Motzkin to Palestine had been an excellent move. His report was thorough, factual and statistical. He had made a complete study of the colonies, and had devoted a great deal of attention to the *Halukkah* Jews, who had for many generations been living in Palestine on the charity collected for them throughout the Jewish world. Motzkin reported that the *Halukkah* Jews could not live on the contributions they received, and many of them were ready and able to take to agriculture. Under the existing legal regulations a mass

immigration of Jews into Palestine was impossible; and infiltration was what Herzl would not have. He called it, in
his opening address, "the smuggling of Jews into Palestine."
There was a third choice: the improvement of the condition
of Palestinian Jewry by colonization and industrialization.
This could be undertaken immediately without running
counter either to the Turkish regulations or Herzl's fundamental principles. Herzl had, in fact, admitted this third
possibility at the first Congress. The resolution formulating
the objectives of the Colonization Commission, yet to be
formed, went somewhat further. It defined the debated
point of the Basle Program as the "programmatic (zweck-
dienstliche) settlement" of Palestine. By this was implied
"colonization to be carried on in accordance with a permit to
be obtained from the Turkish government, and along the
lines to be laid down and supervised by a Commission appointed by the Congress." The seat of the Commission,
which was to be chosen from the various national delega-
tions, and which was to consist of ten members, would be
London. There was no mention in this resolution of a "publicly recognized, legally secured" homeland; but the question
remained open, and much could be read into the "permit"
of the Turkish government, whenever that was forthcoming.

Throughout all this Herzl was aiming at the reconciliation
and unification of opposing elements in the movement. His
opening address was conciliatory in tone, without any surrender of principle. But he was all the sharper in his attack
on the enemies of the national idea, the rabbis "who pray
for Zion and attack it in the same breath," and the leaders
of the religious communities whom they obeyed, in contradiction of the will of the communities themselves, which
were sympathetic to Zionism. Earlier in the same year

Herzl had already considered the idea of a struggle for "the conquest of the communities" and had been strongly supported by Nordau. "Until now," said Herzl, "we have refused, out of brotherly consideration, to bring this contrast to the fore. But in the last analysis this transformation is unavoidable. We can no longer stand by while agitation against Zion is carried on in the Jewish religious communities. It is an impossible, contradictory situation, and we must put an end to it. Wherever the leaders of the communities are not with us, there must begin a fight for elections. Men who have the standing and the capacity to occupy these honorable posts, and who are at one with us in our views, must be elected to the leadership, and inducted into our centers in the name of our national idea. The authority of the religious community, the means which it commands, and the persons who constitute it, must not be directed against the aspirations of the people ... Our next objective is therefore the conquest of the communities."

Even more conciliatory than his opening address was that which he permitted Mandelstamm to deliver on the Zionist program. Herzl had made it a practice to review in advance all important statements to the Congress. Mandelstamm sought to unite the Herzlian with the Ahad Ha-amist concept of Zionism, and spoke of the creation of "a political-cultural and national center ... which shall be a gravitational center for those who are to follow. This center will radiate out its influence upon those who have remained behind, promote the solidarity of the Jews and keep alive their national consciousness ..."

The debate on the financial report of the Actions Committee, held on the opening day, was particularly stormy. The income from the *shekalim* was absurdly small. Herzl was faced — as he was so often destined to be — by a painful dilemma. The foundations of his political action were the negotiations he sought to conduct with Turkey: these negotiations, in turn, were based on the money which he hoped to get by the success of the negotiations! It would therefore have been suicidal for him to permit the world to know that, far from commanding the ear of high finance, his organization could barely meet its current expenses. He was furious when one speaker after another expressed his gratitude to the Actions Committee for "having done so much with so little." He had the balance sheet of the organization reviewed by a Committee, which then reported the balances on hand, without making public the income. This procedure called out vigorous protests, and Nordau too was angry: after all, it was no shame to be poor. Herzl was obstinate on this point and refused to give way. It was only after the third Congress that the details of income and expenditure were made public, though without mention of the names of the political agents.

There were also unpleasant scenes as the result of the dogmatic resolutions and observations by some Social Democrats, among them S. R. Landau and Dr. Nachman Syrkin, who so enraged Dr. Mandelstamm that he submitted a resolution to have these men excluded from the Congress. Herzl refused to put the resolution to a vote, but expressed himself with the utmost sharpness against the tendency to bring division into the national ideal while it was still in process of emergence. He himself, as the defender of the seven hour working day, had, at the opening of the Congress, stressed the social character of the Zionist movement. "Those of us who are most passionately determined to prosecute the movement," he declared, "would regret having taken a single step if it resulted in a new society which was not also a better one."

There were painful interruptions when Herzl had a telegram read to the Congress with the news that Czar Nicholas II was calling a conference for disarmament and permanent peace. Herzl saw in this the first steps toward that international council which would settle the Jewish question. It seemed to him, therefore, that a resolution of support would be a proper move, especially in view of the possibility that there would have to be negotiations with the Russian government. But though the resolution was passed, its effect was completely spoiled by the interruptions of Nachman Syrkin, and the wild scenes to which they led. Herzl found it necessary, at a subsequent session, to make a public explanation to the press, which had of course made the most of these scenes in its reports.

The Congress gave little time to questions of external policy, for Herzl exerted himself to the utmost to exclude such matters from the debates. Only in his opening address he emphasized the relationship of the Jewish question to world politics. He took as his text the recent pogroms in Galicia, which he had also dealt with in *Die Welt*, ("Fire in Galicia") and insisted again that far-seeing statesmen would have to recognize "that the unsolved Jewish problem was a danger to the general social system." The Jews were ready to contribute their share to the solution of the problem by the erection of their own homeland: they had the workers, the materials, the plans. What they lacked was the location, and it was this that the nations of the world would have to bring forward as their contribution.

On the morning of August 31, Herzl closed the Congress with these words:

"We have set out. The moral wandering of the Jews has begun. Whither will it lead us? Into better times, let us hope."

On September 2 he left Basle, completely exhausted, but on the whole satisfied with the results. A stronger and more united organization stood behind him, and it had taken steps toward the creation of a financial instrument.

In this mood he set out for the beautiful island of Mainau on the Bodensee, for an audience with the Grand Duke of Baden.

CHAPTER IX

THE PALESTINIAN JOURNEY

FROM the beginning of his political activity Herzl had dreamed of interesting the Kaiser in his plans. The position of Germany with regard to Turkey was a special one. While most of the western Powers were openly discussing the impending partition of Turkey, Germany was as openly set against it. In the diplomatic complications of the Armenian question, and in the Crete incident of 1896 which led to the Graeco-Turkish war, the attitude of Germany had been extremely helpful to the Turks. The German embassy in Constantinople was the most powerful center of foreign influence. If he could approach the Sublime Porte via Germany, Herzl felt that half the battle would be won.

About the time of Herzl's first audience with the Grand Duke of Baden, he had heard from Hechler that the Kaiser planned to visit Jerusalem for the dedication of the Evangelical Church of the Redeemer. In the summer of 1897 this plan was made public, with one small addition. Besides attending the dedication, the Kaiser would use the occasion to establish a protectorate over the German Catholics in Palestine. But France had always looked upon herself as the protector of the Catholics of Asia Minor. There was a flurry of excitement, there were diplomatic discussions. It soon became evident — as everyone had expected it would — that

276

both the dedication and the establishment of the protectorate were incidentals; there was a deeper political and economic game afoot.

In March 1898, it became known that the Kaiser would be
in Palestine before the end of that year. Thereupon *Die
Welt* published, in its next issue, an editorial which spoke
of the far-sightedness of the Kaiser and suggested it would
be in keeping with his aims to make favorable mention of
the Zionist movement to the Sultan. Herzl sent this issue
of the paper to Lucanus, head of the Imperial Civil Office,
who wrote back that he had passed the publication on to
the Kaiser, and requested that Herzl continue to send him
other issues which might be of interest to His Imperial
Majesty. *Die Welt* then published a series of articles on
the subject of the impending visit to Palestine, all of them
directed at the Kaiser. The political sections of his address
to the second Congress had also been intended for Imperial
consumption.

In his two hour audience with the Grand Duke of Baden
on September 2, Herzl definitely included Zionism within the
oriental sphere of German interest. There could be an
exchange of service between Germany and the Jews via the
founding of the Jewish state. "We need a protector," he
told the Grand Duke, "and German protection would be
welcomed more than any other."

The Grand Duke received Herzl's views favorably. He
told the latter that according to the report of the German
ambassador to Turkey, Marschall, the Sultan was friendly
to the Zionist idea. The Grand Duke himself had given the
Kaiser a complete report on the progress of the movement.
The relationship of Germany to Turkey was such that a word
from the Kaiser would go a long way. But caution was

necessary. Herzl ought to wait for the Kaiser's return from Palestine before he sought an audience. Against this Herzl suggested that if it were at all possible he desired to obtain the audience before the journey, so that the Kaiser might be able to discuss the subject with the Sultan on the basis of adequate information. The Grand Duke thereupon advised Herzl to address himself to the German ambassador at Vienna, Count Philip zu Eulenburg. The general tone of the audience was one of the utmost friendliness and freedom, and toward its close the Grand Duke expressed himself warmly on the subject of Zionism and promised every help. He even gave Herzl permission to publish the fact that the audience had taken place. Herzl did not avail himself of this permission; he wanted to carry on his work quietly, undisturbed by the tumult of a public discussion.

Two weeks later, on September 16, Herzl was received by the German ambassador in Vienna.

Count Philip Eulenburg, the man whose career was afterwards shattered by the attacks of Maximilian Harden, was a friend and confidant of Wilhelm II, and one of the most influential persons in Germany. In the discussion the Count showed himself cool and factual. He began by speaking of the poor soil of Palestine, and the distrustful attitude of the Turks. The Sultan, Abdul-Hamid had, in his timidity, reached the stage of criminality. Herzl unfolded his ideas as he had done in the audience with the Grand Duke, and Count Eulenburg found them new and fascinating. He asked whether the Kaiser ought to raise the subject of guarantees and Jewish autonomy. "No," said Herzl, "I would only want His Imperial Majesty to persuade the Sultan to open negotiations with us."

As to the matter of an audience, the Count did not believe that the impending visit of the Kaiser on the next day, to attend the funeral of the assassinated Austrian Empress Elizabeth, would be a suitable occasion. He promised, however, to use his good offices when he next would see the Kaiser on a hunting party in East Prussia. Meanwhile he thought that Herzl would do well to speak to von Bülow, the German minister for foreign affairs, who happened to be then in Vienna.

The interview with von Bülow took place the next morning. The German minister used his customary technique, an overwhelming and torrential amiability which swept the listener off his feet. He had heard a great deal about Herzl. He had read much of what Herzl had written. "I felt myself becoming weak. Eulenburg had greeted me coolly; I responded with complete control, presented my ideas resolutely and clearly. In von Bülow's presence I unfortunately became a vain litterateur, and was more concerned with polishing epigrams than with speaking seriously to the point." Thus the interview was more in the nature of a chat than a business-like political conversation. Herzl thought it advisable to stress the anti-socialist attitude of Zionism. Von Bülow showed himself well informed on the proceedings of the second Congress. He also showed himself quite aware of the weak points in Herzl's position. Why had the *Neue Freie Presse* been silent and the *Frankfurter Zeitung* so unfriendly? He himself was opposed only "to the destructive Jews." He went on: "The chief difficulty, as I see it, lies in persuading the Sultan to go in with you on this enterprise. It would certainly make more of an impression on him if the advice came from the Kaiser. But we must see to it that no one else hears of it, or else the whole combination may fall to the ground."

A few days later Herzl visited Paris, the Hague and London on business of the Jewish Colonial Trust. From Paris (using, as he noted in his diary, the table on which he had written Der Judenstaat) he addressed a long and detailed letter to Eulenburg, pleading with him once again to obtain an audience for him with the Kaiser before the latter left for Palestine. This was on September 24. A week of nervous tension passed. On October 1, Herzl was in Amsterdam when he received a call to the German consulate. Count Eulenburg's answer had arrived, and it contained much more than he expected: namely, the report of the Kaiser's inclination to take the migration of the Jews under his protection, and his wish to receive Herzl at the head of a delegation in Jerusalem. Details would be forthcoming from Eulenburg in Berlin.

Herzl was stunned. The realization of his plan was practically within reach! Then suddenly he foresaw difficulties. Would not his newspaper, with which he was in constant conflict, dismiss him if, instead of returning to the office in Vienna he set out for Palestine, and became involved in high political adventures? Would it not be better for him to be received in private and secret audience in Berlin? Would not a public demonstration prove premature and therefore abortive? He still did not have the Bank, the financial instrument without which neither the negotiations nor the colonization could be carried on. He read Eulenburg's letter that evening to his friends Wolffsohn and Kann, and pointed out how much more urgent the matter of the Bank had become. In the resolve to push the creation of that institution with the utmost speed, the three men set out for London. Kann told later how, during the crossing, Wolffsohn and Herzl walked to and fro incessantly on the promenade deck and conjured up pictures of the Jewish state that was to be.

On October 3 he addressed a mass meeting in the Assembly Hall, in London, arranged by the *B'nai Zion* Association under Gaster's chairmanship. London had never before seen such a Jewish meeting. Six thousand five hundred Jews gathered in the hall, three thousand five hundred packed the street. The vast majority came from the east side, the first of them four hours before the meeting opened. The *Jewish World* spoke of an enthusiasm "which had something of the legendary about it." A witness reported afterwards: "The souls of these people were in the hand of this man, and with the breath of his voice, which seldom rose above a low tone, he could do with them whatever he liked."

He spoke in German, freely, and without preparation. He transmitted to his audience the feeling of hope and of impending fulfilment which had been aroused in him by Eulenburg's letter. He dealt with the objections which had been raised to Zionism, and of the futile efforts of the "protest rabbis and protest bankers" to hinder the growth of the movement. "Our movement belongs in the first line to the poor, for whom it is preparing a happier future. I do not want to draw a picture of the homeland for you, for it will shortly begin in reality . . . I know what I am saying; I have never spoken so definitely before. Today I declare: I believe the time is not far off when the Jewish people will set itself in motion . . . I ask you to accept my word, even if I cannot make it quite definite. You will remember what I have said to you today, namely, that we have already achieved much. When I return to you again we shall, I hope, be still further on our path." "We are the bodyguard of the truth," he closed with a stirring peroration. "I call upon you to follow the power of the truth, to follow it until the destiny of our people has taken a turn for the better."

The masses responded with a great burst of enthusiasm; they saw the day of deliverance near; he had become the Messiah for them. There were other speakers, among them Father Ignatius, a Catholic believer in Zionism as Hechler was a Protestant believer. Father Ignatius referred to Herzl as "a new Joshua" who had come to fulfil the words of the prophet Ezekiel. "Judaism is Zionism. Zionism is the Judaism of God," he said.

Herzl had not intended to produce this effect with his speech. Personally he did not care for the enthusiasm of the masses, which left him cold, as if someone else were its object. He had always tried to discourage the impression of himself as a messianic figure. When he was in Palestine, a little later, he avoided carefully every opportunity of mounting a white horse or a white ass, and thus help nourish the legend. This mass meeting in London was the only occasion on which he lost his calmness and self-mastery in the public's presence: a circumstance from which we may gather to what a degree he — as well as those who were nearest to him — was convinced, and on understandable grounds, of the immediacy of the fulfillment, and how profoundly he was agitated by the thought. Whatever the causes were, the speech was extremely unwise. It created tremendous excitement among the Jewish masses everywhere. Here and there preparations began for the departure. Suppose this hope were to be falsified?

The original purpose of the meeting had been the promotion of the Bank by a display of the power which stood behind it. Against the advice of everyone except Wolffsohn and Kann, Herzl pushed forward energetically toward the completion of the institution. Despite the growing pains in his heart he was in almost constant conference. A stream of visitors passed in and out of his rooms at the Burlington Hotel. There were legal questions, financial questions and questions of personnel to be settled. At one of the sessions of the Colonization Commission the banker Seligman suggested that in place of a bank there ought to be founded a "Jewish Colonization Society." Seligman had originally offered his help to Wolffsohn for the founding of the bank, but had changed his mind and written against the idea in the *Jewish Chronicle*. Herzl distrusted him, and read into his warnings against over-hasty action the banker's fear of a popular rival institution. He read forth to Seligman "the list of sins of the bankers against the movement ... and threatened war and boycott on the Jewish banking world should it declare itself against the Bank." This threat assuredly did more harm than good. His opponents had a more realistic comprehension of the power of finance and of the will of the masses; Seligman simply laughed at him. In spite of objection in principle, Herzl declared himself ready to abandon the idea of the Bank if Seligman would guarantee the creation of the colonization society. But the answer had to be given within forty-eight hours. Meanwhile, however, he continued with the preparation of the Bank, since he had no faith in Seligman's goodwill.

How hard this preparatory work was, with everything lacking! Herzl, Wolffsohn, Kann and a few others met the initial expenses out of their own pockets. He had taken up the biggest block of shares (2000) in order to show his own confidence in the institution, "even though the investment must not and will not bring me anything."

All these cares retreated into the background before the events of the ensuing weeks. On the evening of October 6 he arrived in Berlin. The expected letter from Eulenburg had not arrived. Thereupon Herzl announced his own arrival telegraphically. He received the reply that the hunting carriage of the Count was waiting for him at the Löwenberg railroad station in north Berlin. From that point he was driven out to the Liebenberg estate.

For the first time in his life Herzl found himself in more intimate contact with those circles of the old aristocracy concerning which he had entertained such high dreams in his youth, and concerning which he had read such discouraging accounts by journalists. There was in him something of the pride of the ghetto Jew at being the first of his kind to enter, erect and self-conscious, into relationship with this exclusive leader-caste for the prosecution of Jewish political plans. He felt himself to be observed on every side, and on this, as on other, similar visits, he laid great weight on the question of clothing, whether he should wear grey or black, which gloves and so on; everything had to be immaculate and discreet, unobtrusively elegant, breathing a natural superiority, as though he had always led this kind of life. The external preparations helped him to conceal from the others his initial uncertainty; but it did not take long before his self-mastery, his psychologically schooled insight into the weaknesses of human beings, his ever-present awareness of great responsibility, restored his sense of inner security and with it its harmonious effect on others.

Count Eulenburg received him in hunting costume. As they strolled together through wood and garden the Count reported on the situation. He had, at the instance of the Kaiser, already written to Herzl on the most important points. "The Kaiser is very warmly inclined toward the project. I was successful in instilling this warmth into him, otherwise it would have no value at all. He must be extremely interested in a matter if he is to prosecute it; for otherwise, what with the multiplicity of his tasks, he naturally loses sight of it." Count Eulenburg had also awakened the interest of von Bülow. In any case, Herzl was to proceed to Constantinople. He might perhaps have an audience with the Kaiser there, and the journey to Palestine would be unnecessary. But the Kaiser wished to receive a deputation of Zionists in Jerusalem. Herzl remarked that only he could present such a delegation. Eulenburg then said that the Kaiser had lived himself completely into the idea of the protectorate. He did not doubt that the Sultan would react favorably to his advice. He believed he could also answer for the favorable response of the German people if he took up the Jewish matter. Herzl ventured to ask whether it would not be better to act a little less demonstratively for the moment; Eulenburg answered that the plan of the protectorate would surely not remain unknown. It was therefore best to promote it openly from the outset. The world would come to terms with the idea. "We can only desire it," added Eulenburg, a trifle more cautiously. "How it works out later is in God's hand. Today we cannot tell whether we shall pursue the matter to its conclusion. Germany will not conduct a war for the Zionists."

Herzl followed these revelations with ever-increasing amazement, exerting himself at the same time to remove the doubts that still lingered in the Count's mind, and to strengthen his confidence in the movement and in himself as its leader. He thanked Eulenburg warmly for his help.

Then he took his leave, without accepting the collation which was brought for him alone. He wanted to make it clear that he had come on business, and that he did not wish to obtrude himself. He pleaded urgent business recalling him to Berlin. "Wonderful, wonderful!" he noted in his diary. "The intervention of Germany, the protectorate, is a *fait acquis*." And to Wolffsohn he wrote: "It is an extraordinary thing, which few human beings have experienced. A dream suddenly comes to realization."

Following Eulenburg's advice, he only left his card with von Bülow. But to the Grand Duke of Baden who, as he learned, was at the moment in Potsdam, he sent a telegram, requesting an audience. Two days later, at 8 A.M. on October 9, the Grand Duke received him in his work room in the castle of Potsdam. He was even friendlier and more intimate than at the last audience in Mainau. Never in all his life, wrote Herzl in his love and reverence for this "wise, good and great man," had he met so distinguished a person; never had he believed that such princes existed. In an interview which lasted almost two hours the Grand Duke confirmed everything reported by Eulenburg. "The Kaiser," he said, "has informed himself thoroughly on the matter, and is full of enthusiasm. The word is not too strong: he is enthusiastically taken by your idea. He speaks of it in the liveliest terms. He would have received you by now, because we have confidence in you, but it was thought better to accord you the reception in Constantinople and Jerusalem. The general situation is good, too. We have received a good report from von Marschall (the German ambassador in Constantinople) and that too is a success. The Kaiser believes that the Sultan will accept his advice . . . He is enthusiastic about it."

In the course of the conversation Herzl said that he wanted to leave it to the German government to make the statement public in whatever form it thought best. "There will have to be a great deal of caution and skill in the presentation." He himself would remain silent for the time being. The Grand Duke then said that he believed it advisable for Herzl to discuss the matter with von Bülow that same day, and told him to wait on him in the nearby Hotel Einsiedel. "As to the form in which the decision would be presented to the public, he believed that it would come best as a statement to the effect that the Kaiser would take the Jewish migration under his care, with the consent of the Sultan."

Herzl went to the Hotel Einsiedel and sent up a note to von Bülow asking to be received. At twelve o'clock the reply came: Foreign Minister von Bülow requests Dr. Herzl to come to the castle, room 149, at one o'clock.

Herzl arrived punctually. In the salon to which he was conducted he found von Bülow, but not alone. There was with him "an old, crooked little figure of a man, whose breast was covered with medals and orders, and who wore a yellow band across his court dress. The two men rose as I entered, and I was introduced to — Reich Chancellor Hohenlohe. I understood at once: a thorough-going, merciless test." Hohenlohe showed himself anything but favorably disposed; his attitude was, in tone and content, anti-Semitic. Bülow too was very cool.

"Do you believe," asked Hohenlohe, "that the Jews are going to throw over their Stock Exchange and follow you?"

"Your Highness," answered Herzl, "not the west side Jews of Berlin, but the Jews of north or east Berlin — I do not know where the poor Jews live — will go with me."

"In any case, it will be the first eastward migration of the Jews, until now they have always migrated westward."

Herzl: "Not at all! This time too it's toward the west. The Jews have circled the globe. East is west again."

Hohenlohe asked what territory Herzl had in mind; up to Beirut in the north, or even further?

Herzl answered, indefinitely: "We ask for that which we need. The more immigrants, the greater the area. The land will naturally be purchased from its present owners."

Hohenlohe: "Who are these?"

Herzl: "Arabs, Greeks, the whole mixed multitude of the Orient."

Hohenlohe: "And you want to found a state there?"

Herzl: "We want autonomy and self-defense."

Hohenlohe: "And what does Turkey say to all this?"

Herzl: "The Grand Duke tells me that he has received favorable reports from Herr Marschall."

Bülow, who had been sitting silent on the edge of the sofa, now put in: "I know nothing of that. I have received nothing from Marschall concerning this matter."

Herzl: "I have reports that the sentiment is favorable. I telegraphed recently to the Sultan and he replied."

To Hohenlohe's question about means, Herzl replied by referring to the various funds, which "in case the matter reaches a serious stage, would unite. One of these funds amounts to ten million pounds."

Bülow: "That's a great deal." And with a half bow to Hohenlohe he added: "The money will do it, perhaps. That's how we'll get at it."

Hohenlohe was silent. Then he rose, as if he was being called to dinner, gave Herzl his hand, and left.

Bülow too was suddenly in a great hurry. "*Auf Wieder-sehen* in Constantinople, Doctor!"

Herzl: "Where will I be received by the Kaiser? In Constantinople and in Jerusalem?"

Bülow: "There will be only one reception."

Herzl: "Shall I then submit the address which I was preparing for Jerusalem in Constantinople?"

Bülow: "*Jawohl*! *Jawohl*!" And already he was in the next room.

The contrast between this audience and the two which preceded leaps to the eye. For Herzl it was of course even sharper. He understood the problem inherent in the situation. Either, he said to himself, these two responsible leaders of German policy were not in agreement with the Kaiser, and did not dare to say it openly, or else they were favorably inclined but not willing to show it. "If it's the first, they are adopting a cool, dilatory attitude, so as to be able to trip me up at the first opportunity, and bring the whole business to nothing. If the second, they are putting on the old, diplomatic show, so as not to let me perceive how much they are interested." What struck him was that Bülow had claimed to know nothing of the report which the Grand Duke had mentioned. Was Bülow, whom Eulenburg claimed to have won over, so cool because he did not yet know what the Grand Duke and Eulenburg had told him, Herzl, of the Kaiser's attitude, which was the primary consideration? "At all events, I must not forget that the most brilliant intentions of this Imperial genius are often corrected and altered beyond recognition by his councillors ... Careful, then! Only, I believe that if it comes to the worst, this idea of ours can be picked up elsewhere as a rejected mistress of the Kaiser, and this adventure can but contribute toward that alternative and help to bring it about."

He stayed only a few days in Vienna. There were again scenes with his publishers which caused him more heartache than his interview with Bülow and Hohenlohe. He met with difficulties in picking his deputation. Finally it was so constituted as to be able to furnish information on the widest possible range of subjects: Wolffsohn, the prospective director of the Colonial Bank, was a merchant; Bodenheimer, president of the Zionist Federation of Germany, was a lawyer; Seidener, the only one with a first-hand knowledge of Palestine, was an engineer; Schnirer, vice-president of the Actions Committee, was a physician. The parting was hard for Herzl. Ben Yehudah, the Hebrew writer and lexicographer, had warned him specifically that the journey was not without its dangers. Would he return in good health? And with what results?

On October 13 he took the Orient Express, without letting even his nearest friends know his destination. He discussed with Bodenheimer the formulation of his demands. Bodenheimer made detailed suggestions on the development and management of the land, and Herzl agreed. But on his arrival in Constantinople the next day he bethought himself that it would be unwise to submit detailed and far-reaching proposals which might at this stage lead only to refusals. His original idea of the Jewish Company fused in his mind with the suggestion made by Seligman in London. "We can ask only for permission to create an organic, initial cell: a Jewish Land Company for Syria (with a charter of rights); this is as much as we can expect, if we are lucky."

His very first step in Constantinople brought him up against bitter disillusionment. While Herzl was delivering Nevlinski's letters of introduction to the Assistant Secretary for Foreign Affairs, Djewad Bey, and the Major Domo, Munir Pasha, he had sent Bodenheimer to the German ambassador, Freiherr von Marschall, to ask when he could be received. Marschall replied that he did not know Dr. Herzl, and that since he had to leave in half an hour for the Dardanelles to greet the Kaiser, he could not receive him at the moment. The Grand Duke's statement about Marschall's report had been wrong, no doubt an old man's error of memory; apparently Marschall was as cool as von Bülow, if, indeed, he knew anything about it at all. The situation was therefore much darker than he had anticipated, the road to the Kaiser more difficult. The next day passed without any activity. On October 17, Herzl decided to request an audience with the Kaiser via the Court Marshal August zu Eulenburg.

"The Imperial reception of the Zionist deputation in the Holy Land," he wrote, along the lines of Philip zu Eulenburg's ideas, "will undoubtedly precipitate much discussion in Europe. Should our demonstration be regarded as evidence of a *fait accompli* — even if its full implications are not revealed — then it will be too late for any hostile intervention that might have been contemplated ... Everything depends on the form which this *fait accompli* is made to take. Consent to the formation of a 'Jewish Land Company for Syria and Palestine' would, in my humble opinion, suffice for the time being ... The acknowledgment of the general political situation would ensue when more emphasis would be laid for public purposes on the German protectorate." The last ship which Herzl could still catch for Palestine and arrive in time was leaving the next morning. He therefore requested the Court Marshal to take immediate action. He also wrote in the same vein to Bülow.

At half past one Wolffsohn returned from the Yildiz Kiosk, the Turkish seat of government. Thanks to his ingenuity he had managed to get past the guards and to reach August zu Eulenburg, who had given him a friendly reception. Bülow had been ill-humored and brusque. Less than three hours later a messenger appeared at the hotel with instructions to Herzl to present himself at half past four at the little palace which had been specially erected for the Kaiser. Five minutes before the appointed time Herzl and Wolffsohn were at the gates. Wolffsohn waited outside, Herzl entered. Not a single one of the German court attendants was to be seen. Herzl stood in the corridor, no one paying any attention to him. After a short interval he asked one of the Turkish adjutants for the Kaiser and was told that the latter was expected any moment. Then he was led into a waiting room — and a guard set over him. Finally, at half past six, he heard the command given to the guard of honor outside to present arms: the Kaiser had come. Five minutes later Herzl was called. Count Eulenburg pointed upstairs. Count Kessel led him past the Empress and von Bülow into the Emperor's working room. Bülow entered behind him. The Kaiser, in dark Hussar uniform, came forward to receive him. Herzl, dressed in a dark frock coat, stood still and made a deep bow. The Kaiser came closer and put out his hand. He was happy to see Dr. Herzl, he said. "Your Imperial Majesty, I am very happy at the honor conferred on me." The Kaiser then went round the table, pushed a chair round to Herzl, himself sat down with his back to the table and crossed his booted legs. Herzl and Bülow sat down, and throughout the interview held their silk hats between their knees, in accordance with form. The Kaiser asked Herzl to speak.

The long awaited moment had come for Herzl. Ever since he had first seen the Kaiser at the manoeuvres in September 1896, he had considered the man and the method of approach. He had observed, in particular, the crippled left arm, a decisive physical characteristic which, strangely enough, very few people noticed. Herzl had then written in his diary (anticipating Emil Ludwig by more than a quarter of a century): "I believe that his condition as a cripple explains his entire character. This supreme war lord would be rejected by the medical officer if he were an ordinary recruit. Hence perhaps his pathological preference for all things military. Nor can he ever carry himself freely, for he must always bear his defect in mind. The truth is that he deceives the majority by the way he holds the reins with his short left hand. Also he loves magnificent, dazzling uniforms, shining helmets which attract and divert the eye. But he seems to me to be a likable man; or, in a single word, a man."

He came closer to the man through his defect. Herzl could feel in him the impulse to exaggeration, the desire to overwhelm; but in this more intimate contact he also was aware of something winning about him — in brief, the entire mixture which captivated those who were admitted to his presence. Herzl considered the Kaiser gifted to the point of genius, and somehow felt a relationship to him: in the love of the theatrical gesture, in the emphasis on the idea of leadership, in the coining of brief, telling slogans, and above all in the high evaluation of technology. Like many of his contemporaries Herzl saw in the Kaiser the prototype of the modern-minded Prince: how few there were who could discern, behind these undeniable virtues, the essential weakness and hesitancy of his nature, his susceptibility to external influence, the lack of seriousness behind his multifarious activities, and the self-regard which the flattery of his courtiers had intensified into delusions of grandeur. Herzl barely noted these negative elements. He was greatly impressed by Wilhelm's great, sea-blue eyes: "I have never seen such eyes. They express a remarkable, daring and searching soul." The entire personality of the Kaiser moved him enormously.

And against this the Kaiser was strongly impressed by Herzl's personality, "one which awakens confidence" as he expressed himself to the Grand Duke of Baden, and as the latter in turn reported to Herzl in December of that year. The impression was confirmed at the meeting in Palestine.

Herzl had expected that the Kaiser would open the conversation. The request that he speak first embarrassed him somewhat. He began by repeating the contents of his letter. The Kaiser soon broke in and explained why the Zionist movement attracted him. The considerations were, as Herzl immediately observed, essentially anti-Semitic.

"There are among your people," said the Kaiser, approximately, "certain elements whom it would be a good thing to move to Palestine. I am thinking, for instance, of the province of Hesse, where usurers are active among the farmers. If these were to take their capital and settle in the colonies, they would be more useful."

Herzl was angered by this identification of the Jewish people with a few usurers; he recovered his coolness, and delivered a speech against anti-Semitism, which, he said, happened to fall most heavily on the best Jews. Bülow parried by speaking of the ingratitude of the Jews; the House of Hohenzollern had always been gracious toward them, and now they were joining the revolutionary party. This gave Herzl his opening for his favorite argument, that Zionism would dissolve the revolutionary parties in the Jewish people. The Kaiser expressed himself as convinced that the Jews would go in for the colonization of Palestine if they knew that he would take them under his protection, so that in a sense they would not really be leaving Germany.

Bülow then adverted to the fact that the rich Jews and the powerful newspapers, among them Herzl's own, were hostile to Zionism. It was evident that he wanted the Kaiser to infer that there was no power back of Herzl. He did not contradict the Kaiser openly — that was not the manner of a court politician. But except that he did not use the word "No," he opposed every conceivable negative to the idea. "'Yes, of course, but'— 'yes, if only'— all masked 'No's,'" as Herzl observed in his diary.

There followed a detailed discussion of the French situation; Herzl felt that the inner weakness of that country would make opposition to the plan impossible. The Kaiser spoke openly of the Dreyfus affair. Herzl expressed no opinion, "but it soon became clear that everyone present considered Dreyfus innocent. It was something utterly astounding."

By this detour Herzl came back to the Jewish question, and unfolded his plan in all its details, and with all the essential arguments regarding the advantages which would accrue to Germany and Turkey. The Kaiser listened, and nodded repeatedly.

"I do not know," said Herzl, "whether I've lost my sense of proportion, but the whole thing appeals to me as being quite natural."

The Kaiser answered: "To me, too."

Bülow objected: "Yes, yes, if they'll only let you, here. You ought perhaps to see the ministers..." he rubbed his forefinger and thumb together significantly. "They all take it here."

The Kaiser threw the suggestion off with a light gesture and said: "It certainly won't fail to make an impression if the German Kaiser shows his concern in the matter... After all, I am the only one who still sticks by the Sultan. I mean something to him."

The Emperor looked at his watch for the second time, and rose to his feet. "Have you another question?" he asked. Herzl brought up the details of the audience in Palestine, the address, or memorial, to be prepared for the Kaiser, and so on. The Kaiser said: "Write your address out and give it to Bülow. I will then work it out with him... Only tell me in brief what you want me to ask of the Sultan."

"A Chartered Company — under German protection."

" 'Good, a Chartered Company,' and therewith he gave me his hand, which is powerful enough for two, pressed mine vigorously, and strode out before us through the middle door."

The secret audience had lasted a full hour. As Herzl went out with Bülow, the latter said: "That is a man of genius!" He advised Herzl to consult with Marschall, and to get full information from him. Herzl promised to do so, and then, immediately after, to work out the address and send it over.

He went at once to the German Embassy, but Marschall had left. Exhausted by the sheer physical strain of the day Herzl returned to his hotel. His heart was rebelling. While Wolffsohn packed the bags he tried to work on the address. At eleven o'clock he gave it up and lay down in his bed. At four in the morning (October 19) he woke, worked for half an hour, and broke off, exhausted. At six o'clock he got up again and worked till half past eight. He sent what he had done, with a covering letter, to Bülow, promising to forward the remainder to Palestine. Then he rushed to the harbor, where Wolffsohn had made all the necessary preparations. At eleven in the morning, under a cloudless sky, the steamship *Emperor Nicholas II* left Constantinople.

A week later, on October 26, 1898, Herzl, somewhat rested and recovered, arrived in the gaily bedecked harbor of Jaffa. As the party mounted the steps of the Hotel Kamenetz they heard the sound of saluting guns. The Kaiser had arrived in Jaffa from the landward side.

Herzl had not come to Palestine for a tour of inspection, but he was naturally anxious to take in whatever he could before the audience. His first visit was to Mikveh Israel, where he was accorded a festive reception by the director of the agricultural school. Herzl conversed with the pupils, visited the grave of Charles Netter, the founder of Mikveh Israel, and then continued on his way to the Rothschild colony of Rishon le-Zion.

The news of his approach travelled before him. No one knew for what purpose he was coming. Some believed that he had merely been sent by his newspaper; others read a much deeper significance into his visit. All the circumstances hinted at great, imminent events, and every colony was excited by his visit. There was the fact that he was coming first to one of the Rothschild colonies, and his negative attitude toward the work of the Baron was of course widely known: that he arrived in the country at the same time as the German Emperor; that the messianic enthusiast Hechler had preceded him, and had woven a mystery, full of vague hints and promises, round his voyage. And there was, on top of all this, the halo which had gathered round the name of Herzl. The young colonists were on fire with enthusiasm, and the flame communicated itself even to the officials of the colonies. The director of Rishon le-Zion was both friendly and distant, keeping a double eye on the colonists and on Paris. Herzl made a thorough inspection of the famous wine-cellars. A deputation then led him to the decorated community house, which was packed with an expectant crowd. A thunder of *Hedad*! greeted him, accompanied by well-meant music. The oldest settler saluted him in the name of the colony. Herzl was visibly affected; this was the first Jewish colony he had set eyes on. In his brief speech of response he expressed his happy astonishment at the work that had been accomplished, and praised the "magnificent generosity" of the Baron. The aim of Zionism was, to be sure, a greater one, the Jewish people was to find refuge here. But it was far from the intention of the Zionists to undertake anything in opposition to the rulers of the country or the direction of the colonies. The colonists only had to go on preparing the soil for the future, no other Zionist work was demanded or expected of them.

Then Herzl visited the individual houses, and was depressed by the wretched condition of the workers. He listened to a report from Dr. Mazie on the fever which raged in the vicinity, and discussed with him the necessity of large scale drainage of the swamps. On the whole, the colony made a bad impression on him. He had never doubted that with money industrial enterprises could be created. But the amounts that had been spent should have shown better results. But what he, whose Zionism was grounded in the feeling for human dignity and freedom, marked with the greatest distress was the relations between the settlers and the management. "Over all broods the fear of the Baron in Paris. The poor colonists have exchanged one dread for another."

The next morning he travelled on in the carriage of the Rothschild managers. In Ness Zionah (Wadi el Chanin), then a tiny settlement, he was received by the entire population, children sang songs, an old colonist came out with bread, wine and salt — the bread and wine grown on his own piece of land. Herzl was compelled to visit almost every house.

They travelled on — preceded always by the breathless announcement of their approach. Outside Rehobot he was encountered by a stormy cavalcade of sixteen young riders, who galloped in wild circles about his advancing carriage, sang Hebrew songs, and shouted *Hedad*! and *Hoch Herzl*! Herzl stopped his carriage and stepped out. His eyes were filled with tears. He was thinking: when would these high-spirited Jewish lads cease to be lonely symbols? In Rehobot itself the whole population was drawn up in two lines, and the songs of the children rose to the skies. Here Herzl saw no bowing and scraping, no fearsome glances, no repression. He remembered this when he wrote, a year later: "There are in Palestine other colonies than those of Rothschild. They cost less and yet they have become self-supporting sooner, and in these freer settlements there grows a sturdier generation. I need only mention the colony of Rehobot which must be regarded, by everyone who has seen it, as superior to, for instance, the more costly Rishon le-Zion."

Herzl returned in the evening to Jaffa, exhausted by the heat and the multitude of impressions. Soon after he received a visit from Hechler, whom he now encountered for the first time in Palestine. Through him he sent a message to Count Eulenburg that he would wait for the Kaiser on the road that ran by Mikveh Israel.

The next morning — it was a Friday — Herzl set out at an early hour for Mikveh Israel. He was not feeling well, and he had to make an effort to remain erect in the intense heat. The thermometer showed thirty-one degrees centigrade in the shade, forty one in the sun (eighty-eight and a hundred and six Fahrenheit). In front of the school the pupils were assembled, and many colonists had come from outlying points to join in the greeting. At nine o'clock the Imperial cortege approached. First came grim Turkish horsemen, then the Kaiser's outriders and finally, among a group of ladies in gray, the Kaiser himself. Herzl gave the signal to the young choir, which broke into the Imperial hymn. Then he stationed himself near a plough and took off his tropical helmet. The Kaiser recognized him from a distance. To the amazement of the assembled he suddenly pulled up his horse, and the entire procession halted. He rode up to Herzl, held out his hand to him, and called, "How are you?"

"I thank Your Majesty. I am taking a look at the country. How has Your Majesty's journey been till now?"

"Very hot! But the land has a future."

"For the moment it is still sick," said Herzl.

"It needs water," answered the Kaiser, "plenty of water."

"Yes, Your Majesty, large scale irrigation."

"It is a land with a future," repeated the Kaiser. He extended his hand again to Herzl and, while the children sang the Imperial hymn again, rode off with his suite.

The scene made the profoundest impression on the assembled, and on Herzl no less. He regarded it as a good omen for the forthcoming reception of the deputation. He returned with his companions to Jaffa. In the fearful heat of midday they set out by train for Jerusalem. The compartment was crowded. Herzl began to feel feverish, and the attack became stronger as the hours passed. He was greatly weakened. The train was late, and so, to Wolffsohn's utter despair, they were still on the train when the Sabbath set in. Moonlight lay over Jerusalem when they arrived. Feverish, supporting himself with a stick, his free arm given alternately to Schub and Wolffsohn, Herzl staggered rather than walked into the Kamenetz hotel. In spite of his exhaustion, the sight of old Jerusalem stretched out in the moonlight made a mighty impression on him. Within the hotel he felt sick, took quinine, retched, and became very weak. Schnirer, as a doctor, attended on him. Wolffsohn was beside himself with distress, and feared the worst. The next morning Herzl woke feeling better, though still weak; Wolffsohn had nothing to fear for the present.

That morning the Kaiser rode into the city, which had made great preparations for his reception. A new entrance had been broken through the Jaffa gate, so that the Kaiser would not have to dismount. The Jews, like the Turks, had put up a triumphal arch. Herzl would have liked greatly to greet the Kaiser under this arch; but the opposition of the hostile orthodox Jews, and the well-grounded fears of responsible Jewish leaders regarding the reaction of the Turkish authorities, made this impossible. So he sat alone in his little hotel room, outlined the conclusion of his address to the Kaiser, entered into his diary his impressions of the visit to Rishon le-Zion, and from his window watched the Kaiser passing first under the Jewish and then under the Turkish arches. In the evening he sent a clean copy of the address, with a covering letter, to Eulenburg, via Wolffsohn, and asked to be informed when he and his delegation would be received.

After the close of the Sabbath Herzl moved to a private house in Mamilla Street, where an entire floor was reserved for him and his entourage. Thither, on the next day, flowed a ceaseless stream of visitors — Zionists, admirers, curiosity hunters, people of the most diverse views and attitudes. Herzl listened attentively to their reports and recitals, and whatever he thought of importance he entered into a little notebook which he kept at hand. In the evening the party made a tour of the old city, under Schub's guidance. At the Wailing Wall, which he visited again the next morning, he was repelled by the sight of "the ugly, miserable, competing beggary," so that his deeper emotions were untouched. When he stood on the Tower of David, which they mounted that evening, he was entranced by the panorama of "the city covered with the first faint twilight of evening." On October 31 he again visited the Old City, and was careful to avoid the Imperial train, which was making its way to the dedication of the Church of the Redeemer. He also inspected a Jewish hospital, and from the gallery of the old synagogue looked out upon the panorama of the Temple site, the Mount of Olives and the city. The Old City, with its oriental filth, left him depressed. He was haunted by constructive ideas. He thought of cleaning out the Old City, and of retaining it simply as an area of religious sanctities. Round about this area would rise, upon the encircling hills, "a glorious New Jerusalem," airy, clean, gracious, in a modern architectural style deriving from the ancient. He returned to this idea over and over again.

Above all these thoughts lay always the shadow of the fear that the delegation might after all not be received. There was as yet no reply from Eulenburg. There were rumors that the Kaiser was breaking off his journey and returning direct to Berlin; France had declared war on England. Those were the days of the Fashoda incident. Herzl sent Wolffsohn and Hechler to the Imperial encampment; at half past seven Wolffsohn and Schnirer reported that Eulenburg had given Hechler the answer: the delegation would be received "tomorrow or the day after." Meanwhile the ship on which Herzl had planned to return left for Europe. On November 1 Herzl hit upon the idea of compiling a photographic album of the Jewish colonies and of sending it to the Kaiser, reminding him at the same time of the audience. Then at last, while Seidener and Schnirer were busy looking for the album, the message came from the German consulate: he was to report to Legation Councillor Kemeth in the Imperial encampment with regard to the address.

The Councillor received him somewhat condescendingly, and handed him back the address with some of the passages crossed out in pencil. This, that, and the other he could not permit Herzl to say to the Kaiser. Herzl was to prepare a new address and to submit it again for the Councillor's approval. Herzl ignored the man's impertinence and in the evening sent him the new fair copy via Bodenheimer. Commenting on a question raised by Herzl, Kemeth remarked that the German government expected no publicity to be given to the audience for the time being.

Extraordinarily enough Herzl was not staggered by the corrections; at least he gives no evidence of it in his diary. Actually all those passages had been deleted which referred specifically to the aim of the Zionist movement, to the desperate need of the Jewish people, and to the petition for the Kaiser's protection of the projected "Jewish Land Company for Syria and Palestine." The address was thereby robbed of a great deal of its character. Herzl seems to have looked upon these changes as intended for public consumption only. He was soon to learn that they meant a great deal more.

On Monday November 2, the exact date on which the Balfour Declaration was to be issued nineteen years later, the audience took place in the palatial Imperial tent.

The Kaiser was wearing a gray uniform, a turban, and gray gloves. In one hand he carried a riding whip, the other he extended in a friendly gesture. Herzl presented the delegation. Then he read out the address, while Bülow followed him in his manuscript. Herzl spoke first of the historic tie between the Jews and Palestine and of the aims of the Zionist movement, without however being permitted to allude to the official program; then he went on to speak of modern technology which made possible rapid colonization, and of the blessing for all humanity which would issue from this enterprise. "This is the land of our fathers," read the main passage, "a land suited to colonization and cultivation. Your Majesty has seen the land. It cries out for men to come and build it. And we have among our brothers a tragic proletariat. These men cry out for a land to build. Now these two crying needs — that of a land and that of a people — may be brought together for the alleviation of both. We believe this enterprise to be such an excellent one, so worthy of the participation of the most magnanimous spirits, that we bespeak for it the high help of Your Imperial Majesty."

The Kaiser in his answer thanked Herzl for the address, which he said had interested him extremely. "In any case," he added, "the enterprise must be made the subject of further investigation and conversation." He then made some observations on such colonization as had already been achieved. "What the land needs above all is water and shade." It was the Kaiser's opinion that the soil was cultivable. "The settlements which I have seen, the German no less than the Jewish, may serve as samples of what can be done with the land. There is room here for all. Only provide the water and the shade. For the native population, too, the colonization will serve as an example of initiative. Your movement, with which I am thoroughly familiar, is based on a sound idea." With the assurance of his sustained interest he closed the official reply, held out his hand to Herzl, and opened a less formal conversation. He referred to the frightful heat. Bülow, whom he had drawn into the circle, repeated the Kaiser's phrase about the great need of water.

"That we can supply," said Herzl. "It will cost billions, but it will bring in billions, too."

The Kaiser: "Well, you certainly have enough money, more than all of us."

Bülow: "Yes, when it comes to money, which is such a problem for us, you certainly don't suffer from a shortage."

The conversation passed to the harnessing of the water power of the Jordan, the hygienic condition of the country, and Herzl's plans for a "New Jerusalem." Then the Kaiser closed the audience by again holding out his hand to Herzl.

This audience was shorter than the one granted in Constantinople. It was also more vague. Certain influences or obstacles must have intervened during that period. The Kaiser assured Herzl of his interest and stated that further investigation was necessary. With regard to the projected protectorate nothing more was said; whether from caution, or to indicate refusal, remained an open question. "He said neither yes nor no." This was how Herzl summarized his impressions in his diary.

That evening Herzl and his friends packed their bags, and to escape observation, left by the early morning train for Jaffa. Herzl was for leaving the city and the country at once, before the news of the audience got abroad and produced dangerous repercussions. He did not feel safe on Turkish soil. It was not only Ben Yehuda's warning that disturbed him; he had received various intimations of the hostile attitude of Turkish officials. In Jaffa and Jerusalem he had observed that he was being followed by the secret service agent, Mendel Krämer; the latter did in fact let it be known afterwards that he had carried about with him an order for Herzl's arrest, to be used in case the visitor behaved suspiciously. Herzl was constantly thinking of the fate of Sabbatai Zevi, with whom he was often compared. On the ship which took him to Palestine he spoke of "the high point of the tragic enterprise" which he was approaching. When he mounted the Tower of David in Jerusalem he said to his friends: "It would be an excellent move for the Sultan to have me taken prisoner here." And when, after waiting a day and a half, he boarded the English orange freighter, the *Dundee*, on the evening of November 4 — this after some unpleasant incidents in Jaffa, and over the protests of his companions (Wolffsohn excepted) who found the boat too small — he wrote in his diary: "Now at last I consider our expedition ended, with, I believe, fairly good results. Palestine was a bit too hot for me, in more than one sense. If the Turkish government were possessed of a grain of political foresight, it would have finished the job there and then."

In Alexandria they abandoned the cockle-shell of a boat, on which all except Herzl and Schnirer had been sick, and transferred to the Italian luxury liner, *Regina Margheritta.* Herzl brooded without letup on the possible causes of the Kaiser's change of attitude. Had external difficulties intruded or had there been a change of feeling in the Kaiser himself? In reply to a cable inquiry, he received from his father the news that the audience had become public. But it was only when they debarked in Naples that they read the official German communiqué, which hid the audience in a closing paragraph among a score of unimportant political announcements, and deprived it of all significance. The communiqué reported first the Kaiser's visits to the Mosque of Omar and to the Roman Catholic and Greek Patriarchs, who received him surrounded by their respective hierarchies. "Later the Kaiser received the French Consul, also a Jewish deputation, which presented him with an album of pictures of the Jewish Colonies in Palestine. In reply to an address by the leader of the deputation, His Majesty remarked that he viewed with benevolent interest all efforts directed toward the improvement of agriculture in Palestine as long as these accorded with the welfare of the Turkish Empire, and were conducted in a spirit of complete respect for the sovereignty of the Sultan."

It was a frightful and sudden descent from the summit of hope into the empty abyss. Everyone was utterly dispirited. Herzl, the hardest hit, kept his head up. He would know what version of the affair to offer to the public. And in this manner of encountering defeat, he also felt himself the leader. "I am neither cleverer nor better than any one of you. But

I am undiscouraged, and that is why the leadership belongs to me." And as his first reaction to the news, he wrote in his diary: "The fact that the Kaiser has not taken over the protectorate is of course excellent for the later development of our enterprise . . . For the protectorate would have been a clear immediate advantage, but not a long range one. We should later have had to pay the most usurious interest for this protectorate."

The later student of events cannot but agree with this appraisal. The successive alienation of Germany from the Western Powers and Russia would have turned a German protectorate into a serious obstacle. The rivalry round Palestine would not have been mitigated; on the contrary, it would have been exacerbated. It would have been impossible to create a peaceful basis for Jewish colonization. Other difficulties of an internal Jewish character would also have arisen; there would have been a clash of patriotisms, and the funds on whose cooperation Herzl counted would, in such circumstances, hardly have been placed at his disposal.

But complications and difficulties would in all likelihood have arisen also within the sphere of German politics. Herzl himself admitted, after the audience at Constantinople, that from this point of view Bülow was perfectly right in behaving coolly toward the plan. As a responsible German statesman he foresaw that, even under the most favorable external circumstances, the practical realization of the plan was endangered by the negative attitude of the rich Jews. Besides, there was the Sultan's dislike of the Zionist policy. It had manifested itself so vigorously when the Kaiser first raised the subject that the latter, as the Sultan's guest, simply could not return to it again. Such was the account given later by Philip Eulenburg; and the Grand Duke of Baden told a Zionist Deputation in 1902 that on this visit the Kaiser made two unsuccessful attempts to broach the subject. It is quite certain that the German ambassador to Turkey, who accompanied the Kaiser on the return journey, influenced his master in the same direction. The whole thing had from the beginning been a personal affair of the Kaiser's, who had been won over by the Grand Duke and Philip Eulenburg. What Eulenburg's motives were remains unclear; they can hardly have been benevolent like the Grand Duke's. The most obvious assumption is that he wanted to put a skillful and prominent journalist under obligation to him. The Kaiser was wildly enthusiastic about the idea, and the reception of the deputation in Jerusalem must have been due to his personal initiative; it was thoroughly in keeping with his passion for theatrical gestures. Bülow, Marschall, Turkish influence and anticipated difficulties with France, England, and Russia, gradually cooled his enthusiasm; to these must be added the bad impression which the Jews of Jerusalem made on him and which the Grand Duke and Eulenburg blamed primarily for his change of heart. He cooled off as swiftly as he had fired up. No one then is to be blamed for the collapse of the protectorate idea; if any blame attaches it is to the Machiavellianism and court flunkeyism of Bülow, who permitted the Kaiser to make promises which were later to be broken. But this was the man all over. As far as he was concerned, the whole business was settled with the communiqué. What did it matter to him that he had landed Herzl in a most difficult situation?

CHAPTER X

THE UNCEASING QUEST

IT WAS one of the most painful moments in Herzl's life. His untimely London speech, the numerous articles—not all of them in the best taste — which had been published by *Die Welt* on the subject of the Kaiser's visit to Palestine, the vague hints of vast things to come which had been spread about by the uninformed during the absence of the deputation — all this had led to immense excitement and tension among friends and foes alike. Now came the communiqué, from which it was not even clear whom it was that the Kaiser had received. Herzl was exposed as a visionary, in fact as a liar who had promised more than he could perform, who had deceived himself and others, a man who stirred up and misled the masses. Was not this what his opponents had always said of him? They were not slow to seize their opportunity now. The Jewish liberal press read its own meaning into the communiqué, to wit, that the Kaiser had taken up a hostile attitude and had sent the Zionists packing. The *Allgemeine Zeitung des Judentums* did manage to find in the Kaiser's words an encouragement of philanthropic colonization, but with it "so decisive a disapproval of political Zionism that the latter, if it ever did possess a reasonable approach, must now be considered as utterly hopeless ... And yet what hopes these visionaries based on the Kaiser's journey to Palestine!"

Similar comments appeared in large numbers of publications.

Herzl's position in the face of these attacks was an extraordinarily difficult one. By publishing the negotiations, letters, and audiences which had preceded the reception in Jerusalem, he could easily have justified himself and strengthened his personal position; but he would also have put the German government in the wrong and perhaps have created considerable diplomatic embarrassment for it. He would, however, have inflicted at least as much harm on himself and the Zionist movement in its relations with the Powers. Germany, instead of being merely disinterested, would probably have become hostile: his indiscretions would also have warned off the other Powers. There was, besides, the question of honor. He had bound himself to silence and his will was set on keeping his word under all circumstances. There is a notation in his diary dated October 1898: "Everyone who comes in contact with me must get the opposite impression of the proverbial Jew."

All he wrote in *Die Welt* was that the purpose for which the delegation had gone to Palestine, namely, to be received by the Kaiser, had been fulfilled; further, that the reception had taken place in the presence of Secretary of State von Bülow — which at any rate indicated its political character — and that the Kaiser had answered his address "in a friendly manner." For the rest he was silent. None of the attacks, neither the few just ones, nor the many unjust ones, provoked him to speech, however hot they made his blood run. He knew his duty, and he fulfilled it with heroic disregard of his own person.

It was only to the larger Actions Committee, which met in Vienna between January 24 and 29, that he unfolded

some of the details of the political events since the second
Congress. Here he could with justice insist that the reception
by the Kaiser had been a triumph for the movement, even
if it had not led to the expected results. After all, the Kaiser
had looked thoroughly into the question, and if he had expressed his benevolent interest it meant that the movement
had been recognized as a reality and not condemned as a
Utopian fantasy; furthermore, all the Protest Rabbis to the
contrary notwithstanding, its legality had been established.
He drew similar conclusions from the comments in the
friendlier or more objective section of the Jewish and the
non-Jewish press. The *Hamburger Israelitisches Familien-
blatt* mentioned the encounter at Mikveh Israel and asked
when had such an honor been conferred before upon a Jew.
"Is it not a greater *Kiddush ha-Shem* than the promotion of
a Jew into the Reserve Officer's Corps?" The *Daily Mail*
discussed the problem of the Holy Places in this connection,
and suggested that the Zionist movement might well prove
the solution which would avert the threatening conflict.

The journey to Palestine was Herzl's first serious political
enterprise. He struggled hard against the realization that
the Kaiser's enthusiasm was by now completely dissipated
and that there was no longer any point of contact between
the Zionist movement and German foreign policy. Despite
the devastating communiqué, which he had evaluated quite
accurately on the first reading, he continued to take seriously
the Kaiser's promise of "further conversations" and to hope
that he would be able to overcome whatever new difficulties
had arisen.

So, for a quarter of a year or more, he still sought to pick
up the thread of the broken relationship. He visited the
German ambassador in Vienna, who was always friendly;

he sought out the Grand Duke of Baden, who remained as constant as ever in his kindliness and understanding, and who even provided him with letters of recommendation to a leading German bank in furtherance of his bank plans. He also gave him letters to the Kaiser, to Bülow, and to Lucanus.

But all of this did nothing to change the situation: Bülow remained cool, and Herzl never saw the Kaiser again. In a letter to the Grand Duke, whom he always kept informed of his steps, Herzl closed this chapter of Zionist history. "I can only assume that a hope which was especially dear to me has faded way and that we shall not achieve our Zionist goal under a German protectorate. I am sorrier than I can tell you."

The German adventure influenced Herzl profoundly in many ways. For one, his journey brought him into closer and more intimate relationship with Palestine. He himself later called it an "organic relationship." This new intimacy was reflected thenceforth in his speeches, as well as in his Palestine novel, which he began about that time. For another, he was deeply changed by the frightful disillusionment which followed so swiftly on highest hope. During the months immediately after his return he was subject to fits of bitter despair. He fought against them and shook them off. And gradually there emerged, in place of these alternating moods, a more even, fatalistic, and wearier condition of spirit. More and more he accepted in all his actions the motto which he had written down after his audience with the Grand Duke in February 1899: *Rien n'arrive ni comme on le craint ni come on l'espère*: nothing happens the way you fear or the way you hope. He worked on with bitter obstinacy, often sharply impatient with others. But more and more frequently he repeated that motto to himself, as if it were an incantation against excessive optimism which threatened to lift him to the clouds only to let him fall again into the abyss. And always he had to pump up more energy against his physical exhaustion and weariness, the results of his overstrained and irregularly working heart. A glimmering of the incurability of this sickness came to him in those days. "A hopeless sickness," he wrote in a feuilleton on the famous health resort of Nauheim, "is nothing other than premature old age." And fourteen days later he noted in Paris (June 19,1899): "Out of piety I always stay in the old house where I wrote *Der Judenstaat* four years ago. What a road I have traversed since then! And what weariness!"

Four weeks after his letters to Bülow and the Grand Duke came the collapse of his last buttress in his first great Zionist action. For fourteen years now Nevlinski had been suffering from heart attacks which became progressively worse. This was why he had not carried out his undertaking to work in Rome during Herzl's Palestine journey. When Herzl returned and met Nevlinski he saw that the man had one foot in the grave; he therefore let him keep the two thousand francs which he had advanced him for the journey to Rome. After the complete failure of his attempts to resume negotiations with Germany, he regarded Nevlinski as his only prospect of reaching the Sultan. Nevlinski declared himself ready, in spite of his condition, to go to Constantinople; his doctor, whom Herzl was careful to consult, raised no objections. A fatal attack might come anywhere, the journey as such made no difference. Herzl even had the impression, and not without reason, that a journey to the south would do Nevlinski some good. He engaged the young

Doctor Poborski as traveling companion and paid the full expenses for Nevlinski's entire family. When his agent left Vienna on March 30, Herzl still could not help feeling that he had assumed a heavy responsibility. Three days later a telegram came from Poborski that Nevlinski had died suddenly.

The news had a shattering effect on Herzl: he asked himself over and over again whether he was not partly to blame for Nevlinski's death. Actually Nevlinski's family found it convenient to assume that he was, and Nevlinski himself seems to have entertained this idea in the event of his death: Herzl would thereby become morally responsible for the welfare of the family. Herzl persuaded the Actions Committee to take over part of the funeral expenses and to vote the Nevlinski family a monthly subvention of 200 gulden until the end of that year. Then he transformed the *Correspondance de l'Est* into a little daily, *Petit Journal de Vienne*, which, under the editorship of Badeni's friend, Kozmian, was to serve for the distribution of news from the Near East.

At first Herzl considered the death of Nevlinski a great loss to Zionism. "He had the best connections with Constantinople, as well as with Rome. Practically irreplaceable," he noted in his diary. *Die Welt* published a eulogistic obituary. Within a few days, however, Herzl's estimate of Nevlinski's role was more moderate. "Whether he ever did anything for us with the Sultan, and whether he was even in the position to do anything, I do not know until this day . . . This mystery he has taken with him into the grave . . . And yet my conscience is clear vis-à-vis my shekel-payers when I ask the Actions Committee for this subvention. Perhaps he could not be of much use; but he could certainly have harmed us a great deal. He once hinted at the fact, and I hastened to make a friend of him before he resorted to blackmail. A single paragraph in the *Correspondance de l'Est* could have put us in the light of dangerous enemies of Turkey or, in the best case, of *blagueurs sans importance.*" Another few days passed, and an examination of Nevlinski's account books revealed that even the second picture was an exaggeration. The *Correspondance de l'Est* had exactly one dozen sub-scribers left. "And still the man was useful to us. His greatest service was that I learned from him to have no respect for *Pashas.*" Two months later Herzl was told by Nouri Bey, a high Turkish official, but, to be sure, not a very reliable witness, that Nevlinski had never submitted his proposals to the relevant authorities, and that he had, on the contrary, offered to serve as their spy within the Zionist movement.

Nevlinski's death occurred at a time when Herzl was greatly agitated by the question of the Bank. The creation of this instrument, with the least possible delay, was an indispenable matter for him. He foresaw the possibility, every time he entered into negotiations, that the demand would be made of him to produce the great sums which he promised before he had them in hand. The practical work was done by others, with Wolffsohn in the lead and Kann assisting him; but Herzl worried over every detail, was continuously urging and driving, complaining that things moved too slowly. He was warned on every side that this was not a matter which could be forced; but, supported by his father, he continued to press. He found the circumspection of his colleagues incomprehensible; he considered them phlegmatic, or ill-disposed; he thought he smelled sabotage, a secret understanding with his opponents. And his opponents consisted of nothing less than all non-Zionist Jewry. But resistance at its worst kept his spirits down only for a few hours or days at a time. On March 3, 1899, he wrote to Wolffsohn: "When difficulties like these arise, we must remain resolute, as in a storm at sea. We are a seafaring people." And two days later: "And now comes the last great effort. I am summoning up my last energies to put the subscriptions through. For God's sake get those subscription offices organized. We have only fourteen days left, before the opening of the subscription lists, and they still haven't sent me the offices for publication in *Die Welt*. Well now, how is it all going to be done? I am profoundly worried, and if I hadn't my obstinacy to fall back on, I would not know where to turn for encouragement."

He inserted notices in *Die Welt*, he wrote innumerable letters to raise the spirits of the Zionists. It was the first Congress all over again; and it was thus that Herzl saw it. By his unceasing admonitions and threats he so far hastened the legal preliminaries in London as to have the Bank registered by March 20. On March 28 the list was opened, and the subscription period extended from the original three days to four weeks. On the latter date Herzl wrote to Wolffsohn: "And now for a prophecy. I may be frightfully mistaken — and it would be my first great mistake in the movement — but I believe that the subscription is going to be a success. On every hand the mood is favorable. There's a kind of Congress mood in the air, but it's for the Bank. Others here share my feelings. We shall see. If the subscription is a failure, we can close our doors. If it is a success, triumphs will follow."

The letter was written two days before Nevlinski's departure for Constantinople; Herzl hoped to be called to the

Sultan while the subscription list was still open, and to exploit his diplomatic triumph for the benefit of the Bank. He hinted definitely at this prospect in the subscription appeal issued by the Actions Committee: "We shall see whether the Jewish people is prepared to put forth an effort in self-help . . . The preparatory diplomatic labors of the Zionist leadership have reached a point which permits us to state that shortly after the closing of the subscriptions we shall be able to take the first practical step toward the realization of our great plan . . ." In a major address in Vienna he expressed himself optimistically about the Bank. He called it the beginning of "the Jewish Chartered Company," which would establish the financial credit of the Jewish people and serve as mobilization center for all creative energies. After the first subscription day he noted in his diary: "I am in the same mood as Faust when he was ready to make any sort of compact with the devil. I am ready to sell ten years of my life to any man who will today promise me the success of the subscription."

Herzl's expectations were disappointed. A few days before the date set for the closing, Wolffsohn estimated that some 200,000 shares had been subscribed, three quarters of them in Russia. This was, in view of the difficulties they had encountered, a respectable enough showing, but it was out of all proportion to the promises and proclamations which had attended the campaign. As a matter of fact, the Bank could not even open for business until 250,000 shares had been subscribed — a precaution which had been embodied in the statutes of the institution. A new effort had to be made. Finally, toward the end of July, and still under Herzl's continuous urging and pleading, which at times became down-

right wounding in their sharpness, the necessary minimum
was obtained. The Bank was officially founded in time for
the third Congress.

Always on the alert for an opportunity to further his
political work, Herzl made use, about this time, of the opening of the Peace Conference in the Hague on May 18, 1899.
He had already greeted the Czar's peace manifesto at the
second Congress. Now the representatives of the various
Powers were assembling in the Hague, and Herzl tried to
turn the event to account. Bertha von Suttner, the famous
peace protagonist, had recently been dropped by the *Neue
Freie Presse*. Herzl, a great admirer of hers, engaged her to
obtain a series of interviews with the leading personalities
of the Conference on the subject of Zionism. His purpose
was "to bring Zionism to the attention of assembled Europe"
without "shocking the susceptibilities of Turkey or in any
way reflecting on her rights." The interviews were published
in *Die Welt*, and in fact the famous pacifist managed to
interest several statesmen in the Zionist movement, to which
she had herself been won over by Herzl. Among them were
Leon Bourgeois, of France, and the American ambassador
to France, Andrew White.

Toward the middle of June, Herzl himself went from Bad
Nauheim, where he took an eight day rest-cure for his heart
and nerves, to the Hague. His main purpose was to make
the acquaintance of the most representative Russian leaders,
and perhaps through them reach the Czar. On the evening
of his arrival the Baroness introduced him to State Councillor Bloch, the man whose initiative was responsible for
the calling of the Conference.

Ivan von Bloch, then sixty-five years old, was of Jewish descent. As banker, railroad builder and writer on political economy, he had achieved wealth and high distinction. In particular he had studied the question of war, and had come to the conclusion, based on a correct understanding of military development but an over-generous estimate of human reason, that the growth of the powers of destruction was bound to lead to an abandonment of war as an instrument of policy. His principal work is devoted to this theme, and leads up to the proposal for general disarmament.

Herzl's views were in general accord with Bloch's. He too had come to the conclusion that the development of the technology of warfare was bound to react in favor of peace. In 1895 he had noted in his diary: "The man who discovers a deadly explosive does more for peace than a thousand gentle apostles." He did not believe that magnanimity and high ideals could improve human beings. And in August 1899 he set down, as his life's slogan: "He who wishes to change men must change the conditions under which they live."

Thus he could agree with at least the theoretical foundations of Bloch's plan. Personally, too, he found the man to his liking. Nevertheless, if he put his pen at Bloch's service during those days, he did it solely with the purpose of placing Bloch under obligation, and thus obtaining a new foothold for Zionism. This was the technique he was to follow in the coming years; to extend help to others in political questions which did not affect him directly, to play to some extent the honest broker, in order to further his own enterprise.

On June 16 an opportunity of this kind presented itself. Germany had entered the Conference reluctantly. Toward the end of May, when the question of the Court of Arbitration was being debated, Germany's attitude became strongly negative. This open hostility, politically clumsy as it was, made it easy for the other Powers to blame the inadequate results of the Conference on Germany, and in fact great play was made of this incident in the anti-German propaganda of the First World War. Herzl was therefore doing both Germany and the Conference a service when he wrote without delay to the Grand Duke, to acquaint him of the anti-German sentiment which was awakening among the delegates and visitors. He pointed out that if a split should come on the question of the Court of Arbitration, with Germany heading the group of non-participants, Europe would be divided into Arbitration States and "Outlaw" States. "I hope," he wrote to the Grand Duke, "that the reckoning is being made without the host, and I should be happy if this modest report of mine contributes something toward averting this danger for Germany."

Herzl showed this letter to Councillor Bloch, and when, two days later, Professor Zorn was instructed by the head of the German delegation, Count von Münster, to report to Berlin, it might very well appear that it was Herzl's warning that had led to the recall of the German delegate. Bloch asked Herzl for a memorandum of his action vis-à-vis the Grand Duke, and gave it to the Russian Minister, de Staal, who telegraphed it to the Czar. Herzl had achieved his purpose; his name had been brought favorably to the attention of the Czar; Bloch promised to try to obtain an audience for him.

His visit to the Hague had another result; it seemed to have opened for him the path to the Sultan. The Turkish delegate to the Conference was Nouri Bey, General Secretary of the Turkish Foreign Office, whom Herzl had already met on his first visit to Constantinople. Nouri Bey now promised him to get together a group of officials (himself included) who could be bribed into arranging an audience with the Sultan. A substitute had been found for Nevlinski.

From the Hague, Herzl went to Paris, where Narcisse Leven assured him vaguely that the Jewish Colonization Association (*ICA*) would cooperate when it came to a question of practical colonization. From Paris he hastened to London, to press action on the Bank. On June 26 he participated in the Conference of the English Zionist Federation, which had been founded the year before, and in the evening addressed a mass meeting in St. Martin's Town Hall.

He spoke in a popular and simple vein; but those who, in later years, are able to reconstruct the setting of the time, can feel in his address the difficulties under which he labored. It was in this same place that, three quarters of a year before, he had made his messianic speech, filled with high promise. He could not justify or vindicate it now, for he could not and would not tell the story of the negotiations. He therefore confined himself to hints and intimations — the result being, once again, that the enthusiastic masses interpreted his political position as being stronger than it actually was.

For the first time he exposed publicly and in some detail the character of his first objective. He put it thus: when a man who intends to build a house finds that he cannot purchase the land immediately, he may still proceed via a lease, or some similar arrangement. "It is my hope that I may be able to come to this kind of legal arrangement, translated into political terms, with the Turkish government. We may properly anticipate the possibility of an agreement, as long as the sovereignty of His Majesty the Sultan is not brought into question, and as long as an ensured immigration into

Palestine will carry with it no challenge to Turkish territory but rather a consolidation and enhancement of its values. I have been successful in winning over, for the furtherance of these plans and ideas, immense influences." "We want to obtain a Charter from the Turkish government, in order to colonize Palestine under the sovereignty of the Sultan."

He spoke in the same strain two months later at the opening of the third Congress. "Our efforts are directed toward obtaining a Charter under the sovereignty of His Majesty the Sultan. It is only when we are in possession of such a Charter, which must carry with it the public recognition and the legal guarantee of our rights, that we can begin a great colonization action."

These utterances made it appear that he had merely changed his tactical approach to the problem. Actually it had become clear, after the collapse of the negotiations, that there was no prospect of obtaining, within a reasonable length of time, either the right to an independent state in Palestine, or even as much as a vassal state under Turkish suzerainty. Nor would the Sultan agree, under any circumstances, to the sale of a land which the Mohammedans, too, regarded as sacred. But it did appear possible to Herzl to obtain, by lease or purchase, colonization rights for a large Company. The problem would then be to incorporate in the document defining these rights — the "Charter," as Herzl called it — such conditions as would, in effect, guarantee him the security he sought, above all, autonomy and self-defense.

Such charters had been in wide-spread use since the beginning of the seventeenth century, and many countries had been colonized in this fashion. The idea was not new even in regard to Palestine. In 1875 General Sir Charles Warren, the famous Palestinian archaeologist, had put it forward, in connection with the Jewish people. He had even spoken of the objective of a Jewish principality "either under the sovereignty of Stambul, or, in case of the partition of Turkey, as an independent kingdom protected by the Great Powers." It is improbable that Herzl knew of this suggestion, but it was in keeping with his general line of thought that he should, unlike the majority of colonizers, envision the political not less than the economic aspects of such an enterprise.

The third Congress, which met in Vienna from August 15 to 18, 1899, differed from the first two in one important respect, namely that the ideological opponents of political Zionism took no part in it. The result was a mitigation of the internal strains and a larger measure of determination, such as Herzl had always aimed at both for the movement and for the Jewish people. What did emerge, however, was a definite oppositional mood directed at Herzl himself, as well as against the particular circle of the Vienna Actions Committee. This need not by any means have been all to the bad. Herzl had become so organically a part of the movement, his leadership was so unchallenged, that his followers no longer needed to sacrifice everything to enthusiastic support of him; they could permit themselves to criticize the details of his proposals. The question was only what the results of such an opposition would be.

In his opening address Herzl rehearsed the significance and tasks of the movement, and reiterated the principle that Zionism did not intend to interfere in the internal affairs of any country. He then went on to speak of the two great successes scored since the preceding Congress. The first was the founding of the Bank, which was, however, only an instrument toward the obtaining of the Charter. The second was the receiving of the Zionist Deputation in Jerusalem. Herzl merely alluded to the fact, without mentioning the hopes he had based on the audience, or the disappointment which had ensued. He begged the Congress not to exploit the incident for purposes of propaganda, and to avoid discussion of it. One point he stressed in particular: "After this incident the complete legality and loyalty of our movement can never again be questioned." These words evoked a storm of applause among delegates and visitors; but neither the words nor the applause could check the rising tide of criticism.

The opposition, which found its strongest and sharpest proponent in Leo Motzkin, was largely directed against three points. Particularly unpleasant was the criticism of Herzl's London speech of October 1898. Motzkin censured it for having been over-generous and over-specific in its promises. Such premature and exaggerated utterances could only send a passing wave of enthusiasm through the people, while the effect which was really desired, that of deeper insight and preparation for patient labor, was rendered impossible. Herzl found himself on the defensive at a Congress for the first time. He justified his London speech by reference to the circumstances in which he had made it; he pointed out, further, that he had set no time limit. He had said only that he "was more convinced than ever that we are on the right path." Occasional words of encouragement like these would do more, in his opinion, to drive the movement forward, than "the mathematically calculated form of propaganda" suggested by Herr Motzkin, the mathematician. "Herr Motzkin," he went on, ironically, directing himself at the opposition, which also accused him of a dictatorial attitude, "would have us remain mathematically and pro-grammatically silent whenever something good happens in the movement . . . I believe that an army on the march needs an encouraging word, a song, a flag . . ."

The second body of criticism hinged on certain of the statutes of the Bank. It was noted first that, despite the resolution of the second Congress, the Bank had not formally restricted its activities "to the Orient, and particularly to Palestine and Syria." Herzl was able to prove documenta-rily that the removal of this restriction had been effected by the London committee of lawyers, over his protests and those of the Actions Committee. As far back as March, Ussishkin had, on these grounds, refused to sign the subscrip-tion appeal, and had been won over only by the assurance that the restriction would be re-introduced. Actually there had been an extraordinary session of the Board of Directors, of which Herzl was President, held in Vienna on August 17. It had been resolved there to change the offending passage to read that, while economic and industrial activity might be carried on in other countries, the Bank could do coloni-zation work only in Palestine.

The point of this criticism being blunted, the distrust of Herzl found sharper expression in the criticism of the manner in which the Founders' Shares had been dis-tributed. In order to safeguard the Zionist character of the Bank, it had been decided that the hundred Founders' Shares which were issued were to be reserved for mem-bers of the Actions Committee; these hundred shares, which would yield no dividends, would ensure the Zionist governing body of one half of the votes at any general meeting of the shareholders. It had been further provided that twenty of these shares were to be reserved for tried and

trusted Zionists, and assigned to them for life, both as a mark
of honor and against possible changes in the character of the
Actions Committee. The opposition, again led by Motzkin,
insisted that this life assignment of Founders' Shares was
undemocratic and dangerous, since there was no assurance
that any holder of a Founders' Share would remain forever
faithful to the movement. The debate became acrimonious.
Herzl was stung by the lack of confidence, which had already
manifested itself before the Congress in all sorts of suspicions; he thought the time had come to show the Congress
that he was not prepared to put up with every attack. He
declared himself ready to submit every resolution to a vote.
But it so happened that of the twenty Founders' Shares
which were to be assigned for life, seven had already been
promised by the Actions Committee to the actual founders
of the Bank. Wolffsohn, who was one of them, was deeply
wounded by the attitude of the Congress, and declared he
and his six co-founders were ready to relinquish the shares.
But Herzl was determined to make this a test question.
If the Actions Committee was to find itself hindered in the
fulfilment of its promises there was, said Herzl, no possibility
of further work. He carried his point; the promise of the
Actions Committee was endorsed, but a resolution was also
passed against the further distribution of Founders' Shares.

The third storm centre of the Congress was the so-called
"cultural question," on which Herzl took a sharper stand
now. Ever since the second Congress there had been growing
dissatisfaction with the indifferent or negative attitude of
the Vienna Actions Committee (with the exception of
Dr. Kahn, one of the chief proponents of that policy) toward
cultural activity. Actually it was never very clear what the
defenders of the idea were aiming at. In accordance with a

resolution of the second Congress, there had been founded the "General Hebrew-Speaking Society." Its work, like the cultural work in general, depended in reality on the efforts of individuals. Now the Congress rang with magniloquent and moving speeches in favor of a renewed Jewish culture. But that was all it came to. The leadership could not be asked for anything more than its general approval of these aims. However, even this degree of cooperation, which would mean the identification of the movement as such with the cultural program, was opposed by the orthodox rabbis. To them the secular character of the work — part of it was, indeed, definitely anti-orthodox — was a contradiction of Herzl's reiterated promise of the complete neutrality of the Congress in such matters. Herzl was forever seeking to anticipate and suppress these debates, which he found premature. "Let us not weaken ourselves," he pleaded, "by emphasizing our differences. Not that these are bad in themselves, but they must be brought out at the right time, that is, when they can be useful as mutual correctives."

Apart from the ratification of the Bank, the most important act of the Congress was the reconstruction of the permanent machinery of the movement, or rather the introduction of a permanent machinery in place of the provisional. The Actions Committee, till then the executive of the Congress, was reconstituted as an Inner Actions Committee of five members and a Large Actions Committee, whose numbers were to be fixed by each Congress. The general organization was divided into national committees, districts and societies.

All in all, this Congress, despite its sharp inner differences, lacked the storminess of the first two Congresses. When Herzl closed the Congress on a late Friday afternoon, well in

advance of the Sabbath, he declared: "Our Congress has
been a quiet one. We did not attain to that level of enthusiasm which marked the former Congresses. But as against
that, we worked all the more. The Congress has passed out
of its boyhood, it has entered the stage of manhood."

One purpose the Congress served which the German
minister in Berne, reporting to the Kaiser, noted in the
precis: "it put an end to oft-repeated assertions that interest
in the Zionist movement would last only as long as the
charm of its novelty." But in spite of all the ovations
which were accorded him at the close of the Congress, Herzl
could not conceal from himself the fact that at least a portion
of the delegates were disappointed at the lack of some great
political triumph. To his own impatience was now added the
impatience of those who were waiting for immediate practical
activity. The double pressure drove him to new and more
feverish efforts.

The day before the Congress, Herzl had been received in
audience by the Grand Duke of Hesse. The arrangements
had been made by the ever-faithful Hechler. Herzl asked
the Grand Duke to use his good offices for an interview with
the Czar, who was expected to visit Darmstadt later in the
year. In October Herzl wrote to the Grand Duke, reminding
him of his request. Possibly the tone of the letter was not
considered subservient enough by the little potentate, for
Hechler, who was again the middleman, was received coolly.
Herzl was not invited. At the end of October, Hechler
broached the subject again, and received a letter in Grand
Duke Friedrich's hand to the effect that the latter had
spoken with the Czar, who had been persuaded by Muraviev
not to grant the audience. Herzl was advised to prepare a

memorial in French; the Grand Duke undertook to transmit
it to the Czar. Herzl wrote out the memorial, which he himself characterized as "a vague, verbose, court document,"
and had it translated by Dr. Marmorek, the bacteriologist.
The Grand Duke sent it at once to St. Petersburg, where it
was read with friendly attention, but produced no results, in
spite of the additional representations made by Nordau and
Bertha von Suttner to Pobiedonostzev, Muraviev and the
Russian ambassador Kapnist. The road to St. Petersburg,
itself a new approach to the road to Constantinople, remained closed.

However, there did seem to be some hope now of a direct
approach. The conversations which Herzl had begun with
Nouri Bey in the Hague promised to bear fruit. Passing
through Vienna toward the end of August, the Turkish
minister came to a definite understanding with Herzl.
The latter was to give him advance baksheesh of ten thousand francs; there was, further, a pledge of thirty thousand
francs, to be divided between Nouri Bey and his equally
honorable colleagues, as soon as the audience was arranged.
Thereafter Herzl heard very little from Nouri himself;
instead he received innumerable letters from Nouri's agent,
Crespi, written in wretched French, and reporting conversations and negotiations with all sorts of important
persons, who were supposed to have been won over. Mid-
December, when the German industrialist George von
Siemens was in Constantinople on the business of the Bagdad
railroad, Crespi wrote Herzl to hold himself in instant
readiness to proceed to the Turkish capital on telegraphic
instructions. Great efforts had been made in his behalf, and
he would be received immediately on his arrival. Herzl
waited and waited. No wire came.

Meanwhile the pressure of his private affairs became increasingly severe. His public work suffered because he was not in an independent position. The *Neue Freie Presse* continued to ignore everything connected with the Zionist movement, and its publishers were forever pressing Herzl to mitigate his efforts on its behalf, or to abandon it altogether. Herzl also feared that his frequent absences from Vienna on Zionist business would one day cause him to lose his post; and with it would go not only his recognized position in the journalistic world, but his independence with respect to the movement. He had been repeatedly urged, both in private and at the Congresses, to give up his profession and to enter the service of the movement. He had refused, decisively, not because he saw anything dishonorable in it, but because he was afraid of his independence vis-á-vis his followers, and of the evil tongues of his opponents. He felt that as creator and leader of the movement for the renaissance of his people he could not permit himself to draw a salary. In fact, he did the contrary: by August 1899, he had used up the larger part of his private fortune for the furtherance of the movement. He had spent, in round figures, fifty thousand gulden (over eighty thousand marks) on *Die Welt* — which never paid for itself — on his travels, on the founding of the bank, and for "advances" of all kinds.

The disappearance of his fortune, which hampered his independence in respect to the *Neue Freie Presse*, and which haunted him also as a crime against his own children, drove him to seek a source of income from the theatre. It was for this, among other reasons, that he had pushed the production of *The New Ghetto*. It was again for this reason that he now went back to old manuscripts which he himself had rejected, and also wrote new pieces more or less of the same character.

In August 1898 he completed a somewhat wry comedy of marriage *Unser Käthchen,* begun in 1891 under the title of *The Fleshpots of Egypt.* Certain overtones of his own marriage can be detected in it. The day before he left for Palestine he read the piece out to the actors of the *Burgtheater,* in case he should not return from his journey, or should return to find himself without a post. The production was forbidden by an overzealous censorship. However, in February 1899, he was present at the first performance in the *Deutsches Volkstheater* in Vienna. It was accorded a friendly reception, and was played again in Prague in June of that year.

Shortly thereafter he dramatized an old feuilleton of his, *I Love You,* and turned it into a light, harmless comedy. In October 1900, he completed a drama in four acts, *Gretel,* or, as he called it at first, *The Sinful Mother.* He notes that, while the Congress was approaching, this piece occupied his attention "more than the Congress, and my uncompleted Congress address, and the Grand Dukes and Princes, and my slave-drivers of the *Neue Freie Presse.*" It is a moral, sentimental piece, but gripping enough. The story deals with a mother who has fallen into immoral ways, has been recalled to a sense of duty and honor by her sick child, and commits suicide because she fears that her husband will deprive her of the child as punishment. The best characterization is of the child, Gretel. One of the characters says of her: "All the gifts and possibilities of the adult are already evident in her. And it is her peculiar charm that she neither knows nor suspects the existence of what is already awake in her. In her glance you read all the measure of intelligence which one needs for life, but happily for her she does not yet know what life is . . . She lacks only knowledge, experience, destiny; otherwise she is a complete human being."

These words are characteristic of Herzl's manner of seeing children. Year after year, since he had thrown himself into the Zionist cause, he had had less and less time for his children, whom he loved tenderly and longingly, and whom, in his over-solicitous way, he was having educated only by private teachers. But the few minutes which he could manage to pass with them in play and conversation, the brief intervals when they were together on summer holidays, sufficed to give him a profound insight into their lives and the life of children in general. His children's feuilletons, which so charmed his contemporaries, still retain that mild, philosophic twilight lustre which surrounds and illumines their sharp, penetrating observations. Equally alive for us are his *Philosophic Stories*, the best and ripest of which he produced at about this time.

We have already spoken of the stories *The Dirigible Airship* and *The Inn of Anlin*. Most revealing for the student of Herzl's history and personal philosophy is the story which he wrote in April 1900, and later dramatized: *Solon in Lydia*. Solon, the great lawgiver, leaves Athens for ten years, in order that he may not be tempted to mitigate the stern justice of the laws which he has instituted, and which, during his absence, are to become flesh of the people's flesh and bone of their bone. While he is on a visit to King Croesus, a boy appears at court reporting that he has found a way of producing flour chemically without using the growth of the field. He is prepared to give up his secret if Croesus will give him his daughter in marriage. Croesus asks Solon for advice. Solon, who conceived an immediate love for the boy, answers: "He must be killed; for he will destroy the order of the world, which is based on the needs and the labor of men. This ill-omened boy would make all men carefree; he would rob them

of the best thing they have, their hunger. What? Shall the
wild days of the Pelasgians return? Shall citizenship and
morality and the settled ways of man be permitted to disappear together with the art of the husbandman? ... A king
must know how to put to death ... And that not only the
wicked, the evil-doers; that is too easy and too pleasant.
He must know how to destroy even the good, if the welfare
of his land is at stake. It is for this that there exists no
earthly power above yours, in order that you may be able to
do even such a thing. That is the unspoken justification of
your power." The King rejects Solon's advice. He experiments, instead, with the free distribution of flour. Labor
and commerce come to a standstill; the populace becomes
lazy, bellicose, dissolute, rebellious. Solon makes one more
attempt to persuade the youth to keep the secret to himself:
the latter, in his high idealism, looks upon Solon's offers only
as a character test. Finally Solon hands him the beaker of
poisoned wine.

This little story is a sample of the innumerable pieces
Herzl was producing at that time in the midst of his political
activity. Their quality was uneven, but there was a steady
ripening of his style into a fine naturalness. They covered
a wide range of subjects: books, plays, expositions, incidents
from daily life, travelogues, moods. There were also political
reviews, with particular emphasis on internal conditions in
France. He could not, of course, avoid the Dreyfus affair,
but he reserved his treatment of its Jewish aspects for
Die Welt. His favorite subject was the technology of the
future and its significance for the individual and social life of
man. So we find feuilletons on the bicycle, a recent invention
to which Herzl himself was passionately addicted, on the

automobile, just emerging into practical form, and on aero-
nautics ("Kress and Zeppelin"). All these pieces, which, like
many others, are not to be found in any collection of his
feuilletons, give us a glimpse of the world which we know
today in its early stages. The hopes and enthusiasms which
he centered on technology interpenetrate also his Palestine
novel, which he began in the summer of 1898, and to which
we shall return in greater detail.

Even so superficial a review as the foregoing shows us that
there was no sharp division between his professional and his
Zionist activities. But he was irked and depressed by the
anomaly of his position. On the one question which gave his
very life its meaning he could not write a line in the *Neue
Freie Presse*, and he who so frequently negotiated with the
world's potentates still remained, in the eyes of the publishers, a dependent employee whom they could dismiss at
will. Little wonder, then, that he was always on the lookout
for an opportunity to put an end to a situation which he felt
to be undignified and unworthy of him. In December 1899,
there arose a rumor that Bacher was preparing to sell out
his holdings on the newspaper and to retire. Thereupon
Moritz Reichenfeld who, besides being Herzl's friend and
relative and financial adviser, was also a bank director,
proposed to raise the money with which Herzl might buy out
Bacher, thus achieving, as co-publisher, a status of greater
freedom. The negotiations which ensued, and which lasted
for many days, were complicated by Herzl's son-to-father
attitude with regard to Bacher himself; there were exciting
scenes, reproaches, reconciliations. The objective which
Reichenfeld had proposed was never attained, but not a little
good was achieved. Herzl's salary became the highest on the

newspaper, he was put in exclusive charge of the literary section, and was given the definite promise that henceforth the purely practical achievements of the Zionist movement could be printed freely in the *Neue Freie Presse*.

Before such achievements could be registered, however, there had to be enough money in hand; above all, the Bank, which was already registered, had to open for business. But according to its own statutes it could not do so until £250,000 had been paid in. The money accumulated slowly, partly because of the vast number of small subscribers — the total was 120,000 — partly because of the economic crisis in Russia, and partly because of political difficulties in that country. In Austria, too, unexpected obstacles arose. The Governor of Galicia forbade the promotion of subscriptions, and Brecher, the Viennese banker who was acting as agent, was called to police headquarters. Following his regular practice, Herzl exploited these difficulties for the purpose of thrusting the work forward.

The Prime Minister of Austria at this time was the recently appointed Ernst von Koerber, who was also Minister of the Interior. Von Koerber, a straightforward, clearthinking official, was, like all his predecessors, greatly preoccupied with the struggle of the various nationalities comprising the Austro-Hungarian Empire. Herzl went to him at first in the matter of the Bank. He found von Koerber sympathetic, understanding, and anxious to be of help. Herzl, on his side, was ready to offer his services to von Koerber in his own difficulties. Herzl's name was of value, his counsel was sound, and he made an excellent impression on the Prime Minister. The two men met eleven times between the end of February and the beginning of July.

Von Koerber opened up to Herzl, told him of his relations with the Kaiser, consulted him on important questions of internal policy. Herzl's ultimate aim was to help solve the minority problems of Austria-Hungary, and to win over the Austro-Hungarian government to a support of his policy in Constantinople, thus finding a substitute for Germany. Herein Herzl was encouraged by the Grand Duke of Baden, who remained unshakeably faithful, and who had begun to look upon his support of the movement as a task entrusted to him by the Almighty.

Meanwhile the Bank was Herzl's most immediate problem, and it was in this connection that he now visited London. But he did not neglect any opportunity to make new connections. He had Nordau introduce him to Alfred Austin, Poet-Laureate of England, who in turn gave him a very friendly letter to Lord Salisbury, the Prime Minister. It was Herzl's idea that if he could win England's support in Constantinople, Germany might once again become interested in the question. Salisbury, however, could not receive him. His worries over the Boer War left him no time.

For months now Herzl had been receiving letters of complaint, most of them anonymous, directed against the Bank management. The work was dragging along, there was neglect, there was failure to register subscriptions, there was duplication of registrations. Graver accusations were not wanting, either. Herzl became increasingly nervous. His own honor and the honor of the movement seemed to him to be at stake; the very existence of the bank was threatened, if he could not restore immediate order and obtain swift action. He pressed, begged, threatened, demanded, and, backed by the Vienna Actions Committee and the Board of Directors, issued orders and instructions. In all this he did not actually overstep the boundaries of his functions as President of the Board, but he did act against the accepted traditions of the business world, which the others understood better than he. He wounded the feelings of responsible officials and co-workers, not excluding Wolffsohn, who begged him again and again to leave the management of the bank to businessmen. When Herzl, still with the support of his Vienna advisers, called a meeting of the directors to London, over the heads of the directors themselves, Kann and Lourie protested by absenting themselves, and even Wolffsohn felt himself driven to a similar protest. "For the first time he has refused!" wrote Herzl in his diary, disappointed. Worried, embittered, deeply agitated, he had the affairs of the Bank reviewed by a certified accountant and by a banking expert.

The investigation disclosed no irregularities in the handling of the monies, but it was the opinion of the expert that the complaints regarding the dragging of the work were justified. Together with those directors who had attended the meeting, but without consulting those who had absented themselves, Herzl issued instructions for the acceleration of the work. There ensued a complicated and embittered correspondence with Kann, who felt that his honor and standing had been impugned. Wolffsohn, too, was deeply wounded, and offered his resignation. "I can no longer give you my advice," he wrote, "for I know only too well that you will not follow it. . . For me, as a Zionist, this is the first dark and hopeless day. I hope God will show me that I am mistaken."

Herzl's answer to Wolffsohn was angry, almost brutal. "You surely are not looking for an excuse to quit, are you? If the moment has arrived, you need no excuse. All you need say is: I've had enough. Then you may go. As regards

Kann, I have stood for more from him than from any other man, even after I recognized his inefficiency. Was your letter of resignation nothing more than a comedy, designed to make me beg on my knees that you remain? I don't understand such jokes. This is a serious matter for me. Nothing remains now but to take the proper measures. We shall have many other great problems in Zionism to solve, and with God's help we shall solve them. *In die Hosen scheissen darf man natürlich nicht, wenn eine Schwierigkeit auftaucht.* Difficulties exist for the precise purpose of rousing in us the strength to overcome them ... As to what you say regarding gratitude, I am completely mystified ... My dear Daade, do not weaken. You are too susceptible to influences. I will give you a key to every situation in which you may possibly find yourself. Only keep on asking yourself whether you still believe in Zionism. If you do, then you may calmly go through thick and thin with me . . . . How you, who know all my views, my readiness to sacrifice myself for the cause, and my paternal anxiety in all Zionist affairs, can speak of my irresponsible experiments with the Bank, I fail to understand. This is not you, but someone else speaking through you. I do not want to be 'my own minister,' i.e., my own bank manager; I want to find the man most fitted for the post. And now, in rejecting your resignation, let me emphasize that what you have said does not constitute acceptable grounds for a resignation. I shall understand you only when you say that you recognize Herr Kann, and not myself, as the leader of the Zionist movement. In that case go with him, in God's name, I shall make no effort to hold you back. But if you happen simply to be tired, like many another, then leave it to me to find a decent, presentable excuse for the rest of the world. Otherwise you will only be disgracing yourself. But you will also be disgracing me, who have so long believed in you and have let you look into the most secret places of my heart."

It is of a piece with Wolffsohn's utter devotion and self-sacrifice that he remained at his post despite the crying injustice of this letter. "I am by no means tired," he replied, "nor am I looking for an excuse of any kind. I will never leave either Zionism or you of my own free will. But if compelling grounds should force me out of the movement, it is a matter of complete indifference to me what reasons are cited for my demission, and what people will think. I have never sought anything in Zionism for myself or my person." He then went on to confront Herzl honestly and manfully with all his errors, which, despite the irreproachability of his intentions, were not the less dangerous because they arose from his complete lack of business experience and his readiness to pay more attention to the complaints and loose talk of outsiders than to his own confidential advisers. "You say you do not want to be your own minister, but would rather find the most suitable men. But even before you have anything like the right number, you push out the few you have acquired. You will never find the suitable men because you measure everybody by your own standard, and find nothing but inadequacy and littleness. If there are some men who, like myself — permit me this immodesty — are capable of doing something, given a free hand, but who out of admiration of you yield on every issue, they are rendered valueless, because their own abilities do not come into play. And if there are men with opinions of their own, who do what they believe to be the right thing, like Kann, then you won't have them. Anything in between must be 'false' and dangerous."

Herzl was deeply moved by these words, and thanked Wolffsohn by wire for his "good letter." But in the matter of the Bank he stood by his guns. On May 16 he directed Wolffsohn to threaten Kann with the loss of his friendship if he did not withdraw from his stand. This Wolffsohn refused to do, since he considered Kann not wrong, but merely obstinate, "which may be said of some of my dearest and most respected friends."

In the midst of these confusions and exchanges, the special conference of the larger Actions Committee and of the Bank, called by Herzl for May 25, took place. Wolffsohn was absent. A new Bank Commission was appointed. It was also decided, against some initial opposition by Herzl, to hold the next Zionist Congress in London. "I suddenly saw," Herzl notes in his diary, "that we have outgrown Basle. I have been growing steadily more intimate with London." Commenting on the resolution in *Die Welt*, he wrote: "Political Zionism is going to London, in order to present itself to the English world and to solicit its support — but only its moral and political support, be it well noted." Then, three days later, he again queried the situation in his diary: "The Congress in London? I am taking my Basle players to London because I have reason to be afraid that I can no longer find an audience in Basle."

On June 19, Wolffsohn came to Vienna, and the two men had a heart to heart talk. There were deep, earnest and disturbing differences to be settled. When Wolffsohn described in all its fullness the confusion which reigned in the Bank's affairs, Herzl finally yielded and entrusted Wolffsohn with full power to proceed to a reorganization. One result of the conference was a complete reconciliation, and even a strengthening of the bond between them. The outward sign of their renewed and deepened intimacy was that Herzl asked his good, dear "Daade" to address him thenceforth by the familiar *Du* instead of the formal *Sie*.

Thus the inner mood was, shortly before the fourth Congress, calmer and friendlier. Externally, too, there was some progress to record, for Herzl managed to win over to the movement no less a personality than Arminius Vámbéry, who had already been approached two years before by Tobias Marcus. Vámbéry, adventurer, explorer, scientist, and secret political agent for England and Turkey, occupied, ostensibly at least, the position of Professor of Oriental Languages at the University of Budapest. He was of Jewish origin, but he changed religions with the same speed and facility as he acquired languages. Years before he had been language teacher to the Princess Fatima, sister of Abdul-Hamid, and had therefore been on intimate terms with the latter since his boyhood. There were certain startling contrasts between Vámbéry and Herzl. They were divided in time by the breadth of a generation, and in their respective attitudes toward Judaism by an immeasurable distance. For all that, they conceived a liking for each other. But it was by no means certain that Vámbéry would do anything for the Zionist leader. Herzl sent letter after letter, pressing the orientalist and explorer to obtain an audience for him before the holding of the fourth Congress. "I know," he wrote, "what it is you wish to construct in your autobiography: nothing less than a royal sepulchre. Let the crown to your pyramid be this chapter: 'How I helped prepare the homecoming of my people, the Jews.' The whole of your marvelous life will then appear as if it had been pointed to this end." When Vámbéry replied that it was impossible to get anywhere with the Turks by means of letters, and in a hurry, Herzl pleaded again: "Disraeli once said to a young Jew: 'You and I belong to a race who can do everything but fail.' My dear Vámbéry Pasha! We can do really everything, but we must be willing. Won't you, Vámbéry *Cácsy?*"

Vámbéry replied the next day that he had written to the Sultan, though he was by no means certain that the letter would reach its addressee. In any case, he did not expect an immediate answer.

And while political success danced tantalizingly in the distance for Herzl, the Jewish tragedy became more and more patent to the world. The Jews of Roumania, pressed by the new outbreak of anti-Semitism which followed the bad harvests of 1899-1900, and which manifested itself in a wide-spread boycott, were caught up in a wave of emigration. The official Jewish emigration agencies were swamped. There was no plan to take care of the new thousands of wanderers. Some were shipped hastily across the seas, others pressed forward blindly into central and western Europe. Finally there was nothing for it but to ask for the closing of the frontiers, and some of the emigrants were even forced to return to their "homeland."

As far back as the spring of that year Herzl had expressed himself openly against the encouragement of emigration as long as there existed no definite objective. This did not prevent the press from accusing him now of having precipitated this migratory flood as a Zionist demonstration.

But the emigrants, too, looked to him for help in a spirit of naive trust. Telegrams poured in on him, pleas for help, requests that he intervene with the frontier officials. Herzl suffered, unable as he was to do anything more than call for help and solidarity in *Die Welt*, and attack the *Alliance Israélite* in Vienna for its lack of system and its undignified treatment of the wanderers. He combined political action with his efforts at relief; he begged Koerber to use his influence with the Sultan to permit the Roumanian Jews to immigrate into Turkey, and at the same time to receive him, Herzl, in order to discuss the question of colonization and settlement. He wrote in similar vein to Vámbéry, who again warned him that it was fatal to try and force the issue with Abdul-Hamid, "the arch-liar," whom Bismarck had called the greatest diplomat of the new age. One had to be armed with patience.

Such was the situation when the fourth Congress convened in London on August 13, 1900. This Congress was supposed to be in the nature of a demonstration, and in that respect resembled the first Congress. There were, however, positive and negative differences. On the positive side it could be recorded that a Zionist Congress was being held in London, that it was given a friendly reception even by the opponents of the movement, that over four hundred delegates participated, two hundred of them from Russia. Herzl was inclined at first to consider it the best Congress held so far. On the negative side, however, it had to be admitted that the demonstration was more forced, even artificial; there was lacking the enthusiasm and fire of the meeting in Basle in 1897, when the Zionists first came together, learned to know each other, and were intoxicated by the mere fact of the encounter. It was a quiet Congress this time, perhaps the quietest. The delegates were conscious of the task which Herzl had laid upon them, of making this demonstration something worthy of the capital of the mighty British Empire.

It was, however, impossible to ignore the fact that there was a certain emptiness in the proceedings. The "cultural question" came to the fore again, and the clash between the orthodox and the "secularist" friends of culture was, if anything, sharper than before. Herzl stood firm by his principles, which called for the suppression of differences and the accentuation of common objectives. "Let us not lose ourselves in squabbles, let us not quarrel with one another. Think rather of the day when we will come before you with the words, 'We are ready,' and ask you, 'Are you ready, too?' "

In this matter Herzl was successful, but there was no doubt that the oppositional mood had grown stronger. Weizmann, distrustful always of fine phrases, criticized the glowing report of the Actions Committee on the growth of the movement. Motzkin, the ever-honest warrior, wanted something more than vague hints on political progress, a field in which Herzl always demanded a sort of blanket vote of confidence.

The one practical achievement of the Congress was the resolution that a Jewish National Fund be founded. Kremenezky was its chief protagonist, and had been fighting for the idea since 1894. With regard to other practical questions, such as the improvement of the economic status of world Jewry, which Herzl submitted for discussion, the Congress showed little interest. His plan for a form of national insurance, which had occupied him before the Congress, and continued to occupy him after it, was never submitted, owing to the opposition of the Actions Committee. His idea had been to create this sort of fund by means of compulsory minimum contributions, so that when Jews were overtaken by a new wave of anti-Semitism, and forced out of their respective countries, they could find at their disposal finances to which they were entitled, and which could not be regarded as charity. Herzl had believed that he could fire the Congress with this plan, making the Zionist movement a participant in the immediate social problem of Jewry and thereby winning over to it the masses of the Jewish people. He could do no more than hint at the idea in his opening address.

For the rest the entire Congress, like Herzl's opening address, was directed largely at that section of the non-Jewish world in which it was being held. This was symbolized by the fact that the first and programmatic part of his address was delivered in English. In his exordium he spoke of England as the one country in which "God's old people" was not confronted by a native anti-Semitism. Yet one could not advise the persecuted ones to immigrate into this country. "Such immigration would constitute a danger to the Jews already here, as well as to those who might follow. For the latter will import in their pitiful bundles the very thing they are fleeing from, namely, anti-Semitism." Then, after a brief review of the aims of the Zionist movement, and its significance for the Jews of the Orient, he rose in a remarkable passage on the wings of prophecy, and foretold the role which England would play in Zionist history. Speaking more intimately and confidentially in German, he cried: "England the great, England the free, England with her eyes fixed on the seven seas, will understand us. From this place the Zionist movement will take a higher and higher flight, of this we may be sure."

He took up the challenging questions of his opponents: "We are building; the structure grows." Then he counter-attacked, and threw up to the philanthropic organizations their failure in the face of the great Roumanian migration "which trails like a bloody thread across the European scene. Where was the accepted officialdom of Jewry, where were the reported great ones of Israel, the pillars of the community? By their fruits ye shall know them." The bankruptcy of assimilation had now been followed "by the insolvency of the philanthropists."

The London Congress had fulfilled the external task which had been laid upon it. The great newspapers took note, reported and discussed; English public opinion was informed and interested. Apart from this general result, Herzl had been introduced by the ever-faithful Sir Francis Montefiore to Barrington, Lord Salisbury's private secretary, and to Lord Lansdowne. He had dined with them and had found them, too, interested in the movement. There had been an excursion of a group of delegates up the Thames, Herzl among them and Barrington accompanying. Passing the flag of Windsor Castle, the Zionists had saluted it by the singing of the *Hatikvah*.

On Herzl himself the London Congress did, in the end, not make a particularly profound impression. The ovations he had received at the mass meeting in the Great Assembly Hall, at the garden party in Regent's Park, and at the banquet of the English Zionist Federation after the close of the Congress, as well as at the Congress itself, left him cold. He had less use than ever for such honors. It had been a tremendous effort for him; he had carried on only by drawing on his last reserves of energy. A few days before the Congress he had had to take to his bed with an attack of fever. Two months before he had had his first attack of anaemia of the brain. It was only during his summer vacation at Aussensee that he began to recover from his sickness and exertions.

The work went forward almost uninterruptedly. In mid-September he went to Budapest, to spur Vámbéry to new activity. The latter again counselled patience, and gave his word of honor that, before next May, Herzl would be received by the Sultan. But this was not good enough for Herzl. He put pressure on Nouri Bey, who had received a considerable advance, and on his agent Crespi. About this time, too, he had been called in again by Koerber, who was seriously interested in Herzl the gifted journalist. At a second conference Herzl laid before him his plan to found a great newspaper which should represent the Prime Minister's views. In mid-October Crespi and Nouri reported to Herzl that the Turkish government was in urgent need of a loan of seven to eight hundred thousand Turkish pounds, and was prepared to pledge its customs receipts for the payment of six to six and a half per cent interest. Herzl was to be the *deus ex machina* for the loan. Herzl took it all very seriously; he wrote Wolffsohn about it, the latter wrote to Kann, then Herzl corresponded directly with Kann. The latter declared himself ready to take up the loan, with the help of his bank. Herzl transmitted this favorable reply to Crespi and Nouri. A long correspondence ensued. Crespi kept changing the conditions of the loan, reported on conversations with the Grand Vizier, with the First Secretary, with the Treasurer; he came — naturally on a solid expense account, which the Actions Committee provided only with the greatest difficulty — to Vienna, said this and that, reported that Vámbéry's letter had been enormously helpful, and told Herzl that a telegraphic invitation was due any day now. Nothing came. Herzl made another trip to Vámbéry, and on his advice prepared two letters for the Sultan. Vámbéry sent them on. Crespi wrote that the Turkish embassy in Berlin would be asked for information. Herzl sent Wolffsohn with a superbly bound copy of his *Philosophic Stories*, which had just been published, to Ahmed Tewfik. Ahmed Tewfik was very friendly, but replied that he had received no instructions from Constantinople; he reiterated his previous opinion, to wit, that the Jews were welcome as immigrants to be scattered throughout Turkish territory, with the exception of Palestine. Herzl's *Judenstaat* had frightened the Turkish government off. Vámbéry, who was also interested financially in the loan, wrote to the Grand Vizier. And thus months passed in protracted correspondence, in a confusion of excitement, hopes and disappointments. Nothing came. Nothing — except, in December, the promulgation of new immigration restrictions for Palestine.

In January 1901, Koerber sent for him again, and informed him that a group of industrialists was interested in buying the *Neue Freie Presse* or in founding a new paper. The negotiations opened auspiciously; Arthur Krupp, a leading industrialist, was of the group; it looked as though Herzl could now look forward to gaining his freedom, acquiring power and influence for the Zionist movement, and building up a fortune for his children. At the last moment the negotiations suddenly collapsed; perhaps because, as Herzl afterwards bitterly reproached himself, his demands had been too high, perhaps because his Jewish politics had given the backers pause, perhaps for other reasons. In any case, by the end of January the incident was closed. "Three months torn piecemeal out of my life, in 'great expectations,'" Herzl wrote in his diary, on January 31, 1901, when all hope was gone either for the Turkish loan or the newspaper. "The wind blows through the stubble. I feel my autumn approaching. I see before me the danger of leaving no achievement to the world and no inheritance to my children."

He forged new plans. He conceived the idea of buying up the Turkish Public Debt, or at least the part of it carried by the Ottoman Bank, so that he might negotiate for the Charter as one Power dealing with another. In February he went to London, to try and win Rothschild over to the idea. But in spite of all the efforts of his English friends, Cowen, Greenberg and Zangwill, Rothschild would not receive him.

Toward the end of February the *Politische Korrespondenz* published the news of further immigration restrictions into Palestine. Once again Herzl exploited a set-back for the purpose of thrusting forward. He wrote to Nordau, to Alexander Marmorek, to Cowen and to Gottheil to work in their respective countries, France, Italy, England and America, for parliamentary intervention against the immigration restrictions. He began to consider seriously the idea of transferring the center of action to England, so that he might free himself of the obstacles created by his Austrian and Viennese environment, and draw more upon the assistance of his able English friends. The publishers of the *Neue Freie Presse* objected, but they were prepared in the end to transfer him to London as the special correspondent of the paper. Wolffsohn, too, was prepared to follow him to London. But there was the question of his parents. They could neither separate from him nor tear themselves away from Vienna. Herzl let the plan fall to the ground. He had never ceased to be a son.

And always, the Bank, worries, labors, frictions, and new worries.

There were days and weeks when his hopes of achievement sank to zero, and remained there. Still he went on working eagerly at his Palestine romance. "My life is no romance today. At least the romance has become my life," he notes. Work on this book draws him into still deeper relationship with Palestine. His heart is on flame to begin the practical work there. He consults with the engineers Kremenezky and Seidener on the problems of the technological development of Palestine. When Seidener suggests the erection of a brick factory, he is passionately enthusiastic about the idea. He is ready to raise the money for it at once. He greets with the same enthusiasm the suggestion of David Levontin, the new director of the Jewish Colonial Trust, to buy up the shares of the Jaffa-Jerusalem railroad; but this enthusiasm soon cools off. He shows more sustained interest in the creation of a branch bank in Jaffa; Kann begins negotiations for the acquisition of the majority of the shares of the German-Palestine Bank, and Herzl throws himself into the task of furthering the branch bank which, for various reasons, he decides finally shall operate as an independent institution under the name of the Anglo-Palestine Company.*

Ever and again he pushes forward in the political field. On April 10 he is in Budapest to see Vámbéry, who himself proposes to go to Constantinople in order to plead personally for an audience for Herzl. Once more there ensue weeks of painful excitement and suspense.

"Today I am forty-one years old," he notes in his diary, on May 2, 1901.

> The wind blows through the stubble,
> I must march now at the double.

It is nearly six years since I began this movement, which has made me old, tired and poor."

---

* Now the Jewish National Bank of Israel.

Five days later a telegram called him to Budapest. He left the next day. Vámbéry arrived an hour later, direct from Constantinople: the Sultan would receive him, not, to be sure, as the Zionist, but as the influential journalist and Jew. But at least he was going to be received — at last, at last, at last!

On May 9, back in Vienna, Herzl wrote in his diary: "I will close this volume here, for I cannot take it along into the country of post-office robbers. I will begin a new volume on the way. What will it contain? Pentecost it will be six years — no! sixty years — that I have been in the Zionist movement."

The next morning he set forth from Vienna once more; first for Budapest, where he was to receive further instructions, and then, together with Wolffsohn and Oscar Marmorek in the Orient Express for Constantinople.

CHAPTER XI

NEW HOPES — NEW DISAPPOINTMENTS

HE SET out with that old fatalistic feeling of his that nothing ever happens as one hopes or as one fears. Five years had passed since he had arrived in Constantinople for the first time, full of hope, naively believing everything that Nevlinski told him; half that number of years had passed since his meeting with the German Kaiser. He was much better informed now, both as to the milieu and the political situation. He knew that Turkey was opposed to the Zionist plan, because it feared the defection of a vassal state, and feared likewise the intervention of European Powers — Russia in particular — on behalf of former subjects. From written and verbal accounts he had formed a more accurate picture of the personality of Abdul-Hamid than he had possessed in the springtime of his Zionist activity. From conversations with Vámbéry and from his correspondence with the treacherous Nouri-Crespi group he had formed a truer estimate of the party struggle in the Sublime Porte, and of the contrast between Tahsin Bey, the first secretary, and Izzet Bey, the second secretary. Vámbéry had placed at his disposal his own confidential agent, Wellisch, a Jewish official in the Turkish sanitation service. And there had been a great inward change in Herzl; not only had he learned much concerning this field, but he had risen

353

to the undisputed position of the recognized leader of that part of the Jewish people which was determined to rebuild its own life; the aesthetic dreamer and onlooker had become the man of action. In 1896 and again in 1898 he had reacted instantaneously to the colorful beauty of the strange capital, Constantinople, "the wonder city," as he called it then. Now days passed before his "hardened mood" responded. "In these years of development," he wrote now in his diary, "I have transformed life from a dream to a battle. The world is no longer imagination; it is will."

On the fifth day after his arrival, i.e., on Friday, May 17, 1901, he was received by the Sultan. Shortly before the reception Ibrahim Bey, the Court Master of Ceremonies, informed him that the Sultan had been pleased to bestow on him the Order of the Medjidje, second class. Herzl thanked the official, but informed him that he did not want any Order; five years before, the Court had bestowed upon him, by error, the same Order of the third class, and he had accepted out of courtesy. Now he would prefer to renounce any Order. The least he could accept would be the first class. A few minutes later Ibrahim Bey informed him that the Sultan had presented him with the Grand Cordon of the Order of the Medjidje, the highest at his disposal. Herzl saw in this a very promising beginning. Again a few minutes passed, and he stood in the presence of the Sultan himself.

The audience lasted over two hours. Against his will Herzl was received as editor — or even as "director" — of the Neue Freie Presse: Vámbéry had advised him not to speak about Zionism, the Sultan did not want to hear about it. But he conducted the conversation, which Ibrahim interpreted in French and Turkish, with such skill and cleverness, that it glided as it were naturally and without hindrance toward his objective.

The Sultan began by saying that he was a constant reader of the *Neue Freie Presse* — without understanding German! — and he was happy to note the friendly relations between Turkey and Austria. Herzl made his first gambit: he said he was devoted to the Sultan because the Sultan was so good to the Jews. Jews everywhere knew this and were grateful. Herzl, in particular, was ready to serve him in every possible way. He would, he promised, make no part of the conversation public, the Sultan could therefore speak to him in all confidence. Abdul-Hamid handed Herzl a cigarette, and remarked that he had always been a friend of the Jews; he relied on Mohammedans and Jews. Herzl lamented the injustices to which the Jews were exposed throughout the world, upon which the Sultan remarked that his Empire had always been open as a refuge to the Jews; the fact was that only recently fifteen hundred Roumanian Jews had been admitted, by his permission and with his assistance, to settle in Anatolia. Then Herzl, adapting himself to the oriental mode of conversation, changed the subject and steered it toward the Ottoman Public Debt with an ingenious device which, as always, he had prepared well in advance.

"When Professor Vámbéry informed me that His Majesty would receive me, I could not help thinking of the charming old fable of Androcles and the lion. His Majesty is the lion, perhaps I am Androcles, and perhaps there is a thorn which I could withdraw." Then, receiving permission to speak more openly, he proceeded to interpret the parable. "I consider the Public Debt the thorn. If this could be removed, then the life-strength of Turkey, in which I have great faith, would unfold anew." The Sultan admitted that ever since his accession he had tried in vain to remove this thorn, which had been left to him by his noble predecessors. If Herzl could help him, that would be very fine indeed. Herzl repeated that he believed he could be of help. The fundamental condition of such help, however, was strictest silence concerning the whole affair. "The ruler lifted his eyes to heaven, placed his hands upon his breast, and murmured: 'Secret, secret!'"

Then Herzl permitted himself to proffer his request. The Powers, he said, were interested in keeping Turkey weak, and would do everything they could to prevent her recovery and to render his efforts vain. But he could carry out the operation on all the exchanges of Europe, through his friends, only with the help of the Sultan. "But this help, again, must take a special form; it must come, at the right time, and in a special manner, as the proclamation of a measure particularly favorable to the Jews."

Upon this the Sultan suggested that he could make a friendly statement on the Jews to his court jeweller, who was a Jew, and have the latter give it to the press. He could also say something similar to the Chief Rabbi, or *Haham Bashi*. Herzl naturally refused to draw the *Haham Bashi* into the affair, for the latter was completely hostile to him and was in the habit, as he had heard, of spitting out at the mention of his name. What Herzl wanted was that such a statement should be issued to the Zionist Congress. He said: "I want to engage the active sympathy of the Jews on behalf of the Turkish Empire. The statement or proclamation must therefore be of an impressive character. The words of the *Haham Bashi* would not be heard outside of Turkey." He would permit himself, therefore, to indicate later the time and manner of the proclamation. The Sultan nodded in agreement, and Herzl took another step forward.

"What this land needs is the industrial initiative of our people. Other Europeans who come here become rich quickly and run away with their booty. Certainly one should make an honest and decent profit out of any enterprise, but one should remain in the country where one's fortune has been made." The Sultan agreed that there was still much untouched wealth in the land. Only that day he had received a telegram from Bagdad, with the news that rich petroleum sources had been discovered. There were ores, too, gold and silver mines. If Herzl remained long enough, the Sultan would advise him to inspect the districts along the Anatolian road. They were like a garden. Then, to Herzl's astonishment, the Sultan asked him to recommend a financier who could create new sources of income for the country.

Herzl replied that he was deeply appreciative of the confidence shown in him. He would, however, only recommend a man whose honesty was as outstanding as his ability. He would think the matter over carefully and advise His Majesty as soon as he had found the man. "Besides," he notes in his diary, "I was thinking that such a man would have to study the financial situation in all secrecy, and then advise me of the conclusions on the basis of which we could proceed to the clearing up of the tangle. But the ruler was of another opinion. He imparted it to the attentive Ibrahim, who in turn transmitted it to me, smiling happily: 'His Imperial Majesty believes it would be better for the man to be given official status; he would be noticed less, then. He should be attached to the Finance Minister — ostensibly as under-secretary — and send in regular reports. His

Majesty could then correspond with you via this confidential
agent.' I recognized the superior strategy of the proposal,
and asked how I was to get my letters through to His Imperial Majesty, and whether I needed a special seal or mark for
that purpose. The ruler replied through Ibrahim that my
seal would suffice.

"The Sultan then passed on to the subject of the funding
of the Public Debt, which was then in the air . . . He explained that this funding would consist of the contracting
of a new debt in place of the old one, whereby a saving of
one and a half million pounds would be effected, to cover the
last year's deficit. 'What?' I exclaimed, shrugging my
shoulders in disappointment, 'so little?' The ruler also
showed his regret, shrugging his shoulders and smiling
sadly. I asked that the funding or unification plan be sent
to me, so that I might judge whether it was worth entering
on if one had something much bigger in view. His Majesty
said that my wish would be met . . .

"Thereafter the conversation wandered from subject to
subject. I interested His Majesty. I gave him the general
outline of a plan for the future, and of all the things that
could be done in this wonderful city and in the Empire . . .
But His Imperial Majesty asked me to put these plans aside
for the time being, and to devote myself to the Public
Debt."

By this time Herzl was exhausted. But he had directed
the conversation as he had hoped; he was certain that the
Sultan would want to hear more from him. He therefore let
the conversation die out, and toward the end only reiterated
his three main requests; first, complete silence; second, a proclamation favorable to the Jews, at the right time and in the

right form, to be indicated by him; third, that a copy of the funding plan be sent to him. Abdul-Hamid promised all three.

The next morning Herzl was called to the palace again. Ibrahim Bey, of whom Herzl did not know whether he belonged to Tahsin's party or Izzet's, invited him to a repast, to discuss certain questions. There was also present Izzet Bey, whom Herzl had until then politely avoided, in order not to compromise his position with the more powerful Tahsin. While they were all at table a blue envelope was brought in: the Sultan sent Herzl, as a sign of friendship, a tie-pin with yellow stones. Clearly, then, Herzl had made a good impression.

When the coffee came, Izzet Bey revealed that he had been officially designated to explain to Herzl the plan for the funding of the Public Debt. A syndicate was to provide thirty million pounds, out of which the government would buy back the bonds of the Public Debt, which amounted to eighty-five million pounds at par but had fallen to a quarter of their value on the Exchange. Herzl, who considered the plan both a piece of thievery and sheer nonsense, listened quietly and replied that he would study the matter and give his opinion later. Then he had himself announced to the Sultan, who sent back word that he was occupied, and regretted that he could not receive him at the moment.

The following morning (May 19) Herzl sent Wolffsohn to Ibrahim with a letter for the Sultan, in which he asked for a final audience before his departure. "The hour has perhaps come," he wrote in French, "for the lion to be liberated from the thorn. If God, the All-Powerful, who is over us, so desires, then Turkey has reached a turning point in its history, and the illustrious government of the Sultan Abdul-

Hamid Khan II, beloved of his Mussulman and Jewish subjects, will cover itself with new glory."

When, at nine o'clock on the morning of May 20, he presented himself again at the palace, Herzl found Ibrahim already waiting for him. The Sultan had read his letter during his afternoon walk. He was eager to hear Herzl's plans and proposals. He had repeated several times the phrase about the lion and the thorn. But as he was too busy to receive Herzl, he begged him to state his views to Ibrahim, who would transmit them to his master.

Herzl unfolded his opinion to Ibrahim, and then dictated to him the following resumé ("for the special benefit," he notes in his diary, "of the weak understanding of His Imperial Majesty of the Khalifate"):

1) Critical Section: a) Izzet's funding plan is unrealizable and the very attempt would be harmful. b) Any attempt at a loan is inadvisable, for in her present condition Turkey would have to submit to the most usurious rates of interest.

2) Positive Section: a) The recalling of the Debt Bonds from the market is to be undertaken quietly by a reliable syndicate, and under the most favorable circumstances could not be carried out in less than three years. b) Meanwhile the immediate needs of the Treasury must be met, and 1.5 million pounds must be obtained by October 1 to cover the current deficit. c) During this period a study must be made of the possibility of new sources of income.

3) General Observation: We Jews need a protector, and it is our desire that this protector (the well-known lion) shall be restored to full strength.

Ibrahim noted Herzl's remarks, made a clean copy of the resumé, and at eleven o'clock went with it to the Sultan. Shortly thereafter he returned with the now very friendly

Tahsin. A few more minutes passed and this time it was Izzet Bey who came out of the Sultan's apartment with the "extremely confidential" resumé — Izzet Bey, "the lean, vicious panther."

"Well, Sir," he addressed Herzl rudely and belliggerently, "in what manner is the funding plan harmful."

Herzl tried to dodge courteously. "I don't say the idea is not good."

"Ah, so the idea is good," cried Izzet scornfully, and turned to Ibrahim with a command. "Write that down!"

Herzl recognized the danger: Izzet wanted to make an impossible figure of him before the Sultan. Assuming that external nonchalance which always came to his rescue in difficult situations, he took up the challenge: "Yes, Your Excellency, write it down! The idea is good and beautiful, just as it would be good and beautiful to be able to fly. Unfortunately, that happens at present to be impossible." Then he repeated briefly his objections to the protocol.

As the conversation continued Herzl employed the specific strategy of being vague about the future and of maintaining the negotiations under all circumstances. With the help of baksheesh they were bound to lead somewhere. The Sultan, said Izzet, was ready to offer the State monopolies to support the loan, and mentioned the sum of four million pounds needed for warships. Then both Izzet and Ibrahim asked, on behalf of their master, what would be the national status of the Jews who came into Turkey. "All of them," said Izzet, "must become subjects of the Sultan. That is also true of those who settle as colonists. They must not only become Turkish citizens; they must also relinquish their former citizenship, and have their renunciation of former citizenship ratified by their respective governments." "And they must do their military duty, too, when the Sultan calls them to the colors," added Ibrahim. "And the colonization," said Izzet, "must not take place *en masse*, but five families here, and five there — scattered, without interconnection."

Herzl had of course not the slightest intention of accepting such conditions. He was cautiously negative, basing himself as it were on practical considerations. Even if he had no objection to such scattered colonization in and for itself, there were certain technical and economic considerations which spoke against it. "Last year," he said, "His Imperial Majesty was gracious enough to admit fifteen hundred Roumanian Jewish refugees into Anatolia. With all my gratitude for this magnanimity, I would not have been in favor of the individual settlement of the refugees, because that lacked an economic basis. Such planless immigration ought not to be encouraged. It leads nowhere. What could be done instead is the creation of a great land company, which should take over uncultivated Turkish territory and settle the newcomers there. There is in Palestine land enough for this purpose. If such a company, which would naturally be a Turkish one, were given the right kind of concession, it could make the land fruitful, settle immigrants on it, and pay taxes. It might even be possible to raise money in advance on the income of such a company."

It was in this innocuous form that he presented to the representatives of the Sultan his desire for a Charter. He considered it enough if they took up these suggestions and transmitted them to their master. Then Izzet went in to the Sultan and brought back greetings and farewell. *The Sultan expected Herzl's positive proposals in the next four weeks.*

Immediately after the audience with the Sultan, Herzl had handed out the sum of forty thousand francs to the

Nouri-Crespi group, for having brought the audience about, though he knew perfectly well that these men had done nothing and probably were incapable of doing anything. But they could harm him. He therefore pretended to believe their lies, and, yielding to Crespi's threats, he even agreed to pay the latter a thousand francs a month for some months to come. In other ways, too, he was prodigal with tips and "expenses," the beneficiaries of the stream of gold being anyone from a door-keeper to a Vámbéry. He wanted to have it known that it paid to work for the Zionists, and that Herzl was a man of his word.

Given the results so far obtained, the money had not been spent in vain. To begin with, he had achieved something which was frequently beyond the reach of ambassadors, to wit, a long audience with the suspicious ruler of Turkey; and during the audience he had made a good impression. The Order conferred upon him was due to his reputation as a journalist, the audience was due to Vámbéry's efforts; but the length of the audience, and its content, were his own doing. He had awakened both the respect and the interest of the Sultan. The later gift of the tie-pin was also his own achievement. Some of the wishes expressed by the ruler even indicated belief and confidence in Herzl. The fact was, indeed, that Herzl had made a good impression. "That Herzl," said the Sultan years later to Vámbéry, "looks altogether like a prophet, like a leader of his people. He has very clever eyes, and speaks prudently and clearly."

Per contra, Herzl carried away a better impression of the Sultan than he had been led to expect by stories and newspaper reports. "My impression of the Sultan was, that he is a weak, cowardly but thoroughly good-natured person. I consider him neither tricky nor cruel, but a profoundly unhappy prisoner in whose name a base, infamous and thievish camarilla commits every shamelessness . . .

"I still see him before me, this Sultan of a dying robber empire. Small, shabby, with a badly dyed beard, which is probably barbered once a week in preparation for the *selamlik*. The hooknose of a Punchinello, long yellow teeth with a big gap in the right upper jaw, the fez drawn down deep over his head — which is probably bald — the protuding ears . . . I see the strengthless hands in the too large gloves, and the big, ill-fitting, colored shirt cuffs. The bleating voice, the diffidence in every word, the timidity in every glance. And that rules! But, to be sure, only nominally and in appearance."

But the consequences of the stay in Constantinople were not confined to these mutual impressions and the honors conferred upon Herzl. The mere fact of the audience, which became known to the public through *Die Welt* and other periodicals, enhanced the standing both of Herzl and of the movement which he represented. Furthermore, Herzl had at last been able to submit his request to the Sultan; admittedly, in very guarded and provisional form; but he had not been rebuffed. On the contrary, he had been asked to submit his detailed proposals for the conversion of the debt and for the compensation which he expected. This was considerably more than Vámbéry had believed to be attainable. Indeed, Vámbéry, who knew the situation, thought the achievement colossal, and expressed the opinion that Herzl would obtain his Charter in the course of that very year, 1901. Herzl was therefore right in expressing himself thus in his diary, concerning the conversation with Ibrahim and Izzet: "With this we have actually entered upon the negotiations for the

Charter. All we shall need now to carry through what I have planned is luck, skill and money."

The great task before him now was to convert his personal success into the success of the movement. Immediately on his return Herzl went to Franzensfeste to report to Vámbéry, and thence to Karlsruhe to see the Grand Duke of Baden, who was trying to get him an audience with the Czar. Such an audience, at this point, would do much to fortify his position in the eyes of the Sultan.

On the night of May 30, Herzl left Karlsruhe for Paris, there to begin the raising of the money (one and a half million pounds) which was to be the first step toward the obtaining of the Charter. His negotiations in Paris were utterly fruitless. Reitlinger, the banker and Zionist, whom Herzl consulted first, despaired completely of being able to interest the rich Jews. A conversation with Zadoc Kahn in Max Nordau's house, revealed that the Jewish Colonization Association (*ICA*) was not to be won over for any kind of work in Palestine beyond the direction of the Rothschild colonies. That organization had even refused to extend a small measure of help to the needy workers in Palestine, and had tried to persuade these workers to migrate to the Argentine.

Zadoc Kahn's efforts to bring about another meeting between Herzl and Edmond Rothschild failed. The attempt unfortunately coincided with the publication of a statement by the banking firm of Rothschild, in the *Financial News*, sharply denying any connection with Herzl. The statement had been precipitated by a false report in the *London Times* that Herzl had, together with "other" representatives of the firms of Rothschild and Bleichröder, been in Constantinople

on the business of the firm. Not less futile than Zadoc
Kahn's efforts were those of Sir Francis Montefiore, who
came specially to Paris for the purpose of arranging a conference between Herzl and the banking family of Pereire.

The sorrowful tale did not end here. Herzl soon learned
that the achievements he had scored in the diplomatic field
were very lightly regarded among some of his closest associates. Kokesch and Alexander Marmorek reported that the
Russian members of the Actions Committee remained extraordinarily cool to the audience in Constantinople, and censured Herzl for having borrowed money from the bank to
carry out this work. Nordau declared that the audience was
a world historic incident, but Herzl had made the mistake
of risking everything on the turn of a card. The opposition
press would soon be writing that he was a new Baron de
Hirsch who wanted to do business with Turkey on the back
of the Jewish people. Nordau expressed himself very severely
to Alexander Marmorek with regard to Herzl's methods;
the latter, he said, was disingenuous and only half outspoken
in his dealings with potentates and with the Jewish people.
Herzl, whose heart and nerves were in such condition that
he collapsed in a faint in the middle of an afternoon's walk,
pointed out to Nordau that what he needed now from his
friends was protection, not criticism. When a man was
standing on a high pillar it was wrong of his friends to make
him dizzy. "Quite right," answered Nordau. "What they
ought to do is hurry up with the mattress . . ."

Herzl's reception in London was better, externally at least.
A banquet was arranged for him by The Maccabaeans in
St. James Hall, with Zangwill as the leading spirit. Vám-
béry, Sir Francis Montefiore, and the wealthy and influential
Jew, Navon Bey of Jerusalem, were also present. Zangwill,

now completely won over to political Zionism, greeted Herzl as "one of the foremost Jews, and the first Jewish statesman, since the destruction of Jerusalem," who had written his name in indelible letters into the annals of the Jewish people. This was a very different reception from those accorded Herzl in 1895 and 1896.

In his address to The Maccabaeans, who were still for the most part in the opposition, Herzl struck a note of reconciliation. "I readily admit," he declared, modestly, "that in the presentation of our cause we have committed some grave mistakes; we have been too unspecific in our utterances, too unskilful in our negotiations; we have not been ready enough to admit gratefully the record of those who have been active for the Jewish people at the same time as ourselves or even before us. But all these misunderstandings and differences must of course sink into the background at a moment which may be nothing less than a turning point in the destiny of the Jewish people."

He made clever use of his own mistake of 1898. He had been reproached with having said too much; he had been attacked as a downright charlatan. A later generation, which would have all the facts before it, would deal with him more justly. But it was useless to appeal to an unborn generation for help in present misery. "I therefore resolved, there and then, never again to awaken the hopes of others even when I myself had the most convincing grounds..." Speaking of the results of his visit to Constantinople, he went on: "My question, my Jewish question, *the* Jewish question, now reads thus: 'Are you prepared to show yourselves equal to the historic help which is being offered you? Are you ready to stand by the man who will stand by you? How generous, how swift, will your readiness prove?' It is precisely the practical men, the calculators, the men who weigh and consider, who will be least astonished if the challenge is formulated in these words: *Do ut des.* One hand can only be washed by the other — if you want to take, give first."

A banker had once told him that businessmen always approached suspiciously any deal in which moral or ideal values were implicated. "He may have been right. It may be that the moral element is a poor recommendation among people who are not acquainted with it. But if the money will not be forthcoming from those who are on top, we shall get it from those who are underneath. Therefore I speak from this hospitable table to those beyond the windows of this room. We need, in the immediate future, about two million pounds. You may remember that this was the sum which we, my friends and I, set for the Jewish Colonial Trust at the time of its founding in London. The results did not come up to our expectations, though enough money came in to enable us to open the Jewish Colonial Trust. If the Jewish people responds to my appeal now, and adds another million and a half to what we now have in the treasury, we can move forward."

But from the point of view of Herzl's purpose, the London journey was a complete failure. His successes were merely social. He was widely invited out, he dined and lunched with "high society" which was captivated by his person. Financially he achieved nothing. True, he had not expected, in response to his vague statements, a flood of gold; but he had looked for a more affirmative attitude than he encountered. Only the banker Seligman, who for some time now had come closer to Herzl's ideas, declared himself ready, on the last day of the visit, to help in the founding of a Land Company with a capital of five million pounds, if the Charter had already been obtained. Herzl was in desperation — so soon after his success in Constantinople, and with such prospects of greater successes if he could only come forward with immediate financial assistance.

He was disheartened to the point of disgust; and with justice. "I have run myself ragged," he wrote on August 18 to his faithful friend, Max Mandelstamm, "and I haven't obtained a hearing from the wretched crew which controls the money. Fire and brimstone must rain from heaven before those stones are softened. It is something utterly unheard of, and fifty years from now people will spit on the graves of these men for it, that I should have been almost through with the question of the Sultan, and that I should have been held up because I could not get the miserable money. But of course we can't make a display of our rage and pain, because then the Sultan would become aware of our weakness, and I must do my best to hold him off, to gain time, trying meanwhile to squeeze water out of stones and scrape gold from the mud. Yes, it would be the easiest thing for me now to drop the whole business and to issue a proclamation: 'Thus it is, Jewish people; in five years I, a poor, helpless journalist, have reached the point where I could conduct these negotiations with the Sultan himself. But you've left me in the lurch; you are nothing but a rabble — the devil take you! I'm through with worrying about you.' This *beau geste*, which would be so easy and comfortable, is forbidden me. I must continue to drag the burden. But the worst of it is that not only opponents and indifferent bystanders, but my own people too make my life a torment. It's impossible to reach a decision with regard to the Bank. There is constant friction, there are personal differences between the directors. If one man proposes something, the other's sure to oppose it. And so on. The result is that I have to play the man of force again, so that something may get itself done ... Things are brewing in the Actions Committee, too. They're talking about 'Youth Zionism' etc. It still is a bit early for us to be having our Young Turk Party. We are, in brief, a very witty people; but that's just what makes me laugh. The time has come for them to throw me out of the movement! Actually I have only one worry just now: money. *Grand Dieu*, where am I to lay my hands on it? I keep racking my brains to find something."

All his efforts came to nothing. On Nordau's and Alexander Marmorek's advice he tried to interest the American industrialist Carnegie and the South African magnate and statesman Cecil Rhodes. All he wanted was the assurance of a loan in case he got the Charter and the income-producing concessions he expected from Turkey; or else it was only the use of these influential names for the Jewish financial groups in question. These steps too led nowhere. He could not get the right kind of introduction to Carnegie; Zangwill's and Cowen's attempts to arrange an interview with Rhodes fell through.

Only the Bank was left, and its condition has already been described. What could he do with the £250,000 which the institution had managed, with infinite effort, to get together? And yet Herzl continued to push forward in the political field, still hoping that a new political triumph would facilitate the raising of the money. From Paris he had written the Sultan that he was making good progress; he was preparing public opinion for practical measures. On June 17 he reported again, this time in more specific terms: in accordance with the suggestion of His Majesty, he was taking steps for the raising of one and a half million pounds, which he considered essential as a substitute for the difficult, if not impossible, funding plan. He was working out, together with his friends, a plan for a Company with a capital of five million pounds, which should engage in business in Syria, Palestine and Asia Minor generally. In return for certain concessions from the Sultan, this Company would guarantee the interest and amortization on a loan of one and a half million pounds to be floated immediately. This loan would, then, cost Turkey nothing; the breathing spell created by it would be utilized for the study of methods of creating larger sources of income. Herzl went on to describe in great detail the advantages which would accrue to Turkey under his plan. He finished up by saying that he was ready to report at once to Constantinople on the request of the Sultan.

This letter, which Herzl might just as well have written in Constantinople immediately after the audience, was intended to give the impression that he had held long and fruitful consultations with his financial friends in Paris and London and was now getting ready for the Charter. That this was the impression actually created may very well be doubted. In any case, he received no answer. Later efforts to arrange another meeting with the Sultan also failed. Only the Sultan's friendly reply to Herzl's telegram of congratulation on the anniversary of his accession to power, toward the end of August, showed that the thread had not been decisively dropped.

So when the fifth Congress assembled in Basle on December 26, 1901 — against his wishes, for he had wanted London again, and had also objected to the date, midwinter — he had nothing to add to his earlier reports to the Actions Committee and in *Die Welt* regarding his relations with the Sultan. He could only rebut the attacks made on him, and that in the most general terms. His opponents, he said, spoke of insuperable obstacles, but every little difficulty was an insuperable obstacle where the will to overcome it was lacking. For five years now the Zionist plan had been public, and nowhere had any nation or government come out against it. "But of course our first question must be, what is the attitude of Turkey and of its ruler? In May of this year I had the honor to be received in a rather lengthy audience by His Majesty the Sultan Abdul-Hamid. The kindliness and cordiality of the reception were such as to justify the highest hopes. The attitude and the language of His Majesty gave me the feeling that in the ruling Khalif the Jewish people has a friend and protector. The Sultan has authorised me to make this statement. Let the Jews of the world hear it, let them understand what prospects this fact opens for them, and may they finally be ready for action which will mean self-help for them and a contribution to the new blossoming of the Turkish Empire."

This was all he said on the subject; he had formulated it in such fashion as to give it the appearance of pro-Turkish propaganda — at least, in the eyes of the Sultan, to whom he sent a telegram of greeting from the Congress, receiving the Sultan's thanks the next day. But the undeniable political success of his audience with the Sultan strengthened his standing with the Congress, which was not as free with its applause and approval as its predecessors. The Russians, disappointed by the empty London Congress, were growing wearier and wearier of waiting for diplomatic salvation; they pressed insistently for practical work in Palestine. There was now, for the first time, an official oppositionist group, the "Democratic-Zionist Fraction"— usually called "the Fraction," for short — whose leading spirits were Motzkin, Weizmann, Victor Jacobson, Martin Buber, Berthold Feivel, Lilien and Trietsch. Altogether it was composed of thirty-seven delegates; its power, however, was out of all proportion to its numbers, for as the only determined group it sometimes dominated the entire Congress. Strongly influenced by Ahad Ha-am, it aimed at the promotion of a more evolutionary, more deeply rooted nationalism, a greater degree of democracy in the leadership of the movement, a stronger influence on the youth and its ideas, and a program of *Gegenwartsarbeit* — immediate, day-to-day activity — of a cultural nature throughout the diaspora.

Herzl was not hostile to these representatives of the youth, nor to the cultural movement as such, even though he was, as we have noted, embittered by this early emergence of an opposition. He had even, about this time, given Feivel and Buber, leading representatives of "the youth," a hand in the management of *Die Welt*; he left them free to propagate their views in the official organ of the movement, and he was generous in his praise for their work. But with Herzl the first consideration was the unity of the Zionist movement and the safeguarding of its political character, which seemed to him to be imperilled by the emphasis on cultural work. At this Congress the clash between Herzl, the prudent political negotiator and imperious leader, and the young, stormy group, came to a head round the long delayed decision on the cultural question.

On the last day of the Congress, Herzl again tried to defer debate and decision on the "culture" resolutions submitted by the Fraction until after the election of the Actions Committee — i. e., until the closing hours of the Congress. To this move the Fraction presented a resolute opposition.

Motzkin, as its spokesman, demanded that the question be put to the vote, even if without debate, so that it might be decided once for all whether the Zionist Organization was going to concern itself with cultural work as a matter of principle. Herzl insisted sharply that he would permit discussion of this issue "only after we have held the elections which are indispensable for the future existence and functioning of the movement ... We must be certain first that the necessary organs exist ..."

When Martin Buber and the artist Ephraim Lilien appealed from this decision to the Congress, Herzl forced his views through in a violent discussion on a question of procedure. This method so embittered the opposition that it left the hall in a body and absented itself for an hour in a protest demonstration.

By this action the Fraction undoubtedly put itself in the wrong, weakened its own demands and created a dangerous precedent. At first Herzl passed over the incident in silence. But later one of the delegates, Bernstein-Kohan, who had not been present during the incident, opposed the holding of any election. Thereupon Herzl took a stand. He declared that the Congress had not declared itself against a program of national education; on the contrary, by refusing to vote on such a program without a full discussion it had expressed its sense of the importance of the issue. He went on to point out vigorously that if every delegate who saw himself voted down would threaten the Congress with secession or withdrawal, there would be an end of all orderly procedure; and he could not concede such an extraordinary privilege even to the oldest and most honored veteran of the movement.

Herzl carried his point, and after the elections threw the floor open to debate on the cultural question. Most of the resolutions submitted in this connection were accepted, Herzl himself demonstratively voting for them, to indicate that the whole affair had left him unembittered. In his closing address he even expressed his happiness at the presence in the Congress of a youth group "which was faithful, sometimes in a rather lively way, and of an older group which was renewing its youth." Thus a break was avoided. But it would be useless to deny that out of all this came an increasing alienation between Herzl and some of the youth.

However, the fifth Congress did produce some valuable results. It completed the structure of the Zionist institutions. Herzl had been able to announce that the Bank was now open for business, even though it was not yet the powerful instrument he had hoped it would be. Herzl was, for this reason, of the opinion that it ought to remain inactive until it had accumulated a larger capital, and that this national asset "ought to be safeguarded with the solicitude which a father brings to the administration of the family fortune." Even more important for the movement was the final creation of the National Fund, the spiritual father of which was Professor Shapira, who had already submitted the idea to the Kattowitz Conference of 1884 and had again pleaded for it at the first Congress. At the fourth Congress Kremenezky had taken the lead in urging its creation, and had worked out its form and the details of its statutes. Herzl himself was mainly responsible for the definitive action of the fifth Congress, intervening energetically at a moment when, as a result of the unskilful direction of Vice-President Tchlenov, it seemed as though a decision would be deferred to the sixth Congress. It was thus that a fund was instituted the importance of which was realized at the time by a small minority only. According to its statutes, the Jewish National Fund was to confine itself to the purchase of land in Palestine, to become the inalienable property of the Jewish people.

Important, too, was the revision and the adoption in final form of a set of statutes for the Zionist Organization. Some of these were already in operation as part of the provisional constitution. Some were new. Such, for instance, was the Congress Court for the settlement of organizational disputes. New also was the provision which called for a biennial Congress, with a *Jahreskonferenz* for the intervening years, composed of the members of the Larger Actions Committee, the Permanent Commission and the Bank directorate. A fundamental change was also introduced into the international structure. Until the fifth Congress the central office in each country had been linked with the directing office in Vienna. From now on fifty Zionist societies with a total membership of five thousand shekel payers could form their own federation and deal directly with the Smaller Actions Committee.

With the creation of the National Fund and the completion of the structure of the Zionist Organization, the fifth Congress closed the initial period of the growth of the movement. Herzl was aware of this turning point in the history of Zionism. "We may in a certain sense declare," he put it, "that we have completed our initial tasks. Our institutions are, to a large extent, only outlined; they are certainly subject to improvement; but they exist. The Jewish people can use them, strengthen them and fill them out, if it so desires. In all our efforts it has been our concern to exclude the element of personality. Only the impersonal can endure. Today no one among us is indispensable. This one or that one may fall out of the ranks; the cause itself goes on."

41. Herzl in Wilna (see p. 450)

43

42. Herzl leaving the Basle synagogue (see p. 454)

44. Herzl with a group of delegates at the sixth Zionist Congress, Basle 1903 (see pp. 453–464)

45. Leopold J. Greenberg, Herzl's diplomatic representative in London (see p. 416)

46. Menachem Ussischkin, leader of the revolt against Herzl's East
African project (see p. 470)

47. Ahad Ha-Am (see p. 177)

48. Herzl looking across the Rhine from his hotel in Basle (1903)

49. The last photograph taken of Herzl

Gruss aus Edlach

Verlag Franz Reinhofer

50. Postcard view of Edlach, with the house in which Herzl died

DAS BEGRÄBNIS Dr THEODOR HERZL am 7 Juli 1904
24 Thamuz 5664

51. Herzl's funeral in Vienna, 1904 (see p. 505)

52. Herzl's coffin arriving in Israel in an El-Al plane, 1949

53. Lying in state in front of the Parliament building in Tel-Aviv

54. The coffin being lowered into its final resting place at Mount Herzl
in Jerusalem

55. Lilien's design for a stained-glass window of Moses,
using the head of Herzl

56. Bust of Herzl, by F. Beer, 1894 (see p. 101.)

57. Portrait of Herzl, by Koppay

58. Portrait drawing of Herzl, by H. Struck, 1903

59. David Ben Gurion reading the proclamation establishing the State of Israel

At the Congresses Herzl was always the recipient of enthusiastic ovations; in spite of growing impatience and discontent, his leadership remained undisputed. He himself avoided such demonstrations as much as possible, finding less and less satisfaction in them. He was only too sensitive to the discrepancy between his will and his achievements. He saw only too clearly how far he still was from his goal — the Charter for Palestine. Between the sending of his telegram to the Sultan on the first day of the Congress, and the receipt of the reply on the second day, he did not cease to tremble lest the Sultan, by ignoring his greetings, indicate the breaking off of the relations. Herzl was forever comparing himself to a horseman crossing a frozen river; the ice had borne him till now: how long would it continue to bear him?

There was, moreover, another dread consideration: his heart. The pauses between the onsets had grown shorter, the attacks stronger. But he worked on. Time was close on his heels.

For months now Joseph Cowen and Israel Zangwill had been working under his direction to get together, with the help of Lord Suffield, a group of financiers. But in this they were as unsuccessful as Herzl himself in his renewed efforts to acquire the shares of the *Neue Freie Presse*. As against this, on February 5, Herzl unexpectedly received a telegram from Ibrahim summoning him to Constantinople to "furnish information" with regard to his proposals. He answered the call. On February 14 he arrived in Constantinople in the company of Cowen, who replaced Wolffsohn because the latter had again fallen temporarily into Herzl's bad graces.

On this occasion Herzl found the invitation to Constantinople thoroughly unwelcome. Apart from the fact that he was worried about his position on the *Neue Freie Presse*, his conscience troubled him with regard to the authorities in Constantinople. He had made public utterances concerning his plans for a Charter in London and Basle; and in actual fact he had raised no money yet. He dreaded that he might be confronted with a genuine offer of the Charter before he was prepared for it. From the outset, then, he was at a disadvantage. He was received in very friendly fashion. Ibrahim even informed him that he was at liberty to regard himself, during his stay in Constantinople, as the Sultan's guest. But with all this the negotiations, which were again conducted, on the Turkish side, by Ibrahim and Izzet Bey, advanced no further.

Izzet Bey touched on the sore spot immediately. What, exactly, had been Herzl's object during his visit in May? Herzl repeated that he wanted to help Turkey. "True," answered Izzet Bey. "And that was how we looked at it. You would give us moral and material assistance, influential as you are in the journalistic and financial worlds. But we've seen nothing of such help. All you have done is make declarations in London and Basle." Herzl parried this thrust by pointing out that before he could proceed to practical measures he had to create a favorable attitude toward the Sultan among world Jewry, and in this he had succeeded. Thereupon Izzet Bey repeated the formal and cautious proposals already offered by the Sultan the year before; to wit, the opening of the country to Jewish refugees, on condition that the latter become full Turkish citizens, renounce all previous allegiances, accept all the duties of Turkish citizenship, and scatter themselves throughout Turkish territory, without mass settlements anywhere. At that, Palestine itself would not come into the picture.

And in consideration for these concessions, the Sultan asked for the creation of a syndicate which should take over the funding of the Public Debt, and undertake through concessions the development and exploitation of Turkish mines.

Herzl asked for time. The next day he responded in writing.

He was ready, he informed Izzet Bey and the Sultan, to continue negotiating with his friends on the question of the exploitation of Turkish mines. However, the funding of the Public Debt, in the form proposed, was in his opinion not practicable, particularly in view of the fact that it was impossible to win over the public at large and the rich Jews in particular with such limited offers of immigration and settlement. "The fact is," he wrote, "there must be a connection between Jewish colonization and the work of unifying and funding the Debt. This connection can, in my humble opinion, be created only via a general concession for a great Colonizing Company." He told Izzet Bey orally that the locale of such colonization had to be left to the Colonization Company. "We are not concerned with individual protection for Jews—we have that already in civilized countries. We are concerned with national protection." What, asked Izzet Bey, was he to understand by this last phrase? Herzl answered: "A great, demonstrative declaration for the benefit of the Jews, such as would be represented by an offer of immigration rights *without any restrictions*."

It was unquestionably a personal triumph for Herzl that he was by now able to communicate his Zionist aims to the Sultan in what was practically open form. It also marked a certain political advance that the Sultan should have offered free land for Jewish colonization in Asia Minor and particularly in Mesopotamia. But Herzl's essential demands were still refused. There could be no mass immigration, and whatever immigration took place would be directed by the Turkish government. Palestine was to be excluded. "A Charter without Palestine! I refused on the spot."

In order not to break off the negotiations abruptly, rather than because he hoped for success along the new line, he made a second proposal to the Sultan the next day: in return for the right to unrestricted immigration he was to found a great Turkish-Jewish bank with branches in all the more important cities, so as to organize the credit system of the country. On the following day the Sultan returned the answer that he could not admit the principle of unlimited immigration under the control of a land company even if he wanted to, for the general opposition would be too great. On February 18, in a closing protocol prepared at the Sultan's request, Herzl repeated his essential demands and declared that the conditions offered seemed to him unacceptable. "But I am still ready to place myself at the service of His Imperial Majesty for further negotiations."

While Herzl was having the French protocol put into a fair copy, a messenger came with a small bag containing two hundred pounds in gold, which the Sultan sent him for his travelling expenses. But there was no invitation to an audience. Nor would the first secretary, Tahsin Bey, receive Herzl. But Izzet and Ibrahim, whom Herzl gave small presents and promised larger ones, declared themselves wholly on his side.

Not as hopeful as on the previous occasion, and yet not entirely disheartened, Herzl left Constantinople. He had kept hoping till the last moment that the Sultan would not let him leave, but would insist on continuing the negotiations. "But it turned out otherwise. With this man it always turns out otherwise than one expects. The Charter, too, will come in unexpected and unpredictable fashion — if it comes at all. That is, if we are not to get it from the Powers after the partition of Turkey."

These February negotiations in Constantinople were the first real ones which Herzl conducted with Turkey; his visit of May 1901 was only a preliminary act. In a sense they might be called negotiations between equals. Their result was that he had to consider his efforts at a direct approach — the Charter in exchange for financial assistance — a failure, for the time being at least. Now arose the question whether there was not an indirect approach. On the day before his departure Izzet Bey offered Herzl a "counsel of friendship." It would be well for him to establish a position of power and influential friendship in the role of financier, and that in Constantinople. Later he could again take up the question of immigration and colonization. "Take our finances in hand, and you will become the master." The best thing would be to begin with the mining concessions.

The idea appealed at once to Herzl, especially because it would give him the means of "flashing some money before these people, without spending any, so that their appetites would be tickled." But he made a show of resistance. His friends, he said, would answer that he was bringing back to them from Constantinople something they had not asked for, while he had failed to bring back what they had specifically requested. However, he continued, he understood Izzet Bey's suggestion that in order to succeed he would have to attach men to himself by linking their interests with his own — and indirectly he permitted Izzet Bey to infer that he was included in that category.

Against the resistance of some of the members of the
Actions Committee — and particularly of Ussishkin — Herzl
proceeded along these lines. He was authorized to obtain,
on the authority of the Colonial Trust, three letters of credit,
each for a million francs, from the Credit Lyonnais in Paris,
the Dresdner Bank in Berlin and Lloyds Bank in London.
These sums were to be deposited in Turkish banks — his
first substantial foothold. The step had a significance beyond
its immediate purpose. Herzl was establishing the principle
of indirect action. Its implication was that the Zionist objective could and might be reached by a detour; and the results
of such an implication were to be made evident a year later.

Meanwhile the actual consequences of his action were of
little importance. The cards were stacked against him.
While he was negotiating with Ibrahim for changes in the
form of immigration which would be permitted him, the
French ambassador to Turkey, Constans, was offering the
Sultan a more substantial and reliable solution of the problem of the funding of the Public Debt. The three million
francs deposited in the Turkish banks got Herzl no further.
Tahsin Bey informed him, through an intermediary, that
the money had been deposited as the result of a misunderstanding. "I knew that well enough," wrote Herzl, in closing
the tenth volume of his diary. "I only wanted to show these
people the color of my money, so that they wouldn't forget
me." On April 14 Tahsin's intermediary, Mahmud, called
Herzl to him again. Herzl had used the two hundred pounds
which the Sultan had sent him for his expenses on the trip
to Constantinople, as a contribution to the Hedjaz railway
fund. Tahsin instructed Mahmud to return the money to
Herzl. It seemed by now that the connection with Constantinople was severed.

There followed a brief interlude of diplomatic calm, during which Herzl concentrated on his Palestine novel, completing it on April 30. Immediately thereafter he resumed negotiations with Turkey, and one notes with interest how he made use of every chance opportunity which presented itself. He took up the project which had been sponsored by Weizmann, Buber and Feivel, for a Jewish university in Jerusalem, and submitted it to the Sultan, with the observation that such a center of learning could also be open to Turkish students, who would thenceforth not have to visit foreign universities where they were exposed to all kinds of revolutionary influences. Izzet informed Herzl through Wellisch that his plan had been studied by the Sultan. Herzl was asked what plans he now had for the regulation of Turkish finances under conditions more favorable than those submitted by the French. Herzl answered that he did indeed have such plans. But he would not submit them otherwise than personally in Constantinople. He saw clearly through the manoeuvre; he was only being used by the Sultan to force better terms out of the French. Still, it meant that he would remain in contact with Constantinople.

Then a new turn came in his efforts.

As far back as 1894, and again in 1898 with greater earnestness, the British Conservatives had brought to the fore the question of Jewish immigration into England — or, as the more cultivated called it, the immigration of poor aliens. Since those years there had been a steady influx of Jews from Eastern Europe. It had never acquired any considerable volume. Greenberg's report to the fifth Congress showed that between 1890 and 1902 the total Jewish immigration had been 25,000. But public opinion in England was concerned with "the growing threat of cheap labor." Press and Parliament became busy with it, and in 1902 the British government appointed a Royal Commission to investigate the question.

The situation was skilfully exploited by Greenberg, one of Herzl's most devoted followers. Early in March 1902, he began his efforts to have Herzl invited to testify as expert before the Commission, in the belief that this would have a tremendous propaganda effect. By the beginning of May, when Herzl was in Berlin on the business of the Bank, Greenberg telephoned him that the invitation could be expected any moment. But a few weeks passed before the call actually came, despite the raging opposition of Lord Rothschild, a leading member of the Commission.

The date was June 4. Herzl was in Paris, exhausted in body, weary in mood. "I am again in Paris," he had written in his diary. "An aging and famous man. The days of my youth were, in spite of their attacks of melancholy, more desirable." But the invitation of the Commission sent his spirits up again. He perceived at once that its essential significance was not propagandistic. "It is the encounter — leading to battle or reconciliation — with Lord Rothschild: that is its profound significance." He instructed Cowen and Greenberg to try to arrange a meeting with Lord Rothschild; he would use his presence in London in order to promote a mining concern for the exploitation of the Turkish concession.

On June 9 he arrived in London, full of high hopes; the long-sought interview with Rothschild was to take place at last, on the day following the next. But when he returned to his hotel that night, after a visit to the theatre, he found a telegram from his wife. "Papa very sick. Come Vienna immediately." He understood in a flash. It was death. The night which followed he himself described as one of the darkest in his life. True, his father was not an exceptional man. What was exceptional was the bond between them, a bond which had never been strained, and which had grown ever stronger with the years. It was possible that the father, with his simple and straightforward mind, had not always understood what his son was seeking and doing; but he had understood all the more what his son needed: quiet loyalty and frank counsel. This he had given in full measure. On February 15, 1896, when the *Judenstaat* appeared in print, and everyone whom Herzl consulted shrank back in timid caution, Herzl wrote in his diary: "Now my good father is my only support... He stands there like a tree." Thus he stood, too, when the Bank was being organized, when unpleasant attacks were being directed both against the institution and its creator. "How much he has gone through with me! How much he has supported me, comforted me, after having given so many years to my upbringing and education. The travels on which I learned so much I owe to him. And now I am not at home at the moment when his eyes are closing for ever ... How deeply I am indebted to him, though I have not been a bad son. What a buttress he has been to me, year after year, what a counsellor. He stood there like a tree" — he repeats his phrase of 1896 — "and now the tree is no more."

The next day he received a telegram which extinguished the last glimmer of hope that his father had had nothing more serious than an attack of pneumonia. He could not contain himself, but broke down and sobbed. Then he pulled himself together. Julie Herzl had telegraphed Wolffsohn to accompany her "poor husband" from Cologne to Vienna.

Herzl refused this offer. "He can't help me." From the road he telegraphed to Kremenezky: "Please help my mother. Shall be there tomorrow evening. Funeral to take place at Türkenschanz cemetery ... Omit speeches. Only Hebrew songs."

A week later Herzl sat again in Altaussee at his table, poorer, lonely, aged. "I am finding myself again slowly," he wrote on June 19 to Cowen. "But I am still shattered." And to Wolffsohn a week later: "I would rather not write you about my state of mind. My work, and the worries which you cause me, must help me past it."

Early in July, Greenberg called him again to London, and on July 4 the meeting with Rothschild took place. Another step forward!

Nathaniel Mayer, Lord Rothschild, the son of that Lionel Nathan Rothschild who, after a long battle, had won the right to sit in Parliament as an unbaptized Jew, was, for his part, the first Jewish member of the House of Lords. It was understandable that he should oppose tooth and nail everything which, in his opinion, endangered the emancipation which had been won by so much labor. As head of the English banking house of Rothschild, member of the Board of Directors of the Bank of England and President of the United Synagogue, he was the outstanding figure in English Jewry and a man of immense influence generally. Until this time his attitude toward Herzl had been sharply negative; he had curtly rejected the suggestion to meet with him, and had fought bitterly the proposal that this "demagogue" be called before the Royal Commission, on which he was the only defender and representative of the Jews. If he now consented to receive Herzl in his business office, it was in the hope of anticipating and preventing any dangerous public statements by this man who was twenty years younger than himself. The interview was conducted in a loud tone of voice because Rothschild was hard of hearing; at certain points it was also agitated. Herzl had been invited, declared Rothschild, so that the opponents of the Jews might be able to say: "Dr. Herzl is undoubtedly the best Jew, and it is his opinion that a Jew can never become an Englishman." Herzl replied: "It would be a piece of stupid arrogance on my part to give the Commission a lecture on the characteristics of a real Englishman. I shall simply tell them what frightful wretchedness reigns among the eastern Jews, and that the Jews must either die or get out. The misery of the Roumanian Jews is well known since 1897; the petitions to the Zionist Congress have everywhere been ignored. In Galicia conditions are perhaps even worse. In that country we have some 700,000 destitute Jews. These too will set themselves in motion."

"Milord answered: 'I wish you would not say that to the Commission. It will lead to restrictive laws.' At this point I became solid: 'Certainly I shall say it. Most certainly. You may rely upon me to say it.' Thereupon his jaw dropped, he rang the bell, and sent for his brother Leopold. When the latter appeared I repeated what I had said and added that Jewish charity had become a machine for the suppression of the Jewish cry of misery. Milord wailed: 'That's what he wants to tell the Commission!' I went on: 'I would be a wicked sort of person if I would say only that which might lead to the restriction of immigration. But I would be one of those wicked persons to whom the English Jews ought to raise a monument, because I would be protecting them from an influx of eastern Jews and therefore perhaps from anti-Semitism. But I have a plan of help, and

I want to submit that to the Commission.' Thereupon milord interrupted me and asked whether I would take lunch
with him. 'With pleasure.'

"After the coffee I went to his desk and asked: 'Would
you now like to hear my plan.'

'Yes.'

I pushed my chair round on the side of his better ear and
said: 'I want to ask the British government for a Colonization Charter.'

'Don't say Charter. The word has a bad sound.'

'Call it what you like. I want to found a Jewish colony
in British territory.'

'Take Uganda.'

'No. I can only use this ...' and since there were other
people in the room I wrote on a scrap of paper: 'Sinai
Peninsula. Egyptian Palestine. Cyprus.' Then I added:
'Are you in favor?'

He considered, with a pleased smile. 'Very much.'

That was a victory."

Three days later, on July 7, Herzl appeared before the
Royal Commission. He submitted his principal statement
in written form, to be read out, Greenberg having translated
it. He began by pointing out that as leader of the Zionist
movement he was in a position to understand the life and
social condition of Jewry at large; then he outlined briefly
his view of the Jewish question. The mere fact of the appointment of the Commission had created a difficulty. "For,
as a result, the Commission must either recommend restrictive legislation or not. If the former, and its recommenda-
tions are given effect, then England will break away from the
great principle of free asylum to the oppressed which hitherto
has been its glory, although the endeavour to keep out the

poor, oppressed Jews cannot, I believe, be successful. But if restrictive legislation is not recommended, the mere fact of the Commission having sat will give an impetus to immigration to England" — it will have formed an additional certification of the desirability of England as a place of refuge.

Jewish philanthropy, which in the past had sufficed to take care of needy Jews forced out of their place of residence and compelled to seek new homes, was incapable of dealing with the flood of modern migration. The only way out of the present difficulty was the Zionist solution, to which he wished to direct the attention of the Commission, even though it lay outside its field of investigation. "The Jews of eastern Europe cannot stay where they are — where are they to go? If you find they are not wanted here, then some place must be found to which they can migrate without raising the problems that confront them here. Those problems will not arise if a home be found for them which will be legally recognized as Jewish. And I do submit that whether the Commission can directly influence that solution of the problem or not, they must not omit to consider it and give it the high value of its opinion."

In answering the questions put to him by the Commission after the reading of this statement, Herzl was confronted by the difficulty that he did not wish to say anything which might be used as an argument in favor of restricting immigration into England, and that he did not wish to give the impression of meddling in English affairs. He therefore declined to offer his advice as to actual decisions to be recommended by the Commission, and strove again and again to direct its attention to Jewish migration as a world problem. Asked what the aim of Zionism was, he quoted the Basle Program.

But he added at once that "there are moments when immediate help or a direct step forward is out of the question. The Zionists therefore consider themselves obligated to try, under all circumstances, to mitigate the hard fate of the Jews by appropriate measures."

The plan he had indicated to Rothschild, with regard to Sinai, El Arish and Cyprus, he submitted privately the next day to the chairman of the Commission, Lord James. The latter pointed out that the plan could be carried out only with the assistance of Lord Rothschild.

That same afternoon Herzl had his second, lengthier interview with Lord Rothschild. He submitted the details of a Colonization Company for the development of the mentioned territories. Rothschild showed himself seriously interested, and asked for a written outline of the plan. He wanted to discuss it with the English Minister for the Colonies, Mr. Chamberlain.

Three days later, on July 12, 1902, Herzl sent Lord Rothschild an English outline of the plan for Chamberlain, and a German outline of the financial side of the plan for Rothschild himself. The latter provided for the creation of a Jewish (Eastern) Company with a capital of ten million pounds, of which, however, only ten or twenty per cent was to be paid in.

In the accompanying letter Herzl noted: "To avoid all misunderstanding now and for the future, I wish to make it clear that I have submitted this plan only because you are against Palestine. You are the greatest effective force that the Jews have had since their dispersion, and I consider it my duty to place my modest advice at your disposal if you are at all interested in doing something of value for our unfortunates. I cannot permit myself to refuse the cooperation of my advice on grounds of principle. But apart from this human interest of mine, there exists also a political interest. A great Jewish settlement in the eastern Mediterranean strengthens our position in regard to Palestine . . . Whether I myself can cooperate in the carrying out of this plan, i.e., whether I can place the Zionist Organization at its disposal, depends on the decision of my party."

As a second, private plan he suggested settlement in Mesopotamia, as proposed to him by the Sultan, and as supported by the American ambassador in Constantinople, Oscar S. Straus. This, however, he would keep in reserve, because of its weaker legal guarantees, in case the English plan fell through.

Lord Rothschild answered that he wanted to examine the Sinai plan more closely. The idea called for exact investigation and study. There was not the money for its carrying out on a large scale.

Soon after his arrival in London (July 4), Herzl had been advised by the Turkish ambassador to England that the Sultan had asked telegraphically that he proceed at once to Constantinople. Herzl made a show of indifference. There were rumors that the negotiations with Rouvier, the Frenchman, for the conversion of the Public Debt, were about to fall through; Herzl did not want to appear on the scene as a competitor who would be used as pressure against Rouvier. But when, after a stormy exchange of telegrams, the Turkish government insisted on his presence in Constantinople, he accepted the invitation. He left on July 22, 1902, again in the company of Wolffsohn.

The reception in the Yildiz Kiosk was even friendlier than in February; Tahsin himself, who had been so evasive in

February, came forward to assure Herzl that he was to consider himself the guest of the Sultan, and that a court carriage had been placed at his service. The negotiations, too, had a more serious character. Once more Herzl was asked to submit his plan for the unification of the Public Debt. Herzl made his proposal one and a half million pounds cheaper than Rouvier's, and asked, as recompense, the granting of a Charter for Mesopotamia and "for the territory of Haifa and in the region of Palestine." His financial plan was translated into French by the famous Turkish statesman Karatheodory Pasha.

Two days later he was conducted to the Grand Vizier, Said Pasha, who received him coolly and played the same game with him as Hohenlohe had done in 1898. The financial report now had to be translated into Turkish, reported Said Pasha, at the Sultan's request. And it was only now, also, that Herzl's book, *Philosophic Stories*, which he had given Ibrahim for the Sultan in February, was transmitted to that potentate.

In a second conversation with the Grand Vizier, Herzl spoke openly of the significance of Palestine for the Jews. The Grand Vizier suggested that the debt plan be separated from the colonization plan, inasmuch as it was not worth while breaking off with Rouvier for the sake of the saving of one and a half million pounds. To this, too, Herzl agreed. But it was quite clear that these long drawn out negotiations had only one purpose, namely, to squeeze better terms out of Rouvier. Ibrahim told Herzl that the Sultan had the highest personal regard for him; but his offer went no further than that made in February, i. e., scattered settlement of the Jews under the direction of the government. Herzl expressed gratitude for the renewed offer, and answered that he would have to consult his friends. The Sultan then asked Herzl to accept a subvention for the *Neue Freie Presse* and to submit a statement of his expenses for the voyage. Herzl naturally rejected the offer of a subvention. As regards reimbursement of his expenses, he would consider himself hospitably treated if the hotel bill were paid. In spite of this, there came again a little bag of gold, which he could not refuse, and which he said he would distribute among the poor Jews.

For the first time he gave a detailed report in *Die Welt*.

"The negotiations," he wrote, "have again led to no results. However, the Sultan expressed his high regard and sympathy to Dr. Herzl. The connection is by no means broken off. On the contrary, we may still hope that the advantages which would accrue from a publicly recognized, legally secured settlement of the Jews in accordance with our program, will still be recognized in all its bearings by the Turkish government. The Zionist Organization must prepare itself for that moment; our propaganda must be carried on unceasingly, and the material means must be accumulated. The more capable our movement becomes of action, the sooner and the more certainly shall we reach our goal."

Herzl himself came to the conclusion, as a result of these last negotiations, that the direct road to Palestine was for the time being blocked. He hoped to advance, therefore, by the indirect road of El Arish. "I hope," he noted in his diary, recording the idea which he had mentioned to Ibrahim, and in which the latter had concurred, "that when I have succeeded in setting up the Jewish Eastern Company, His Majesty the Sultan will sing another tune. For I shall then have become a neighbor with whom it would be well to have friendly relations."

Meanwhile he had received a discouraging letter from Lord Rothschild, filled with warnings against ambitious and over-hasty plans, and characterizing the idea of Palestine as a myth, while, however, expressing recognition of Herzl's work. To him Herzl wrote, on August 13: "Ah, if you had some idea of the immeasurable wretchedness of our decent poor people — I am not speaking of beggars and riffraff — you would listen to me more sympathetically." Rothschild wrote him again, in friendly disagreement, expressing himself in favor of scattered settlements among non-Jews, because otherwise "there would only arise a new ghetto, with all the disadvantages of a ghetto;" and Herzl answered, on the 22nd: "I cannot admit that the Jewish commonwealth which I seek to create will be small, orthodox and illiberal. For three years I have been at work on an answer to these and similar fears. It is in the form of a book which I have called *Altneuland*. It will appear in a few weeks, and you will be among the first to whom I will send it."

Six weeks later, on October 5, 1902, he sent Lord Rothschild, among others, his Palestine romance, just off the press.

CHAPTER XII

ALTNEULAND

IT WILL be remembered that at the time when the idea of the Jewish state first began to haunt Herzl, and during the days when its outlines were emerging for him from the mist of inspiration, he toyed with the idea of conveying his message in the form of a novel. He decided in favor of a pamphlet, for he felt that a novel would not lead to that act which his spirit demanded. As he wrote in 1899: "People would have spoken about it in drawing rooms and railroad compartments, many would perhaps have laughed at the moody concept, others would perhaps secretly have wept into the pages. But what would have been achieved? One more fairy tale added to the Arabian Nights of literature. No, no, what I wanted was reality and the act. The Jewish people had to be shaken out of its torpor, not lulled into deeper sleep. And indeed, it was shaken out of its torpor, it stretched its limbs, it began to move, it started that movement which we call Zionism in accordance with its aim. And now," he adds, "I feel the time is here to tell it the fairy tale of the days to come."

The impulse toward the writing of the novel was provided by his visit to Palestine. He made the first outline on July 2, 1899, on three slips of paper, in a railway carriage between Paris and Frankfort, as he was returning from London. The framework of the story was definitely fixed; the title was to be: "The New Zion." On August 30, 1899, he found a better title. He records the inspiration in his diary. "Today, on the rattling omnibus, the title of my Zion novel came to me: *Altneuland* — a throwback to the *Altneuschul* of Prague. It will become a famous word."*

The work went forward very slowly, and amid repeated interruptions. It was only toward mid-March 1901, when failure in London and bad news from Constantinople led to deferred hope, that he threw himself energetically into the production of the novel. Then once again the excitement of political activity in Constantinople, London and Basle thrust the book into the background. It was more than a year later, on April 30, 1902, that he finally completed it, and another half year passed before it appeared in print.

It is definitely a book with a purpose, a utopia novel. Its purpose is to body forth the Palestine of the future, to show "how much justice, goodness and beauty can be created on earth if only there is a decent will to it."

It has the weaknesses of every tendencious novel, the weaknesses of all of Herzl's plays: the figures are not full-grown and three-dimensional, they are types embodying a specific outlook or expressing a specific view. This does not, however, alter the fact that most of the fictitious persons are based on living personalities, whose characters or peculiarities have been incorporated in this or that protagonist. Indeed, it was Herzl's purpose to memorialize his friends, as well as some of his opponents; the truth remains, however,

---

Altneuland — *Old-New Land*. Sokolow, who translated the novel into Hebrew, gave it, by a play on words, the title *Tel Aviv*, which afterwards became the name of the first modern all-Jewish city.

that most of the *dramatis personae* are figures in a play; the
entire work has something of the stage about it, and proceeds
in scenes rather than by way of narrative. We perceive in it,
as in all of Herzl's literary productions, his special ability to
arrest a moment in time and to outline swiftly and simply
the elements of a situation or subject; we perceive also that
he lacks the breath, endurance and patience to master a great
literary form, as well as the creative power to round out and
fill with life the figures which he presents. Regarding himself Herzl said, in his diary, that he was "a writer of great
mold," who "had not put forth his full strength because he
had been disgusted and discouraged." But the truth seems
to be that he overestimated his literary gifts. His talent was
of another kind: he had a flair for development and growth,
he saw the full fruit in the seed, the future lying concealed
in the present. He pictured forth the future, he showed the
way to it, he called upon others to tread the path, and he
himself courageously led the way — a road-builder and
banner-bearer.

The action of the novel begins as of the close of the year
1902. We meet the lawyer Friedrich Loewenberg, who in
some respects embodies Herzl's mood at the beginning of
his Paris period, but who in the main is also a portrait of
his friend Heinrich Kana. Loewenberg, weary and disgusted
with life, meets a former German officer by the name of
Kingscourt, who is in the same spiritual condition. Kingscourt, who has accumulated a large fortune in America, in-
vites Loewenberg to accompany him to a lonely island in
the Cook Archipelago On their journey, as they pass the
vicinity of Palestine, Kingscourt proposes a visit to that
country, which interests the Prussian aristocrat more than
it does the embittered Jewish intellectual. They spend a

few days in "the ancient homeland of the Jews," and see
there what Herzl saw in 1898: a land in deep decline, decayed
as the Jewish people has decayed. Kingscourt says what the
Kaiser said in 1898: "The land needs only water and shade,
and it can still have a great future." In answer to Friedrich's question he adds what the Kaiser should have said
in 1898, but did not: that it was for the Jews to bring this
water and this shade to the country.

In Jerusalem, as the two men are walking through the
moonlit night from the station to the hotel, just as the
feverish author had done four years before, Friedrich is suddenly and incomprehensibly overcome by the panorama of
this unknown city. His boyhood awakens in him; he sees
himself once more accompanying his father to the temple,
the sanctity of the Passover evening sends a sudden shaft
through his soul. "It overwhelmed him. He came to a halt,
and the tears coursed slowly down his cheeks."

By daylight there was, to be sure, much that repelled him
in Jerusalem, in particular "the revolting sight of the energetic businesslike mendicants." He enters into conversation
with an old Russian Jew, the eye-doctor Eichenstamm—
who is, of course, none other than Professor Mandelstamm
of Kiev, the Russian eye-doctor and Zionist who had a special place in Herzl's heart. Eichenstamm tells Loewenberg
of the new Jewish settlements, which the travellers must
on no account miss seeing. "Our ancient soil is bearing fruit
again." They go on an excursion to the colonies, they see
"Rishon le-Zion and Rehobot lying like oases in the midst
of the withered landscape." Kingscourt is inspired to high
enthusiasm by the wild riding exhibition of the boys of Rehobot, even as Herzl was in 1898; the weary Jewish intellectual scarcely responds. The non-Jew, with his healthy, honest

naturalness, sees the significance of Palestine and the tasks
and abilities of the Jews with a sharper, clearer eye than the
resigned and depressed Jew at his side. Later, when Kingscourt and Loewenberg are travelling through the Red Sea,
the former remarks that if Moses were to come again he
would laugh grimly to see what little use people knew to
make of the world's technical progress. "Everything exists
for the creation of a better world. Man alive, do you know
who could show the way? You! You Jews! You have nothing to lose. You could build up the world's experimental
country — over there, where we were, create an old new
land, *Altneuland*, on the ancient soil." But the representative of the Jews, to whom these words are addressed, has
celebrated the turn of the year by drinking more wine than
he can carry. He does not hear the call. He is asleep.

Thus closes the first book of the novel, entitled "An Educated Young Man," an attempt at a cross section of Jewry
in decay. The following sections of the novel are placed
twenty years later, in the year 1923. The travellers have
passed two decades in happy isolation from mankind. They
return now from their lonely island to take one more look
at the world. His life with nature has turned Friedrich
Loewenberg into "a tree of a man." They learn that Palestine is no longer a desolate country, and they decide again to
make a detour for a few days in order to confirm the report
with their own eyes.

They land in Haifa, which Herzl did not see in 1898. Haifa
is now "the safest and most comfortable harbor in the Mediterranean," an international world city. Hardly have the
travellers landed than they are addressed by a man whom
Loewenberg had rescued from the deepest need before his
flight from the world. David Litvak — this is his name, in

honor of David Wolffsohn — was one of the first to come to Palestine; he started as a peasant, and is now a ship-owner, a wealthy and respected man. The travellers must of course become his guests, and learn from him, in his house, about the new Palestine. They are so profoundly affected by the life about them that they decide to remain in the country.

Friedrich wins the love of the schoolteacher, Miriam Litvak, David's sister — modelled on Herzl's sister, Pauline. Loewenberg-Kana does not have to shoot himself, he does not have to sink into despair, as of old in real life. He finds a place for himself, he finds remunerative work, and a natural, healthy life. For in that twenty-year interlude there has taken place the return of the Jews.

Let us take a look at this Palestine of 1923. Its territory lies east and west of the Jordan; its northern and southern boundaries are not clearly indicated, but in the north it stretches as far as modern Syria. The dead land of 1902 is now thoroughly alive, with great cities and a flourishing agriculture. All that is most modern in technology has been installed here. Numerous railroad lines traverse the country, "like a canalization of human energy," and connect with great world systems; Palestine, lying at the crossroads, has become a focal point of world transportation. Transportation within the country is for the largest part electrified. The electricity for this purpose is drawn from the water-power of the country; to be exact, it derives from the streams which begin in the Lebanon and Hermon mountains, as well as from the difference in level, more than a thousand feet, between the Mediterranean and the Dead Sea. These two bodies of water are connected by a canal, passing in part under tunnels; a power house on the shore of the Dead Sea transforms the force of the falling water into electricity. The chemical wealth of the Dead Sea is exploited, and has become the world's greatest production center for bromium and potassium salts. The bituminous limestone of the region yields "the best asphalt in the world." Sulphur and phosphates are obtainable in inexhaustible quantities; deep borings have uncovered petroleum sources.

The water is also used, of course, in enormous quantities for irrigation purposes. "The real creators of *Altneuland*," says David Litvak, "were the irrigation engineers. Drainage of swamps, irrigation of the desert regions, and above all the system of power houses — there was the answer."

Technology, and in particular electrical power (the significance of which was only beginning to be understood in Herzl's day) has given a new form to general labor. Agriculture, handicrafts, lighting, building, road-laying — everything carries the stamp of the new technology.

But it has done more than beautify the life of the individual. It has made possible, it has even compelled, a new social and economic order, a new form of human community.

The economic order in *Altneuland* is described by the word "mutualistic," whereby Herzl indicates a cooperative economic organization. Private property and currency are not abolished, but are made fruitful for the land as a whole by the cooperative system. This he describes as "the mediate form between individualism and collectivism." Here Herzl's ideas, which had been ripening since his Paris period, come very close to those of Franz Oppenheimer, with whom he had been in frequent contact, both by letter and in person, before he finished the novel, but after he had finished the definitive chapter.

In *Altneuland* nearly everything is organized on a cooperative basis. For the cooperative makes possible a just economic order without encroaching on the freedom of economic
man more than is essential for the common good. Social and
communal forms are cooperative, too; what has been created
is not just a State, but "the New Society"— the apotheosis
of the "Society of Jews" mentioned in the *Judenstaat*. Every
member of "the New Society" must devote two years of his
life to public service, generally from the age of eighteen to
that of twenty. As against this, there is no military service;
the youth is trained, as in Switzerland, by way of games and
sports, the idea of self-defense is propagated via relevant
societies. Women enjoy equal rights with men. Unmarried
girls are no longer exposed to ridicule as "old maids," for the
entire "Department of Social Service" is in their hands.
Care is provided for the sick, work for the healthy. Everyone
has the right to work — but also the duty to work. All
members of "the new society" carry accident, sickness, old
age and life insurance.

Education in the schools up to the Zion University is free.
Punishment of criminals has been transformed into re-
education. Prisoners are trained on a model farm and become
accustomed to healthy work; the system is highly successful,
and many prisoners do not want to return to the city.

Agriculture is practiced only on a large scale and through
the medium of producers' cooperatives, such as Franz
Oppenheimer had advocated; the architect Steinek (Marmorek) calls these new farms "open-air factories." All work
in the Jewish villages is done by the Jews themselves. The
land is public property and is leased only for periods of fifty
years (until the jubilee year).

Commerce and industry are directed by a Department of Industry, as is the entire economic system, according to definite plans and controls, with all freedom for the individual. Every effort is made, however, to avoid compulsion, but rather to guide human activity in the desired direction by the use of mass psychology.

In addition to the world-city of Haifa, mention is made of the modern spa of Tiberias, the winter resort of Jericho, and, above all, the new Jerusalem. The ancient city Zion has been left essentially unchanged; it has only been cleaned, and the streets and alleys have been paved with new stones. "There were no more private residences in the old city. The buildings were either for charity or religious devotion." But round about the old city "modern suburbs had arisen, broad, tree-shaded boulevards and parks, institutes of learning, markets, architectural showplaces and places of amusement . . . a world-city in the spirit of the twentieth century."

Culturally, too, the land ranks with the best in the world. Culture and philosophy have their independent institutes. There is a Jewish Academy of forty members, modelled after the *Académie française*, its insignia a yellow ribbon for the buttonhole. "That color shall remind us of the darkest days in our history, and bring humility in the days of our triumph."

Matters of faith have been definitively removed from the sphere of public influence. The Sabbath is, however, the general Jewish festival; the Temple is reared once more in Jerusalem, though not on its ancient site — for of course the Mosque of Omar remains where it was — and in a new form: a modern synagogue with choir and lute. The festivals, too, are observed by the Jews according to tradition.

Tolerance is the basic principle of the new society. "The stranger must feel at home among us," are the last words of the dying President, Eichenstamm. "Whatever we possess," says David Litvak, "we owe to those that labored before us. It is incumbent upon us to remember and meet this debt. There is only one way of meeting it: supreme tolerance."

There are no race antagonisms. The Arabs live in friendship side by side with the Jews. The incoming of the Jews has been nothing but a gain for them, first through the sale of superfluous lands and by well-paid work in the draining of swamps, a work for which they, adapted as they are to the climate, are better fitted than the Jews. But on top of that they have learned much from the Jews in the way of new economic organization; the filth of their villages has disappeared under the influence and through the example of adjacent Jewish settlements. The introduction of new methods of production and superior transportation has increased the orange export tenfold. "The Jews have enriched us," says David's friend, Reshid Bey. "Why should we have anything against them? They live with us like brothers, why should we not love them?"

Such is the picture of Altneuland itself. But for the Jews who have remained scattered through the world, we are told, the results have also been favorable. Jewish competition with non-Jews has declined, Jewish intellectuals have ceased to occupy the same field as non-Jewish intellectuals, having found a more attractive outlet in Palestine; the consequence is a complete elimination of anti-Semitism. It is only now, "when the harassed Jews have found peace in their own land" and, being in the majority, demonstrate their tolerance, that the emancipation becomes a reality everywhere.

And thus it was made clear that the Jewish problem could be solved if only there was the will to it. Indeed, the motto which Herzl chose for his novel was: "If you will it, it is no legend." And he closed with this warning: "But if you do not will it, then it remains a legend which I have recited. Dream and action are not as widely separated as many believe. All the acts of men were dreams at first and become dreams again."

Altneuland did not produce that effect which Herzl had promised himself from it. Very definitely it carried conviction to only a tiny number of Jews, or awakened in them the will to a new life. Even within the Zionist movement the book did more harm than good. Many of those who stood closest to Herzl were disappointed that the novel should have been so thoroughly interpenetrated with the spirit of western civilization. Nor did the opponents of the book, Zionist or non-Zionist, fail to take advantage of its weakest points, its inconsistencies and improbabilities. The sharpest and deadliest critic was Ahad Ha-am.

Ahad Ha-am had followed with close and critical attention every development in political Zionism. He had scored a great success at the Minsk Conference of the Russian Zionists, and his cult of spiritual Zionism had begun to exert an influence on the western wing of the movement; in particular it had found expression in the propaganda of the "young Zionists," like Weizmann, Feivel and Buber. Ahad Ha-am saw nothing of the positive side of Herzl's new work; he perceived neither the brilliant prophetic vision of the development of the country, nor the profound love for Palestine, nor the faith in the land and the people; he felt nothing of its creative joy or of the earnest ethical impulse which informed every page.

He saw only the weaknesses of the book; these he singled out with the keen eye of the born critic and exposed with cruel irony. First he remarked on the impossibly short stretch of time within which the return of the Jews to Palestine had been compressed. He chose, as the second point, the excessive emphasis on the idea of tolerance, not wrong in itself, but played up out of all proportion in a desire to please the non-Jews. It was an old reproach of his that Herzl, in all his work, kept one eye on the anti-Semites and did his best to win their sympathetic approval.

But the focal issue was, for Ahad Ha-am, the cultural question; and it was from this point of vantage that he declared all the labors of the "New Society" to be a sustained flight from the national self — all in order to avoid displeasing, at any cost, the non-Jews. Why, he could and did ask, was it so necessary to emphasize, with regard to all the new methods employed in Altneuland, that they had not been created by the Jews, but had been prepared by other peoples? And what did the author mean by having a "Jewish Academy" which devoted itself almost exclusively to general human questions while it ignored the Hebrew language and literature, quite unlike the pre-occupation of its model, the *Académie française*, with the French language and literature? "Presumably that would have been interpreted as 'national chauvinism.' Why, then, call it the 'Jewish Academy?' Perhaps because only Jews have that attitude toward their own language and literature," is the tart suggestion.

And in reality there is very little mention of Hebrew throughout the book. Herzl's indifference toward the renaissance of the Hebrew language, his failure to recognize its focal significance both historically and currently, was well known. But now that this significance was, so to speak,

made official and programmatic in his novel of the future,
the effect on the protagonists of the revival was extremely
painful.* Ahad Ha-am had some cutting observations to
offer on that passage in the book which deals with the
achievements of Steinek (Marmorek), the bacteriologist.
Steinek is shown working on the great anti-malaria campaign, which is to make possible the resettlement of Africa
and the return of the American negroes to their ancient
homeland, which will bring with it the solution of the negro
problem on the heels of the solution of the Jewish problem.
Ahad Ha-am follows up the picture. "We could very well,"
he suggests, "imagine a negro movement, with the Zionist
leader at its head, writing another *Altneuland* which embodies the ideals of the negroes after twenty years: and we
would like to ask wherein the negro Altneuland is to be distinguished from the Zionist Altneuland. I do not think I
exaggerate when I say that the author would have to make
very few changes in the book ... To copy others, without
showing a spark of original talent; to avoid 'national chauvinism' in such fashion as to leave no trace of the character
of one's own people, or of its literature and spiritual creations; to gather oneself together and retreat into a corner
merely to show others that we are tolerant, tolerant to the
point of wearisomeness — that can be done by the negroes
too. And yet, who knows, perhaps they too would be incapable of such a performance."

Comparing the book with the Hebrew novel *Journey to
Palestine in the Year 5800* (2040), by Levinsky, which had

---

*It should be noted that Herzl himself made repeated attempts to learn Hebrew,
and that, in particular, he had had his children taught the language. He was by
no means an opponent of the Hebrew renaissance; but he was not a protagonist
either.

appeared ten years earlier, Ahad Ha-am says of the latter that it "pulsates with a fresh national life based on all-human foundations. As against this," he says, "we find in *Altneuland* nothing but mechanical aping without a touch of national character; it is a book which breathes that atmosphere of 'slavery within freedom' which is characteristic of the western spirit. True, Levinsky's book is placed in the year 2040, this one in the year 1923; which means that a renaissance which is to be specifically Jewish cannot be carried out overnight, by means of a stock company and cooperatives. A historic ideal calls for historic development, and historic development takes time."

In this formulation of his views Ahad Ha-am may have been quite correct on many individual points; but it misses the essential foundation of the book. Herzl was not less eager than he in his hopes for a national life, a national art; but he believed that these would develop of themselves only on the basis of a free existence, and he saw it as the task of the Zionist movement to create that free existence. He held it to be true of the spiritual not less than of the economic field, that only the preliminary conditions had to be created: "Conditions, not things." The latter must be left to the free play of forces. Therefore, in describing the New Society, he had limited himself to the bare essentials. In the matter of "tolerance," too, his views were far deeper and more earnest than Ahad Ha-am suspected.

Herzl might not have reacted to a purely objective criticism of his book; but Ahad Ha-am's observations were something more; they were a sharp attack on his authority as the leader of the Zionist Organization. He could not put up with this kind of ironic and condescending criticism. But since he himself could not reply to an attack which he considered

personal, he sent a German translation of the article to
Nordau, with the request that the latter issue a defense of
Herzl against "this spiteful attack."

Nordau acceded to the request — perhaps with more
enthusiasm than was called for. He had, indeed, every right
to define as a Zionist one who occupies himself with the
creation of a Jewish homeland, but he certainly went too far
when he described Ahad Ha-am as a secular protest rabbi
and bitter anti-Zionist. He was right in pointing to the fact
that political Zionism had created a platform for Ahad
Ha-am's ideas; he was unjust in asserting that Ahad Ha-am's
sole merit was that he wrote a good Hebrew. Finally, it was
quite absurd to retort that Ahad Ha-am opposed Herzl's
ideas of tolerance because he himself wanted to institute the
Russian knout and the Inquisition.

We do not know whether Herzl saw this article before it
was published. When Buber justly observed that this sort
of retort was not in keeping with Herzl's character, Herzl
replied evasively, justifying Nordau's furious counter-attack
as a response not to Ahad Ha-am's literary criticism, but to
the assault on the movement. This reply, on top of the angry
emotions unleashed by the two articles, caused Weizmann,
Buber and Feivel to publish a protest in *Ha-Zeman*, the new
Hebrew periodical. A large number of signatures was attached to this protest. Thereupon articles began to appear
in various journals, but particularly in the Hebrew press;
some defended Nordau and Herzl, others defended Ahad
Ha-am. The rift between Herzl and the opposition became
wider, and Herzl expressed the opinion that the opposition,
which until then he had considered a healthy and helpful
one, was weakening the political force of Zionism by its
emphasis on the cultural program.

Altneuland was translated into many languages, and widely read; but it did not produce the effect Herzl had hoped for. The results were, indeed, very different. The furious discussion in the Zionist press accentuated the differences between the two tendencies in the movement; they strengthened the opposition to Herzl and prepared the way for the developments of the sixth Congress which cannot, in fact, be understood without reference to this accentuation of the controversy.

The immediate precipitating cause of these developments, however, was the turn which Herzl's political methods had taken since the summer of 1902.

CHAPTER XIII

EL ARISH, KISHINEFF, UGANDA

WHEN Herzl first conceived the idea of his *Judenstaat* he still believed that the locale of its realization was unimportant. He considered essential only the creation of a national home for the Jewish people, in which it could develop its forces once more and assume the control of its own destiny in freedom and honor. Contact with the *Hoveve Zion* leaders led to the recognition of the fact that actually there was only one country to be considered, namely, the one to which the Jews had a historic claim, their ancient homeland, Palestine. His journey to Palestine in 1898 transformed this recognition into an emotional relationship. Since that time he had been continuously occupied with Palestine, had given loving consideration to its development, had expressed in *Altneuland* the apotheosis of the people's longing, and had left no stone unturned in his efforts to open the gates of that country to a systematic, publicly recognized, legally secured settlement by the Jews.

He began, however, by underestimating considerably the political difficulties in the way of this program. It was only after continued and serious negotiation with the Sultan and his advisers that he understood what obstacles confronted him.

Until then he had refused to entertain any suggestions for colonization elsewhere than in Palestine. At the close of 1897, Davis Trietsch, who had long been a student of the problem of Jewish migration, had proposed to him a plan for the settlement of Cyprus. Trietsch had been propagating the idea since 1895. Cyprus, formerly Turkish, and since 1878 under British administration, lies close to Palestine; the assumption was that the British would not raise the same difficulties as the Turks. Herzl replied that he had given careful consideration to this "interesting proposal." But, he added, "I do not consider the time opportune to discuss it, as we have better prospects in view."

In the summer of 1898 he obtained his first direct glimpse of the tragic need of the Jewish masses, and the impression was profound: a series of pogroms took place at that time in Galicia. During those weeks, finding that he could make no progress in his political efforts, and feeling the accumulation of Jewish suffering into a volcanic mass, he gave serious thought to the idea of "finding a closer territorial objective for the movement, while retaining Zion as the ultimate aim." "The poor masses," he noted in his diary on July 1, 1898, "need immediate help, and Turkey is not yet in such desperate condition as to accede to our wishes . . . What we must do first, then, is set an immediately accessible goal, without yielding any of our historic rights. We can perhaps ask England for Cyprus; we may even consider South Africa or America, until the day of Turkey's dissolution comes."

The Palestinocentric spirit of the delegates to the Congresses, particularly among the East Europeans, and the political progress which marked his Palestine journey, pushed these thoughts into the background. They came to the front again after the collapse of the hopes he had reposed in Germany. On July 25, 1899, he wrote to Gustav G. Cohen: "Just a short note, in deepest confidence. I am thinking a great deal about Cyprus." And a few weeks later he exerted himself to influence the delegates to the third Congress at least to listen quietly to Trietsch's exposition of his Cyprus plan. It was all in vain; the *Hoveve Zion* would hear nothing of any plan relating to another land than Palestine, even if it lay as close to it as Cyprus.

This was enough to hold Herzl back from pressing the plan, which he considered, in and for itself, a reasonable one. He wrote in this sense to Trietsch, who at that time was conducting a lively but not always responsible propaganda for his plan among the Roumanian Jews: as the leader of a party Herzl had not the same freedom as a private person to launch upon what might prove to be a dangerous experiment. At the same time he noted in his diary: "This is how I see immediate developments: if, by the time of the Fourth Congress, I shall have made no progress with the Turkish government, I shall have my Cyprus plan ready to hand; I shall then visit England, speak with Salisbury, and have the Congress decide to go to Cyprus next. In any case I believe that after the next Congress we shall proceed in a practical way to the land, any land."

In the spring of 1900 the misery of the Jewish masses again rose up before him in the form of the Roumanian migration, which moved "like a bloody trail" across Europe. The cry for help became more and more urgent; his delegates were becoming more and more impatient. Thus the Cyprus plans swam up to the surface again, and in January 1901, they took on, for a brief moment, fantastic form: he dreamed of the settlement of Cyprus, from which the Jews would then take Palestine by force "as it was once taken from us." The next morning he abandoned this impossible vision; but he proposed to himself, in the event of an increasingly negative attitude on the part of Turkey, to submit his Cyprus project to the fifth Congress. He even began to think out the logical approach to the subject in his Congress speech. "I declared that it would be the fusion of the Palestine hope, deferred for the present, with immediate action, indispensable as it was for the present, for the sake of our neediest... I further explained to the Fifth Congress that Cyprus was only a station on the road to Palestine; that Turkey would then begin to take us seriously, and so on. I could already hear opposition and agreement in the Congress."

The reception by the Sultan and the consequent revival of his hopes with respect to Palestine put off the plan beyond the fifth Congress. But very shortly thereafter the prospect of the Wadi el Arish, in Egypt, came up in all seriousness for the first time as a center of settlement; Trietsch, the protagonist of the Cyprus plan had already spoken of this territory, both to Herzl privately and in public. It was the old frontier land of Palestine, the "brook of Egypt" mentioned in the Bible, situated in the Sinai Peninsula, so richly filled with Jewish history and legend. In Herzl's day the locality was called "Egyptian Palestine." On January 25, 1902, Herzl proposed to Franz Oppenheimer that he attempt in El Arish the creation of a model cooperative colony in the form he had long been advocating in *Die Welt*.

Some six months later Herzl held those conversations with Lord Rothschild and Lord James which have already been reported at some length. It was then that Herzl put on the *tapis* the idea of the colonization of the English administrated territories of Cyprus, El Arish and the Sinai Peninsula, feeling that, with Lord Rothschild's opposition to Palestine, he himself could not, at a time of such dire Jewish need, stand inflexibly by his principle. He hinted at this view, too, in his appearance before the Royal Commission. This was the first time that the acceptance of another locale than Palestine, with reservation of ultimate right to the latter, was mooted before representative English and Anglo-Jewish circles.

Actually Herzl was putting out feelers, with the intention of driving further in this direction if the indications were favorable. Primarily he made use of the opportunity afforded him by the British immigration problem for this purpose; without it, he might perhaps have waited longer. Then his last visit to Constantinople brought with it the resolve to proceed with the matter energetically. He could see now that there was no likelihood of reaching a satisfactory arrangement with Turkey within a reasonable period. It seemed further to him that the break-up of Turkey, which he had believed in 1897 to be very close at hand, had been put off indefinitely, to no small extent as a result of the financial arrangement with Rouvier, the Frenchman. Thus the strongest point in his argument, that the Jews would be able to rescue Turkey from her wretched financial situation, had fallen away. He tried to console himself with the thought that new financial difficulties would arise, that he would be called again, dismissed, called a third time, and so on until he obtained what he wanted. But such vague prospects could not satisfy a movement occupied with the settlement of large masses of human beings whose misery increased from day to day; nor could they still the impatience of a man afflicted with a serious sickness of the heart, a man who found his daily writing stint a revolting task, and whose soul longed for fulfilment in creative reality, in colonization, direction and planning. And then, again, there was the consideration that colonization of adjacent territory to Palestine's, the appearance of a new, serious but friendly neighbor, would lead to more rapid concession of rights within Palestine itself. It was not a renunciation of Palestine; it was, on the contrary, a strategic move toward it. Nor did he, while pursuing the strategic detour, cease to press the direct approach. In particular he occupied himself with the obstacles opposed by Russia, and made use of every occasion which presented itself for the improvement of his political position.

Meanwhile he went systematically about the business of preparing the ground for the new departure in Zionist policy. The detailed report in *Die Welt* on the status of the negotiations in Constantinople had a double purpose: to prepare public opinion for an abandonment of hope with regard to Turkey, and to create a favorable approach for a new strategy. It was with the same ends in view that Herzl delivered his detailed review of the unsuccessful negotiations before the *Jahreskonferenz* in October 1902. "We are convinced that we are on the right path. If obstacles are opposed to us here and there we shall do our best to find new paths, until the goal, which remains constant for us, has been reached."

He could make this statement, with its ring of confidence, because he had already registered definite progress in England. He had had the good fortune to acquire, in Leopold Greenberg, as excellent a diplomat and ambassador as he could have wished for; it was he who, at Herzl's request, succeeded in arranging a meeting between the Zionist leader and Colonial Minister Chamberlain.

On October 22, 1902, the conference, which was to have far-reaching results for the Zionist movement, took place.

Joseph Chamberlain, a rich manufacturer who had entered politics late in life, had become the head of the Colonial Office in 1895, and had retained this post when Salisbury's government was replaced by that of Arthur James Balfour. An early protagonist of the idea of Imperial preference and of a customs union between England and the colonies, Chamberlain had left the Liberal for the Conservative party. He was extraordinarily popular with the British people. On the other hand he had shown considerable understanding of the Jewish problem.   In his letter to the "Roumanian Bulletin," reprinted in *Die Welt* for July 24, 1902, he had indicated that he regarded the Jewish question as a national one. Thus Herzl, following up in his conversation with him the views he had already set forth in a written memorandum, encountered no difficulty in the setting forth of his concept of the essence and solution of the Jewish problem.

Chamberlain listened with immobile features, but with every evidence of deep interest, as Herzl held forth in his somewhat stumbling English, following, in his discourse, the line he had already laid down before the Royal Commission. Palestine was the ultimate goal, he said, and in this connection he was in constant negotiation with the Sultan. But the negotiations were dragging, as was only to be expected when one was dealing with Orientals. "Now I have time to negotiate, but my people has not. They are starving in the Pale. I must bring them immediate help." And then he submitted his plan for the colonization of Cyprus and the Sinai Peninsula, including El Arish: Jewish settlers under a Jewish administration.

Chamberlain replied that he could speak definitely only about Cyprus; the Sinai Peninsula lay within the competence of the Foreign Office. But conditions in Cyprus were not promising. The Greeks and Mohammedans would object to this new competitive element, and it would be his official duty to side with them, though he was very remote from the anti-Semitic movement and was completely opposed to it.

However, he took a more affirmative attitude on the El Arish proposal — though he had to ask Herzl to point to the territory in question on the map. Herzl told him that in his last negotiations with Turkey he had asked for the region round Haifa, and he believed that he would come to a more rapid and cheaper arrangement if he turned up in the Wadi el Arish, the "brook of Egypt." Chamberlain then observed that Herzl would encounter the same difficulties with the population of Egypt as with that of Cyprus. "No," said Herzl, "we will not go to Egypt. We have been there." Chamberlain laughed, and understood what Herzl was driving at: a gathering place for the Jewish people in the vicinity of Palestine. "In El Arish and Sinai there is empty land," said Herzl. "England can give us that. In return we promise an increase in her power and the gratitude of ten million Jews."

Chamberlain declared that the most important step now for Herzl was to speak with the Foreign Office; the upshot would depend essentially on the goodwill of Lord Cromer, the British Consul General in Egypt, and actually the vice-regent of that country. Chamberlain further declared himself ready to arrange a meeting between Herzl and Lord Lansdowne, the head of the Foreign Office. Herzl was to return the next day.

Chamberlain was as good as his word. When Herzl appeared at the office the next day, he was greeted in the friendliest fashion. Chamberlain had arranged the meeting with Lord Lansdowne. The appointment was for four-thirty that afternoon. "I have prepared the way for you. You will lay the whole matter before him. You will reassure Lord Lansdowne that you are not contemplating a Jameson raid from El Arish on Palestine." "I will reassure him, Mr. Chamberlain!"

From Chamberlain Herzl went to Lord Rothschild, where he was admitted at once to the dining room. At first there was nothing more than empty table talk. After the meal, in the library, Herzl told the story of his meeting with Chamberlain. Rothschild was dumbfounded. He declared he would visit Chamberlain the following week, and ask him about the status of the question. Fundamentally, Rothschild was more favorably inclined toward the colonization of Cyprus than of El Arish, but he raised no objections when Herzl gave him Chamberlain's reasons for preferring El Arish as a beginning. Rothschild seemed by now to be completely captivated by Herzl's personality. He had recently written to someone that the well-to-do Jews of Austria were at fault, in the matter of the Galician and Roumanian Jews, in not listening to Herzl, "who may be an enthusiast, but is a great man." Rothschild told this to Herzl. "What?" exclaimed the latter. "You embarrass me." "No," answered Rothschild, "it is really my opinion. You are a great man." Visitors were announced. "If we get the concession, said Herzl, "we shall have to found the Company with five million pounds. Without that it will be difficult, perhaps impossible." Rothschild neither agreed nor objected. They would talk about that later.

In the afternoon Herzl proceeded to his appointment in the Foreign Office. Lord Lansdowne accorded him a friendly reception; from Barrington, Lansdowne's secretary, Herzl

learned that Chamberlain had shown himself greatly concerned about arranging the meeting. Herzl was free to talk
now. Lansdowne listened with interest, raised very few
objections, and finally asked Herzl for a written exposé.
He, for his part, would like to assure himself of the goodwill
of Lord Cromer. Thereupon Herzl repeated the suggestion
he had already made to Chamberlain, to wit, that he would
like to send his confidential agent, Greenberg, to Cromer
without delay. Lord Lansdowne declared himself ready to
arrange the meeting. The interview ended as cordially as it
had opened.

The next morning, October 24, 1902, after leaving detailed
instructions with Greenberg, Herzl left for Vienna. On the
train he began his memorandum to Lord Lansdowne, but
following the advice of his English friends, he did not send it
off at once. He arrived in Vienna in time to begin the *Jahreskonferenz* which has already been mentioned. Of the resolutions passed during the sessions the most important was the
one sanctioning the Anglo-Palestine Company, which could
begin operations in the summer of 1903 with the opening of
the Bank in Jaffa under the direction of S. D. Levontin.

The journey to London, and the conference immediately
following it, placed a tremendous strain on Herzl's health.
During the conference itself he was troubled several times
by the condition of his heart. When the conference was over,
he was in a state of collapse, incapable of writing a single line.
On November 7 he reported himself sick to the office of the
Neue Freie Presse. On the same day he received a telegram
from Greenberg, who had left for Egypt on October 31 with
the recommendation of Lord Lansdowne. All was well, the
telegram stated. Herzl's entry in his diary for that day reads:
"Is this the eve of an *English* Charter, and of the founding

of the Jewish State? The exhaustion of my energies makes it plausible." Then he added immediately: "In his discussion of *Altneuland* Dr. Ganz remarks very finely: 'No Moses ever enters the Promised Land.' "

This was Herzl's mood when he went for a rest cure to Edlach, a little village at the foot of the Rax Alps, which two years later was to be the scene of his last earthly sojourn.

By November 12, refreshed and ready to resume his labors, he received a visit from Greenberg, who came to report on his Egyptian journey and to take counsel with him on the next steps. Greenberg had achieved as much as could be achieved at this stage. Lord Cromer had been friendly, had given him all the information he needed, and had provided him with a letter of introduction to the Egyptian Prime Minister, Boutros Ghali Pasha. Greenberg had laid Herzl's plan before the latter, too, without being turned down. The strongest counter-argument raised by both Cromer and Boutros had been the pitiful failure of an attempted Jewish colony undertaken in 1891–2 in the region of ancient Midian. The director had been Paul Friedmann, a converted Jew; the human material had been utterly unsuitable, the means and methods inadequate. There had been political complications and border disputes with Turkey. At that time Turkey had laid claim to the whole Sinai Peninsula, a claim which Lord Cromer had rejected; but the frontier problem had not been settled. Greenberg could counter, of course, by pointing to the entirely different character of Herzl's enterprise, which was not to be compared with the ill-planned, ill-executed though well-meant fancy of an ambitious, assimilated Jew. Subsequent negotiations proved, however, that it was not so easy to dispose of the effects of that early failure.

Still, the fact that the colonization project was receiving serious attention represented a great success for Greenberg, as Herzl warmly recognized. It was with Greenberg's help, too, that he put his memorandum to Lansdowne in final form.

After expressing his gratitude for Lansdowne's and Cromer's friendliness, Herzl made a declaration of the Zionist program, and proceeded to a discussion of the projected settlement in the Sinai Peninsula. He observed that while the need of the Jews in Galicia and Roumania was steadily increasing, public opinion in England and America, the two countries which still offered possibilities of refuge, had become perceptibly anti-immigrationist; in England this negative attitude had found expression in the Royal Commission. This was the situation which moved Herzl to the proposal he was now submitting. "In the southeast of the Mediterranean a country, at present worthless and almost uninhabited, could be made by the influence of England a place of refuge, a home for oppressed Jews, if England will favor the establishment of a Jewish colony such as I have referred to.

"My proposition will tend to solve the Jewish question of Eastern Europe in a manner that, while reflecting fresh honor upon England, may also benefit her materially. We have chosen the Sinai Peninsula largely because of its historical associations which would form an attraction to the best class of colonizing Jews."

The practical steps, the document went on to explain, would consist first of a land concession granted by the Egyptian government — the details to be worked out later — and a colonization agency, the Jewish Eastern Company, with a capital of five million pounds.

"This company would undertake colonization on a regular system. Prior to starting colonization work, a staff of technical and agronomic specialists will be dispatched, the building of streets, roads, harbors, etc., prepared, the land taken up and parcelled out for distribution.

"The immigration would begin slowly and would be carefully organized. We have many thousands of Zionist associations spread throughout the world. These are united in each country into local federations. All the federations are now centralized. Through these we can turn every branch society into an emigration bureau with absolute reliance and unity of system. The immigrants will be selected for us by the local bodies and each body will answer for the suitability of the people selected. The purpose of this is to ensure a secure ground stock of pioneers. The colonizing would be done on the most modern principles which science and experience can afford. The capital of the Company and the labor of the carefully chosen pioneers would build up only the beginnings of the colony."

It is in this formulation that Herzl's plans for the transfer and colonization of the Jews, which he had incorporated in *Der Judenstaat* and in *Altneuland*, were first submitted in a serious political document. It is here, too, that the demand for Jewish statehood is first submitted to a government as a practical measure.

"But were this all," the document continues, "this settlement would partake of the artificiality and insignificance of other, earlier experiments in Jewish colonization. Its greatness and future promise lie in the guaranteeing of colonial rights. Here lies the powerful attraction for the Jewish people. It is not merely the Jews of Eastern Europe in search of work that would migrate thither. People with capital at their disposal would also establish enterprises, in a land where they could be certain to enjoy the fruits of their labor. From Russia and the east of Europe, indeed, some of the richest Jews would join the migration — I speak here from precise and personal knowledge."

The most important task now was to obtain the consent of the British government to the sending out of a commission, and in turn to have this consent transmitted to the Egyptian government and approved by it. No effort would be spared, Herzl stated, to make the project one worthy of British support.

While the memorandum was being studied in London and Cairo, and while Chamberlain, early in his African tour, was consulting Lord Cromer, Herzl wrote to the Sultan in order to keep the record straight and to anticipate political opposition. He also sent the Sultan a copy of *Altneuland*, a vision of the happy results which would flow from the successful Jewish colonization of Palestine.

A month later Herzl received an answer from London, dated December 18, 1902. It was written, on behalf of Lord Lansdowne, by Sir T. H. Sanderson, Permanent Undersecretary. Lord Lansdowne had heard from Lord Cromer, who favored the sending of a small commission to the Sinai Peninsula to report on conditions and prospects. From information he had received, Lord Cromer feared "that no sanguine hopes of success ought to be entertained." However, should the report of the commission turn out favorable, the Egyptian government would certainly offer liberal terms for Jewish colonization, such as tax exemption over a period of years for cultivated land. On the other hand, however, the Zionist leader should understand that he would be expected to meet the cost of a defense corps, and to guarantee the administration. Further, inasmuch as the frontier dispute between Egypt and Turkey had not been settled, the colony would have to lie westward of the furthest points claimed by the Turkish government.

In Lord Cromer's opinion the most important question at the opening stage of the negotiations was that of the rights which Herzl expected for the projected settlement. "In your letter of the 12th ult. you state that 'its greatness and future promise lie in the guaranteeing of Colonial rights'. It does not appear from your letter what is implied by these words or what would be the nature of the rights which it is proposed to ask for in behalf of the Colonists." Lord Lansdowne therefore asked for more exact information.

Finally Lord Lansdowne touched on the question of the new citizenship of the settlers, and it was here that Herzl encountered an unexpected turn. At first he had believed that he would have only Englishmen to deal with, since England had become more and more the master of Egypt. One of the results of Greenberg's journey had been to make it clear that the Egyptian government also played a role. On top of this it was also revealed that there was a Turkish suzerainty of Egypt with certain legal implications. Lord Cromer confirmed that the Egyptian government would make it an essential condition that the incoming settlers should become Turkish subjects, bound by Egyptian law; otherwise complications would arise in connection with the "Capitulations." However, as long as the British occupation continued the settlers would always be certain of fair and unbiased treatment.

Herzl was, on the whole, thoroughly satisfied by this letter, and with reason. He had every right to describe it as "a historic document." In it the British government had recognized him, and the movement represented by him, as a negotiating party, and had declared its readiness to be of assistance if the natural resources and condition of the territory passed muster. That this would be the case was something that Herzl did not doubt at that time. He already saw the "Egyptian Province of Judaea," under a Jewish governor, with its own defense corps under Anglo-Egyptian officers; already his imagination was busily at work with plans for the upbuilding of the country; he would ask the Sultan, in exchange for the Turkish citizenship of the settlers, for a slice of Palestine — under English guarantees.

He sent off a brief acknowledgement of Lansdowne's letter, and on New Year's Day, 1903, set out for Paris, where he took counsel with Nordau, Greenberg and Alexander Marmorek on the reply to Lansdowne and on subsequent action. Nordau outlined the reply, Greenberg translated it. Herzl opened by stating that after consultation with his colleagues he accepted the proposal of a Commission of Experts. In order to head off the consequences of a not very favorable report, he went on to point out that the Jewish tragedy was in itself a force which could make a success of a colonization enterprise which might normally be considered discouraging. Having none of the alternatives which were open to other peoples, the Jews would readily accept land which others would consider unsuitable — if only "the administration, even while completely subject in every way to existing rule, shall yet be of such a Jewish 'atmosphere' as to secure for them as Jews liberty, safety and justice. Your Lordship will readily appreciate that invaluable sentiment of national consciousness which, despite all, has saved our people from the lowest forms of degradation in the past, and is certain to raise them in the future from the undesirable state in which we find them today." The means and men would be forthcoming if the Jewish immigrants knew that there would be assured them a free, honorable life as citizens of a permanent and definitive homeland. What civic liberty meant, it was not necessary to explain to Englishmen, whose ideal in that field had been held up for so long to all other peoples. It would not be difficult to reach an agreement with regard to the conditions to be incorporated in the Charter. As to the other points, such as citizenship, frontiers, etc., he declared himself in agreement with the wishes of Lord Cromer and of the Egyptian government respectively.

From Paris Herzl went to London, where he began the preparations for the expedition. This visit was on the whole successful, though he failed to speak in person with Lord Lansdowne. He was received instead by the Permanent Undersecretary of the Foreign Office, Sir Thomas Sanderson, with whom he had been in correspondence, "a lean, angular, clever, suspicious old man." When Herzl spoke to him of colonial rights for the settlement, he became frightened; there could be no question of an international guarantee, at most it would be a Charter granted by the Egyptian government. Herzl would have to settle the details with Cromer. "The English government will go as far as Cromer, no farther."

Lord Rothschild seemed to be completely won over by now. When Herzl asked for a meeting, the old banker, who two years before had refused to meet the Zionist leader, now visited him in his hotel. Herzl showed him his correspondence with the British government, then asked him to get three million pounds from the *ICA* for the Jewish Eastern Company which was to be founded. The other two million would be obtained by public subscription. The "good old man," for whom Herzl had developed a great affection, promised his assistance, telegraphed to Claude Montefiore, who declined "because of sickness," and arranged a meeting in his house between Herzl and Herbert Lousada, an influential member of the board of governors of the *ICA*. The result of the interview, at which Rothschild supported Herzl warmly, was a statement by Lousada that the enterprise would have to be examined when the concession and the report were completed.

The essential task in London had to do with the getting together of the Commission, the discussion of its tasks and of its route, the technical equipment and so on. Herzl was concerned with every detail; he made the contract with Cook's, with the insurance companies, with the individual members of the Commission;* he became deeply absorbed in maps of the locality; he worked with members of the Commission, and with friends who were in London, on the question of irrigation, which he had been studying for weeks, and on which he prepared plans and drawings. He had suggestions in every field of the inquiry, to serve as guides for the members of the Commission. A condition of participation in the expedition was a promise to Herzl not to publish or to recount anything without his permission.

While this was going on, Greenberg left for Cairo to carry on the political negotiations until the Charter was granted.

---

* The director of the Commission was the South African Zionist and engineer, Kessler; The Egyptian Government was represented by the chief inspector of the Egyptian Survey Department, Humphreys; Colonel Goldsmid was to report on the land, and Dr. Soskin, who was acquainted with Palestine agriculture, was to study agricultural possibilities; architect Oscar Marmorek was to investigate building and housing problems and to act as general secretary; Dr. Hillel Joffe, of the Jaffa hospital, was entrusted with the problems of climate and hygiene.

The basis for his negotiations was to be the outline of a Charter worked out by Herzl and the members of the Vienna Actions Committee. The expedition passed through Vienna on January 28, and took along this outline, to be delivered to Greenberg in Cairo. On February 3, Herzl sent Greenberg a letter of authorization, empowering him to act in his name and that of the Actions Committee. This letter never reached Greenberg, and was only returned to Herzl, marked "Undelivered," five months later. This unfortunate circumstance contributed considerably to the tension which developed between Greenberg and Herzl in the ensuing months. There were, however, other factors.

Greenberg's first telegrams were encouraging. Then, on February 16, he reported that according to information he had received from Lord Cromer, the Turkish commissioner in Cairo was opposing him vigorously. On that same day Herzl, after a delay forced on him by his professional duties and other preoccupations, had once more applied to the Sultan, the Grand Vizier, Ibrahim, Izzet and Tahsin Bey, for a Charter of Colonization to cover the *sandjak* of Akko (Galilee), and had included the outline of such a Charter in French and in Turkish. The Turkish translator, a poet and a member of the Young Turk Party, had offered Herzl to arrange for the bribing of the Turkish minister.

To Greenberg's telegram Herzl replied — in code, of course, as was their practice with all diplomatic telegrams, and even letters — that he was to get round Turkish opposition by bribery. A day later Greenberg cabled back that a Charter could not be obtained from the Khedive; he had submitted "an alternative," was acting in accordance with instructions from Cromer, awaited the consent of the Khedive, and hoped to be able to leave on the following Monday.

Herzl had no idea what Greenberg meant by his "alternative," and cabled an inquiry. He understood just as little why Greenberg wanted to return after he had again been told by cable on February 11, that he was to stay until he had obtained the signature of the Egyptian government to the Charter. Herzl's suspicions were thoroughly awakened when Greenberg cabled again that he would not be able to touch at Vienna on his return because of lack of time, although Herzl, consulting the schedules, established that no loss of time would be involved by this route. He was getting the impression that Greenberg wanted to push him out, and to emerge as the single-handed winner of the concession. Nor was this suspicion lessened by the detailed report which Greenberg sent him from London, or by the personal dispute which ensued when they met again; but by this time it was already March, for Herzl, wounded by what he thought had happened, had refused to receive Greenberg till then.

A careful examination of Greenberg's letters to Herzl — Herzl's replies have for the most part been lost — and of Herzl's observations in his diary, side by side with later developments, shows that objectively speaking Greenberg was in the right. He had left for Cairo without having received instructions from Herzl regarding the details of the demands to be included in the Charter. The outline provided by Herzl did not correspond to the possibilities as he discovered them in Cairo, and subsequent instructions never reached him. Boutros Ghali, the Egyptian Prime Minister, asserted that the *firman* of the Sultan, on which the authority of the Khedive rested, did not extend to the granting of a Charter. Under these circumstances Greenberg showed himself a skilful negotiator when he asked for right of settlement on part of the territory, with municipal rights for the settlers.

Boutros agreed, and Greenberg even obtained this agreement in a letter from the Prime Minister.

If Greenberg was in the right to the extent that he had obtained the maximum possible under the circumstances, Herzl was justified in asserting that the Prime Minister's statement hardly represented any gain. On the contrary, it contained many restrictions and, against these, only hypothetical promises. Herzl could further insist that precisely because of this, it was important for Greenberg to have waited for the return of the Commission; apart from which a longer stay would have permitted him to cultivate the friendship of the men in power.

Against this Greenberg could retort that Herzl had issued his instructions without knowledge of the circumstances, and that he, Greenberg, had followed Cromer's suggestion in hastening to London, where he might obtain English intervention against Turkish opposition before the cabinet in Cairo took up the matter. This would serve a double purpose; the British government would feel itself more strongly bound to the Zionist policy, perhaps as a matter of honor, and if the project fell through, might feel itself obligated to help the Zionists in some other way. In any case, the statement of the Prime Minister was only a beginning; political negotiations were conducted in the Orient like purchases in a bazaar. Above all, the offer was not to be thrown overboard. Cromer had repeatedly pointed out that haste could only lead to failure; he considered it unwise for the work to be pushed in Cairo; until the Commission had rendered its report, efforts should be concentrated on London.

All these arguments, cogent as they were, could not overcome Herzl's feeling of mistrust. The truth was, that this sprang from various sources. To begin with, Herzl felt that he had received a personal setback. It went against his pride to have to sit in Vienna, as literary editor, while a luckier man than he achieved a political triumph. He felt himself humiliated, too, in a general way, when his employer, Benedikt, called him "a man all but lost," because he had not read a speech by the Prussian Minister of the Interior in the evening edition of his own paper. And then, when Greenberg stated that he could not pass by Vienna without serious loss of time — which actually turned out to be the case — he felt himself slighted as leader, the more so as Nordau and Marmorek in Paris, Zangwill and Cowen in London, sided with Greenberg. He was accustomed to command, he could put up with discussion and persuasion from his faithful followers, but not with sharp contradiction and opposition. He wrote to Wolffsohn, in February 1902, that the latter was for him "the prototype of the faithful and blindly obedient follower," and had won his confidence because he had declared that he would continue to follow Herzl even when he believed him to be in the wrong. "I must, indeed, be the leader in reality, and not merely at public demonstrations for which I care nothing, not being either a fool or a clown." And to his independent friend Cowen, whose free-spirited outlook he prized highly, and to whose counterpart in *Altneuland* he had entrusted the most important task, he now wrote (March 4, 1903): "It is a heavy time, full of worry and labor. You, my friends, can help me only by following me. I do not want the honors of a leader; I want only the obeying of my wishes or, let us say, the fulfilling of my requests. Don't call me 'Chief' and don't act against me. Call me 'donkey,' 'jackass' or anything else you like—but obey and follow me."

Something else must be added openly if this conflict is to be made intelligible. Greenberg had let himself be paid, and very well paid, for his journey. If Herzl, who had sunk all his fortune in the movement, had from the beginning felt this to be somewhat objectionable, he now began to feel, for a variety of reasons, that Greenberg was using the situation for the purpose of straightening out his own finances. At first Herzl had always followed Greenberg's advice. Now he suspected, behind anything Greenberg proposed, all sorts of obscure personal motives, and was therefore inclined to do the exact opposite. The heart to heart talk for which Greenberg came to Vienna on March 16 was therefore essentially fruitless; Herzl's distrust was not overcome — any more than that of the overzealous and petty Viennese membership of the Actions Committee — and against Greenberg's warnings and entreaties he resolved to proceed to Egypt himself, without delay, in order to bring the negotiations to a conclusion.

Impatience and the feeling of responsibility drove him to this decision; he was concerned about the work, he was afraid it might remain undone. In all his actions, and sometimes in his spoken words, he revealed that he knew how it stood with him: the cold hand of death was already on his shoulder. He wrote to Lord Rothschild on February 10: "Moreover, our life-span is a short one, and we must hasten, if we desire to do something good, as long as we tread the earth."

Herzl's journey to Egypt, on which he set out two days after Greenberg's visit to Vienna, in no wise improved the situation. From March 24 on he dealt with Lord Cromer, who was very cool toward him, with Boutros Ghali, the Egyptian Prime Minister, with the legal adviser of the Egyptian government, McIlwraithe, and with others. On the 26th and 27th he received the general report of the Commission, just then returned, and the reports of its individual members. The main report summed up the results of the investigation in the observation that "under existing conditions the country is quite unsuitable for settlers from European countries;* but ... that were a sufficient water supply forthcoming, the conditions of soil, hygiene and climate are such that part of what is now desert would be capable of supporting a considerable population. *In short, the whole question is one of water supply.*" The creation of a water supply would be costly, and would differ from zone to zone. The relatively simplest task would be the irrigation of the area round the Wadi el Arish, where it would be a question of erecting dams to prevent the overflow of water to the sea, and then of distributing the supply thus obtained. The most difficult area would be the plain of Pelusium (Tineh), the coastal stretch between Port Said and the Sirbonian Sea, the "Sin" district of the Bible, which would have to be irrigated from the Nile.

On March 27 Herzl sent the report with a covering letter to Lord Cromer, who received Herzl and Goldsmith the next day for a short conversation, and advised them to apply for the concession now. He recommended, as their legal representative for this purpose, the Belgian lawyer Carton de Wiart. On the day following Herzl worked out, with Wiart, the main lines of the concession. In accordance with Lord Cromer's suggestion he stayed mainly within the limits of Boutros's statement, from which he quoted the paragraphs dealing with citizenship and administration. But he did attempt to go beyond the Boutros letter in asking for full rights to the territory which was to be leased for 99 years — the Company was to be permitted to act as if the land were

---

*At first Herzl wanted to have this negative opening section of the report suppressed, but could not carry his point.

its property. Developed land was to be tax-exempt for a number of years; the Company was to have the right to construct harbors and all kinds of roads. The question of irrigation was held over until the return of Lord Cromer's irrigation expert, Garstyne.

The representatives of the Egyptian government with whom Herzl was negotiating did not receive the outline of the concession at all favorably: they saw in it the Charter, in disguise. The negotiations were, it seemed, going to continue for some time, and Cromer had shown, by his attitude toward Colonel Goldsmith and Greenberg, that he preferred to deal with Englishmen; Herzl therefore withdrew from Cairo on April 4, leaving behind him Colonel Goldsmith as his representative with full power of action: a piece of self-conquest!

He went by way of Paris, where he conferred with Lord Rothschild, Zadoc Kahn and other members of the directorate of the *ICA* on the method of its participation, to London, in order to push his project with the British government. On April 23 he was received in very friendly fashion by Chamberlain, who had only just returned from his African journey. Chamberlain listened while Herzl gave him an account of the situation. Then he spoke of the Commission report, which Herzl had sent him the day before.

"Not a favorable report," he said. "Yes," said Herzl. "It is a poor country, but we will make something of it."

"On my travels," said Chamberlain, "I saw a country for you: Uganda. On the coast it is hot, but in the interior the climate is excellent for Europeans. You can plant cotton and sugar. I thought to myself: that's just the country for Dr. Herzl. But *he* must have Palestine and will move only into its vicinity."

"Yes, I must," replied Herzl. "The base must be in or near Palestine. Later we can also settle Uganda. For we have enormous masses ready to migrate. But we have to build on a national foundation, that is why we must have the political attraction of El Arish." He pressed on with his negotiations. "Man's life is short," he said.

Chamberlain promised him to ask Lansdowne to use his influence with Cromer to hasten the negotiations.

Lansdowne received Herzl that same afternoon, and listened, as Chamberlain had done, to a report on the situation. Later in the day Lord Rothschild told him that he had written Zadoc Kahn in support of the Sinai plan, that Alphonse Rothschild was opposed to it but that Edmond Rothschild was delighted by it. He had also written to Jacob Schiff, in New York.

On his return journey Herzl stopped again in Paris, and consulted with five members of the directorate of the *ICA*. They did not take a definite stand and their interest was confined to the Pelusium project, but they left with Herzl the impression that they would not go as far as he had asked, namely, three million pounds; they would come forward with one million. But before the next meeting of the *ICA* directorate, which was due in June, the negotiations in Egypt had taken a turn for the worse.

On May 1, Herzl, again in Vienna, received a telegram from Goldsmid advising him that the situation had not yet been clarified. The irrigation experts were investigating the terrain. On May 5, Herzl cabled back: "Go ahead all you can. You can rely upon Chamberlain and Lansdowne. Please hurry. I have British government." From May 6 on cable after cable arrived from Goldsmid, each worse than the last. Then on May 11, Goldsmid cabled that Lord Cromer had informed him that the Egyptian government was rejecting the plan. On May 12 he cabled again that the negotiations were coming to an unsuccessful conclusion. Then, on May 13, arrived his detailed letter, in which he explained what had happened. The irrigation expert of the Anglo-Egyptian administration, Sir William Garstyne, had, on the basis of careful computation and long experience, come to the conclusion that the Pelusium area would need five times as much water as had been set by the Commission's expert, Stephens. The Egyptian government had decided that it could not permit the diversion of such a quantity of water from the Nile; furthermore, the laying of the pipes would interfere with traffic on the Suez canal for several weeks, and the prospects of success for the entire project seemed to be slender. Garstyne had therefore pronounced against the plan, and the Egyptian government had confirmed his rejection.

For the third time Herzl was confronted by failure: the Kaiser, Turkey, Egypt! On May 11 he wrote in his diary: "It's simply done for." And five days later he added: "And I thought the Sinai project so certain that I would not buy any more space in the Döblinger cemetery, where my father is provisionally laid to rest. Now I consider the plan so definite a failure that I have been at the district court and have acquired vault 28."

When his father's body was being exhumed and transferred to its new resting place, Herzl attended, in the company of A. H. Reich, the secretary of the Zionist office. Toward the end of the ceremony Herzl pointed to the family vault and said to Reich: "Soon, soon I too shall be lying down there."

During the days of the collapse of the Sinai project, the western world was learning of the incidents which had taken place in Russia throughout the Easter week. In Kishineff, under the eyes of the city administration, a mob which had been systematically incited to the deed carried on, for several days, a bloody pogrom, the first of a series which was to sweep across the country. The reports which reached the western world, the stories of barbarity, rape, and bloodlust, filled it with horror. When the hurricane had subsided, the tale of savagery in Kishineff could be summed up in cold figures: forty-five dead, six hundred seriously wounded, about five hundred lightly wounded, fifteen hundred houses plundered and destroyed.

On Herzl this catastrophe, which only confirmed what he had been saying for years, had a shattering effect. Again ten thousand, a hundred thousand, Jews would be set in motion. Whither?

But what affected him more than the incident was its consequences and implications. "Think of it," he wrote to an American statesman. "Seven million outlawed human beings who have again begun to tremble! After what has happened we have no right to reproach them with their fear. They are not allowed to arm, they are not defended, they feel themselves surrendered up — and to what a rabble!"

Herzl felt resting upon himself the urgent responsibility of finding swift help. "Let us save those who can still be saved," he pleaded a few months later with the sixth Congress. "It is high time."

His search moved in two directions. He wanted to enter into negotiations with the Russian government, which, it seemed to him, was necessarily interested in the question of Jewish emigration, and to obtain its support for his proposals in Constantinople. At the same time he intensified his efforts to find a territory as an immediate place of refuge for the Jews who were being thrust out of their present homes.

Together with Greenberg, who, restored to confidence, was again acting as his empowered representative in London, he decided not to give up wholly, as yet, the Sinai project, but to continue the negotiations at least for the El Arish valley (which did not need any of the waters of the Nile); he would also continue to ask for Cyprus. In any case, he would try to keep the British government linked with the Zionist movement. While he was having a counter-report on the irrigation question prepared, he instructed Greenberg to see Chamberlain and transmit a written message: in view of the situation in Russia, which was about to set off a new wave of immigration, he asked Chamberlain to take up anew the question of a Charter for Cyprus. The colonization would begin there, and later, when the resistance of the Egyptian government had been overcome, it would be continued in the Sinai Peninsula.

On May 20, 1903, Greenberg held a one hour consultation with Chamberlain, in which he agitated the question of Cyprus, though he did not work out the written message asked for by Herzl. Chamberlain answered that in principle he was prepared to help. Kishineff had shown him how right Herzl had been in his demand for a regulated migration of the Jews out of eastern Europe. The only question was: whither? Greenberg answered that the goal was Palestine. But swifter help was necessary. He pointed to El Arish and Cyprus. Chamberlain remarked that any further intervention on his part with Lord Cromer, with whom he had spoken in Egypt, could only be harmful. He had little faith, too, in the effectiveness of an international congress to be called for the purpose of solving the Jewish problem via Palestine, as Greenberg proposed. Cyprus was out of the question, as he could testify from a knowledge of the situation. But as against this there was, as he had told Herzl, the possibility of a territory in East Africa, with a good climate and other favorable conditions for the creation of a large colony with room for at least a million souls. He had not wanted to urge it upon Herzl because he had sympathized with his longing for Palestine and had thoroughly understood the significance of the El Arish plan in that connection. "But if nothing comes of it, I hope that Dr. Herzl will take my suggestion seriously." Self-administration would be granted, and the governor could definitely be a Jew, said Chamberlain in reply to Greenberg's question. In any case, Herzl should think the matter over. The territory was, at the moment, under the competence of the Foreign Office, but it could be transferred to his, the Colonial.

On May 20, Greenberg sent a detailed report of the interview to Herzl. As a convinced supporter of Palestine, Greenberg himself would not take a definite stand toward the proposal until he had heard from Herzl. "But it seems to me," he wrote, "no small gain from the political point of view to be able to say that the British government has offered us a refuge territory, and I believe it could be used as a drill ground for our national forces."

Herzl was won over. Telegraphically and by mail he advised Greenberg of his agreement with the latter's point of view. Greenberg was to ask more definitely where the territory lay. It would, of course, have to be fruitful land. "We will see what they offer us. Even if, under the pressure of immediate need, we accept such a proposition, we still do not give up Sinai." When, in accordance with Herzl's

ZIONISTEN-CONGRESS.

Vorläufige Anzeige.

Am 25., 26. und 27. August 1897 findet in München ein Weltcongress der Zionisten statt. Zweck dieses Congresses ist, eine Annäherung und Verständigung zwischen allen Zionisten herbeizuführen und dem gemeinsamen Bestreben einen einheitlichen Zug zu verleihen.

Der Congress wird die Wünsche unserer an verschiedenen Orten bedrängten Brüder entgegennehmen und die Mittel zur Abhilfe berathen.

Wer am Congress theilzunehmen gedenkt, hat sich bis spätestens 15. August anzumelden. Die Anmeldestellen in den einzelnen Ländern (Landescomités) werden demnächst bekanntgegeben. Vorläufig können Anmeldungen an das Centralbureau des Congresses (Verein „Zion", Wien II. Rembrandtstrasse 11) gerichtet werden. Die Angemeldeten werden die Eintrittskarten rechtzeitig zugestellt erhalten. Für Unterkunft der Congresstheilnehmer in München, wird auf Wunsch Vorsorge getroffen werden.

Die officielle Einladung zum Congresse wird, von sämmtlichen Einberufern unterfertigt, an Vereine und Körperschaften verschickt werden, sobald die Tagesordnung endgiltig feststeht.

Den Congress wird der Alterspräsident eröffnen. Hierauf erfolgt die Constituirung. Die Verhandlungen sollen nach den Grundsätzen einer vernünftigen und würdigen Redefreiheit geleitet werden.

Für jeden Punkt der Tagesordnung wird ein Referent aufgestellt, an den schon jetzt direct oder durch Vermittlung des Vereins „Zion" in Wien, Mittheilungen gerichtet werden können.

Die bisher bestimmten Referate sind:

a) die Lage der Juden in den einzelnen Ländern (ein Specialreferent für jedes Land), ökonomische, sociale und politische Zustände. Referent Herr Dr. Max Nordau, in Paris, (34 Avenue de Villiers)

b) die Colonisation, ihre bisherigen Ergebnisse und ferneren Aussichten. Agrarische, industrielle, commercielle, technische Fragen. Referent Herr Willy Bambus, in Berlin, (W. Bülowstrasse 89)

c) die Aufgaben der jüdischen Wohlthätigkeit in Palästina. Referent Hr. Dr. Hirsch Hildesheimer in Berlin,

d) Finanzfragen, Referent Herr Dr. Max Bodenheimer in Köln a. Rh. (Hohenzollernring 18)

e) die Judenfrage und der nächste diplomatische Congress der Grossmächte. Referent Dr. Theodor Herzl in Wien (IX. Berggasse 6)

f) eine Beschickung der Pariser Weltausstellung 1900 mit jüdischen Colonialprodukten.

Die weiteren Punkte der Tagesordnung sind später zu publiciren.

Die officiellen Delegirten der eingeladenen Vereine und Körperschaften werden zur Congresszeit in München eine besondere Berathung abhalten und deren Ergebniss dem Congresse mittheilen.

Viele praktische Fragen, welche den Congress beschäftigen werden, enthalten ein Element von Actualität und können desshalb nicht Monate vorher formulirt werden.

Findet es der Congress für nöthig, so wird er ein Executivcomité zur Führung der jüdischen Angelegenheiten bis zu seinem nächsten Zusammentritt einsetzen.

So erhalten die gemeinsamen Bedürfnisse ein Organ. Es wird ein Zufluchtsort für die Wünsche und Beschwerden unserer Brüder geschaffen. Die Judensache muss dem Belieben vereinzelter Personen — wie gutwillig diese auch seien — entrückt sein. Es muss ein Forum entstehen, vor dem Jeder für das was er in der Judensache thut und lässt zur Rechenschaft gezogen werden kann. Dem wird sich kein redlicher Mann widersetzen.

Wir sind der Theilnahme aller Menschen gewiss, die unseren Gedanken richtig verstanden haben. Es handelt sich darum, eine dauernde, gesicherte Heimat für diejenigen Juden zu schaffen, welche sich an ihren jetzigen Wohnorten nicht assimiliren können oder wollen.

Der Congress zu München wird zeigen, was der Zionismus ist und will. Dass er etwas ist und dass er etwas will.

Dr. Theodor Herzl
Wien, IX. Berggasse 6
Im Namen der vorbereitenden Commission.

1. Preliminary notice of the meeting of the First Zionist Congress, 1897
(see p. 218)

Verte!   6 IV 97

Sehr geehrter Herr Professor!

Herzlichen Dank für Ihren Brief vom
26 III.

Ein grosses Gewicht lege ich auf die
Betheiligung der russischen Zionisten.
Darum haben wir den Congress nach
München einberufen, weil wir glaubten,
die Russen würden nicht gern nach
Zürich kommen.

Es ist selbstverständlich, dass Ihre Wirk-
samkeit sich nicht auf das bulgarische
Landescomité zu beschränken braucht.
Agitiren Sie überall wo Sie können!
für: Beschickung des Congresses mit mög-
lichst viel Delegirten, Veranstaltung
von Kundgebungen u. Massenpetitionen
mit Unterschriften an den Congress.

Der Congress in München ist mehr
als das umstehende vorläufige Pro-
gramm sagen kann u. will.

Es ist die erste jüdische National-
versammlung!

Ich bitte um Berichte über den
Fortgang Ihrer Arbeiten.

Mit herzlichen Zionsgrüssen für
alle Freunde   Ihr ergebener
                         Th. Herzl

2. Letter from Herzl to Prof. G. Belkowski, written on the back of the
'Preliminary Notice'

Programm.

Der Zionismus erstrebt für das jüdische Volk die Schaffung einer rechtlich gesicherten Heimstätte in Palästina.

Zur Erreichung dieses Zieles nimmt der Congress folgende Mittel in Aussicht:

I. Die zweckdienliche Förderung der Besiedlung Palästinas mit jüdischen Ackerbauern, Handwerkern und Gewerbetreibenden.

II. Die Gliederung und Zusammenfassung der gesamten Judenschaft durch geeignete örtliche und allgemeine Veranstaltungen nach den Landesgesetzen.

III. Die Stärkung des jüdischen Volksgefühls und Volksbewußtseins.

IV. Vorbereitende Schritte zur Erlangung der Regierungszustimmung, die nötig sind, um das Ziel des Zionismus zu erreichen.

3. The Basle programme as distributed among the First Zionist Congress. Note the correction in the second line (see p. 238-9)

aber in der Geschichte wachsen
wird — an meine Eltern u.
Frau u. an jedes meiner Kinder,
Pauline, Hans u. Trude eine
Congress = Korrespondenzkarte.
Das ist vielleicht die erste Kinderei
die ich in der ganzen Bewegung
seit zwei Jahren beging.

———

3 September

Wien

Die letzten Tage, die wichtigsten seit
der Empfängnis der Idee damals in
Paris, sind nun vorübergerauscht. Ich
war in Basel u. auf der Rückreise
zu erschöpft, um Aufzeichnungen zu
machen, die doch nöthiger sind als je
weil auch Andere schön merken, dass
unsere Bewegung in die Geschichte
eingetreten ist

Fasse ich den Basler Congress
in ein Wort zusammen — das ich
mich hüten werde öffentlich aus-
zusprechen — so ist es dieses: in Basel
habe ich den Judenstaat gegründet.

49

4. Notes in Herzl's Diary after the First Zionist Congress, 1897 (see p. 243)

wenn ich das heute laut sagte, würde
mir ein universelles Gelächter ant-
worten. Vielleicht in fünf Jahren,
jedenfalls in fünfzig wird es Jeder
einsehen. der Staat ist wesentlich
im Staatswillen des Volkes, ja selbst
eines genügend mächtigen Einzelnen
(l'état c'est moi Ludwig XIV) be-
gründet. Territorium ist nur die
concrete Unterlage, der Staat ist
selbst wo er Territorium hat immer
etwas Abstractes. Der Kirchenstaat
besteht auch ohne Territorium, sonst
wäre der Papst nicht souverän.

Ich habe also in Basel dieses Ab-
stracte u. darum den Allermeisten
Unsichtbare geschaffen. Eigentlich mit
infinitesimalen Mitteln. Ich hetzte
die Leute allmälig in die Staats-
stimmung hinein u. brachte ihnen
das Gefühl bei, dass sie die Na-
tionalversammlung seien.

Eines meiner ersten Ausführungs-
gedanken schon vor Monaten war

50

5. Continuation of Notes in Herzl's Diary

(see p. 286)

TELEGRAMM

an herrn william h. hechler
geistliche an der englischen
botschaft in wien elisabeth
strasze =

+ ss wien da mainau 3b 92 1 8 20 n =
bin ihnen sehr dankbar fuer ihres ausfuehrlichen werthen brief .
ich habe sehr befriedigende antwort erhalten und
sehe nun die sache als gesichert an .. das protectorat wird eintreten
die vermittlung beim herrscher des gesuchten Landes wird
erfolgen. der impfang der abordnung am zielpunkt ihrer reise ist
zugesagt. sagen sie das alles an den der mit ihnen bei mir war
damit er selbst an die spitze der abordnung trete reisen sie
gluecklich und kehren sie gesegnet heim = friedrich groszherzog +

6. Telegram from the Grand Duke of Baden to the Rev. Hechler, 1898 (see p. 286)

The Subscription List will be opened on the 28th March, 1899, and closed on or before the 28th April, 1899, in London, at The London & Provincial Bank, Limited, and its Branches and Agents, and at The Jewish Colonial Trust (Juedische Colonialbank), Limited, and its authorised Agents in all parts of the World. The Bank of Africa, Limited, and its branches will receive subscriptions throughout South Africa.

THE JEWISH COLONIAL TRUST

(JUEDISCHE COLONIALBANK)
LIMITED.

(Incorporated under the Companies Acts, 1862 to 1898, whereby the liability of Shareholders is limited to the amount of their Shares.)

CAPITAL - - - £2,000,000

DIVIDED INTO

£1,999,900 ORDINARY SHARES of £1 each, and
£100 FOUNDERS' SHARES of £1 each.

THE FOUNDERS' SHARES will be vested in the Council of the Company or their nominees and can only be transferred with the approval of the Council. They will not confer any right to participate in the profits of the Company.

PRESENT ISSUE—£1,999,900 IN £1 SHARES

Payable at the option of the Applicant in any one of the following modes, namely :—

(a) 20 per cent., or 4s. per Share, on Application, and the balance in four instalments of 20 per cent., or 4s. per Share, each at intervals of 3 months from the date of the first payment, with 6 per cent. Interest in the meantime payable with the last instalment.

(b) 20 per cent., 4s. per Share on Application, and the balance on Allotment.

(c) The full amount of £1 per Share on Application.

The Council

Dr. THEODOR HERZL,	Littérateur,	VIENNA.	Dr. I. BERNSTEIN KOHAN, Doctor of Medicine, KISCHINEW.
Dr. MORITZ SCHNIRER,	Doctor of Medicine,	VIENNA.	SAMUEL PINELES, Merchant, GALATZ.
Dr. OSER KOKESCH,	Counsellor at Law,	VIENNA.	I. H. ELLMANN, Merchant, BRAILA.
Dr. LEOPOLD KAHN	Counsellor at Law,	VIENNA.	Dr. ALEX. MARMOREK, Doctor of Medicine, PARIS.
OSKAR MARMOREK,	Architect,	VIENNA.	WLADIMIR TEMKIN, Engineer, ELISABEDGRAD.
Dr. MAX MANDELSTAMM,	Doctor of Medicine,	KIEW.	CARL HERBST, Civil Servant, SOFIA.
Dr. RICHARD GOTTHEIL,	Prof. in Columb. Univ	NEW YORK.	Dr. E. W. TSCHLENOW, Doctor of Medicine, MOSCOW.
Dr. ISRAEL JELSKY,	Doctor of Theology,	LODZ	Dr. SALOMO ROSENHECK, Doctor of Medicine, KOLOMEA.
Dr. I. W. JASSINOWSKY,	Counsellor at Law,	WARSAW.	SAMUEL SCHUR, Doctor of Chemistry STANISLAU.
Dr. M. I. BODENHEIMER,	Counsellor at Law	COLOGNE.	MICHAEL USSISCHKIN, Engineer, EKATERINOSLAW.

And three other persons to be appointed by the Council.

Board of Directors.

DAVID WOLFFSOHN (Messrs. Bernstein & Wolffsohn), COLOGNE.
J. H. KANN (Messrs. Lissa & Kann, Bankers), The HAGUE.
S. L. HEYMANN (Messrs. Heymann & Martin), LONDON, and (Messrs. Heymann, Gordon & Co.), SOUTH AFRICA.

GREGORIE LOURIE, Manufacturer, PINSK
HEINRICH ROSENBAUM, Banker, JASSY
S. BARBASCH, Banker, ODESSA.
SALOMO SACHS, Manufacturer, DWINSK.

LEIB SCHALIT, Merchant, RIGA.
Dr. RUDOLPH SCHAUER, Counsellor-at-Law, MAYENCE.
ABR. HORENSTEIN, Merchant, KIEW

} Governors.

Two of whom will be represented in London by their Attorneys.

Bankers.

LONDON AND PROVINCIAL BANK (LIMITED), 7, Bank Buildings, Lothbury, London.

Solicitors.

BENTWICH WATKIN WILLIAMS & GRAY, Corporation Chambers, Guildhall Yard, London.

Auditors.

JACKSON, PIXLEY, BROWNING, HUSEY & Co., 58, Coleman Street, London.

Secretary.

JAMES H. LOEWE.

Registered Offices.

BROAD STREET AVENUE, LONDON, E.C.

7. Prospectus of the Jewish Colonial Trust 1899 (see p. 317)

An den Vorsitzenden
der amerikanischen Zionisten-Conferenz.

Herr Präsident!

Zum erstenmale versammeln sich die Zionisten Amerikas zu einer Conferenz. Es geschieht in einem Augenblicke, wo Europa mit noch mehr Spannung als sonst nach dem jungen Staatswesen dort drüben jenseits der Meere ausschaut. Wenn wir hier jeden Abend lesen, was dort am Morgen geschehen ist, ...

... so zweifeln wir nicht am Siege dieses Sternenbanners der Union, das so hoch fliegt. ...

... und wenn wir dabei die geschichtlichen Zusammenhänge betrachten, wird uns, besonders uns Juden ... zu Muthe. Die neue Welt, die heute so gewaltig aufragt, ruhte noch unentdeckt auf dem Ocean, ...

8. Message from Herzl to the First Conference of American Zionists, 1898

I   1899 23 Juli 6 uhr morgens
Das neue Zion - im coupé von
                    Paris nach Frankfurt

cap. Das letzte Experiment
Dr Friedrich Löwenberg liest
im Café die annonce: Gebildeter
u. verzweifelter junger Mann
wird gesucht, der bereit ist
mit seinem Leben ein letztes
Experiment zu machen.
Ferner antisemdebatten im
n.ö. Landtag. Judenexcesse in
Galizien. Fall Dreyfus.
Verstimmt geht er weg. Das neue
Ghetto. Goizaggasse u. Rosaner
Lände. Typen des neuen Ghetto
Vortheil u. Vergnügen. Else verlobt.
mit einem Geschäftsjüngling.
Friedrich kehrt Nachts in das Café

9. First page of Herzl's outline of his idea of Altneuland (see p. 395)

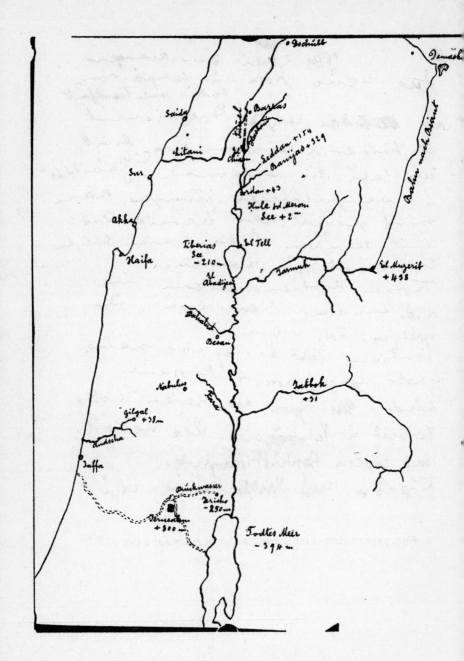

10. Map of irrigation of Palestine, used by Herzl for the description in Altneuland (see p. 400)

Extra-Ausgabe.

Die ✡ Welt

Erscheint jeden Freitag.

Redaction
und Administration:
WIEN
IX., Türkenstrasse Nr. 9.
Telephon 14199.

Zuschriften sind nicht an einzelne Personen, sondern
an die Redaction oder Administration: Wien, IX.,
Türkenstrasse Nr. 9, zu richten.
Unfrankierte Briefe werden nicht angenommen und Manuscripte
nicht zurückgesandt!
Sprechstunden der Redaction: Montag, Mittwoch und Freitag
von 3–4 Uhr.

Preise der Anzeigen:
Die viermal gespaltene Petitzeile
30 Heller.
Der Inseratentheil
wird Donnstag abends geschlossen.
Einzelne Nummern 30 Heller.

Bezugspreise: Oesterreich-Ungarn: ganzjährig 12 Kronen, halbjährig 6 Kronen. Für das Ausland: Deutschland
ganzjährig 13 Mk. 70 Pf., halbjährig 6 Mk. 85 Pf. England ganzjährig 14 Shg., halbjährig 7 Shg. Russland
ganzjährig 7 R., halbjährig 3 R. 50 Kop. Schweiz, Frankreich, Italien, Turkei, Rumanien, Serbien, Griechenland, Aegypten
ganzjährig 17 Frcs., halbjährig 8 Frcs. 50 Cts. Amerika ganzjährig 3 Doll. 40 Ct.

Constantinopel, 17. Mai 1901.

Doctor Theodor Herzl, Präsident des zionistischen Actions-Comités, wurde heute von Sr. Majestät dem Sultan in längerer Audienz empfangen.

Herausgeber und verantwortlicher Redacteur Berthold Feiwel   Buchdruckerei „Industrie" (S. Bergmann).

11. Special issue of Die Welt, announcing that Herzl had been received by
the Sultan (see p. 354)

FOREIGN OFFICE,

December 18th, 1902.

Confidential.

Sir:-

I am directed by the Marquess of Lansdowne to
acknowledge the receipt of your letter of the 12th
ultimo,which was left at the Foreign Office by Mr.
Greenberg, relative to the proposed establishment
of a Jewish Colony in the Sinai Peninsula.

I am to inform you that Lord Lansdowne communicated with His Majesty's Agent and Consul General at
Cairo in regard to your proposals and that he has now
received a despatch from the Earl of Cromer on the
subject.

Lord Cromer strongly advises that before any
further steps are taken in the matter the organizers
of the project should send a small Commission to the
Sinai Peninsula to report on the situation and to
form some opinion as to whether the undertaking is

likely

Theodore Herzl, Esq., M.D.,
29, Haizingerstrasse,
Vienna-Währing,
Austria.

12. First letter from the British Foreign Office to Herzl (see p. 424)

Entwurf

Charter

welcher von der Regierung Sr. Königl.
Hoheit des Khedive von Egypten dem Prä=
sidenten des Aufsichtsrathes des Londoner
Jewish Colonial Trust (Jüdische Colonialbank)
Limited, Herrn dr theodor Herzl in Wien
verliehen worden ist.

I

Zum Zwecke der Cultivirung der brach-
liegenden (uncultivated) innerhalb der nach-
stehenden Grenzen :

. . . . . .

. . . . .

gelegenen Provinz überläßt die egyptische
Regierung dem J. C. T. und seinen Rechts=
nachfolgern ~~dem~~ (rightful oder legal suc=
cessors) diese ihre Provinz zur Colonisation
durch Juden.
Zur ökonomischen Durchführung der
Colonisation hat der J. C. T. innerhalb
Jahresfrist eine Landgesellschaft (Land
company) mit etwa fünf Millionen ₤
Actiencapital zu begründen :

13. Draft of the charter of the Sinai peninsula (see p. 429)

Die ✡ Welt

Erscheint jeden Freitag.

Redaction
und Administration
WIEN
IX., Türkenstrasse 9.
Telephon 14199.

Zuschriften sind nicht an einzelne Personen, sondern
an die Redaction oder Administration: Wien, IX.,
Türkenstrasse Nr. 9, zu richten.
Unfrankierte Briefe werden nicht angenommen und Manuskripte
nicht zurückgesendet.
Sprechstunden der Redaction täglich von ½12—½1 Uhr.

Preise der Anzeigen
laut aufliegendem Tarif
Der Inseratentheil
wird Dienstag abends geschlossen.

Bezugspreise: Oesterreich-Ungarn: ganzjährig Kr. 12.—, halbjährig Kr. 6.—, vierteljährig Kr. 3.—. Für das
Ausland: Deutschland ganzjährig Mk. 13.70, halbjährig Mk. 6.85, vierteljährig Mk. 3.45, England
ganzjährig Shg. 14.—, halbjährig Shg. 7.—, vierteljährig Shg. 3.10, Russland ganzjährig R. 7.—, halbjährig R. 3.50, vierteljährig R. 1.75, Schweiz, Frankreich, Italien, Türkei, Rumänien, Bulgarien, Serbien, Griechenland, Aegypten ganzjährig
Fres. 17.—, halbjährig Fres. 8.50, vierteljährig 4.25, Amerika ganzjährig Doll. 3.40, halbjährig Doll. 1.70, vierteljährig Doll. .85.

Basel, 29. August 1903 — 6. Elul 5663.

Eine Erklärung der englischen Regierung.*)

Sir Clement Hill, Chief of Protectorate Dept. to Mr. L. J. Greenberg. | **Foreign Office.**

Aug. 14th 1903.

SIR.

Mr. Chamberlain communicated to the Marquess of Lansdowne the letter which you addressed
to him on the 13th ultimo containing the form of an agreement which Dr. Herzl proposes should be entered
into between His Majesty's Government and the Jewish Colonial Trust Ltd. for the establishment of a
Jewish settlement in East Africa.

His Lordship has also had under his consideration the remarks made by you on 6th Just. on
the occasion of your interview in this office with Sir E. Barrington and Mr. Hurst.

I am now directed by His Lordship to say that he has studied the question with the interest
which His Majesty's Government must always take in any well-considered scheme for the amelioration of
the position of the Jewish Race. The time at his disposal has been too short to enable him to go fully
into the details of the plan or to discuss it with His Majesty's Commissioner for the East Africa Protectorate, and he regrets that he is therefore unable to pronounce any definite opinion in the matter.

He understands that the Trust desire to send some gentlemen to the East Africa Protectorate,
who may ascertain personally whether there are any vacant lands suitable for the purposes in question,
and, if this is so he will be happy to give them every facility to enable them to discuss with His Majesty's
Commissioner the possibility of meeting the view which may be expressed at the forthcoming Zionist
Congress in regard to the conditions upon which a settlement might be possible.

If a site can be found which the Trust and His Majesty's Commissioner consider suitable and
which commends itself to His Majesty's Government, Lord Lansdowne will be prepared to entertain
favourably proposals for the establishment of a Jewish colony or settlement on conditions which will
enable the members to observe their National customs. For this purpose he would be prepared to discuss
if a suitable site had been found and subject to the views of the advisers of the Secretary of State in
East Africa) the details of a scheme comprising as its main features: the grant of a considerable area of
land, the appointment of a Jewish Official as chief of the local administration, and permission to the Colony
to have a free hand in regard to municipal legislation and as to the management of religious and purely
domestic matters, such Local Autonomy being conditional upon the right of His Majesty's Government to
exercise a general control.

There is no need at present to consider the details of the terms upon which the land would be
granted, whether by sale or lease, but His Lordship assumes that no portion of the administrative expenses
of the settlement would fall on His Majesty's Government, and the latter would reserve power to reoccupy
the land if the settlement should not prove a success.

I am, Sir,

Your most obedient

humble servant

*) Der englische Originaltext.

(signed) **Clement Hill.**

14. Page from Die Welt publishing a letter from the British Foreign Office
on the establishment of a Jewish settlement in East Africa (see p. 446)

WOLF'S VILLA IMPERIALE

Franzensbad den 6 Mai 1904

Lieber Daade,

dies der Rest meines Briefes,
den ich dir nach London schrieb;
das Andere, das auf einer
irrigen Voraussetzung beruhte,
habe ich annullirt.
Ich gebrauche hier die Herz=Kur.
meine <u>Mutter</u> weiss nichts davon,
glaubt, ich sei nur zum
Ausruhen hier...
macht keine Dummheiten,
während ich todt bin.

   Herzlich grüsst Dein
   zu Schanden gearbeiteter

            Benjamin

15. Letter to David Wolffsohn, written by Herzl shortly before his death
(see p. 499-500)

Im esch koboch

Jeruschalaim

tischkach jemini

16. "JERUSALEM, IF I EVER FORGET THEE, WITHERED BE THIS MY HAND" (Psalm 137). The Hebrew wording, written by S. Pineles in Roman lettering at Herzl's request, was quoted by Herzl in his closing speech to the Sixth Zionist Congress, 1903 (see p. 464)

communications, Greenberg asked about the borders of the
territory in question, Chamberlain answered that as yet he
had no definite territory in view. But in his opinion it ought
to be the stretch between Nairobi and the Mau escarpment;
that was the most favorable. But, he went on, should Herzl
take up the proposition seriously, it would be necessary for
him to make an investigation of the British East African
Protectorate.

Herzl meanwhile was again submitting plans to Constantinople; through Izzet Bey he was pressing for a Charter for
Mesopotamia and the *sandjak* of Akko; he was making
efforts, in various directions, without success, to hinder the
Rouvier funding plan, so that he might be called to Constantinople; he was also preparing, on Greenberg's suggestion,
a statement of his objections to the Garstyne report. And
at the same time he instructed Greenberg to write to Chamberlain that he, Herzl, wanted to send a commission of investigation to the British East African Protectorate without
delay. However, he suggested the signing of a provisional
agreement before the sending of the commission. Chamberlain declared himself ready to receive the outline of such an
agreement.

Even before he received his answer, Herzl forwarded the
outline to Greenberg. In order to avoid infringement on the
Bank statutes, which confined its colonization activities to
Syria and Palestine, Herzl asked, in the proposed Charter,
that the offer be made to him personally to create a Colonizing Company; the British government was to place at the
disposal of this Company a territory, to be indicated in more
detail, as a "place of refuge for those Jews who, for any
reason, are compelled to leave their present places of domi-
cile." The territory was to be the permanent property of

the Company, in so far as it was not as yet in private possession. The settlers were to be given self-administration in
local affairs at first, while the Foreign Office was to provide
a Governor chosen by the British government; after five
years there was to be complete autonomy. In his letter to
Greenberg Herzl said: "We treat the matter *not as a financial
but as a political concession*, and I beg you to place all emphasis on this point of view in all your negotiations." The
request was unnecessary, for Greenberg observed in his
letter, which crossed Herzl's, that he placed even sharper
emphasis on the point. The East African offer had little real
value, but its political significance was correspondingly great,
if it were only exploited properly.

While Greenberg was having the Charter proposals put
into correct legal form, Herzl received Lord Lansdowne's
reply to his rebuttal of the Garstyne report. It proved the
correctness of Herzl's suspicion that the irrigation question
had only been brought forward as a pretext. Lord Cromer,
said the letter, stated that the objections of the Egyptian
government were so serious, that they could only be overcome by greater pressure than the circumstances warranted.
Even so, neither the British nor the Egyptian officials
believed in the possible success of the enterprise — here the
failure of the Friedmann project played its part!— and would
not accept responsibility. Furthermore, the administration
of Egypt was already complicated enough, without adding
to it the difficulties which would be created by "the establishment of a large cosmopolitan society." These objections were,
in Cromer's view, so cogent, that he considered it useless
to continue the negotiations. Four weeks later the Foreign
Office forwarded a note from Cromer, in which he said that
the estimates of his irrigation expert had been proved to be

right. Lord Lansdowne declared that he could not put further pressure on the Egyptian government.

Nothing remained now but the East African project, which had logic on its side but nothing more, and which was to prove so fateful for Herzl and for the Zionist movement. It was only after long consideration and against strong inner objections that Herzl agreed to the submitting of the outline of the Charter; but that done, he pressed for swift work, so that he might be able to place the results before the Congress. Greenberg had had the Charter prepared by the firm of Lloyd George, Roberts and Co., because Lloyd George, as a member of Parliament and one who had a knowledge of Uganda, could consult the Foreign Office and find out in advance what would be acceptable. The name of the settlement was to be "New Palestine;" it was to be created "for the encouragement of the Jewish national idea" and the "promotion of the welfare of the Jewish people." The lawyers pointed out that it would be difficult to have the concession offered to Herzl personally, since he was not English. Against his original wishes and intentions the concession therefore had to be offered to the Jewish Colonial Trust; he agreed only upon the assurance that the contract could readily be transferred to another Company, which he could found, if he thought it necessary.

He did not communicate this plan to Nordau until the beginning of July, either because he had really forgotten, as he himself wrote on July 6, or because he had wanted to shield the plan, in its initial stages, from Nordau's sharp criticism. Toward the end of June he had merely asked Nordau to prepare an address for the Congress on the migration question. It was only on July 2, when Nordau had refused because there were no reliable data, that Herzl

acquainted him with the plan, and wrote him his reasons for
accepting. It was necessary, he said, to show the Sultan
that the Jews were prepared to go elsewhere. Every other
means — except money, which was not being placed at his
disposal — had been exhausted. This was to be his last offer,
as it were. "But apart from the question of diplomacy, we
have to come to a decision on the actual question of migration. Our program for immediate help is not to be confused
with the small settlement idea (the *Hoveve Zion* say Palestine, the philanthropists say *n'importe où*); it is the publicly
recognized, legally secured plan of settlement, transferred
elsewhere, but we still hold aloft — yes, and higher than
ever! — the flag of Zion, beneath which we and our forces
assemble." For this program of immediate help Herzl
reverted to his original idea of a Jewish state, because he saw
no other prospect of quick relief, and because he believed
that the Zionist movement, as the core of the Jewish people,
could not stand by inactively at such a time of national need.
"We must give an answer to Kishineff, and this is the only
one . . . We must, in a word, play the politics of the hour."

Nordau objected. He had a more accurate prevision of
the resistance which would arise among East European
Jewry, brought up as it was in Jewish tradition and history.
Herzl, who was not afraid of external resistance, replied that
this precisely was the task of leadership, "to set the people
on the path which, by seeming detours, leads to the goal.
Moshe Rabbenu followed the identical course." Wherever
the building of the house might begin, the Jewish state,
which had been and still remained his objective, remained
an unalterable principle. If it proved impossible to begin
with Palestine, which would have been very beautiful,
proceeding afterwards to the establishment of autonomous

colonies — the way England had done with her superfluous masses — then one had to invert the process: one began with colonies and used them as political-national points of support and training for Palestine: "an inverted England in miniature." The first such political colony with this significance would be represented by the settlement between Kilmanjaro and Kenya. "This British East African beginning is politically a Rishon le-Zion," and thus nearer in spirit to a national Palestine than Edmund Rothschild's creation. He developed the idea further on July 19. "If we acknowledge Chamberlain's offer with thanks, retaining the mentioned conditions, we strengthen our position in his sympathies, we involve him in the necessity of doing something for us in the event that *our* commission (which is under our control) brings in a negative recommendation; and we have, in our relationship with this gigantic nation, acquired recognition as a state-building power (cf. in international law the quality of a war-waging power)." Charters from other states would follow, new "power-stations" would be created, whose political and colonizational significance would be quite unaffected by the question of geographic distance.

It is fascinating to watch Herzl's fantasy at work in the creation of a comprehensive plan which should make Chamberlain's offer plausible to himself and Nordau. The fact that his feelings were not touched off by the proposal may be deduced from one circumstance: he did not draw up a special plan of colonization, as he had done in the case of the Sinai project, to which he made repeated efforts to return. On July 20 he wrote Greenberg to make use of Lord Cromer's presence in London to do whatever was possible to revive the Sinai enterprise. "We must indeed take East Africa, or at least the Charter, but we must not deceive ourselves as to the fact that all the non-English Jews are against East Africa. I shall have to use a great deal of patience for it, whereas El Arish is popular." And then, following up his image of an "inverted England in miniature," he even prepared steps to approach the Portuguese government for a Charter for Mozambique, the Belgian for a territory in the Congo, the Italian for a section of the plain of Tripoli.

At no time did he lose sight of Palestine. The contrary was in fact the case. Though he did not believe that serious, productive work could be done in Palestine without a Charter, he showed the liveliest interest in the work of David Levontin, who left Vienna on June 8 to open the Jaffa branch of the Jewish Colonial Trust — since 1948, the Jewish national bank in Israel. He hoped that this bank would serve both to strengthen the Jewish position in Palestine and to open a path to new relationships with Turkish governmental departments. He transmitted to Levontin, for examination and approval, various plans of practical work which had been submitted to him. He also gave his support to certain efforts aimed at the purchase of Palestinian land, when such purchases were being made cautiously and unofficially.

At the same time Greenberg, acting in his name, pressed the British government for an early reply to his outline of a Charter for East Africa, so that it might be laid before the impending Zionist Congress, which was to open August 14.

A reply came, in Lord Lansdowne's name, from Sir Clement Hill, permanent departmental head. In his letter Sir Clement Hill declared that Lord Lansdowne had "studied the question with the interest which His Majesty's Government must always take in any well-considered scheme for the amelioration of the position of the Jewish race." But time had been too short for a closer examination of the plan and for its submission to the British representative for the East African Protectorate. "Lord Lansdowne assumes," the letter continued, "that the Trust desire to send some gentlemen to the East Africa Protectorate, who may ascertain personally whether there are any vacant lands suitable for the purposes in question, and, if this is so, he will be happy to give them every facility to enable them to discuss with His Majesty's Commissioner the possibility of meeting the view which may be expressed at the forthcoming Zionist Congress in regard to the conditions upon which a settlement might be possible.

If a site can be found which the Trust and His Majesty's Commissioner consider suitable and which commends itself to His Majesty's Government, Lord Lansdowne will be prepared to entertain favourably proposals for the establishment of a Jewish colony or settlement, on conditions which will enable the members to observe their National customs. . . ." The document went on with an offer — subject naturally to the consent of the relevant officials — of a Jewish governorship and internal autonomy.

This first official declaration of a government directed to the Zionist movement, and this first recognition of the Jews as a people, reached Herzl in Russia. The letters he had written, immediately after the Kishineff pogrom, to Plehve and Pobiedonostzev had remained unanswered. But when he learned, toward the end of June, of a secret circular of Plehve's calling for the suppression of the Zionist Organization, after the sale of Bank shares had already been forbidden, he set everything in motion to get to Russia. He was strengthened in this resolve by the appeal of Jassinovsky, the Russian member of the Actions Committee, and it was a Polish lady, Korvin-Piatrowska who, at the instance of Jassinovsky, managed to obtain for Herzl an invitation to an interview with von Plehve, Minister of the Interior.

In many circles this journey of Herzl's to Russia was bitterly condemned later on: no Jewish leader, it was said, should have negotiated with Plehve, who was regarded as responsible for the pogroms. Herzl properly took another view. Political action was not directed by sentiment. If, as he hoped, he could help the Jewish people, he did not dare to let this opportunity pass. On August 5 he left for Russia, and on the 7th arrived in St. Petersburg.

He was received twice, in a very friendly manner, by von Plehve, and obtained from the Minister of Finance, Witte, the promise that the prohibition of the sale of Bank shares would be withdrawn if a branch of the Bank would be opened in Russia, which Herzl had intended to do in any case. From the Director of the Asiatic Department in the Foreign Office, Hartwig, he obtained the assurance that the latter would plead with the Russian ambassador in Constantinople for support of the Zionist aim. But his most important achievement was his acquisition of Plehve as a supporter of Zionism. The Minister showed himself to be well informed on the subject; he knew the tendencies within the movement, and their leaders; he was aware of the inadequate support which the Russian members of the Actions Committee brought to the Vienna leadership. Herzl compared their attitude to that of Columbus's sailors before land was sighted. He pleaded that the Russian government help him reach land, after which he would find it easy to maintain discipline.

Plehve stated that the Russian government was interested in the definite emigration of the unassimilable portion of the Jewish people, which created serious problems for Russia;

he himself, who had grown up among Jews, was by no means an enemy of the Jews; but it was extremely simple for the other states to complain of the cruelty of the Russian government toward the Jews and at the same time to close their gates against Jewish immigration. The Russian government had therefore been sympathetic in its attitude toward the Zionist movement, as long as it had been a movement of emigration. But of late, and particularly since the Minsk All-Russian Zionist Conference of September 1902 — in which Ahad Ha-am had taken a leading part — the cultural question had pushed the migrational so far into the background that the movement had become objectionable to the government as opposing its efforts to create a homogeneous population in Russia.

Herzl skilfully exploited von Plehve's concern over the foreign reaction to the Kishineff pogrom to obtain his tolerance, and even support, of the Zionist movement if it returned to its old program of action. He proposed that von Plehve write a letter, to be put before the Congress, stating that the Zionist movement could count on the government's "moral and material assistance if some of its measures lead to the diminution of the Jewish population of Russia. This assistance would consist of Russian protection of Zionist accredited agents vis-à-vis the Turkish government, and the facilitation of the tasks of emigration societies."

This declaration of von Plehve's had been approved by the Czar. In his second interview with Herzl, von Plehve promised he would take up with his master the question of including Kurland and Riga in the Russian area open to Jewish settlement, and of giving them — that is, the communities, not individuals — the right to acquire land there. Von Plehve further agreed to receive Dr. Katzenelson of

Libau, Herzl's confidant and agent, who accompanied him throughout his Russian journey, for future negotiations.

The negotiations in Petersburg, which later aroused such hostility toward Herzl, were undoubtedly a significant political success. On Herzl personally a much stronger impression was produced by what he saw in Russia outside governmental circles. Since the first Zionist Congress he had learned to know the Russian Jewish intelligentsia to the extent that it was Zionist; now he saw the Jews in every stratum, the Jewish masses, on the spot. Even on his hither-ward journey, concerning which he had imparted nothing to the press, he found numerous followers waiting for him at the railroad stations in Warsaw and Vilna. "Things are so bad with them that a poor devil like myself seems to them to be a liberator." In Petersburg he met Jews from all circles. At the banquet arranged for him by the Zionists of St. Petersburg, on August 11, he listened attentively to all the speeches and learned all he could about the Zionist work. In the somewhat lengthy speech which he himself delivered he issued a warning against admitting to the Zionist program other tendencies, and particularly radical ones. For, he explained, such an admixture would give rise to the belief — he said this, of course, with an eye on von Plehve's state-ments — that the Basle Platform was only a cover to other aims. There would be time enough to exercise the right to build socialist parties once the Jewish people was in Pales-tine. In the diaspora the support of the socialist parties would help the Jews as little as the support of liberalism by the western Jews had done.

On his homeward journey he made a stop in Vilna on August 16. He had been warned that this was dangerous; the members of the Bund, the Jewish socialist-revolutionary

movement, were furious with him because of his visit to
Plehve and because of his Petersburg address. From many
towns inquiries were directed to Petersburg whether Herzl
was really dead. His visit to Vilna was announced in advance. A tremendous ovation awaited him; the streets
through which he rode were almost impassable because of
the throngs of spectators. The terrified police forbade all
demonstrations, listened in on all his telephone conversations, and kept close watch on all his movements. His
projected tour of the Jewish quarter, the banquet in the town
hall and the visit to the Great Synagogue had to be abandoned on instruction from the police. He did however ride
through "tumultuous Jewish streets" to the community
house, where a dense crowd of representatives and deputations awaited him. One of the leaders greeted him as "the
greatest son of the Jewish people," then read out a Hebrew
address from a parchment scroll which he afterwards presented to him. Old Reb Shleimele lifted his hands over the
Zionist leader and pronounced the Priestly Benediction.
The historian W. Javitz presented him with a small Torah
scroll in a carved holder as a gift of honor from the Vilna
community. "There was in all these greetings a spirit which
so moved me that I managed to keep back my tears only by
thinking of the newspaper reports. The numerous addresses
overpraised me fantastically, but the wretchedness of these
oppressed people was genuine enough." Deeply touched, he
thanked the deputations for the honors which, unfortunately, he had not yet merited, for the great work which he
saw as the sole solution of the Jewish problem had not yet
been completed, though he did not doubt its ultimate success.

The evening of that day a secret banquet was tendered him
in the village of Verko, eight kilometres from Vilna. On the

journey Herzl asked his companions, I. Goldberg and V. Katzenelson, to show him the houses of the poor Jews. The sight so shook him that this time he could not keep back his tears. He was not less moved when a poor Jew refused with thanks the gold coin which he offered him, saying that he had only wanted to see Herzl. While the banquet in Verko was in progress, there suddenly appeared, outside the house, Jewish boys and girls of Vilna, who had made a pilgrimage through the night to see and hear him. They sang Hebrew songs. One young worker proposed a toast in which he spoke of the time when "King Herzl" would reign.

At one o'clock in the night Herzl went from the hotel to the train. The city was awake. Thousands of Jews were in the streets and on the balconies of the houses. At the station there was a dense throng. The police appeared. Brutally they dispersed the crowd. Herzl was aghast. Deathly pale, completely broken, he reached the station, which had been roped off. A number of Zionists managed to get past the guard as "passengers with baggage." Herzl forbade any kind of demonstration; he did not want his visit to add to the sufferings of a single Jew. His last words to the Vilna Jews were: "Gentlemen, do not lose courage; better times are coming, they must come; that is what we are working for."

At Altaussee, where his family was passing the summer vacation, he took just one day's rest. Then he set out for Basle and the sixth Congress.

CHAPTER XIV

UGANDA, CATASTROPHE AND DEATH

THERE has been much discussion as to whether — and if so in what form — Herzl ever obtained the permission of the Greater Actions Committee to lay the Uganda offer before the Congress. It is, however, certain that on Friday, August 21, he reported to this body on the British offer and on his journey to Russia. In his diary Herzl notes bitterly that it did not even occur to any of the participants that his labor and success in England and Russia "merited so much as a word or a smile of thanks." Jacobson, Tshlenov and Belkovsky had reproaches to offer. The extremely brief official minutes of this session record that almost all the Russian members of the Actions Committee were doubtful as to the value of von Plehve's promises. With regard to the East African offer Bernstein-Kohan, who came from Kishineff, remarked that in their present circumstances the Jews of Russia would even go to hell. Jassinovsky agreed. Tshlenov, the leader of the Russian federation, disagreed. Bodenheimer pointed out that the consideration of the project by the Congress would signify a change in the Basle Program, which confined itself exclusively to Palestine. The sharpest opposition seems to have come from Alexander Marmorek, Herzl's personal friend. On his motion it was resolved that a second session of the Actions Committee be held, that the members take a stand individually, and that the decision be made subsequently.

The next morning was a Sabbath, and following his usual custom at the Congresses, Herzl attended the services in the Basle synagogue. It was immediately on the conclusion of the services that the famous meeting took place in Joseph Cowen's room to which Herzl invited a limited number of leaders — among the Russians, Mandelstamm, Yelski, Bernstein-Kohan and Tshlenov, besides Wolffsohn, Marmorek, Cowen and Zangwill — in order to win them over to the project. He placed the English document before them. The impression was powerful. Tshlenov stood up and made the *Sheheheyanu*, for the document was the first recognition of the Jewish people as such since its dispersal; it was also the expression of England's confidence in the creative capacity of the Jewish people, and the promise of Jewish autonomy. There followed, for four hours, an agitated discussion, during which Herzl absented himself so as not to influence by his presence the opinions of the participants; the final decision was — to lay the offer before the Congress.

At the second official session of the Greater Actions Committee, which took place on Saturday evening, there does not seem to have been a thorough discussion of the East African project in connection with the formulation to be contained in Herzl's Congress address; there was instead much talk concerning Kishineff and von Plehve's letter. The letter of the British government could be seen by the members in Herzl's room. Nevertheless it was Herzl's claim, frequently reasserted, that he was empowered to lay the offer before the Congress.

There the first reaction of the majority of the delegates to Herzl's speech was one of profound emotion. A storm of applause swept through the hall. "It could not have been greater," wrote one reporter, "if Herzl, instead of submitting a proposal which obviously thrust the Basle Program into the background, had announced to the Congress: 'Palestine is ours, the masses can set out.' " Shemarya Levin, who, as one of the secretaries of the Congress, could survey the scene from the platform, saw on the faces of the delegates "amazement, admiration — but not a sign of protest . . . The first effect of the magnanimity of the British offer was to eclipse all other considerations." The strategy of surprise, which Herzl liked only too well, had begun with a victory.

It was only in the sessions of the separate federations, and particularly that of the Russian, the strongest at the Congress, that critical reconsideration and opposition emerged, to find more and more powerful expression from hour to hour in the debates on the floor of the Congress itself.

In the carefully formulated opening speech which followed on the political report, Herzl had emphasized, at the very outset, that the East Africa project was in no wise intended as a substitute for Palestine. Palestine remained the unchangeable goal, and this had been made abundantly clear in his negotiations with the British government and all its agents. It was nevertheless his opinion that a method could be found of making use of this offer: "The offer has been extended to us in a way which cannot but contribute to the improvement of the condition of the Jewish people, without our relinquishing any of the great principles on which our movement is founded . . .

"Zion this certainly is not, and can never become. It is only a colonizational auxiliary or help — but, be it noted, on a national and state foundation. This will not give the sign to our masses to set themselves everywhere in motion. It is, and must remain, an emergency measure which is intended to come to the rescue of our helpless philanthropic enterprises and prevent the loss of these detached fragments of our people."

He emphasized in particular that through his negotiations in St. Petersburg, and in the official promise of von Plehve to support the Zionist effort in Constantinople, a new political path to Turkey had been opened. "With renewed courage, and with better prospects than ever before, we can continue our efforts for Palestine." Then, in closing, he proposed the appointment of a small commission which should make a thorough investigation of the East African offer. "Whatever may be the decision, I know I can comfort myself with the thought that our hearts are filled with the deepest gratitude for the statesmanlike generosity which Great Britain has displayed in these negotiations toward the Jewish people."

Max Nordau, who was at bottom opposed to the plan even now, but who had been impressed by Herzl's plea for an objective attitude toward the British offer, and was, moreover, reluctant to abandon Herzl in this difficult moment, delivered an ambitious oration in support of Herzl's arguments; he coined, for the prospective colony in East Africa, the not altogether fortunate phrase *Nachtasyl* — a night shelter for the hundreds of thousands of Jews who were being thrust out of their homes and to whom Palestine could not yet be offered. "It will, however, be a night shelter in which the inhabitants would find something more than food and lodging; they will find there the means for a political training, to educate themselves and the world to the idea that we Jews are a people capable, willing and ready to take upon ourselves all those tasks which characterize an honorable and independent people."

On the majority of the delegates all this made but a slight
impression. Although the official debate was directed to the
resolution to appoint an investigation commission, and although even the defenders of the resolution were for the
most part convinced that there would be no East African
colonization — indeed, their intention was to find an honorable way out for Herzl by burying the project via the commission — the resistance of the delegates became more determined from hour to hour. Curiously enough it was from the
Russian representatives, among whom were the Zionists of
Kishineff, who showed themselves unalterably opposed to
permitting the Zionist Organization even to negotiate for
any other immigration center than Palestine. It signified
a departure from the line laid down at the first Zionist Congress, a break with the Basle Program. The problem of
meeting the pressure of Jewish need was not the business
of Zionism, whose task it was to concentrate on the achievement of its ultimate objective even if it could not, in the
interim, be of any assistance to the suffering Jewish masses.
Every compromise, every deviation from the road which led
straight to Palestine, seemed to the protagonists of the viewpoint to be a surrender of fundamental principle. The debate
became converted into a question of principle: Palestine or
Uganda.

Herzl himself took no part in this debate. He played the
observer; he held private conferences with his supporters
in the various federations in the hope of winning over a
majority to his side; from time to time he was forced to
suspend this activity because of heart attacks. Then, to
break the tension, he opened the Wednesday session by
giving the floor to Professor Franz Oppenheimer, with whom

he declared himself to be in perfect agreement. Oppenheimer's thesis was that the upbuilding of Palestine had to
begin with the founding of peasant cooperatives, and that
only when the foundations had been laid in this wise was
mass immigration to set in.

After a second speech by Nordau, closing the debate,
Greenberg submitted a detailed report on the negotiations
with England.

Greenberg's address and the letter of the British government made a profound impression. The Congress rose and
applauded. Rabbi Pines declared that he would make the
contribution needed to inscribe the British government in
the Golden Book of the Jewish National Fund, opened for
the first time at the sixth Congress.

It was a quarter to two in the afternoon. Herzl suspended
the session for an hour and called together the Greater
Actions Committee to deliberate on the exact formulation
of the resolution. For now, after the long debate, the original
formulation was wholly inadequate. The new resolution entrusted to a commission of nine members, as yet to be
elected, the task of "cooperating with the Smaller Actions
Committee, but without voting power, on the sending of an
expedition to the territory to be investigated." The money
for this enterprise could not be drawn from either the Bank
or the National Fund. The decision on the actual colonization of the East African territory was to be left to a Congress
especially called for that purpose. At the session of the
Greater Actions Committee, Herzl, against the resistance
of the Russian members, had forced through the unit rule,
so that the Committee voted en bloc, the members not having the right to vote separately in the Congress. The reso-

lution having been accepted by a majority, Herzl laid it before the Congress at a quarter past four.

The actual voting, which was by roll call, was preceded by an earnest introduction on the part of Herzl. He considered it "the duty of a leader not to evade a responsibility, but to take a definite stand; and I am certain in the knowledge that our future work will be made enormously difficult, if not impossible, unless the extraordinary weightiness of this resolution is fully grasped; I therefore wish to emphasize the profound gravity of the issue and of your vote." The resolution was translated into the most important languages, including the Hebrew. Then the roll call began, and lasted about half an hour. There were 295 affirmative votes, 177 negative. The negatives were for the most part Russians, with a small admixture of westerners. The affirmatives were composed of the delegates of various federations, under the leadership of the German, supported by a majority of the Mizrahi fraction, the Socialists and individual Russians who were especially close to Herzl or who wished to express by their vote their enduring confidence in his leadership. About a hundred delegates abstained, among them men of the standing of Nahum Sokolow, Herbert Bentwich, and the Mizrahi leader, Reines.

The vote was a clear victory for Herzl. But it was a Pyrrhic victory. The announcement of the vote was accompanied by deafening applause, followed by a turmoil. In the session of the Actions Committee, Herzl had committed the grave error, when forcing through the unit rule, of seeking to obtain unanimity by declaring that any member voting against the resolution could no longer remain a member of that body. He was now to pay the price. The Russian members of the Actions Committee, Tshlenov, Tiomkin, Bernstein-Kohan, Belkovsky, Jacobson, Bruck and Goldberg handed him a declaration to read out to the Congress, wherein they stated that in the session of the Committee they had voted against the sending of the expedition. Herzl read forth the declaration. The signatories rose, stepped down from the platform and marched down the central aisle and out of the hall. Their followers on the floor applauded, rose likewise, and accompanied the procession. All the "Negatives," the entire body of the opposition, left the Congress. The delegates remaining in the hall were restless and agitated. Herzl had to suspend the session for an hour, and then Sir Francis Montefiore was able to deliver his dull paper on organization and propaganda. At eight o'clock Herzl closed the session, after announcing the final results of the voting (295 to 178), and after again explaining that the acceptance of the resolution did not signify the acceptance of the colonization plan, but only its investigation. "Let this be thoroughly understood; for if it is thoroughly understood I cannot understand why a number of delegates should have withdrawn from the hall in this fashion. In the absence of these gentlemen, whom I expect back shortly, I will permit no further discussion of the matter."

Meanwhile the "Negatives," or, as they called themselves, the *Zione-Zion*, had assembled for counsel in the small hall where the first Congress had held its sessions. The secession had, in spite of its appearance of preparation, been a spontaneous act precipitated by the withdrawal of the leaders. Deep depression reigned; to all assembled here it seemed that the ideal had been betrayed, Palestine abandoned or thrust to a side; the more excitable broke into tears; some sat down on the floor as if in the mourning rites of Tish'a b'Ab. Such was, on them, the effect of the resolution.

Late that evening Herzl learned of the mood which had seized the seceding minority. He at once resolved to sacrifice his pride and to go to the "Negatives." It was a closed session. A motion had to be made and passed on whether they should admit and hear the President of the Organization, on whom they were sitting in judgment. Herzl waited in the corridor outside until he was admitted. No applause greeted his entry; a voice was heard: "Traitor!" Herzl listened to a report of what had happened at the session, then he took the floor. His speech was not humble, but rather that of an admonishing father. He began by saying that he had looked upon the withdrawal from the Congress as a demonstration, and he had therefore been inclined to ignore the "Negatives" as he had ignored the withdrawal of the "Fraction" from the fifth Congress. "But then they came and told me: 'Those people outside are weeping!' Then I understood that you had not staged a demonstration, but that you had followed a spontaneous impulse, because you believed that the Basle Program had been violated. That is why I have come to you, in order to offer an explanation. The Basle Program remains integral and unaffected."

He then told them of his journeys to Constantinople. In 1901 he could have obtained the Charter if he had had enough money. But when he had asked in London for one and a half million pounds, they had sold shares for eighty thousand. "When one gives this sort of answer to this sort of appeal one ought to be more restrained in one's criticism than one customarily is in our organization. That is my situation. Money you do not give me. There remains diplomacy;

but in the last two days I have seen how you help me, how you support me in my diplomatic moves." He then spoke of the emergence and political significance of the British proposal, of the renewed hopes bound up with the prospect of Russian support, pointing toward Palestine still. For all that, the Congress ought not to turn down the investigation of the project: "Had you done that you would have placed me in a frightful position; no one would have negotiated with me again, seeing that I had not even influence enough to have the Congress look into my proposals seriously . . .

"And *I* am supposed to have violated the Basle Program? Never! Not I, but others have violated it a hundred times, when they formed themselves into separate groups with remote and irrelevant objectives. I have always stood, I still stand, upon the Basle Program; but I need your faith in me, not your distrust. And one thing more I must tell you: in this achievement which I have given to you I have always left a retreat open: the possibility of descending from the tribune at a moment's notice. You may drive me out if you wish; I shall return without complaint into the longed for tranquility of my private life. I have only one wish for you: may no one accuse you with justice of having misjudged my motives and rewarded me with ingratitude."*

These words of Herzl's, calm, impressive, self-controlled and controlling, did not fail of their effect. The next day, at a conference with representatives of the minority, a compromise was reached. The opposition reappeared in the

---

*Jabotinsky, who took down the speech verbatim and published it in *Die Welt* in 1914, added the observation: "With his first sentence I understood, from the expression which almost every face took on, from the extraordinary silence which fell immediately, the significance of that historic phrase of Lomonosov's, 'I can expel the Academy rather than it me.' "

Congress, and Shemarya Levin read forth a declaration to the effect that the withdrawal "had not been intended as a demonstration, but had been the spontaneous expression of a profound spiritual shock." Thereupon Herzl accepted, in the name of the Actions Committee, the resolution of the opposition that *shekel* funds, too, were not to be used to finance the expedition, and that the report of the expedition was to be submitted to the Greater Actions Committee before a new Congress could be called for the purpose of making the final decision.

Thus the last two days of the Congress passed off quietly. The remainder of the agenda was transacted without any incidents. One important step was the appointment of a Palestine investigation commission consisting of three members (Professor Warburg, Professor Oppenheimer and Dr. Soskin), with a definite budget of 15,000 francs. The re-election of Herzl as President of the Organization was carried with only three negative votes.

In his closing speech Herzl declared that the sixth Congress had been a hard but a great one. It had been made evident both in agreement and opposition that one could count on the Zionists. "But I must remind you that it is not always possible to follow an airline..." Nor did he believe that the masses must sink into deeper misery before they could become strongly Zionist. Strengthening them meant strengthening Zionism.

Then his speech took a familiar, an almost intimate note, and instead of the formal *Sie*, he used the closer form of address: *Ihr*. "And when it seemed to me, in one of those difficult moments which were not lacking, that all hope was lost of retaining an immediate or visible goal, that is, one which could be attained within our lifetime, then I wanted to come to your rescue in your sore need, and to lift up your hearts, which had been opened up to me, with a word in the language of our forefathers, a word which meant both encouragement and duty: '*Im eshkahech yerushalayim tishkah yemini. If I forget thee, O Jerusalem, may my right hand wither.*'" He uttered the words dolemnly, his right hand uplifted, as if he had himself fashioned the ancient oath on the spot. The Congress was swept by a storm of applause. "But," he continued, "when I was about to utter this comforting word, I found that you did not need it at all; for, as I have told you, a new prospect of help toward Palestine has been opened by the promise of help from the Russian government. There is no break then, no alteration, no defection from the Basle Program. But if I should need to offer you a guarantee then — this is perhaps the first occasion on which you will be able to accuse me of immodesty — I myself am the guarantee, I who worked for the formulation of the Basle Program . . .

"We have already put upon our program reforms which in certain other places are still in the realm of dreams; we have accepted the principle of freedom of conscience, equality of rights for women, cooperative union for the weak, and many other points. The Congress is our first national institution, and it is my desire that it shall remain our best, our highest and our noblest, until the day when we shall transfer it to the Land of our Fathers, which we do not need to investigate in order to love."

These were his words in public. But before his friends Zangwill, Nordau and Cowen, he drew the logical consequences of what he had observed, learned and felt. "I want to tell you now," he said to them in Cowen's room, and it was obvious that he was physically and spiritually exhausted, "what my speech before the seventh Congress is to be — if I live till then. By that time I shall have Palestine, or else I shall have recognized the complete futility of all further effort in that direction. In this latter case the summary of my speech will be: It was not possible. The ultimate goal has not been reached and cannot be reached within the calculable future. But we have a compromise achievement — this land in which our suffering masses can be settled on a national foundation with autonomous rights. I do not believe that for the sake of a beautiful dream or a legitimist flag we ought to withhold relief from the unfortunate. But I understand at the same time that this has brought a decisive split into our movement, and this division passes right through my person. Although I was originally a Jewish statist, no matter where, I did later on lift up the flag of Zion, and I myself became a lover of Zion. Palestine is the one land where our people can come to rest. But hundreds of thousands are waiting for immediate help. There is only one way of resolving this contradiction: I must resign the leadership. I will, if you so desire, conduct the next Congress; after that, elect two Actions Committees, one for East Africa and one for Palestine. I shall not stand for election in either. But whoever should devote himself to the work can always have my counsel for the asking. And my best wishes will always follow those who devote themselves to the fulfillment of that beautiful dream.

"That which I have done has not made Zionism poorer, but Jewry richer."

He worked on without a moment's respite. On his return from the Congress he visited once more the Grand Duke of Baden and gave him a two hour report. "We would be glad," he said, "to renounce the good land of East Africa for the poor land of Palestine. I in particular would see an honorable rescue for our poor Jews if this exchange could be made." It might be that the Kaiser, what with the favorable attitude taken up by France and England, would be ready to place himself again at the head of the movement. This suggestion did not elicit a response from the Grand Duke, but he declared himself ready to see to it that Herzl's Basle address, together with Plehve's letter and that of Sir Clement Hill, should be brought to the attention of the German government. Germany would be more inclined to associate herself with a diplomatic move on the part of Russia.

Sick, and troubled by the condition of his heart, Herzl returned to Altaussee. But he took no measures to guard his health. On September 5 he was already writing at length to von Plehve. The Congress, he said, had proved clearly the correctness of what he had told Plehve in Petersburg. "Emigration without return can only be directed to Palestine." Now his hopes were based on Russia's promised support in Constantinople; should these hopes be disappointed, he would lose his influence in the Zionist movement, and the revolutionary parties would triumph. He therefore proposed that the Czar send him a statement favoring Zionism which he could lay before the Sultan; at the same time the Russian ambassador in Constantinople was to be instructed to support Herzl's moves. Germany and England would associate themselves with these steps.

He wrote in similar vein to von Hartwig, the departmental head of the Russian Foreign Office, to General Kireyev, who had introduced him to von Hartwig, to the German ambassador Philip zu Eulenburg, to the Grand Duke of Baden, to Koerber, and to the Austrian Prime Minister, asking the last to help him with the Foreign Minister, Count Goluchovsky. He also began action leading, as he hoped, toward obtaining the agreement of the Pope to the Jewish colonization of Palestine through the extra-territorialization of the Holy Places. Thus he closed the circle of his diplomatic relations regarding Palestine, the acquisition of which seemed once more to move into the realm of the tangible future.

At the same time (September 15, 1903) he instructed Greenberg in England to strike while the iron was hot and to press for the East African Charter. But ten days later he wrote to Colonel Goldsmith asking him to see Carton de Wiart, his legal adviser in Cairo, who happened to be on a visit to London, and to discuss with him the possibility of raising again the El Arish project.

The East African prospect had taken a sharp turn for the worse since Herzl's last letter from the British government, dated August 14. To the obstructive resistance of the Russian Zionists, which had raised doubts in the mind of the British government as to the possibilities of success, was now added the opposition of the English colonists in East Africa. Already on August 28 the *Times* had published a telegram of protest from Nairobi, capital of Uganda, signed by Lord Demarest: the offer of such excellent land on the Uganda road, built with British money, to foreigners, was unjust to the British taxpayers and would lead to clashes with the natives. The influential publicist Lucien Wolf, too, wrote a letter to the *Times*, summarizing all the arguments of the assimilationist Jews against Herzl and the East African plan. Wolf was more English than Chamberlain, the founder of the plan, who at this time had withdrawn from the government the better to propagate his project of Imperial preference.

Sir Harry Johnston, who as African explorer and one-time commissioner for East Africa was a leading authority on the territory, expressed himself against the project in a letter to the *Times*, while showing himself not unsympathetic to the Palestinian aims of the Zionists. He repeated these views in an interview with the correspondent of the *London Jewish Chronicle*, and, like Lucien Wolf, pointed to the fiasco which Theodore Hertzka, the Viennese writer, had made of his utopia, "Freiland," in the same territory. Only twenty per cent of the area in question was suitable for colonization by whites. Lord Hindlip, who had only just returned from a journey to East Africa, supported this statement of Johnston's in an interview with the correspondent of the Reuter Telegraphic Agency. It was quite true, he admitted, that Sir Charles Eliot, the English High Commissioner, had asked for suitable settlers — from this and from sundry other utterances made public at that time it is possible to deduce the origin of the offer! — but it was no response to this request to send out unsuitable people who would afterwards have to be re-transported to their homes at the expense of the administration.

Thus the attitude of the English government became perceptibly cooler. Lord Lansdowne's advice to Greenberg was that Herzl ought to send an envoy to Sir Charles Eliot, the High Commissioner, to clarify the situation, for no progress was possible until his views had been definitely ascertained. At bottom this attitude on the part of the British government was not unwelcome to Herzl, and it was not without his own purpose that he republished in *Die Welt* all the antagonistic opinions expressed in England. Both orally and in his letters he told Greenberg, who visited him in Vienna at the beginning of October, that he "would gladly revert to the Sinai plan and would accept East Africa reluctantly only as a last resort." According to one of his letters, written on October 14, he was of the opinion that Lansdowne was only looking for a pretext; before he was permitted to use it, however, one should extract the maximum advantage from the situation. What he had in mind was to swing Lord Lansdowne toward the Sinai plan again, in exchange for the abandonment of East Africa. This would have a double advantage: Sinai was close to Palestine and could be made to evoke a great Jewish enthusiasm; what was equally important, the *ICA* had expressed itself in favor of this enterprise, at least in principle.

On the other hand, his first efforts to engage the interest of the *ICA* in the East African project had been without success. In reply to his inquiry, addressed in a circular to the members of the governing board, whether the *ICA* would meet the costs of the expedition to East Africa, for which the funds of the Zionist Organization were unavailable, he received the reply that the *ICA* could only offer its assistance when the project was of a purely philanthropic and not of a political character.

Herzl's English friends did not respond to his suggestions. Both Goldsmid and Greenberg informed him that Lord Cromer had, in view of the negative report of his experts, and of the general resistance to the project, sharply refused to reconsider the subject. As long as he governed Egypt there was nothing to be done. Moreover, this indecision between two plans would make a bad impression on the English as well as on other governments; the Foreign Office would drop both ideas and Herzl would fall between two stools. There was only one thing to be done — proceed with the East African plan, and as the next step send an envoy to

Sir Charles Eliot. Greenberg expressed himself ready to go. It was necessary, also, to proceed to the raising of the money for the expedition, and not less necessary for Herzl to issue a reply to the attacks. There had to be a clear, decisive policy.

This was the situation when Herzl received Ussishkin's fateful letter of protest. Menahem Ussishkin, born 1863, was of that group of Russian Zionists whose resolute unity had made such a deep impression on Herzl at the first Congress. He was one of the earliest members of the *Hibat Zion* movement, had already as a schoolboy belonged to the *Bilu*, later became a member of Ahad Ha-am's Order *B'nai Moshe*, and had remained one of the most active members of the Odessa Committee, whose President he later became, in 1906. At all times faithful to the religious tradition, he had, as an engineer, responded more to the practical than to the cultural aspect of the work. It was from this standpoint, too, that he judged Herzl.

Ussishkin had aligned himself with the new movement from the day when the propaganda began for the Zionist Congress; he had remained one of the most vigorous workers, and his district, Ekaterinoslav, was held up as the best example of Zionist organization in Russia. For all this, his attitude toward Herzl and his views had always been critical, and he was forever on the watch lest the latter divert the movement from its exclusively Palestinian character. He was forever pressing the importance of a strong line of practical work in Palestine. We have had occasion to note his opposition to the making out of the three letters of credit, at one million francs each, for deposit in various Turkish banks, in connection with Herzl's diplomatic activity in 1902. He was hard and obstinate in defense of his views, but at the same

time frank and devoid of subterfuge. Mendel the peasant, in
Herzl's *Altneuland*, a coarse but honest character with narrow nationalist views, is a rough portrait of Ussishkin. Had
he been present at the sixth Congress, the clash would probably have been a sharper one, but he would undoubtedly
have compelled a clearer decision.

As it happens, however, Ussishkin had left for Palestine
in June 1903, to make land purchases for the *Geulah* Committee, and at the same time to organize the *Yishub*. While
the sixth Congress assembled in Basle, Ussishkin assembled
in Zichron Ja'acob some sixty Hebrew teachers and seventy
delegates of the Jewish settlements, and laid before them
a plan of organization similar to that of the world Zionist
body, with elected representatives of the colonies and a
Greater and Smaller Actions Committee. The telegram of
greeting which Ussishkin sent from Zichron Ja'acob to the
Congress, and which Herzl read forth after the return of the
"Negatives," was only too significant an anticipation of the
future; for it had the character of a communication between
two powers; the assembled representatives of the Jewish
people within Palestine, and the assembled representatives
of the Jewish people in the lands of the dispersion. The
telegram was received with tumultuous applause by the
Congress, which did not notice, however, that Herzl's reply
was so worded as to restore the proportions: "The Zionist
Congress expresses its thanks to those brothers who are already settled in Palestine for their greeting, and hopes
that they will not long remain an isolated group in their
labor for the rehabilitation of the sacred soil of our forefathers."

Herzl's concern over Ussishkin's activity found clearer
expression in his letters to Levontin, the director of the

Anglo-Palestine Bank in Jaffa. There was some danger at that time (September 1903) that the Bank would be forbidden to operate; only the English consul could avert this danger, which Herzl attributed to the incautious public action of "Ussishkin and other unpolitically-minded *Hoveve Zion*." Herzl warned Levontin, Ussishkin and his friends to exercise the utmost care in avoiding acts which might be interpreted as provocative.

Ussishkin arrived in Odessa on October 4, filled with Palestinian impressions. In an interview which Benjamin published in *Die Welt* he expressed himself with extraordinary optimism regarding the situation in Palestine and its future. "If only the will were present," he said, much like Herzl in *Altneuland*, "our future would be assured." The practical work was to be pursued intensively; the Charter, he believed — in contrast to Herzl — was to be built "upward from below." He went on: "When we in Palestine shall have created a healthy Jewish core, we cannot fail to have the Charter, which we shall acquire by action from Palestine outward." It may easily be seen that the reports of the Uganda project, impinging on this mood of Ussishkin's, called forth an even more unfortunate reaction than might normally have been expected; equally comprehensible — and from his point of view justifiable — was his opposition.

What was wrong, however, was the way he set about it. Without advising either Herzl or the Vienna Actions Committee, he sent out to the Zionist press, with a request for the widest publicity, an open letter addressed "to the delegates to the sixth Zionist Congress." Therein he declared that he accepted his election to the Actions Committee, but regarded the principle resolution, authorizing the sending of an expedition to East Africa, as not binding upon him.

"I oppose this resolution with all my being, and I shall do everything in my power to prevent its execution. A Congress majority can be decisive in regard to any particular act or enterprise, but not in regard to the principle and the ideal. And even as all the majorities in the world cannot divert me from Israel's faith and Israel's Torah, so the majority of the Congress cannot divert me from *Eretz Israel;* for only those who have been dazzled by diplomacy and political fireworks have failed, in their simplicity, to observe that the resolution of the Zionist Congress to send an expedition to any other country is a renunciation of Palestine and a separation from it. You will learn shortly of my propaganda and activity in this cardinal question."

Ussishkin's letter came upon Herzl when he was confronting something more than a difficult political situation. Himself exhausted, physically and spiritually, he had been held in Altaussee by the all but mortal sickness of his wife, which lasted until October 24. This event, as well as his constant expenditures for the movement, had brought him into financial difficulties, and compelled him to sell five hundred shares of the Colonial Trust. On top of this there was an accumulation of disappointments with the inadequacy of human beings and the failure of hopes; he had planned the opening of a branch of the Colonial Trust in New York, hoping thereby to tap new sources, but it had come to nothing. Nervous and irritable, brooding day and night on methods of furthering the Zionist cause, he reacted to Ussishkin's letter in a burst of anger. Before leaving, on October 27, for Edlach, the little town to which he resorted with increasing frequency for rest and concentration, he wrote a sharp reply to Ussishkin's sharp challenge, and published the two in the October 30 issue of *Die Welt.* "Herr Ussishkin of Ekaterinoslav expresses an urgent wish to have the following declaration published. He will also be answered on the spot."

He began by censuring the breach of discipline. Together with the rights of a member of the Actions Committee, Ussishkin had also accepted the duties. "He can present his views in Committee, then submit to the will of the majority, as all of us have done. If he does not want to observe party discipline, and would rather go his own way, nobody will hold him back. But in such a case the proper thing is to resign." The violence of Ussishkin's action was not a new thing to Herzl; and if he singled out this occasion for vigorous counter-action it was because on this occasion Ussishkin had overreached himself and given aid and comfort to the enemy. He would only assume, for the honor of Ussishkin, that the latter did not know whom his attack was serving. "But nothing in the world gives him the right to assume that he is a better *Hovev Zion* than I and my friends." He had nothing to add on the subject itself to what he had said in Basle. Ussishkin's prejudice against "diplomacy and political activity" reminded him of the prejudice of certain worthy folk against educated people. "According to this the uneducated would be superior to the educated, and in a cause of a political character, which can be furthered only by political methods, how shall one proceed except diplomatically? On this point I simply do not understand Herr Ussishkin. Perhaps he will say: Acts, not words! And then with a magniloquent phrase he will point to his 'workers in Palestine,' to his 'activity on the hills of Judaea.' But let us take a closer look at these acts."

And Herzl — repeating what he had already written to Levontin — criticised sharply his opponent's activity in Palestine. By his "little secret gathering in Zichron Ja'acob," which had been pompously called a "Palestinian Congress," Ussishkin "had endangered, on his Palestine journey, those brothers who dwell in that country," and on this point Herzl did not wish to dwell. It was enough to repeat, for the benefit of the participants in that "so-called Congress," his earnest warnings against unreflecting action.

He then passed over to the question of land purchases in Palestine. This had its grave as well as its lighter side. The grave side consisted of the ancient error contained in the belief that one could acquire a land by the piecemeal purchase of lots. He had pointed out a thousand times that there was a vast difference between private and national acquisition, "and it is precisely this difference which constitutes the crux of our movement." If Ussishkin were to buy up every lot in Ekaterinoslav, the locality would still belong, politically, to the ruler of Russia, and Ussishkin could not undertake any enterprise which ran counter to the laws and decrees of the country, or even to the rules and regulations laid down by the governor and the chief of police. Admittedly, and as Ussishkin well knew he, Herzl, had supported the *Geulah* in its efforts to purchase land, but he had done this on the condition that such purchases were to take place in a quiet and orderly business atmosphere, which would not encourage land speculation, as would happen if emphasis were laid on the importance attached to these purchases. "What the extent of Herr Ussishkin's diplomatic ability is, I do not know, but I do know that he is a poor buyer. He is without question an honest man: even at this point, when I make such accusations, I do not for a moment challenge his honorable intentions. It only happens that he is unsuited for such enterprises, and if the *Geulah* still intends

to make land purchases in Palestine, it would do well to
entrust its orders to a man who is not quite so noisy and
obtrusive."

Then Herzl turned to the East African project and, without naming it specifically, alluded to it as a method of pressure for the acquisition of Palestine. He drew a parallel in
the private purchase of a house. In such a transaction he
would not make himself dependent on the whim of the seller;
should the latter show himself obdurate, the best procedure
would be to declare that one was giving up the idea of the
purchase; one was going to move into another neighborhood,
close at hand, or even at a distance. "And I would even
begin to conduct serious negotiations with such an end in
view, nor would I be deflected from my course if a few people,
less wise or more ill-intentioned, should rail at me." He could
not tell how the transaction would wind up, but he considered the conduct of it much cleverer than Ussishkin's; and
if Ussishkin knew of a quicker and more direct method of
acquiring Palestine for the Jews as a publicly recognized,
legally secured homeland, it was not at all nice of him, as a
good Zionist, to keep the information concealed from the
Jewish people. On the other hand, if he did not know of such
a method, "then it was up to him not to disturb, with his
empty phrases, the unity of Zionism, which was worth more
than a couple of lots in Palestine."

It can hardly be said that this rebuttal was either convincing at all points or worthy of the writer; intelligible as
Herzl's agitation was, it did not justify him in replying
harshly to a harsh attack. The cutting and condescending
tone of the reply cannot but recall Nordau's retort to Ahad
Ha-am. Had Herzl taken a lower flight, responded calmly
with a review of the objective factors, with an appeal to

Zionist discipline, he would have had opinion on his side. As it was, giving utterance to his personal irritability and to inner uncertainty — features which Zionists were not accustomed to in him — he awakened doubts in others as to his own conviction of rightness. To some, again, his open reference to the dangers of the Palestine conference smacked of denunciation to the authorities. And thus, in the storm of correspondence which ensued on the publication of Ussishkin's open letter and Herzl's rebuttal, the rift was widened. It became clear that Herzl had underestimated the significance of the attack, and that while many had disagreed with the form the attack had taken, they were in sympathy with its substance.

Within two weeks of the publication of the letter, Herzl, then in Edlach, drew up the outline of a "Letter to the Jewish People," the intention of which was to make public the utterances which he had permitted himself before the small group of friends at the close of the last Congress. But the tone of the outline is so much warmer than the reply to Ussishkin, the inner division is so much clearer, the love of his people so much deeper and more humble. "We have come," he says, "to the parting of the ways, and that parting passes through the personality of the leader. We must draw the logical consequences of this fact." Again he unfolds his view point, tells of his transformation from a Jewish statist to a Zionist. Palestine, which the Jews might have acquired in 1901 if they had heeded his cry, was now beyond their reach, as far as the tangible future was concerned. "Because you did not will it, it remains a legend, for this period." "But since we are together, we want at least to do something to meet our need, waken the people more, and strengthen those who are awake. But this can be done only if there is firm ground — land — under our feet." But he, as a *Hovev Zion*, could direct the movement in its East African enterprise only as long as all Zionists were decided in that sense. "But should a split come, my heart remains with the Zionists and my reason with the Africans. This is a conflict which I can resolve only by my withdrawal.

"I shall withdraw without any feeling of bitterness or discontent. It is true that I have often been attacked, but even my most implacable enemies cannot accuse me of having sought or obtained in the movement material advantage, and therefore I can put up calmly with their attacks.

"But as against this I can say that I have been richly rewarded in the love of my people, which has been granted me in a measure seldom achieved even by those who have had much more of a claim to it than I. It is a good people, but unfortunately an unhappy people. God help it on."

Herzl did not publish this letter; for shortly after he drew it up he received, in Vienna, the first excited and agitating reports of the Charkov Conference of the Russian Zionist leaders, from which it was clear that the split in the movement had gone deeper, and that the proud boast with which he had finished his unpublished letter was branded as a lie! The closing of the sixth Congress had been comparatively peaceful in externals only. Herzl's festive closing speech had not tranquilized the Russian Zionists, who were not content with his declaration that he would continue to work for Palestine, or would put Palestine in the first place. What they wanted was exclusive concentration on the historic fatherland, and every declaration in its favor which Herzl made only provoked them to remember his interest in other territorial projects. Distrust of him had, moreover, been strengthened by certain speeches which others had made, among them Zangwill, Greenberg, and certain of the German Zionists. It was reported that Herzl was at work on the preparation of the expedition: what was going to happen if its report was a favorable one?

There was also an older history of discord. For years the Russian members of the Actions Committee had objected to what they called Herzl's dictatorial direction of political action; in 1899, 1901 and finally in 1903, they had protested officially through the Actions Committee. At the Congresses, too, voices had been raised in regard to this point. Until then, however, such objection and protest had stayed within narrow limits because, as Tshlenov put it in a circular, "the uncontrolled will, the enthusiasm and the gifts of our leader were concentrated exclusively on the acquisition of a Charter for Palestine." But after the sixth Congress this feeling of certainty had been destroyed. "Incalculable danger now faces the Zionist movement," the circular proceeded. This was, with few exceptions, the dominant mood among the Russian members of the Actions Committee; and the mood was strengthened by Ussishkin's propaganda. At the Congress certain considerations connected with the hostile attitude of the Russian government to the Zionist movement — though internal Russian Zionist forces had something to do with it, too — had led to the formation of a Russian committee consisting of "Negatives"— Bernstein-Kohan, Tiomkin, Ussishkin and Victor Jacobson. The direction of the financial bureau, which controlled the *shekel* collections, had been taken from Herzl's friend, Professor Mandelstamm, of Kiev, and transferred to Vilna. It was this new Russian committee which had called the conference in Charkov.

The outcome of the fiery debates which marked the Conference was that, in submitting the East African project to the Congress, Herzl had violated the Basle Program and that therefore "the activity of Dr. Herzl as President of the Actions Committee had violated the principle of cooperation with its members." The resolution then went on to disclaim responsibility on the part of the Russians for all actions entered upon by those following the East African line, and declared them justified in attacking all decisions taken by Dr. Herzl on questions which lay within the competence and jurisdiction of the Actions Committee.

Three men were chosen by the Charkov Conference to call upon Dr. Herzl and to acquaint him with its demands, if necessary in the form of an ultimatum. These demands fell into two sections. The first had to do with Herzl's attitude toward the Greater Actions Committee. Herzl was called upon to give up "his method of authoritarian decision" and to submit to the majority decisions of the Committee. He was to promise that in future he would submit every serious project to the Actions Committee, at least one month before its meeting. Further, the Smaller Actions Committee was in future to be responsible not to the Congress direct, as had been the case hitherto, but to the Greater Actions Committee.

More important still were the demands in connection with the East African project. Herzl was to promise "in writing . . . in the form of a letter or a protocol" that, "as President of the Actions Committee, he would not lay before the Congress any territorial projects other than those connected with Palestine or Syria;" further, "that he would drop the East African project completely, and take it off the agenda of the Zionist Congress." He was, moreover, to call a meeting of the Actions Committee, for the purpose of cancelling the authorization to send an expedition. This was not put directly. The form of the demand was, that the expedition was not to be sent until the Actions Committee had changed the statutes of the Bank which forbade the participation of that institution in any colonization activity outside of Palestine and Syria. Then followed a series of decisions (not formally passed) connected with practical work in Palestine, and the delimitation of Herzl's effective powers. Funds were no longer to be forwarded to Vienna. Propaganda was to be started throughout the Jewish world for the organization of the opposition. A separate Congress of the "Negatives" was to be convened. Public claim was to be made for the control of the financial institutions of the Zionist Organization, in case the latter became transformed into a territorialist organization. The claim was to be pressed, if necessary, before the English and Hague courts.

There cannot be any doubt that the demands of the Charkov Conference were dictated by grave concern for the welfare of the movement, and that these objective motives far outweighed whatever personal impulses may have moved some of the delegates. But just as little can it be doubted that, from the formal point of view, the resolutions represented usurpations of power, and that the conference was guilty of precisely those errors which it accused Herzl of committing. For it sought to impose the will of a minority on a majority, and trespassed upon the competence of the Congress to make its own decisions. If the participants were seriously inclined to believe that Herzl would yield to such demands, presented in such form — apart from the question whether he agreed with their contents — then they did not understand the man, his character, his pride and his feeling for authority. It would have meant, once and for all, the renunciation of his leadership. It was the most unskilful form in which the demands could possibly have been presented. True, the secessionists had declared that they would prefer not to launch a mass agitation against Herzl: but the hint conveyed by such a declaration was a greater blow to his dignity than a hundred public attacks. And again: if they were so profoundly concerned with the situation, and with the execution of their decisions, action had to be prompt. But private and personal reasons led to the loss of months, and it was not before December 31, 1903, that the delegation elected by the Charkov Conference, consisting of Professor Belkovsky, engineer Tiomkin and attorney S. Rosenbaum, arrived in Vienna. It could have spared itself the trouble, for it must have known in advance that it came in vain.

The resolutions of the Charkov Conference had not been passed unanimously. Professor Mandelstamm had accepted the invitation to the Conference, but only for the purpose, as he wrote Herzl, "of acting as a check on Orlando Furioso Ussishkin." He had left the Conference in protest. Jassinovsky, too, had not agreed with its decisions. From these, and from others, Herzl received, shortly after its close, detailed reports of the proceedings of the Conference.

To him it looked like rebellion and mutiny, motivated by "personal ambitions." His first reaction was to authorize the organization of an opposition to the opposition. He sent the reports he had received, without publishing them, to those Russian Zionists who were faithful to him, pointed to their infringement on the authority of the Congress, and asked for meetings of protest against the "disrupters of unity." He demanded that the *shekel* moneys be paid direct into the indicated offices of the Colonial Trust, so that they might not be used illegally for a fight against the Organization. "The Russian Zionists," he said in a letter, "have the opportunity of proving whether they want me to continue working for them. Should I fail to be vindicated in a striking fashion, I shall know what to do."

While all this was going forward, Herzl held a consultation with his envoy, Greenberg, who came to Vienna on December 5, on the subject of the line of activity to be pursued in England.

The latest negotiations between Greenberg and Chamberlain had brought to light the fact that in the territory which had been discussed by the latter, and in which, according to his statement, there was room for one and a half million Jews, concessions had already been granted to others, and that the extent of suitable land remaining was about as large as an English county. Since such a restricted area was, in Herzl's and Greenberg's view, useless for mass colonization, Sir Clement Hill proposed the Tanaland district; this was certainly large enough, but as Herzl established, unsuitable for white settlement. Herzl and the Smaller Actions Committee now had the definite feeling that the English government, strongly influenced by the opposition within the Zionist ranks, was in effect withdrawing the East African offer. Kokesch, a member of the Actions Committee, was so delighted by this turn of events — we may see from this how wide of the mark the Russians were in their distrust of the Palestine sentiment of Herzl and his followers — that he made a contribution to the Jewish National Fund to celebrate it! Herzl too was glad at the prospect of being able to withdraw from the East African affair without loss of prestige for himself and the Zionist Organization. He immediately instructed Greenberg to take up the suggestions he had made in October, and which had not been followed: i. e., Greenberg was, in view of the inadequacy of the British African offer, to press once more for Sinai and El Arish. Only if this led to no results, was he to follow up the East African project and ask for the allocation of a suitable territory, so that the expedition could investigate this without having to cover all of British East Africa.

As soon as Greenberg left Vienna, Herzl took up once more his diplomatic work for Palestine. On December 11 he asked for an interview with the Austrian Foreign Minister, Goluchovsky. On the same day he wrote again to von Plehve, repeating his request that the Russian ambassador in Constantinople be directed to give his support to the Zionist demands. He admitted, in his letter, that he did not believe that such steps would be successful; what would be of significance, however, would be an open declaration of attitude on the part of the Czar. Two weeks later he wrote to the Russian ambassador in Constantinople, quoting von Plehve's reply to himself. Meanwhile he pursued his efforts to open a branch of the Jewish Colonial Trust in St. Petersburg, where Dr. Katzenelson, his envoy, was received in friendly fashion by von Plehve. He also informed von Plehve of rumors which were current abroad concerning impending pogroms against the Jews. Herzl gave these rumors wider currency in the English and American press in the hope of heading off the actual events. He also maintained his contact with the Grand Duke of Baden, whom he advised of the favorable action of Russia in Constantinople. He also renewed his correspondence with Izzet Bey — and in a private letter promised him ten thousand pounds after the signing of the Charter.

So strong was the impression which Herzl's distaste for the East African project had made on Greenberg, that shortly after his return to London the latter advised Herzl to make public his attitude, and to renounce East Africa finally. The method was to be the writing of a letter to Sir Francis Montefiore, which was to be given to the press. Greenberg made a draft of the letter, in which the Zionist leader was to make his acceptance of East Africa dependent on the fulfilment of four conditions, reasonable enough in themselves, but by now obviously beyond anything that the British government contemplated. Herzl refused to make public such a letter. He remained firm in his view that the Foreign Office had either to withdraw the offer or make a satisfactory substitute offer. Moreover, it seemed at this moment to Herzl that the situation in Constantinople was more favorable than ever before. Russia had promised its support, Plehve had called Dr. Katzenelson to St. Petersburg. In England Lord Percy, Under-Secretary in the Colonial Office, seemed to be interested in Palestine. From Italy, Margulies, the Chief Rabbi of Florence, reported that the King had expressed himself as ready to grant an audience to Herzl. In Vienna, the Turkish military attaché, General Shukri Pasha, had promised to write to his father, the Turkish War Minister, that the obstacles in foreign countries had been overcome.

This was the situation when Herzl learned of the attempted assassination of Max Nordau. On the evening of December 19, at a Hanukkah ball arranged by the Paris Zionist society *Mevaseret Zion*, a twenty-seven year old student, Chaim Zelig Louban, approached Nordau, cried out "Death to Nordau, the East African" and fired two shots, at almost point blank range. The shots missed. A bystander was wounded in the leg. A panic ensued, in the midst of which Nordau alone remained calm.

The next morning the papers reported the attempt on the life of the famous writer. It was soon established that the attacker was mentally unbalanced, but the attempt served to show how far-reaching had been the effects of the anti-African agitation. "Yesterday evening," wrote Nordau to Herzl, "I got an instalment on the debt of gratitude which the Jewish people owes me for my selfless labors on its behalf. I say this without bitterness, only in sorrow. How unhappy is our people, to be able to produce such deeds."

The moment he received the news of the attempted assassination, and before Nordau's letter reached him, Herzl telegraphed Greenberg (December 20, 1903) to make use of the proposed letter to Sir Francis Montefiore — but to emphasize its original date (December 14) lest the impression be created that he was yielding on the African project under the influence of the attempt on Nordau's life. But now Greenberg counselled against making the letter public; for in the interim he had stated to the Foreign Office that Herzl was expecting the fulfilment of the promises made in Sir Clement Hill's letter, or else the withdrawal of the offer and the substitution of another. Herzl's public renunciation of the East African offer would look like double-dealing. There was an exchange of telegrams between Herzl and Greenberg, the upshot of which was that Greenberg made the letter public in imperfectly edited form: in principle the original content remained, but the conclusion that Herzl was giving up the African project was omitted. At first Herzl was furious and threatened to publish the letter in its original formulation in *Die Welt*. In his final declaration, however, he merely insisted once again that Greenberg press with the utmost energy for the substitution of territories — Sinai in place of East Africa. Then, in the December 25 issue of *Die Welt*, which took on the character of a general assault on the opposition, Herzl published, not the edited letter to Montefiore, but a speech of Greenberg's delivered on December 14, which gave the substance of the letter, almost word for word, but as Greenberg's point of view, advising the surrender of the project. At the same time Herzl sent out a confidential circular to all the members of the Greater Actions Committee acknowledging the collapse of the British offer.

These actions were designed to prove, at this point, that the opposition had no objective basis, and that the East African project had been only a pretext concealing the operation of personal motives. "The Gasters, Ussishkins, Jacobsons, Bernstein-Kohans, etc.," wrote Herzl to Nordau, "saw in it the instrument for ridding themselves of us. Poor devils! They do not know how willingly we two would have gone away. Not now, of course. If there is shooting, we remain where we are. And if a shot is aimed at you, there's a bullet for me too . . . It would be hard to show a direct connection, but in my opinion Louban's revolver was loaded in Russia. The ultimatum which was delivered against me in Charkov cocked the pistol."

A tone at once more cautious and more biting characterized Dr. Werner's leading article, which Herzl published in *Die Welt*, under date of December 25. The shot itself, wrote Dr. Werner, may have been fired by a half-demented person, who was therefore only partly responsible for his act. No such mitigating observation could be made concerning the unscrupulous agitation which had heated his faith in the ideal to the point of fanaticism, and thus made him capable of any sort of action. "These people have assumed a frightful responsibility, and have inflicted untold harm on Zionism. Woe to us if we do not at once expel such friends of the movement, woe to the future of our people if such incompetents as the inciters of this fanaticism can exercise even the slightest influence upon our masses!"

Side by side with the report of the attempted assassination Herzl published in *Die Welt* an account of the Charkov Conference, together with a declaration by a number of Congress delegates of Vienna calling upon those men who had voted for the ultimatum at Charkov to surrender their mandates. In a subsequent issue appeared a digest of the minutes of the Conference.

A storm of indignation passed through the Zionist world against the "conspirators," "traitors" and "destroyers of unity." In England and in Russia there sprang up "Committees for the Defense of the Congress," or of the Organization. Protests and expressions of confidence poured in from every side, and the Zionist press was shaken by an indescribable excitement. It seemed now that the Organization was about to split, with the larger half opposed to the Charkov group. At the beginning of all this excitement, a week after the publication of the reports, the Charkov deputation finally arrived in Vienna. Herzl hesitated to receive it under its own designation; there was no such thing as a Russian Actions Committee, and he could not recognize a delegation from a non-existent body. However, he invited the individuals in their capacity as members of the Greater Actions Committee to visit him privately and to attend a session of the Smaller Actions Committee "after it had been officially established that they neither came as delegates nor had an ultimatum to deliver," as he wrote in a letter to Pasmanik.

The private negotiations and the agitated discussions in the Actions Committee gave Herzl a deeper insight into the motives and purposes of the opposition, but neither side managed to convince the other. The deputation turned home with nothing accomplished. Herzl, formally victorious, remained in Vienna, embittered. "The God of Israel protect me from ever becoming dependent on the movement," he wrote to Wolffsohn, who was forever trying to detach Herzl from the *Neue Freie Presse* and have him devote himself exclusively to Zionism. "The idea fills me with an insuperable disgust, and if I had not had this disgust hitherto, one look at the Charkov delegation would have taught me what people I am dealing with. I kicked them out with superb politeness ..." The struggle continued, furious and personal on both sides.

But, just as in the Congress debates, Herzl himself did not take a personal part in these polemics, in which the official party organ continued to publish the statements of the opposition. His situation was becoming increasingly desperate. Glad as he would have been to dissociate himself now from the project which threatened to break the organization he had created with so much labor, he could not renounce it without creating the impression that he was capitulating to the rebels. His friends in Vienna, Nordau in Paris, counselled him repeatedly to publish the statement that the negotiations had collapsed, and thus to prevent a split which would make it impossible for either half of the movement to exist separately. Greenberg, who had continued the negotiations with the British government — without, however, sending in clear reports — declared that the confidential circular sent out to the Actions Committee on December 27 was based on a misunderstanding, asked for

its withdrawal and demanded a definite and consistent policy. Cowen, for his part an opponent of the East African
plan, was irritated by Herzl's partiality for the Russians;
even more irritated was Zangwill, who was gradually becoming an out and out territorialist. On top of these internal
difficulties came a report from Constantinople that the Russian ambassador, requested by his government to support
the Zionist program, had declared such action to be difficult
and hopeless, and had therefore not undertaken it. Herzl
refused to be discouraged. He worked, worked, worked
daily to the point of exhaustion, always looking for new
approaches, disregarding his deteriorating physical condition. "My sleep is becoming steadily worse," is the only
observation he makes on this point in his diary.

On January 19 he set out for Italy, remained in Venice
for one day, and continued to Rome. On January 22 he was
received by Merry del Val, the Papal Secretary, and on
January 25 by the Pope himself, who accorded him a lengthy
audience. The outcome of these negotiations was that Merry
del Val promised to take under consideration the matter of
supporting the Zionist aspirations.* The saintly Pius X,
who some six months before had succeeded the combative
Leo XIII, declared that he could not support the return of
the infidel Jews to the Holy Land. "If you come to Palestine
and settle your people there, we want to have churches and
priests ready to baptize all of you."

---

*A few weeks later York-Steiner succeeded in obtaining from the Papal Secretary
of State the promise that the Apostolic See would place no obstacles in the way
of the colonization of Palestine, which he regarded as a humanitarian work.

Between these two audiences there was a one hour reception by the Italian King. Victor Emanuel III showed, during a very lively and informal conversation, that he had a serious interest in Zionism and much sympathy for its leader, whose *Altneuland* he asked to have sent him. The decision as to what measure of political support Italy could offer in Constantinople he left to his Foreign Minister, Tittoni. The latter, having been thoroughly informed on the subject by his monarch, asked for a memorandum (which Herzl forwarded later from Vienna), declined to take active measures, but promised to write the Italian ambassador in Constantinople to associate himself with the steps taken by Russia. But in view of the reply which the Russian ambassador had returned to his own government, this meant very little.

On January 27, a day after his interview with Tittoni, Herzl received Greenberg's telegram to the effect that the British government, with which he had continued to negotiate, had now made a definitive offer. Shortly thereon followed a letter with the details. The new territory, in Nandi, was even better than that which had been offered at first, and was well adapted to mass settlement. It did not lie on the road, but in one place was only five miles off. Greenberg advised immediate acceptance and the sending of an expedition before anything intervened. The colonization was, he suggested, to be carried out by a company specially founded for that purpose; in this wise the Zionist Organization would be relieved of the burden.

To Herzl this offer came as something unwelcome. On February 3 he telegraphed back that he could take up the proposal only after the most careful investigation. In a letter which he wrote to Greenberg, but which has not survived, he seems to have reproached the latter with not having directed the negotiations toward the Sinai Peninsula, for a letter of Greenberg's, dated February 8, explains in detail that no other policy had been open to him than the one he had followed. Then, on February 9, Greenberg cabled Herzl to accept without delay; a governmental change was impending, and without an immediate acceptance all might be lost. Under this pressure Herzl cabled back the demanded consent. But on the following day he cabled Greenberg again to undertake nothing until he received his, Herzl's, written instructions. However, on the night of the ninth Greenberg had signified the acceptance in principle to the Foreign Office.

And thus Herzl, who had begun to hope that he could use the East African project merely as a political counter, found himself chained to it as a political reality. His friends in London urged the immediate organization of the expedition and the recall of the misleading circular according to which the British government had withdrawn its East African offer; in the Zionist world the struggle round the question continued; within the Smaller Actions Committee, before which Herzl laid the plan on February 10, after his cable of consent to Greenberg, opinion was divided as to whether the project accorded, in principle, with the one which Herzl had submitted to the Congress, and whether Herzl was therefore justified in having accepted it. The cleavage of which he had said, two months before, that it passed through his person, became deeper and deeper. Was he to see his creation crumbling, out of the pride which held him back from meeting the opposition half way? During these weeks a frightful struggle must have taken place in him. He knew that the stretch of life lying before him was not a long one: was he to end up as one who had destroyed his own achievement, that Jewish cause to which he had dedicated his life ever since the day of his awakening? York-Steiner, like others who visited Herzl about that time, was startled by the change which had taken place in him during those painful months, and particularly since his Italian journey. "The imposing figure," writes Steiner, "now stooped, the face was sallow, the eyes, those mirrors of a fine soul, were darkened, the mouth was drawn in pain and marked by passion." Thus, almost on the brink of the grave, he decided to rescue his work before it was too late, and to hold out the hand of understanding and reconciliation to his opponents. Toward the end of February he called the Greater Actions Committee to Vienna for April 11, 1904.

"I have undertaken," began his opening address, "to bring you a word of peace. I know what distress and anxiety reigns among the masses of our fine, good, faithful Zionists throughout the whole world, and particularly in Russia; I know with what concern they follow these negotiations, how profoundly they fear that these beginnings of a national organization, brought about with so much labor for the benefit of the national cause, may suffer injury. As far as I am concerned, I am without obstinacy; I pass the sponge across whatever has been said against me personally, and will say not another word about it. But I am aroused when it is a question of safeguarding our organization, completing our work, guarding our unity and fulfilling the obligations to which we pledged ourselves in accepting our mandates to the Congress." He then recapitulated the events during and after the Congress, alluded to the undecided attitude of some of the leaders, and reminded his audience that he had submitted to the Actions Committee the question whether he ought to put the East African question before the Congress. "My personal point of view was and is that we have not the right simply to reject such a proposal, fling it back without even asking the people whether they want it or not. I do not want to use the much debated word 'Night Refuge' in describing the English offer, but say rather: 'Here is a piece of bread.' I, who perhaps have cake to eat, and in any case can always have a piece of bread, have not the right to reject the piece of bread which is being offered to the poor because I don't need or want it. Perhaps I personally can be moved to great enthusiam by the fact that there are some people who, in the midst of their need and hunger, are strong enough in their idealism to say: 'No, we don't want that bread.' But I am obligated at least to transmit the offer to the people. That is my conviction."

He admitted that the existence of an opposition at the Congress, and even its secession, had not made too deep an impression on him, "for, gentlemen, here in Vienna I tore myself loose one day from that which had been my life till then, from my friends and acquaintances, and devoted myself to that which I considered right. I do not feel the need of a majority. What I do need is that I shall be at one with my own convictions. Then I am content, though not even a dog will take a piece of bread from my hand." What had shaken him, however, and filled him with consternation, was the belief that he had given up Palestine. That was why he had gone to the "Negatives" and spoken with them as with brothers whose sorrows were his own. And again in his closing address to the Congress he had pointed out that the vote was not on the acceptance of the project, but on the sending of the expedition. "In this confidence, which I reposed in my colleagues, I was sorely disappointed."

At the same time he could declare that the Actions Committee had done all that was possible for Palestine. Only a few weeks before this session he had sent Levontin and Dr. Kahn to Izzet Bey, though their negotiations had not borne fruit. His passion for Palestine needed no one's admonition. "But there is another passion which moves us, and that is, to sustain, if at all possible, without surrender of principle or neglect of our duty, the unity of our organization." A condition antecedent to such unity was that the opposition accept as binding upon itself the decisions of the Congress. He closed with a reference to Solomon's judgment in the case of the rival mother claimants. "The one who was prepared to cut the baby in two was not the real mother."

The debate, agitated and vigorous, lasted two whole days, covering all the practical and theoretical aspects of the case. There were sharp attacks, bitter reproaches. Herzl answered with immeasurable patience. "I am stronger than you," he said, "and therefore I am conciliatory." He closed with a long address on the evening of April 12. He dealt with the objections of his opponents and once again condemned the Charkov Conference. Against attacks made with loyal intent he had no objection. At the Congress, he promised, he would exercise no pressure in favor of East Africa; he only wanted the objective judgment of the people on the basis of the facts.

"We want the continuous growth of Zionism, we want Zionism as the representative of the people. Why do we want this? Because we believe that we cannot achieve our goal without great forces, and these great forces are not to be found in a federation of little societies. Such a federation you had twenty years ago, and you are always telling me that you were already Zionists twenty and twenty-five years ago. You are always throwing that up to me. But what do you prove thereby? What could you achieve as long as you did not have political Zionism? You lived in little groups and collected money. Undoubtedly your intentions were magnificent, your idealism unchallengeable. Nevertheless you could not achieve anything because you did not know the path to the objective. This path is the organization of the people, and its organ is the Congress. That is why you must submit to the Congress, even though you may be utterly dissatisfied with its decisions."

He would not, he said, go to East Africa, even though the suspicion had been voiced that he wanted to be viceroy of Uganda. He had exerted himself in favor of Palestine among all the leading states. Even so, no one could accuse him of being unfaithful to Palestine if he did choose to go to Uganda. "It was as a Jewish statist that I presented myself to you. I gave you my card, and there the words were printed: 'Herzl, Jewish Statist.' In the course of time I learned a great deal. First and foremost, I learned to know Jews, and that was sometimes even a pleasure. But above all, I learned to understand that we shall find the solution of our problem only in Palestine . . . If today I say to you, 'I became a Zionist, and have remained one, and all my efforts are directed toward Palestine,' you have every reason in the world to believe me . . ."

He closed: "Gentlemen, I have certain things to forgive you, for in certain matters pertaining to me you are to blame. But let me pass over that. I ask nothing more than that you do your duty as organized Zionists, without doing violence to your convictions. Fight as much as you like, think of every device which may obtain for you a majority at the Congress, but do not do it with the help of the instruments of the movement; do it in your personal capacities. If you should create a majority of votes, a party, against me, I would certainly be grateful, but only on condition that you really do get a majority. I counsel you: submit to the Congress decisions, as the rest of us have to do. Until now I have not conducted a fight against you. If you should leave this session of the Actions Committee and agitate against the Congress, then I shall carry on an agitation against you, and I promise you that you will be defeated. Please believe me that this effort at reconciliation, the trouble I have taken, the words I have uttered not altogether consonant with my dignity, do not indicate that I am in any way afraid of the struggle. We have a tremendous majority on our side. But what I want is that you shall be able to come home and say to your people: We have received reassuring declarations, we know that the Executive in Vienna is working, and we know what the leader wants. Do not fix your eyes on an uncompleted house, just begun; wait till it is ready, and put your confidence in those men whom you have trusted till now and who have done nothing to lose your confidence."

These efforts of Herzl's, together with the will to an understanding which existed among elements in both camps, were crowned with success. The following resolution was adopted almost unanimously: "The Greater Actions Committee notes with satisfaction the continuous labors of the Smaller Actions Committee on behalf of Palestine. The Greater Actions Committee assumes that the Actions Committee will concern itself with the task of sending an expedition to East Africa, in the spirit of the resolution of the sixth Congress. Inasmuch, however, as the question of the colonization of East Africa is still to be decided at the seventh Congress, this, like all other pending questions, remains open to free discussion."

The resolution went on to state that a thorough discussion and clarification had taken place of the misunderstandings which had arisen in the preceding months as the result of the too fiery debates, and which had been harmful to the work of the movement. Further, it was agreed that all suggestions emanating from the Russian membership of the Actions Committee, and not related to the East African project, were to be considered and weighed by the Actions Committee. An amendment brought in by the Smaller Actions Committee was directed against the continuation of personal attacks in the discussion of the East African project. The remainder of the session was devoted to practical Palestinian questions, and Herzl took a leading part in urging the erection of a model farm on the principles formulated by Franz Oppenheimer. Tshlenov, the leader of the opposition, had the closing word in the sessions: "I am happy," he said, "to have been convinced by the declarations of Dr. Herzl, that the Actions Committee and its chairman are making every effort to further the work in Palestine programmatically, energetically and wisely. We can now return calmly to our homes, to take up the task with renewed spirit." Complete clarification, said the speaker, had not yet been achieved, but he hoped that it would be by the next session. He then moved a resolution of complete confidence in the Smaller Actions Committee.

Herzl closed the session and thanked the participants, not in his own name nor in that of the Smaller Actions Committee, but in that of the movement. "I hope that at our next meeting," he said, "I shall be able to inform you of gladdening progress in our movement."

This reconciliation conference was Herzl's last great achievement, humanly speaking perhaps the greatest of his life. But it may well be said that it also finished him. Before the opening of the sessions his appearance had terrified his friends. With that energy which was peculiar to him, he had managed to pull himself together, so that few of the participants knew how matters stood with him, and to what extent the negotiations were exhausting him and using him up. When the sessions closed he went on ignoring his own exhaustion. He made preparations to proceed early in May to Paris and London in order to arrange the financing of the expedition. To this end he made contact with the New York financier, Jacob Schiff. On April 30 he had a long interview with Goluchovsky, the Foreign Minister, who had given evidence of an earnest interest in Zionism and who advised Herzl to work in England for a Parliamentary expression of opinion in favor of Palestine. A second meeting between the two men was agreed upon.

That meeting was never to come about, nor was Herzl ever again to visit Paris. Immediately after this audience a consultation of his doctors established that an alarming change for the worse had occurred in the condition of his heart muscles, and he was ordered to Franzensbad for a six weeks' cure. To his mother, from whom he had always concealed the gravity of his condition, he wrote harmless letters, saying that he already felt much better, and that he was enjoying deep, unworried rest, and even boredom. He wanted to be free, he said, for some time at least, from kings, popes, ministers, politics and newspapers. But his letter to Wolffsohn, dated May 6, reads in part: "I am taking the heart cure here. My mother knows nothing about it, she thinks I'm only here for a rest." Then immediately follows the queer sentence: "Don't do anything foolish while I'm dead." Three days later, on May 9, he said to Katzenelson, after a severe heart attack: "Why should we fool ourselves? The bell has rung for me. I am no coward and can face death calmly, all the more . . . as I have not spent the last years of my life uselessly. I was not altogether a poor servant of my people, don't you think?" Then, as Katzenelson tried to change the subject, he added: "There's no time left for joking, it's in deadly earnest now."

Katzenelson discussed with Herzl the results of his trip to London. Schiff had declared himself ready to negotiate a loan for Russia if the latter proved ready to do something for the Jews. Now Katzenelson was to place the proposition before von Plehve in Herzl's name, and leave for Petersburg the next morning. At five-thirty the next morning Herzl met him, by appointment, at the spring; he brought with him a heavy manuscript, the memorandum for Katzenelson's journey. He had sat all night at his writing desk. "Is this how you expect to restore your health?" asked Katzenelson, reproachfully. "Yes, yes, my friend," answered Herzl. "You saw yesterday that there is no time to lose. The last weeks — or days. We must hurry . . ." Nor was this the only piece of work he did. He wrote numerous letters to friends and to political personalities in Italy, Vienna, Russia. His diary breaks off with a report to Jacob Schiff on May 16.

The cure in Franzensbad did him no good; his condition grew worse. He returned to Vienna, but a rest at home brought no improvement either. On June 3 he left with his wife and Kremenezky for Edlach, on the Semmering. He knew that this was his last journey. On top of a heap of correspondence on his writing desk he spread, before his depar-

ture, a sheet of paper on which he had written, in English:
"In the midst of life there is death."

For all that, his condition seemed to take a turn for the
better as a result of the devoted ministrations of his wife.
Those about him, and he himself, too, began to hope. Then,
suddenly, there were grave symptoms of irregularity in the
heart functions, accompanied by a painful shortage of breath.
Again his body fought its way through; he was even able to
get on his feet and take a walk in the garden. As late as
June 30 he had a telegram sent to Gustav G. Cohen, in
Hamburg, advising him that he had decided to make a visit
to the cure resort of Blankensee, on the North Sea. His
friends in Vienna were expecting him the next day. Then,
about noon, Oscar Marmorek received a telegram asking him
to proceed to Edlach with two doctors; Herzl had suffered
a severe setback as the result of a bad coughing fit. The
consultation, held by Drs. Konried, Bondi — the family doctor — and Gustav Singer, established the fact that bronchial
catarrh had set in. He had a bad night, with high temper-
ature and shortage of breath. Herzl had often meditated
on death; he had written about it in countless feuilletons, in
Altneuland and in his diaries. He had often discussed it
with his friends, and had pictured it as a gentle, gradual
decline into unconsciousness. "I always believed," he said,
"that I knew what terror and horror can be. But everything
that exists, and everything we can conjure up, is as child's
play by comparison with the worst horror of all, with the
fight for breath." Exhausted by the frightful fits of coughing
and spitting of blood, he sank now and then into a half hour
of troubled sleep. Once he sat up suddenly, stared before him
with wide-open eyes, his body rigid; he struck the bedcover
with his right hand, as if he were swinging the gavel at a

Congress, and called in a ringing voice: "Ad loca! Ad loca!"

On Saturday morning he began to urge that they call his mother, who had been kept in ignorance of his condition, and his younger children. His oldest daughter, Pauline, had been with him in Edlach for some weeks. To the faithful Hechler, his prophet, aid and friend, who was permitted to visit him, he said: "Give them all my greetings, and tell them that I have given my heart's blood for my people." As the afternoon deepened into evening he became more and more excited; he begged repeatedly to have his mother and children brought to him at once on their arrival. "Yes, dear Reich," he said to the secretary of the Congress office. "Soon you will have a great piece of work. Soon you will have to call a Congress together."

By Sunday morning, July 3, his condition had become worse. Pneumonia had set in on the left side, his heart had weakened, there were signs of approaching exhaustion. He kept imploring those about him to keep him alive until he could see his mother again. Once he sat up with an imperial gesture on his disordered bed, pointed proudly to the students who were on guard in his room and said to Dr. Singer, in a solemn tone of voice: "They are good, splendid men, my folk-brothers! You will see! They will settle in their homeland."

Finally, at midday, his mother arrived. Herzl, whom Dr. Werner had observed only a few minutes before in a condition bordering on collapse, sat up straight when she entered, his eyes wide open. He held out his hand to her, and said, in a calm tone of voice: "It's nice, dear mother, to have you here. You're looking well. I'm not looking so well, but that'll soon be over." He kissed his mother who, controlling herself, uttered some words of encouragement. When the two younger children, Hans and Trude, came in, he was almost cheerful. After a few minutes he sent mother and children out, and sank back, exhausted.

In the afternoon he felt better again. His wife spent some time with him, his mother could pay him a second visit, and he could receive his friends Marmorek and Kremenezky. Then he said, "And now, my dear friends, leave me." At five o'clock Dr. Werner, who had taken his eyes off the patient for a moment to prepare an injection, heard a deep sigh. As he whipped round he saw the head sink on the breast.

Herzl was dead.

CHAPTER XV

EPILOGUE

THE news of Herzl's death struck like a thunderbolt. It was known, indeed, that his health had been undermined; but there were very few who knew how serious his condition was, and those few fought until the last moment against the realization of the inevitable. For those who were not close to him the end came as a shattering surprise. His public bearing, which he had maintained until the last, had deceived everyone. Perhaps the struggle round the East African project would have lost some of its bitterness and acerbity if it had been known how it stood with him. "Unhappily," lamented Shemarya Levin at the great memorial meeting in Vienna, "the Jewish people learned too late of the sickness which had attacked the heart of its leader." The pain was now all the deeper. Among friends and leaders the first impulsive reaction was that an irreplaceable Zionist and human force had been extinguished, the force which had held them all together to a degree which none of them had understood till that moment.

Among the masses of East European Jewry the dread announcement had something of the effect of a new destruction of the temple. The repercussions rolled through the world. Telegrams and letters poured in by the hundred to the Actions Committee, to *Die Welt*, to the *Neue Freie Presse*, which

504

now at last permitted itself a couple of lines on his life's activity. These communications ranged all the way from simple condolences to long and detailed encomia. The general press, in all parts of the world, reported the event; the Jewish press, even in that part of it which had been hostile, praised his memory, and the Zionist press devoted its columns to the story of his life and achievements.

The funeral, which took place on Thursday, July 7, was an overwhelming expression of public sentiment. In his will, written in 1900, and again in his last testament, dated March 5, 1903, Herzl had expressed the wish "for a burial such as is customary among the poorest classes. No speeches, no flowers." He asked to be laid next to the metal coffin of his father, "and to remain there until the Jewish people shall transport my remains to Palestine." Thus, the funeral cortege was without adornment. Behind the simple hearse came the women of the family, in a carriage. All the other mourners and participants walked, in spite of the blazing heat. And what an extraordinary funeral train it was, moving from the house on the Haizingergasse to the Döblinger cemetery: leading figures from the literary world, men high in politics, Zionist deputations from Vienna, from all the towns and cities of Austria, and from all the countries of Europe. And behind these the countless masses of the unbidden, who came in no one's name, young and old, pietists and atheists, plain folk and "society." *Die Welt* reported the number at six thousand. Never before had a Jew been accompanied thus to his grave. It was as if the Jewish people had lost its father.

It needed his death to reveal to many what Herzl had been. They learned it from the emptiness created by his disappearance, and from the love and adoration which was manifested by the Jewish masses throughout the world. For it was the simple folk which had best understood him from the beginning. It had been won and held spellbound by something more than the touch of the exotic and mysterious in his outward being, by more than his bearing, his fascinating graciousness, the contrast of kingliness and modesty, of energy and softness; by more than the courage which he awakened, the sorrow which spoke from his dark Jewish eyes, the European perfection of dress and the black Assyrian beard, the frankness and clarity of his speech, which nevertheless left behind it an intimation of the mysterious, the simplicity of his words and the pathos which informed them. That something more which the masses felt at once was compounded of his love, his goodness, his unsleeping solicitude for his people, his self-sacrificing labors. All this was shot through, in the mass mind, with little characteristics illuminated by anecdotes, with the stories of his encounters with ministers and princes, so that there emerged, even during the lifetime of Herzl, a picture which lay beyond the truth. That picture was the mirror of the longing of the masses; they had transmuted Herzl into a king, a *Messiah ben David*, who was to lead them out of darkness and destitution and oppression into light and freedom, into the land of their dreams, the Land of Promise.

It was Herzl's opponent, Ahad Ha-am, who had seen most clearly this effect on the masses. During Herzl's lifetime he fought it; after Herzl's death he accepted its positive valuation. We see this in the third volume of his collected works, in which he had gathered his essays on Herzl, most of them hostile. He did not believe that Herzl's work would endure, he did not believe in the stability and success of Zionism as a political movement, he negated, now as before, Herzl's outlook. But he knew that Herzl had given the Jewish people something which transcended ideas and political achievement: his person had become a center of crystallization for the longings of the Jewish people. The significance of the instruments he had created — Congress, organization, Bank, National Fund — would be judged by the future. But his image was lodged for ever in the fantasy of his people, and there it would continue to grow until it became the perfect and stainless embodiment of the national longing for freedom and honor — an heroic figure pointing the way to liberation and rebirth.

Time fulfilled this prevision of Ahad Ha-am's. It was true that immediately after Herzl's death the philosophy of his opponents came to the fore within the organization, so that it seemed as though his lesson would be forgotten, and its place taken by a purely cultural theory of Zionism, or by the continuation of the Palestine work in the spirit of a preceding epoch. But his image grew swiftly in the heart of the people and assumed more than mortal proportions. The Jewish date of his death, the twentieth of Tammuz, became a national memorial day, and in the mind of his people a line ran straight back from this heroic figure to the far off time when the Jewish homeland still flourished: but the face was turned forward, in sign of the beginning of a new epoch in the people's history.

Slowly at first, but with increasing insistence as the development of the Jewish problem confirmed what Herzl had formulated and foretold, the lesson which he had taught sank home. Today all thinking minds recognize its prophetic clarity.

Thus the historian will finally associate himself with that popular judgment which was born more of instinct than of intellectual insight: with Herzl's emergence there actually begins a new epoch in the history of the Jewish people. Since the destruction of the second Jewish State there was no Jewish history in the real sense of that word. There were, it is true, great Jewish achievements in every walk of life; it is also true that in the centuries of their dispersion the Jews suffered untold persecution, and that they demonstrated their endurance as a people by evincing a faith in a future without which they would have been broken. But it was only with and through Herzl that the Jewish people entered again as an active factor into world history. From that moment on it was no longer content with the role of the passive endurer. Led by a minority which looked upon itself not as a party but as the vanguard, it began to shape its own life, and took its future into its own hands.

Only by means of this approach can it be fully understood why, at the very outset, Herzl posited the necessity of a specific Jewish policy. To him it expressed the rebirth of the Jewish people as a people, it was for him the condition precedent for the solution of the Jewish problem. Accepting this evaluation of the Jewish problem and its solution, he put himself in diametric opposition to his Jewish contemporaries and to the interpretation of history springing from the epoch of emancipation and assimilation. As one of those authentic historic figures through whom, in Hegel's phrase, the concealed spirit of history beats at the Present and seeks to break through, he initiated a new chapter in the history of the Jewish people, a chapter to which the immediate present still belongs.

Modern Jewish history begins with the French Revolution, as does the nineteenth century, within which modern Jewish history unfolds.

The great revolution of 1789 liberated the rising capitalist economy from the bonds of an outlived, semi-feudalistic epoch, lifted the individual out of the limitations of the guilds and crafts, and by the famous Declaration of the Rights of Man — itself an extension of the American Declaration of Independence — conferred upon him the rights of economic man, responsible for himself and his destiny. This system of liberal thought made the individual the basis of its ideology, and first principles were directed toward the maintenance of his freedom against the encroachment of the all-powerful force of the State. But the idea of the sovereignty of the people, and of representation, made a stronger bond than ever between the individual and the State; it filled him with the idea of civic liberty, and on the other hand identified him completely with the State's will to power and domination. Thus it was that under the very aegis of liberalism there grew up the essentially illiberal concept of the homogeneous National State, which could demand from its citizens something more than the fulfilment of their civic duties. This concept of right and law permitted the dominant people of the State to rob other folk-groups within the territory of their cultural independence, to demand their assimilation and amalgamation, using both force and the ostensibly peaceful instruments of a cultural policy, propaganda, language and schools.

Into this world the western Jews were ushered by the French Revolution, and behind them, at a considerable distance, the upper strata of eastern Jewry. Until then the Jews had lived in the ghetto, close-pressed within and despised without, but held together and fortified by religious tradition, folkways and an uninterrupted historic consciousness: a scattered people, but a people, a people of God.

This narrow but self-enclosed world, with its mixture of poverty-stricken reality and mystic hope, broke under the impact of the new idea. The Jews left the ghetto, and entered the surrounding world. This they did, however, not as a group, but solely as individuals; they were emancipated not as Jews, not as members of the Jewish people, but as "human beings." That term implied equality with the citizens of the nations in the midst of which they lived; they were to become similar to these citizens in all respects except their religious worship — itself a phenomenon often regarded with none too friendly eyes. According to the ancient legend it is the curse of the "eternal Jew" to be forced to wander eternally, without being able to die. This curse was, in both its aspects, to be lifted from the shoulders of the Jewish people by the emancipation. The Jew was to be made at home in the State in which he lived — but at the same time he was to die, or cease to exist, in his capacity as member of the Jewish people.

The Jews made the most strenuous efforts to fulfil this pact honestly. Simultaneously with their entry into the economic and civic order, they entered also into the cultural life of the surrounding people; with all their energies, and with an extraordinary degree of success, they participated in its development, and they lived themselves so thoroughly into it that they believed themselves to be completely at one with it. They did their best to forget their past as a unified people, and to forget with it all those hopes and dreams which until then had sustained them in suffering and persecution. The Jews, so they themselves declared and believed in increasing measure, were from now on no longer a people: what connected them with the Jews of other lands was their religion, a bond on no way different from the one between a

French and German or Italian Catholic. If the dispersion of the Jews had once been regarded as a divine punishment, it was now to be given an aim in the fulfilment of a "mission:" through them the Jewish lessons of humanity and justice were to be spread through the world. The establishment of these human ideals would lead to the final disappearance of the last differences dividing the nations, which would then be absorbed into a unified humanity.

But all these hopes and efforts did not yield the desired result: in the eyes of the surrounding world, at least, the Jews persisted as a recognizable and separate group, held together by closer bonds than those of a different religion. The surrounding world stood away from them, closed off the entry to its social ranks and higher administrative positions, and never permitted them to forget that they lived where they did because of a special indulgence, this despite all legal civic equality. Anti-Semitism provided a rationale for this instinctive aversion, a rationale which frequently destroyed itself by its own inner contradictions; it also organized the aversion, wherever it happened to be tacit and subdued, into a clamorous and brutal movement. In countries which harbored large Jewish masses it provoked outbursts of physical violence.

Anti-Semitism brought with it the utter disillusionment of the "emancipated." They had cut themselves loose from their own past and future; now they were being thrust violently and unintelligibly out of the new connections to which they had fastened all their hopes and beliefs. The reaction to these attacks was of various kinds. There were some who believed that it was necessary to carry their assimilation further, to emphasize and re-emphasize their patriotism, and to dissolve in the baptismal font their last link with their origins. Others founded defense organizations, protested, remonstrated, argued, proved — without ever penetrating with their arguments to anyone except those who had no need of them. And the majority hoped that the attacks were a transient phenomenon, and that anti-Semitism would soon disappear.

Herzl had passed through the process of assimilation. He too had suffered deeply from anti-Semitism in his youth; like most of his contemporaries he had hoped and believed that the phenomenon was transient, and that a kindlier and more humane era was at hand. His development, as we have sought to depict it in these pages, throws a clarifying light on the nature of that phenomenon; it condenses into the experience of a few years, almost in symbolic form, the efforts of three generations to vindicate their hope of an emancipation. The Dreyfus affair shattered that hope irreparably.

We must ask ourselves why it was precisely Herzl who was affected by it in this decisive manner. There were hundreds and thousands of Jews who followed the affair step by step, without being led to these radical conclusions. The answer is — the peculiar sensitivity of his nature, which distinguished him from his contemporaries. He sensed the coming convulsion, felt and recognized the subterranean forces at play which would someday break forth with volcanic fury. He understood in a flash which elements in the Jewish question were external and apparent, which were deeper and causal. And he gave utterance to this cognition in clear words of warning and admonition.

Yet Herzl in no wise denies the emancipation. Quite the contrary. As long as he lived he was aware of what he owed to it, and what the Jews owed to it. But he transvalued its historic significance. For him the emancipation is not what it is for the liberal Jews, the ultimate goal of development; it is only a transitional stage. Its historic purpose is to loosen the rigidity of Jewish life. Simultaneously with the precipitation of the Jewish problem in its modern form, it creates the preliminary conditions for its solution. By inducting the Jews into the modern world it has given them a new bearing, provided them with the courage and capacity for political action, instructed them in modern science and technology, and thus opened for them a larger prospect of laying new foundations for their continued existence as a people.

The emancipation had placed the Jews as individuals in a new environment, and at the same time had taken from them the support which they had possessed in previous ages of persecution, namely, their common life in the ghetto. Complete solution into the surrounding world was out of the question, in part because the nations would not permit it, and in part because great sections of the Jewish people were impelled by their unbroken folk-instinct to recoil from it. Legal recognition had been bestowed upon the Jews as human beings; the problem now was to attain recognition as Jews. The emancipation of the Jewish individual had to be followed by the legal recognition of the Jewish people, and the dispersion of the Jews among all the peoples by their new reconcentration. This was not to be done by a return to the ghetto, but, on the contrary, by transcending that "New Ghetto;" this was the significance of the ingathering of the people on its own territory, and the founding of a Jewish State. There all persecuted Jews, all Jews "who could not or would not" assimilate in their present places of residence, could find a real homeland, a life of freedom, labor and honor. There the

Jewish people could find renewal, and by the erection of a model state render greater service to mankind, fulfil a truer mission, than by its continued dispersion and assimilation.

These thoughts had, indeed, been expressed by many others before Herzl, and by some of them, as for instance Pinsker, in a form by no means inferior to his. But until Herzl's time there remained the intellectual property of scattered and circumscribed groups. Herzl's power of persuasion and will to action succeeded in conveying this perception to tens of thousands, transforming it thereby into an instrument for the realization of his political plans.

He believed at the outset that the Jewish people in its totality would endorse his plans enthusiastically. His disappointment in this belief was his first great disillusionment. What he found was hostility, and some small groups of powerless Zionist devotees, who shared his views, but in miniature, and without his courage. To these he imparted his own courage, his profound faith in the realization of his demands, his sense of certainty and his clear vision of objective and means. He gave them a program, he organized them: he created the Congress as the central organ of a new Jewish world policy, and the Zionist Organization as the embodiment of a people on the march; and he conceived the Bank as the instrument of power of the movement, the focalization of the one power which he thought the Jewish people then possessed, if it could only be concentrated and applied. These institutions proved to be more enduring than Ahad Ha-am, who did not understand their significance, foresaw.

It was the Congress which best fulfilled the task for which it was designed. It was for a long time the center of assembly for that section of the Jewish people which believed in a Zionist policy, in the policy of a national future in Palestine;

it united the Jewries of east and west on the platform of
Jewish national endeavor, and from it issued, in struggle
and cooperation, the slogans for the labors of the individual
groups. The idea of democratic representation and self-
determination spread from it to other Jewish institutions;
the free discussion of the condition and destiny of the Jewish
people penetrated into ever wider circles which opposed the
Zionist movement or endorsed it only in an attenuated form.

It was, as we have noted, only a small minority of the
Jewish people which at first did this work and responded to
these slogans, and not the people as a whole, to which Herzl
had confidently made his appeal. But national unity is
always created by minorities, all national movements are
borne by them; and how could it have been otherwise with
the Jewish people, which found and still finds itself in such
an abnormal situation? But this minority Herzl welded into
a firm, ever-expanding organization, which was free in the
election of its representatives and executive organs, and from
whose members he demanded the disciplined acceptance
of all its decisions.

The Jewish Colonial Trust, the Bank, into which Herzl
put so much effort, corresponded least to what he had desired
and previsioned: it did not become an instrument of power.
The fact that it did not do so, the fact that the financial
powers and the great funds held off from him, was the
greatest obstruction to his policy, and may even be said to
have taken away its foundation.

In order to acquire Palestine as the legally secured homeland of the Jewish people, two things were needed: the consent of the Powers and the consent of Turkey. It was an
altogether extraordinary achievement of Herzl's that he
should, in a brief period of eight years, have obtained the

consent of the more important Powers, and that he should have won for the Zionist Organization, which he had created out of a multitude of little groups and circles, the recognition of the political world as the representative of the Jewish people. He aimed at securing the consent of Turkey by financial aid. To this it might have been objected that he took too rationalistic a view of the rulers of that country and of their policies in assuming that they would sell to the Jews the land which was sacred to all religions and desired by all the States. It is impossible to determine the validity of this criticism, for the Jewish people did not place at Herzl's disposal the means which he demanded, and no man can go forth to do battle armed with the wooden sword of a Don Quixote. Herzl himself always insisted that in the spring of 1901 he could have obtained the Charter for Palestine in exchange for the moneys asked of him. The fact that he could not fulfil the expectations which were entertained in Constantinople doomed his subsequent negotiations to failure. Nothing remained after that but to wait for the dismemberment of the Turkish empire.

This, together with the impression created on him by the unfolding tragedy of Jewish need, moved him to accept a mediatory solution, the founding of a Jewish State, of an autonomous Jewish settlement, on some other territory. It was said of Herzl that it was his good fortune not to have known the Jewish people: this gave him the courage to act. It is probably true. But this ignorance was also his misfortune, since without it the Uganda conflict could never have arisen. For there cannot be any doubt that the Uganda policy was a misstep. Historically-rooted Jewry revolted against it. For the first time a large group of the most devoted Zionists refused to follow Herzl, and had adequate grounds for it. With this proposal he brought confusion into Zionist ranks; east and west, which he had brought together with so much labor, threatened to break away from each other; the discipline of the organization, which he deemed essential to its survival, threatened to disappear. For these developments, which grew out of the tragic coil of circumstance, and for which he was not to blame, he paid the penalty like the hero of some ancient tragedy.

And what irony of fate it was that precisely in connection with this misstep he should have attained his highest political triumph: England's recognition of the Jewish people and of its national aspiration. From this achievement he proceeded further, with Greenberg's help, to make connections with England's leading political figures. These connections were never completely severed, and they attained a significance which was hardly appreciated in later years. Balfour, who, as Foreign Minister, issued the famous Declaration in 1917, was Prime Minister when Herzl was negotiating with the British cabinet. Lloyd George, who was Prime Minister at the time of the issuance of the Balfour Declaration, was the lawyer who drew up the terms of the Charter for East Africa in 1903. There is a direct political line out of those early days to the upbuilding of the new Palestine "as the national homeland of the Jewish people."

In the *Judenstaat* and elsewhere, but particularly in *Altneuland*, Herzl gave utterance to ideas and projects which at many points took on astounding actuality in the light of the upbuilding of Palestine. He foresaw with the utmost clarity the difficulties which would be created by an immigration not backed by adequate preliminary political guarantees. He recognized the importance of the time element as a political factor, and wanted immigration and upbuilding to be carried through in the shortest possible period. He saw, similarly, that only by the exploitation of all the most modern technological resources could place and possibility be created for large settlements; he strove to apply great plans for systematic construction on an economic basis, directed by the Jews; he desired the maximum of social justice, he saw the national revival as a social revival, a blessing for the Land and beyond that for the world.

Herzl had the daring to make clear and open declaration of the political aim of the Zionist movement: the founding of the Jewish State. At the same time, Zionism was for him something more; he gave to it the name of "The Eternal Ideal;" even after the acquisition of Palestine it would not cease to be an ideal. "For in Zionism, as I understand it," he wrote three months before his death, in his introduction to a youth publication, "there is not only the striving for a legally secured soil for our poor people; there is the striving for moral and spiritual perfection." In this striving for moral and spiritual perfection he himself led the way.

His greatness as symbol and leader derives from the fact that he not only gave utterance to his perceptions, but gave himself utterly to the task of their realization. He devoted to it his private fortune, so that after his death David Wolff-sohn had to make a national appeal for a fund to provide for his family and pay for the education of his children. He gave to the last ounce of his strength — and beyond. "Why is it," he asked in an essay, shortly after he had made the great resolve, "why is it that the best must always fall? It is because they give to the last ounce of their strength — and beyond — that they are the best." Thus, though he was tied to his profession until the last, he grew out of himself as distinguished journalistic observer and commentator to become a monumental figure. The man of contemplation became the man of incredible will-power, and the great task burned away gradually the little human weaknesses and vanities, and in the end absorbed and transmuted all his ambition. "Poetry is the pictured experience of the individual," he wrote on the threshold of the fruitful Paris period during which he became what he was. "The power of imposing such an experience on others, so that they take it for their own — that power is called genius." In this sense Herzl was a genius. He was, however, more: an all-human exemplar, tied down to no party, not to be monopolized by a party, towering above all and leading the way for all. He raised aloft the banner of his people and carried it in the van, a servant of the light whose flames in the end consumed him.

Deep spiritual suffering gave birth to his perceptions and provided him with the strength to turn them into realities. As a man of belief, convinced of the significance of all human events, he likewise perceived in the suffering of the Jewish people a source of strength which could work wonders if only it were shown the right direction. That direction he showed it, and from that time on nothing could shake his belief in the ultimate triumph of the Zionist ideal. Driven by the power of desperation, and seeing before it the goal of two thousand years of longing, the Jewish people would, despite all resistance and obstacles, return to its historic land, and there, with the labor of its hands, construct a homeland for itself and a cultural heritage for humanity.

The truth of these predictions, both in their positive and negative implications has become manifest only during the past two decades.

Having analyzed the situation objectively and fearlessly, Herzl concluded that the Jewish problem in Europe — and he always had Europe primarily in mind when he spoke of the Jews and the Jewish problem, since that was where the great majority of the Jews lived — must end catastrophically unless it were speedily resolved through emigration and the concentration of the Jews in a state of their own. This is why he had written *The Jewish State* and why he had entered upon his life's work. He tried to forestall the impending tragedy; he wanted to turn into fruitful channels that vulcanic force which he saw imprisoned in the unsolved Jewish problem; he sought to transform Jewish need into a source of power for the self-liberation of the Jewish people and its revival on a land of its own, lest this need drive the Jews to despair and result in their joining the forces of revolution against the existing social order. A Jewish state was for Herzl the only way out; and, what is more, it could be realized quickly, if only the Jews and the world willed it. Delay heightened the danger; and Herzl urged speed. His impatience, so incomprehensible to co-workers and opponents, symbolized in his own life the need for speed on the part of the Jewish people. Time was short; there was none to lose. Death was imminent.

The burden of this prophecy, and the urgency with which he clamored for aid to avoid calamity, were understood by few. Had the Jews responded more quickly and vigorously and had the world taken his call to heart sooner, who knows but that some of the most unspeakable events of the recent past might have been avoided. Herzl himself was conscious of this interrelationship between delay and tragedy from the very beginning of his Zionist work. He wrote in his diary, on October 11, 1895: "That which I want to attain through

my constructive ideas will be forced on us by compelling
events."

Actually, the events of our day exceeded in horror Herzl's
darkest forebodings. He had already been deeply affected
by the Jewish problem when studying Dühring's book in
which National Socialism was presaged and the means for
realizing it outlined. As some of his writings indicate, Herzl
had clearly recognized the threat of degeneration which faced
the population of Central Europe. Yet not even a Herzl
could foresee the organized bestiality that would result when
modern technology, organization and science combined with
barbaric ideas about mankind and human rights, so that,
under German direction, six million European Jews could be
exterminated in gas-chambers, like bacilli. Murder and
expulsion were within his experience, and he could conceive
of them even in intensified measure; but, fortunately for him,
he was still so bound up with the traditions of culture — as
Jew, as European, and as Liberal — that he could never have
imagined such mass-murder as eventually took place. Indeed, he was convinced that the status of legal equality,
wherever it had been granted the Jews, would never again
be denied them, and that a modern state and a modern
economy could never restrict and certainly not rescind the
rights of free movement and of personal property. The rise
of a totalitarian state, with its attempted reduction of all
differences to uniformity and its rigid control of thought and
action — and the tragic consequences of this for the Jewish
people — exceeded anything that the most critical analysts
of the close of the 19th century could imagine.

Yet this very unimaginable catastrophe for European
Jewry, along with the growth of the Zionist effort in Palestine, led to the solution for which Herzl had hoped, namely,

the establishment of the Jewish State. Jewish tradition had always heard the footsteps of the Messiah in the days of suffering. Herzl had repeatedly emphasized this connection: want, suffering, and the power of despair were bound to lead to self-liberation and a national renaissance, if only the goal were always clear and the existing forces properly directed. With this in mind, he said, at the First Zionist Congress, that the goal of Zionism was "to turn the Jewish question into a question of Zion," and to take good care, moreover, that the question was solved "within the councils of the civilized nations." At the conclusion of that Congress, which Herzl always viewed as the national assembly of the Jewish people, on September 3, 1897, he summed up its results in the familiar words that in Basle he had actually founded the Jewish State. Within fifty years this was to be clear to everyone. Almost exactly fifty years after these words had been written down, on November 28, 1947, the United Nations — "the council of the civilized nations" — recognized the right of the Jews to a state of their own in Palestine, and one half year later, on May 14 (5th Iyyar), 1948, the State of Israel was proclaimed. Victoriously defying armies which far outnumbered its own forces, the new State made Herzl's prediction come true, namely, that under the banner of Zionism the Maccabeans would again come to life.

The State maintained itself. It opened wide its doors. Hundreds of thousands of Jews from all over the world streamed into it. The State of Israel, moreover, fulfilled Herzl's last personal wish, expressed in his will: for in August 1949, an Israeli airplane of the newly-established Israeli airline brought his remains to Israel. In front of the house where the Israeli parliament met, before the offices of the Central Zionist World Organization, the citizens of the new

State paid their respects to the departed leader. A ceremonial procession carried his coffin to a hilltop in Jerusalem which was renamed for him. His remains were interred there in their final resting place. Goal of pilgrimage, stirring place of meeting, the grave compels the visitor to stop and meditate.

Each person must solve his problems in his own fashion, and so must each age. No personality, however great, should be considered so sacred and infallible that his teachings may be permitted to harden into dogmas. His example, nevertheless, must be permitted to influence those who follow; and his teachings, in which truth found its expression in a form limited by time and place, must ever serve as a source of honest thought, inducing later generations to undertake fearless re-examination of their own situation and so attain a solution appropriate to their own time and circumstance.

Herzl recognized that the Jews shared a common fate as a people among peoples. "We are a people; *one* people!" This was the basic observation with which he introduced his writing on the Jewish State, and this insight has become common property. From this viewpoint he analyzed the Jewish problem, and his analysis has withstood the test of time. From this standpoint he evolved his plan for the problem's solution. In his opinion it was the task of Zionism to free the Jewish people from the abnormal situation into which history had led it and which had become a burden both to the Jews and to the nations of the earth.

The means for accomplishing this task was to be the establishment of a state in Palestine. As Herzl envisioned this state — he expressed himself often on this point — it was to be a land which blossomed brilliantly, loved liberty, was at peace with its neighbors and with the world, exercised tolerance, provided a true home for all who settled within its borders. The freedom which prevailed in it, the beneficent institutions which distinguished it, the feeling of security which it offered the Jews as Jews were to act as a magnet to attract the Jews from all over the world. The amount of the immigration would be in direct proportion to this power of attraction and to the repelling forces in the lands of the Diaspora. It would depend, in other words, on such natural forces as operate among all peoples and nations. "The solution of the Jewish difficulty," said Herzl in 1902 before the Commission on Alien Immigration in London, "is the recognition of Jews as a people and in the finding by them of a legally recognized home to which Jews in those parts of the world where they are oppressed, would naturally migrate, for they would arrive there citizens just because they were Jews and not aliens." There can be no doubt that Herzl was convinced that the majority of Jews, whose densest population was in Eastern Europe, would eventually come to reside in the Jewish State, and that the Jews would not fail to take advantage of the opportunity which the establishment of such a State would afford them. But, he often contended, he never envisaged a total emigration of the Jews from the lands of their habitation; he merely hoped for a "regulation of the Jewish problem." The mere fact that the Jewish State would be open to every Jew who might want to leave his homeland, either out of external pressure or inner conviction, would serve to normalize the relations between Jews and non-Jews.

The first step toward curing the ills within the body of Jewry was to create a Zionist movement, that is, to arouse the national will-to-live among the Jewish people and to organize it for self-help. The second decisive step would be the establishment of the State. This was to be the goal of the eternal wandering; in it the wandering would find its end — the wandering of the individual Jew as well as the homelessness of the Jewish people.

The unity of the Jewish people stood forth as the starting point for Herzl's conception of Zionism; the same unity was also a goal, since the Jewish State would exert a unifying power over the Jews wherever they might be. In our day, the truth of this insight of Herzl is a common experience. Never was the Jewish people so united in the face of the entire world as at the moment when the Jewish State came into being. In those rather recent days, and time and again since then, it has been perfectly clear that the Jews are bound together in a common fate, whether they become part of the Jewish State or continue to live in the Diaspora. Both types of Jew needed one another: those of the State needed the moral and material support of the Jews in the rest of the world, and the latter needed the State which had been created for them and without which, once it has been established, they can no longer exist. The State will in increasing measure become the point of gravity for Jewry the world over, the home to which one may go without being asked for credentials but simply because one is a Jew, even as one may enter one's parental home without first asking permission. The mere fact that such a homeland exists, and that it can at any time become the home of any person, whether by his own choice or through the force of circumstances, will, once it sinks deep into the consciousness of the individual Jew, restore the health of the Jewish people. We cannot know where and when times of distress will descend upon the Jew; but this we do know: such periods will never again find him helpless and aimless as did the pogroms of

Kishinev in Herzl's day or the murderous crematories of Hitler in our own time.]

Two of Herzl's stories, culled from his literary remains, deal with right living, with correct judgment, with just exercise of power. Herzl's life was a struggle for truth, right and dignified living. His sense of honor, which drove him to take a stand for his people, derived from his sense of insulted humanity. The state for which he strove was to restore to the Jews their honor and their rights — their rights as individuals and as members of their people. By freeing themselves, they would free the world from the burden of the unsolved Jewish question. Taught by the experience of their own suffering, they would build a state founded on justice and thus offer an example to men and nations. "The existing condition of the Jews," he declared in his address at the Third Zionist Congress, "can lead in any one of three directions. One is to continue dumbly to suffer insult and distress. The second is to rebel against and hate the stepmotherly society about us. Our way is the third. We want to raise ourselves to a higher standard of life, to spread well-being, to build new highways for communication among peoples, and to find new expressions for social justice. And just as our beloved poet (Heine) created new poetry out of his very pains, so we are preparing, out of our suffering, to create progress for mankind, which we serve . . . "

A NOTE BY THE AUTHOR

In the present work, which reproduces in somewhat condensed form the Hebrew and German versions of the same subject, I have sought to create as clear and objective a picture as is possible on the basis of existing records, of Theodore Herzl, the man, the writer and the creator of the modern Zionist movement, covering his development, his ideas and his effective influence.

Apart from the published writings of Herzl himself — including his diary — and the enormous literature about him, I have drawn upon the rich, unpublished material which has been collected by the Central Zionist Archives in Jerusalem. The first place must be given of course to Herzl's own legacy, his diaries, letters and manuscripts. After this come the archives of the Viennese Zionist Central Office in Herzl's time, and the archives of David Wolffsohn, Max Mandelstamm, Max I. Bodenheimer, Arye Leib Motzkin, and others. To these must be added the Herzl letters in the Schwadron Collection of Autographs in the National Library. I have also had access to certain private collections, and have taken full advantage of numerous conversations with Herzl's contemporaries.

Before settling in Palestine I was able to consult the relevant records of the German Foreign Office and of the Rathenau Archives in Berlin, and made use of some hundreds of photostat copies of Herzl's articles in the *Wiener Neue Freie Presse*. For the special benefit of the English edition I had the advantage of the great collection of Herzl letters which the Central Zionist Archives in Jerusalem assembled under my direction, and which already contains several thousand original holographs or copies.

For access to this material, as well as for assistance in other ways, I am indebted in the first line to my friend Dr. Herlitz, Director of the Central Zionist Archives, to engineer Johann Kremenezky (whose passing I must now record with sorrow), one time guardian of the Herzl Archives in Vienna before their transfer to Jerusalem, and to Director Moritz Rosenfeld. For the publication of the book in its German and Hebrew editions my thanks are due to that noble spirit and fine Zionist, now, alas, also no longer among the living, Dr. Hugo Herrman, to Mr. Mordecai Newman and Mr. Elias Newman. I have also derived great help from the able criticism and cooperation of my wife.

Nor must I fail to add the expression of my gratitude to the readers of previous editions of this work, and to the critics who have drawn my attention to errors contained in them. I have made every effort to incorporate their corrections, as well as those suggested in my subsequent researches into the subject, in the present version, which, however, differs in no essential respect from the versions which have preceded it.

ALEX BEIN

Jerusalem,
March, 1940.

BIBLIOGRAPHY

This bibliography is not meant to be exhaustive, but rather to make it possible for the reader to check on statements by reference to published material. Works of general history have been entirely omitted, although naturally extensive use was made of them.

I. WORKS BY HERZL

A. Dramatic Works:*

1. Kompagniearbeit, comedy in one act, Vienna, 1880.
2. Die Causa Hirschkorn, comedy in one act, Vienna, 1882.
3. Tabarin, comedy in one act, (1884).
4. Muttersöhnchen, comedy in four acts, (1885). (Later "Austoben" by H. Jungmann).
5. Seine Hoheit, comedy in three acts, (1885).
6. Der Flüchtling, comedy in one act, (1887). Reklams-Universal-bibliothek No. 2387, Leipzig.
7. Wilddiebe, comedy in four acts, in co-authorship with H. Wittmann, (1888).
8. Was wird man sagen?, comedy in four acts, (1889), Vienna, 1890.
9. Die Dame in Schwarz, comedy in four acts, in co-authorship with H. Wittmann, (1890).
10. Prinzen aus Genieland, comedy in four acts, (1891), Vienna, E. Pierson's Verlag, 1892.
11. Die Glosse, comedy in one act, (1894), Dresden-Leipzig-Vienna, 1895.
12. Das Neue Ghetto, drama in four acts, (1894), Vienna (Verlag der "Welt"), 1898, new edition, Vienna-Berlin (R. Löwit Verlag), 1920.

---

*Dates in brackets represent the year of origin; other dates represent the year of publication.

13. Unser Kätchen, comedy in four acts, (1898), Vienna, 1899.
14. Gretel, comedy in four acts, (1899).
15. I love you, comedy in one act, (1900), Vienna.
16. Solon in Lydien, drama in three acts, (1901), Vienna-Leipzig (Wiener Verlag), 1904.

B. Collected Feuilletons, Stories, Sketches, etc.:

1. Neues von der Venus, Leipzig, F. Freund, 1887.
2. Das Buch der Narrheit, Leipzig, F. Freund, 1888.
3. Das Palais Bourbon, Bilder aus dem französischen Parlamentsleben, Leipzig, Duncker und Humblot, 1895.
4. Philosophische Erzählungen, Berlin, Gebrüder Paetel, 1900; new edition, Berlin-Vienna, Benjamin Harz, 1919.
5. Feuilletons, 2 vols., Berlin, 1903; second edition, with an introduction by Raoul Auernheimer, Berlin-Vienna, Benjamin Harz, same year.

C. Zionist Works:

1. Der Judenstaat, Versuch einer modernen Lösung der Judenfrage, Leipzig-Vienna, M. Breitensteins Verlagsbuchhandlung, 1896; numerous editions and translations.
2. Der Baseler Kongress, Vienna, Verlag der "Welt," 1897.
3. Altneuland, a novel, Leipzig, Hermann Seemann Nachfolger, 1902; English translation by Jacob de Haas, in *The Maccabaean*, New York, 1902/3.
4. Zionistische Schriften, published by Leon Kellner, 2 vols., Berlin, Jüdischer Verlag, 1905; second edition, one volume, 1920.
5. Theodor Herzls Tagebücher, 3 vols., Berlin, Jüdischer Verlag, 1922/23.
6. Theodor Herzl: Gesammelte Zionistische Werke. 5 vols., Tel-Aviv, Hozaah Ivrith, 1934/35.
7. מבחר כתבי הרצל (Selected Writings), 12 vols., Tel-Aviv, Hozaat Mizpa, 1934; second edition 1939.
8. Herzl, Theodor: יומן הנעורים (Diary of his Youth). Tel-Aviv, Hozaat Mizpa, 1934.
9. Theodor Herzl: נאומים ומאמרים (Addresses and Statements), Tel-Aviv, Hozaah Medinit, 1937.

10. Herzl, Theodor: מכתבים (Letters), Tel-Aviv, Hozaah Medinit, 1937.
11. Herzl-Worte, compiled by Felix A. Theilhaber, Berlin, 1921.
12. Herzl, Theodor: The Tragedy of Jewish Immigration, New York, 1902; second edition, New York, 1920.
13. Herzl, Theodor: The Congress Addresses, translated from the German by Nelly Straus, New York, Federation of American Zionists, 1917.

II. BIOGRAPHIES OF HERZL

1. BEIN, ALEX, Theodor Herzl Biographie, mit 63 Bildern und einer Ahnentafel, Vienna, Fiba-Verlag, 1934; popular edition, Vienna, 1935; Hebrew edition, 2 vols., Tel-Aviv, Mizpah Publishing Co., 1934; second edition, Tel-Aviv, 1939.
2. BINJAMIN, RABBI, Theodor Herzl — מלחמת חייו (His Life's Battle), Tel-Aviv, 5689.
3. BRAININ, RUBEN, חיי הרצל (A Life of Herzl), vol. I, New York, 1919.
4. CITRON, S. L., Herzl — חייו ופעוליו (His Life and Achievements), Wilna, 1921.
5. DE HAAS, JACOB, Theodor Herzl: A Biographical Study, 2 vols., New York, 1927.
6. FRIEDEMANN, ADOLF, Das Leben Theodor Herzls, Berlin, 1914; second edition, 1919.
7. GEORG, MANFRED, Theodor Herzl, Sein Leben und sein Vermächtnis, Berlin, 1929.
8. HAGANI, BARUCH, Le Sionisme Politique et son Fondateur, Paris, 1917.
9. KELLNER, LEON, Theodor Herzls Lehrjahre, Vienna, 1920.
10. THON, OSIAS, Theodor Herzl, Berlin, (1914).

III. MONOGRAPHS AND COLLECTIONS OF ESSAYS ON HERZL

1. DIAMANT, PAUL, Theodor Herzls väterliche und mütterliche Vorfahren, Jerusalem, 1934.
2. ERDTRACHT, D., Theodor Herzl und der Judenstaat, Vienna, 1921.
3. FISHMAN, Z., בנימין זאב בן יעקב הרצל — ערך ביאוגרפי וביבליאוגרפי (Herzl: A Biographical and Bibliographical Evaluation), reprint from Hator, Jerusalem, 1924.

4. FRÄNKEL, JOSEF, Theodor Herzl, des Schöpfers erstes Wollen, Vienna 1934.

5. Freie Zionistische Gruppe, Die Wahrheit über Charkow, Berlin, 1904.

6. GORELIK, SH., Herzl in seinen Tagebüchern, Berlin, 1929.

7. Theodor Herzl: Ein Gedenkbuch zum 25. Todestage, hrsgg. von der Exekutive der Zionistischen Organisation, Berlin, 1929.

8. LANDAU, SAUL RAPHAEL, Sturm und Drang im Zionismus, Vienna, 1937.

9. LEVONTIN, S. D., לארץ אבותינו (To our Fatherland), vol. II, Tel-Aviv, 1925.

10. MARCUS, AHRON, Dr. Theodor Herzls "Judenstaat." Hamburg, 1897; second edition, 1919.

11. MEDZINI, M., המדיניות הציונית מראשיתה עד מותו של הרצל (Political Zionism from its Beginning to the Death of Herzl), Jerusalem, 5634.

12. NUSSENBLATT, TULO, Zeitgenossen über Herzl, Vienna, 1929.

13. NUSSENBLATT, TULO, Ein Volk unterwegs zum Frieden, Vienna, 1933.

14. NUSSENBLATT, TULO, editor, Theodor Herzl Jahrbuch, Vienna, 1937.

15. JAFFE, LEIB, editor, ספר הקונגרס (The Book of the Congress), Jerusalem, 1923.

16. Souvenir of the Herzl Room at the Head Office of the Keren Kayemeth le-Israel. Text by A. Bein, Jerusalem, 1937.

17. VARDI, A., מלכי בציון (My King in Zion), Tel-Aviv, 1931.

18. "Warum gingen wir zum ersten Zionistenkongress," published by the Berliner Büro der Zionistischen Vereinigung, Berlin, 1922.

19. WEISGAL, M., editor, Theodore Herzl — A Memorial, New York, 1929.

20. ZANGWILL, ISRAEL, Dreamers of the Ghetto, London, 1899.

IV. ARTICLES ON HERZL

1. BEIN, ALEX, "Theodor Herzl," Encyclopedia kelalit, Tel-Aviv, vol. III.

2. BEIN, ALEX, "Herzl und der Dreyfussprozess," Die Stimme, Vienna, Oct. 5, 1934.

3. BEIN, ALEX, "Herzl und Lassalle," Die Stimme, Vienna, July 3 and 12, 1935; Hebrew in Moznayim, vol. 4, no. 1.

4. BEIN, ALEX, "Theodor Herzl und Palästina," in Herzl und Bialik, Erzieher des Volkes, Berlin, 1935, Keren Kayemeth le-Israel; Hebrew in Ha-aretz, July 21, 1935.

5. BEIN, ALEX, איך נעשה הרצל לציוני (How Herzl Became a Zionist), *Ha'olam*, July 1, 1937.

6. BEIN, ALEX, "Herzls sittlich-soziales Wollen," *Herzl-Jahrbuch*, 1937, pp. 224–231; Hebrew in *Ha-aretz*, 14.7.1936.

7. BEIN, ALEX, כיצד קם והיה הקונגרס הראשון (Origin of First Congress), *Ha-aretz*, Aug. 3, 1937.

8. BEIN, ALEX, "Theodor Herzl u. Max Mandelstamm," *Ha'olam*, May–September, 1939.

9. BEIN, ALEX, ההתקשרות המדינית הראשונה עם אנגליה (First Political Contacts with England), *Ha'olam*, July 6, 1939.

10. BEIN, ALEX, הרצל, ארץ ישראל והברון הירש (Herzl, Palestine and Baron de Hirsch), *Ha'olam*, July 6, 1939.

11. BEIN, ALEX, "Theodor Herzl und Walther Rathenau." *Jüdische Weltrundschau*, July 7, 1939; Hebrew in *Ha-aretz*, July 7, 1939.

12. BEIN, ALEX, לתולדות הקונגרסים הראשונים (History of the First Congresses), *Ha-aretz*, August 18, 1939.

13. BEIN, ALEX, "David Wolffsohn," *Mundo Israelita* (Buenos Aires), September 30, 1937.

14. BEN AMI, "Erinnerungen an Theodor Herzl," *Die Welt*, 1914, p. 688.

14a. FRÄNKEL, JOSEF, "Theodor Herzl und die akademische Burschenschaft Albia," *Die Neue Welt*, 1932, no. 235, 236, 238.

15. FRÄNKEL, JOSEF, "Wie das neue Ghetto entstand," *Selbstwehr* (Prag), July 15, 1938.

16. FRIEDEMANN, ADOLF, "Der Prophet Theodor Herzls" (Hechler), *Jüdische Rundschau*, July 26, 1931.

17. GELBER, N. M., "Herzls diplomatischer Agent Newlinski." *Jüdische Rundschau*, 1928, no. 53.

18. "Herzl und der Sozialismus," *Die Neue Welt*, 1929, no. 97.

19. "Theodor Herzls tragischer Kampf um den politischen Zionismus," *Die Neue Welt*, 1930, no. 148 ff.

20. HOFMANN, MARTHA, "Arthur Schnitzler und Theodor Herzl," *Die Stimme*, May 14, 1937.

21. JABOTINSKY, SEEV, "Herzl bei den Neinsagern," *Die Welt*, 1914, p. 671.

22. KAZNELSON, SIEGMUND, "Theodor Herzl: Der Mensch und sein Werk," *Die Welt*, 1912, p. 813.

23. Kaznelson, Siegmund, "Theodor Herzl, der Denker: Politischer oder Kulturzionismus, *Jüdische Rundschau*, 1935, no. 58.
24. Kellner, "Was Herzl vorfand," in Heimkehr, *Essays jüdischer Denker*, Czernowitz-Berlin, 1912.
25. Kohn, Hans, "Der junge Buber und der Herzlsche Zionismus," *Der Jude*, Febr., 1928.
26. Kohn, P., "Geheimberichte über Herzls Besuch in Wilna 1903," reprinted from *B'nai B'rith — Mitteilungen für Oesterreich*, XXXVIII, July 6, 1928.
27. Nussenblatt, Tulo, "Aus Herzls Schul- und Universitätszeit," *Die Neue Welt*, 1932, nos. 229, 231, 232.
28. Prinz, J., "Herzl — der Erneuerer des Volkes," *Jüdische Rundschau*, 1934, no. 35.
29. Schmitz, S., "Theodor Herzls Feuilletons," *Die Welt*, 1912, p. 51.
30. York-Steiner, "Theodor Herzls Mutter," *Die Neue Welt*, II, no. 42.

V. NEWSPAPERS

1. Neue Freie Presse, Vienna, 1891–1904.
2. Berliner Tageblatt, 1886–1889.
3. Jewish Chronicle, 1896.
4. Die Welt, 1897–1914.
5. Zion, Zeitschrift für die nationalen Interessen des jüd. Volkes, Berlin, 1895–1896.
6. Clippings in the Herzl-Archiv.
7. Herzl issues of Die Welt, 1904, 1910, 1914; Ost und West, 1904; Jüdische Rundschau, 1904; Die Neue Welt; Ha'olam; Ha-aretz; Davar; Haboker; New Judea; and other newspapers annually on the anniversary of his death.
8. The special issue of the Neue Freie Presse on the 50th anniversary of the newspaper's establishment, August 30, 1914.

VI. LITERATURE ON THE HISTORY OF ZIONISM AND BIOGRAPHIES OF HERZL'S CO-WORKERS

1. Ahad Ha-am, Ten Essays on Zionism and Judaism, translated from the Hebrew by Leon Simon, London, 1922.
2. Ahad Ha-am, על פרשת דרכים, vols. I–III, Berlin, 1921.
3. Ahad Ha-am, אגרות, vols. I–III, Berlin-Jerusalem, 1923–1924.

4. BEIN, ALEX, אריה לייב מוצקין, reprint from *Sefer Motzkin*, Jerusalem, 5699(1939).

5. BEIN, ALEX (ed.), ספר מוצקין, Jerusalem, 5699(1939).

6. BEIN, ALEX, Der Zionismus und sein Werk, Prague, 5699(1939).

7. BEIN, ALEX, Introduction au Sionisme, translated into French by Jacques Torczyner, Paris, 1938; second edition, 1939.

8. BEIN, ALEX, Het Zionistsche Kolonisatie-Werk, Amsterdam, 1940.

9. BIRNBAUM, NATHAN, Ausgewählte Schriften zur jüdischen Frage, 2 vols., Czernowitz, 1910.

10. BÖHM, ADOLF, Die Zionistische Bewegung, 2 parts, Berlin, 1920–1921; second edition, 2 vols., Tel-Aviv-Jerusalem, 1935-1937.

11. BUBER, MARTIN, Die jüdische Bewegung, vol. I, Berlin, 1920.

12. CITRON, S. L., תולדות חבת ציון, Odessa, 1914.

13. CITRON, S. L., לכסיקון ציוני, Warsaw, 1924.

14. DINABURG, BENZION, חבת ציון, 2 vols., Tel-Aviv, 1932-1934.

15. DINABURG, BENZION, ספר השנה לארץ ישראל, 1923.

16. DRUYANOW, A., חבת ציון, Encyclopaedia Judaica, vol. V, p. 439 ff.

17. DUBNOW, SIMON, Weltgeschichte des Jüdischen Volkes, vol. X, Berlin, 1929.

18. FRÄNKEL, JOSEF, Dr. Sigmund Werner: ein Mitarbeiter Herzls, Prague, 5699(1939).

19. GELBER, N. M., Vorgeschichte des Zionismus, Vienna, 1928.

20. GLÜCKSOHN, "Das Werk der Chowewe-Zion," *Die Welt*, 1910, nos 41–42.

21. GOLDRING, Zur Vorgeschichte des Zionismus, Frankfort, 1925.

22. GOODMAN, PAUL, Zionism in England, London, 1929.

23. GOTTHEIL, R. I. H., Zionism, Philadelphia, 1914.

24. GUR ARI, הרב י. ה. אלקלי, Tel-Aviv, 1929.

25. HERRMANN, LEO, Nathan Birnbaum, Berlin, 1914.

26. HESS, MOSES, Rom und Jerusalem, Leipzig, 1862.

27. HESS, MOSES, Rome and Jerusalem: A Study in Jewish Nationalism, translated from the German by Meyer Waxman, New York, 1918.

28. KLAUSNER, JOSEPH, ספר פינסקר, Jerusalem, 1921.

29. KOHN, HANS, Martin Buber, 1929.

30. LEVIN, SHMARYA, The Arena, London, 1932.

31. LURIE, M., הרצל והשקפותיו הפוליטיות והחברתיות, Tel-Aviv, 1927.

536   THEODORE HERZL

32. NORDAU, MAX, Zionistische Schriften, Berlin, 1909; second edition, 1923.
33. NORDAU, MAX, Erinnerungen, Erzählt von ihm selbst und von der Gefährtin seines Lebens, Leipzig-Vienna, n. d.
34. PINSKER, LEO, Autoemancipation, Berlin, 1882; fourth edition, Berlin, 1932; in English, edited with supplements and afterword by A. S. Eben, London, 1938.
35. ROBINSOHN, A., David Wolffsohn, Berlin, 1921.
36. SCHÖN, LAZAR, editor, "Die Stimme der Wahrheit," *Jahrbuch für wissenschaftlichen Zionismus*, Würzburg, 1905.
37. ספר טשלנוב, Tel-Aviv, 1937.
38. SOKOLOW, NAHUM, History of Zionism: 1600–1918, 2 vols., London, 1919.
39. SOKOLOW, NAHUM, אישים (Personalities), 3 vols., Tel-Aviv, 5695 (1935).
40. SOKOLOW, NAHUM, חבת ציון (The Love for Zion), Jerusalem, 1935.
41. STEIN, LEONARD, Zionism, London, 1932.
42. Stenographische Protokolle des 1–7 Zionistenkongresses. Vienna, 1897–1904.
43. VAN PASSEN, PIERRE, Days of Our Years, New York, 1939.
44. WEIZMAN, CHAIM, The Jewish People and Palestine, London, 1939.
45. ZANGWILL, ISRAEL, Speeches, Articles, Letters: selected and edited by Maurice Simon, With a Foreword by Edith Arton Zangwill, London, 1937.
46. ZLOCISTI, THEODOR, Moses Hess. Berlin, 1921.

VII. MISCELLANEOUS WORKS

1. GELBER, N. M., Aus zwei Jahrhunderten, 1924.
2. Die Grosse Politik der Europäischen Kabinette, published by the Deutsche Auswärtige Amt, B.X/2.
3. MORAVITZ, Die Türkei im Spiegel ihrer Finanzen, 1903.
4. SCHAPIRA, J., Der Antisemitismus in der französischen Literatur, 1927.
5. SCHWARTZKOPPEN, MAX VON, Die Wahrheit über Dreyfus, published by B. Schwertfeger, Berlin, 1930.
6. TEWELES, H., Theater und Publikum, Prague, 1927.
7. TIETZE, HANS, Die Juden Wiens, Vienna, 1933.
8. MAYER, S., Die Wiener Juden, Vienna-Berlin, 1917.
9. YORK-STEINER, Die Kunst als Jude zu leben, Leipzig, 1928.

INDEX

Abdul-Hamid, Sultan of Turkey, 166, 194, 195, 198–201, 231, 245, 251, 277, 278, 279, 285, 286, 287, 288, 296, 307, 308, 314, 315, 318, 321, 322, 323, 342, 343, 344, 348, 352, 353–364, 369, 370–371, 372, 377, 378, 379, 380–381, 382, 383, 391, 392, 393, 414, 417, 424, 426, 429, 430, 444, 466; audience with Herzl, 354–358, 363, 364, 372, 373.

Abeles, Lazarus, ancestor of Herzl, 7.

Abeles, Theresa, great-grandmother of Herzl, 7.

Actions Committee, 240, 246, 247, 264, 267, 268, 272, 273, 290, 311, 315, 318, 324, 326, 327, 328, 337, 341, 345, 348, 366, 370, 372, 373, 376, 382, 429, 433, 447, 448, 458, 462, 472, 474, 479, 480, 481, 483, 488–9, 492, 494, 495, 497, 498; Greater, 376, 453, 454, 458, 459, 460, 462, 480, 487, 488, 493, 497, 498.

Address to the Kaiser, 303 ff.

Address to the Rothschilds, 138–9, 140, 149, 151, 154, 159, 220, 252.

Adler, Chief Rabbi Hermann, 220.

Admat Yeshurun (Zion Society), 186.

Agliardi, Count, Papal Nuncio, 197–8.

Agrarian Bank in Palestine, 216.

Agriculture, Jews in, 83, 128, 205, 270.

Ahad Ha-am (Asher Ginsberg), 177–8, 256–264, 268, 272, 373, 405–9, 449, 470, 476, 506, 507, 514.

Ahavat Zion, Society of Borislav, Galicia, 184.

Ahmed Tewfik, Turkish ambassador, 199, 255, 349.

Akademische Lesehalle, 25–32, 77.

Albia fraternity, 30–31, 39–42, 185.

Alkalai, Yehuda ben Solomon Hai, 5, 15, 173.

Allgemeine Israelitische Wochenschrift, 180.

Allgemeine Zeitung des Judenthums, 180–1, 218, 310.

Alliance Israélite Universelle, 152, 173, 344, 346–7.

Altneuland, 22, 68, 394, 395–410, 421, 423, 424, 432, 471, 472, 491, 501, 517.

America, migration to, 173.

American Investigation Commission on persecution of Jews in Russia, 84.

Anglo-Jewish Association, 203, 206.

Anglo-Palestine Company (Bank), 351, 420, 472.

Anti-Semites en France, by Mermeix, 86.

Anti-Semitism, 71, 136, 152, 156, 160, 162, 165, 169, 173, 175, 197, 198, 204, 219, 223, 224, 233, 249, 252, 294, 345, 346, 387, 404, 406, 508, 509–514; in America, 422; in Austria, 87, 101, 117–118, 148, 152; in England, 160–161, 386, 388–389, 418, 422; in France, 80–82, 83–101, 108–119; in Germany, 16, 30, 35, 36, 37, 38, 59, 80, 163, 179, 287; in Hungary, 15, 16, 19, 26, 29, 40–41; in Roumania, 343; in Russia, 129, 173–177, 274, 438 f., 447, 484; see also Persecution, Pogroms.

Anti-Zionism, 211, 212, 213, 217, 219 ff., 224, 241, 246 ff., 256, 264, 267, 268, 271, 279, 281, 283, 295, 301, 308, 316–317, 356, 365, 368, 386, 390, 409, 414, 514.

Arab cooperation, 403.

"Ararat," proposed State of, 172.

Hill, Sir Clement, 446, 466, 483, 486.
Hindlip, Lord, English diplomat, 468.
Hirsch, Baron Moritz de, 84, 120–133, 135, 138, 141, 145, 148, 195, 211, 366.
Hirschkorn Case, play by Herzl, 43, 49.
Hofburg Theatre, 43.
Hohenlohe, Reich Chancellor, 287–288, 290, 392.
Holy Places of Palestine, 166, 228, 312, 467.
Holzmann, Dr. J., 215.
Hoveve Zion (pre-Herzlian Zionists), 124, 152, 174, 176, 177–9, 181, 183, 187, 190, 206, 207, 211, 213, 224, 227, 228, 231, 232, 238, 239, 241, 259, 263, 264, 411, 413, 444, 470, 472.
Humphreys, Inspector of Egyptian Survey Department, 428.

Ibrahim Bey, Court Master of Ceremonies, 354, 357, 358, 359, 360–2, 377, 378, 380, 382, 392, 393, 429.
ICA (Jewish Colonization Association), 83, 84, 118, 124, 126, 156, 158, 205, 209, 213, 241, 264, 322, 346–7, 365, 427, 428, 435, 436, 469.
Ignatius, Father, Christian Zionist, 282.
I Love You, play by Herzl, 332.
Illness, Herzl's, 98, 214, 264, 283, 290, 296, 301, 314, 347, 366, 377, 384, 415, 420, 433, 457, 466, 490, 493, 499–503.
India and Zionism, 263.
Industrialization of Palestine, 271.
Inn of Anlin, story by Herzl, 333.
International politics, 72, 197, 263, 274, 276–7, 308, 309, 311, 319, 320–1, 353, 356, 381, 415, 424, 466; see also Politics and the Jews.
Israelit, journal, 180.

Ish-Kishor, J., 206.
Italy and Zionism, 446, 485, 491; Zionists in, 350.
Izzet Bey, second Turkish secretary, 353, 359, 360–2, 378–9, 380, 381, 383, 429, 441, 484, 495.

Jabotinsky, Vladimir, 462.
Jacobson, Victor, 373, 453, 460, 479, 487.
Jaffa, 173.
Jaffa-Jerusalem Railroad, 351.
Jahreskonferenz, 376, 416, 420.
James, Lord, chairman of Royal Commission, 390, 414.
Jassinovsky, Israel, 447–8, 453, 482.
Javitz, W., historian, 451.
Jensen, Wilhelm, author of *Jews of Cologne*, 32, 34 f.
Jewish Chronicle; see *London Jewish Chronicle*.
Jewish Colonial Trust, 167, 216, 240, 252, 253, 254, 264, 267, 269–270, 275, 280, 290, 313, 316–318, 322, 324, 326, 327, 331, 336–341, 350, 351, 368, 369, 382, 384, 420, 441, 443, 446, 447, 448, 458, 473, 481, 482, 507, 514, 515.
Jewish Colonization Association; see *ICA*.
"Jewish Company," the, 165, 167.
Jewish Eastern Company, 422, 427.
Jewish National Fund, 240, 345, 375, 376, 458, 483, 507.
Jewish Question, The (Herzl's diary), 134–135.
Jewish State, The, by Herzl, 159.
"Jewish State and Jewish Need," by Ahad Ha-am, 260.
Jewish World, newspaper, 230, 281.
Jews, medieval, 35, 38.
Joffe, Dr. Hillel, 428.
Johnston, Sir Harry, Commissioner for East Africa, 468.